Lecture Notes in Computer Science 13009

More information about this subseries at http://www.springer.com/series/7410

Hyoungshick Kim (Ed.)

Information Security Applications

22nd International Conference, WISA 2021
Jeju Island, South Korea, August 11–13, 2021
Revised Selected Papers

 Springer

Editor
Hyoungshick Kim ⓘ
Sungkyunkwan University
Suwon-Si, Korea (Republic of)

ISSN 0302-9743 ISSN 1611-3349 (electronic)
Lecture Notes in Computer Science
ISBN 978-3-030-89431-3 ISBN 978-3-030-89432-0 (eBook)
https://doi.org/10.1007/978-3-030-89432-0

LNCS Sublibrary: SL4 – Security and Cryptology

Preface

The 22nd World Conference on Information Security Application (WISA 2021) was held at Jeju Island, Korea, during August 11–13, 2021. The primary focus of WISA 2021 was on artificial intelligence-driven security including all other technical and practical aspects of security applications. This year, in particular, we invited prominent researchers working on artificial intelligence (AI) and system security who are keen on addressing fundamental security challenges to participate. The conference was hosted by the Korea Institute of Information Security and Cryptography (KIISC). It was sponsored by the Ministry of Science, ICT and Future Planning (MSIP) and the National Intelligence Service (NIS), and co-sponsored by the Electronics and Telecommunication Research Institute (ETRI), the Korea Internet & Security Agency (KISA), and the National Security Research Institute (NSR). The program chair, Hyoungshick Kim (Sungkyunkwan University), prepared a valuable program along with the Program Committee members listed here. We received 66 submissions, covering all areas of information security, and finally selected 23 outstanding full papers. The excellent arrangements for the conference venue were led by the WISA 2021 general chair, Jaecheol Ryou (Chungnam National University), and organizing chair, Kyungho Son (Kangwon National University).

We were specially honored to have the two keynote talks by Ross Anderson (University of Cambridge), on "Security Engineering and Machine Learning," and Surya Nepal (CSIRO Data61), on "Building Trustworthy Deep Neural Networks." Both talks were geared toward the roles of computer security in machine learning and artificial intelligence applications. Many people contributed to the success of WISA 2021. We would like to express our deepest appreciation to each of the WISA Program Committee and Organizing Committee members. Thanks to their invaluable support and sincere dedication, WISA 2021 was a success. We also thank the authors for their patience and cooperation during the back-and-forth process of comments and revisions requested by the editor and the reviewers, especially since the process slowed down at the onset of the COVID-19 pandemic. Finally, we thank the Springer team for the assistance for the LNCS proceedings.

September 2021   Hyoungshick Kim

Organization

General Chair

Jaecheol Ryou   Chungnam National University, South Korea

Program Committee Chair

Hyoungshick Kim   Sungkyunkwan University, South Korea

Program Committee

Ki-Woong Park	Sejong University, South Korea
Yonghwi Kwon	University of Virginia, USA
Junghwan Rhee	University of Central Oklahoma, USA
Sang Uk Shin	Pukyong National University, South Korea
Qiong Huang	South China Agricultural University, China
Seonghan Shin	AIST, Japan
Muhammad Ejaz Ahmed	CSIRO Data61, Australia
Simon Woo	Sungkyunkwan University, South Korea
Sang Kil Cha	KAIST, South Korea
Siqi Ma	The University of Queensland, Australia
Yansong Gao	Nanjing University of Science and Technology, China/CSIRO Data 61, Australia
Min Suk Kang	KAIST, South Korea
Kyu Hyung Lee	University of Georgia, USA
Dongseong Kim	The University of Queensland, Australia
Joonsang Baek	University of Wollongong, Australia
Kouichi Sakurai	Kyushu University, Japan
Kazumasa Omote	University of Tsukuba, Japan
Younghee Park	San Jose State University, USA
Hsu-Chun Hsiao	National Taiwan University, Taiwan
Ulrich Rührmair	Ruhr University Bochum, Germany
Naoto Yanai	Osaka University, Japan
Toshihiro Yamauchi	Okayama University, Japan
Kangkook Jee	University of Texas at Dallas, USA
Dongwan Shin	New Mexico Tech, USA
Marcus Peinado	Microsoft, USA
Byoungyoung Lee	Seoul National University, South Korea
Taejoong Chung	Virginia Tech, USA
Dooho Choi	Korea University, South Korea

Kirill Morozov	University of North Texas, USA
Jin Hong	University of Western Australia, Australia
Eul Gyu Im	Hanyang University, South Korea
Ji Won Yoon	Korea University, South Korea
Masakatsu Nishigaki	Shizuoka University, Japan
David Mohaisen	University of Central Florida, USA
Hojoon Lee	Sungkyunkwan University, South Korea
Kevin Koo	Sungkyunkwan University, South Korea
Chung Hwan Kim	University of Texas at Dallas, USA
Byung-Chul Choi	ETRI, South Korea
Heeseok Kim	Korea University, South Korea

Organizing Committee Chair

| Kyungho Son | Kangwon National University, South Korea |

Organizing Committee

Hyojin Jo	Soongsil University, South Korea
Taejin Lee	Hoseo University, South Korea
Hwanguk Kim	Sangmyung University
Changhun Lee	Seoul National University of Science and Technology, South Korea
Jin Kwak	Ajou University, South Korea
Dongguk Han	Kookmin University, South Korea
Jung Taek Seo	Gachon University, South Korea
Donghwan Oh	KISA, South Korea
Seongjae Lee	KISA, South Korea
Byungchul Choi	ETRI, South Korea
Yousung Kang	ETRI, South Korea
Hyeongcheon Kim	NSR, South Korea
Woonyon Kim	NSR, South Korea

Contents

Hardware Security

Application Security

Machine Learning Security

LOM: Lightweight Classifier for Obfuscation Methods

Jeongwoo Kim[1], Seoyeon Kang[1], Eun-Sun Cho[1(✉)], and Joon-Young Paik[2]

[1] Department of Computer Science and Engineering, Chungnam National University,
Daejeon, South Korea
{201502038,sy.kang}@o.cnu.ac.kr, eschough@cnu.ac.kr
[2] Tiangong University, Tianjin, China
pjy2018@tiangong.edu.cn

Abstract. Obfuscation is an important technique that renders it difficult to analyze programs and has been developed for copyright protection. When an obfuscation is applied to a program, the logic of a program can be very complex and de-obfuscation can be very difficult. However, obfuscation can be used to conceal malicious codes in malware. Therefore, de-obfuscation for binary codes is required for malicious code analysis. In addition, the type of obfuscation technique applied to a program must be identified as it determines the de-obfuscation solution. However, it is difficult to acquire information regarding obfuscation from binary codes, where various obfuscation techniques are mixed. Herein, we propose a lightweight neural network-based classifier (LOM) to detect obfuscation techniques. LOM involves only a lightweight procedure using an opcode histogram, which is designed based on the effects of obfuscation methods on opcodes. It is experimentally shown that LOM yields competitive performance compared with other obfuscation technique classifiers.

Keywords: Opcode histogram · Neural network · Deobfuscation

1 Introduction

Obfuscation is a technique that converts the logic of a program to be the same but difficult to read. It is used for software security and prevents unauthorized program copying. Several different obfuscation techniques change the operations or control flows in the original code. Furthermore, obfuscation is used for malicious codes [1, 2]. In other words, it is difficult to analyze the original behavior of the obfuscated malicious code; as such, the response to malicious codes is delayed. However, because de-obfuscation is extremely difficult, the intervention of highly skilled experts is required instead of automation. In particular, the obfuscation technique applied to malicious codes must be identified before de-obfuscation. If various obfuscation techniques are applied simultaneously, then it would be extremely difficult to determine the applied obfuscation techniques in the programs. The goal of this study is to classify obfuscation techniques applied to obfuscated binary codes.

© Springer Nature Switzerland AG 2021
H. Kim (Ed.): WISA 2021, LNCS 13009, pp. 3–15, 2021.
https://doi.org/10.1007/978-3-030-89432-0_1

Some previous studies [3–5] on de-obfuscation have targeted obfuscated programs of high-level programming languages. They typically exploit high-level semantics (e.g., strings). Although it is challenging to extract meaningful features to identify obfuscation techniques from binary files, many researchers are focusing on de-obfuscation with various methods [6, 7]. OBFEYE [8] uses a deep-learning-based model to identify obfuscation techniques applied in obfuscated binary codes. Binary semantic information of structures such as "long dependence" and "strong structure" [8] were used to construct the model. However, such information might be overly specific and complex, thereby not justifying its high cost for analysis. For instance, the superfluous code chunk introduced by obfuscation is ad hoc and random, necessitating a detailed analysis that may not provide too much information.

Herein, we propose LOM, a lightweight neural network-based obfuscation technique classifier that enables the identification of obfuscation techniques in obfuscated binary code. One of the primary functions of LOM is to use minimal information from obfuscated codes to ensure a lightweight process. First, it focuses on the effects of changes on control flows and operations yielded by individual obfuscation techniques. In addition, LOM relies only on selected key opcodes in obfuscated binary codes, which are processed into histogram representations and input into the neural network-based classification model. The superiority of the proposed LOM was demonstrated experimentally; its performance is comparable to that of the existing complex obfuscation technique classifier while requiring much lower costs, owing to the simple neural network that we adopt.

The remainder of this paper is organized as follows: We present the background of obfuscation, previous studies, and our research motivation (Sect. 2). Next, we analyze the change in the opcode level due to obfuscation and then describe the process of converting it into an opcode histogram and the model using this histogram as input data (Sect. 3). Subsequently, we describe the configuration for the experiment (Sect. 4) and present experiments that classify obfuscation methods (Sect. 5). Finally, we provide the conclusions in Sect. 6.

2   Background and Motivation

2.1   Obfuscation

Obfuscation complicates the control flow graph and operations or inserts a dead code to render the program difficult to read. When the code is obfuscated, the control flow of the obfuscated code becomes much more complicated than that of the original code. For example, the obfuscation techniques supported by *OLLVM* [9] manufactured by INRIA in France include instruction substitution, bogus control flow, and control flow flattening, which can be used multiple times. We focused on these three techniques as they are the most representative obfuscation techniques. The obfuscation technique is as follows:

Instruction Substitution. Instruction substitution complicates general operations, as in Eq. (1), and the Mixed Boolean-Arithmetic (MBA) expression is often used for this purpose. The MBA expression mixes logical and arithmetic operations to render simple arithmetic operations difficult to read.

$$a = b + c \rightarrow a = b - (-c) \tag{1}$$

Control Flow Flattening. Control flow flattening is an obfuscation technique that flattens the control-flow graph. When control flow flattening is applied, one basic block is partitioned into several blocks and controlled by the switch statement and variable.

Bogus Control Flow. Bogus control flow is an obfuscation technique that modifies the function call graph by inserting fake control flow branches. The newly created fake control flow branch is implemented using opaque predicates. Opaque predicate is a condition that is always true or false. For example, if a branch has a condition that is always false, then a true branch block is not executable. Bogus control flow is an obfuscation technique involving dummy code insertion [10].

2.2 Existing Obfuscation Detection Methods and Motivation

Studies to detect obfuscated codes for analyzing malicious codes have been conducted. First, features that can appear in the code are extracted to analyze the obfuscated code. The authors of [4] and [5] effectively analyzed strings appearing in the obfuscated code to detect the obfuscated JavaScript code. Furthermore, obfuscated codes were detected based on the entropy that can appear when a string is encoded. The structural features of obfuscated codes were identified in some studies. The author of [3] utilized the AST context of JavaScript to identify the obfuscated JavaScript code.

OBFEYE [8] obtains semantic information from binary files by leveraging deep learning techniques with an awareness of the basic blocks in the disassembled code. It demonstrated good performance for the classification of obfuscation techniques. However, this method has several disadvantages. First, OBFEYE exhibits a complex architecture that comprises a convolutional neural network and long short-term memory network with complex layers. Second, its extraction of semantic information such as long dependences and strong structures is costly and not straightforward. Finally, the detailed semantic information may hinder the classification of sophisticated obfuscation techniques. The information is based on the relationship between neighboring instructions and basic blocks in a program, whereas obfuscation strategies may randomly distort the information because of the instructions and basic blocks. Hence, the approach is highly sensitive to even slight deliberate actions of obfuscators (e.g., instruction reordering and ad hoc dummy block insertions). Moreover, because the validity of disassembly is not guaranteed for obfuscated codes, using excessive specific information regarding program structures (e.g., basic blocks and control flow graph) from incomplete disassemble codes is not recommended.

The goal of this study is to observe the change in the instruction code for obfuscated binary codes, effectively express it as a histogram, and implement the obfuscation technique classification model by feeding these histograms.

2.3 Research Using Opcode Histogram

Binary opcode refers to the operation of the instruction to be executed. The binary opcode histogram encodes the frequency of the occurrence of opcodes into one-dimensional data. This representation is extremely simple in comparison with other complex encoding methods and does not involve executions or the appearance order. As such, it is used extensively in various fields, such as program analysis and similarity classification. In [11], an opcode histogram of the Java byte code was proposed, and a model that uses the opcode histogram and classifies similar programs was constructed. In addition, opcode histograms were used as training data for deep learning models to perform malicious code classification and detection [12–14].

In this study, only binary opcodes were used as a feature to classify the obfuscation technique. Once the original codes are manipulated through obfuscation, any changes in the opcodes will affect the opcode histogram representations. For instance, the bogus control flow increases the values of the opcodes related to the control flow branches in a histogram representation. In addition, the opcode histogram is resilient to any opcode reordering of obfuscation techniques.

3   Classification of Obfuscation Method Using Opcode Histogram

3.1   Overview of Our Approach

The aim of this study is to implement a lightweight model based on minimal information and to classify the obfuscation techniques of obfuscation tools *OLLVM* that are widely used by malicious code developers. Our choice to target OLLVM is reasonable because the effect of OLLVM has already been shown in previous study [15]. Herein, we propose the opcode histogram, which can be obtained by focusing on the disassembly code and selecting only opcodes that change because of obfuscation.

An obfuscation technique classification model was trained using an opcode histogram as input data. The obfuscation techniques to be classified were control flow flattening (fla), bogus control flow (bcf), and instruction substitution (sub), which are supported by *OLLVM* [9]. This includes the application of multiple techniques. The details of the dataset are described in Sect. 4.

3.2   Changes in Opcode Frequency Based on Obfuscation Techniques

To observe changes in programs due to obfuscation, we extracted the opcodes from the dataset. To obtain the opcodes from the dataset, we disassembled binary programs using the Linux command *objdump*. Next, after parsing the opcode appearing in the assembly, the frequencies of each opcode were counted.

If all opcodes defined for a binary program are considered, then the number of opcodes will increase, and the histogram will become extremely large. Hence, only the first byte of the opcode was considered in a previous study [12]. However, this method is not suitable because various opcodes with a length of two or three bytes exist, and they perform completely different operations. For example, in the case of "20," the code is "and" when expressed as a mnemonic code and is regarded as a 1-byte instruction code; however, it may appear as a "mov" instruction code when considering a two-byte instruction code [16]. To solve this problem, we reduced the number of opcodes using another method.

First, the number of opcodes was maintained appropriately by considering only the opcodes appearing in the dataset and then observing the change due to obfuscation. Figure 1 shows an example of a histogram showing the frequencies of the opcodes in one program. Among the 403 opcodes that appear in our dataset, only a few opcodes appeared in one program. Therefore, if the entire opcode is trained, then many unnecessary opcodes can be included in the dataset.

Fig. 1. Example of histogram (using all opcodes appearing in dataset)

Second, only some of the opcodes affected by obfuscation were used in learning. When obfuscation is applied, only a few opcodes are affected by obfuscation. In this study, by comparing the difference between the opcode histogram of the obfuscated file and the original file, it was discovered that only some of the opcode frequencies were affected after obfuscation. Table 1 shows the average increase in the opcodes due to different obfuscation techniques. For files to which OLLVM's Bogus control flow (bcf) was applied, opcodes such as or, add, and test increased by 14 or more on average compared with the number of opcodes in the original files. In addition, the change in the opcode used for obfuscation differed for each obfuscation technique.

Table 1. Opcode changes in file based on obfuscation technique

Option	and	or	test	je	add
fla	0	0	0	19	0
bcf	14	15	16	0	7
sub	8	8	0	0	2

The entire process of the proposed opcode selection is described as follows.

First, we denote F and Op as the set of all binary programs and the set of all opcodes in binary programs, respectively. Assume that the size of Op is K, which implies that the number of opcodes is K. For a file f within F, freq (f, op) denotes the number of appearances of the opcode op within Op in file f. Accordingly, a "frequency vector" is the tuple $freq_f = (freq(f, op_0), freq(f, op_1)\ldots freq(f, op_{k-1}))$ for f within F, which enumerates the number of appearances of each opcode in f. The arity of $freq_f$ is K. Let PlainF is the subset of or equal to F denote the set of all original binary programs considered for our experiments and assume that the number of PlainF is N. It is noteworthy that $freq_{fi}$ is denoted as $freq_i$, where f_i within PlainF.

ObfusM is the set of obfuscation methods considered herein. In this study, the size of ObfusM is 3, and obm_0, obm_1, and obm_2 represent the instruction substitution, control flattening, and bogus control flow, respectively. For a file f_i within PlainF, the obfuscation method obm_j within ObfusM is used, where j is 0, 1 and 2, and obm_j (f_i) denotes the obfuscated file earned after the application of obm_j to f_i. It is noteworthy that $freq^{fi}_{obmj}$ is denoted as $freqobm_i^j$. For file f_i and obfuscation method obm_j the tuple $Diff_j$, whose arity is K, is defined as follows:

$$Diff_j(i) = |freqobm_i^j - freq_i| \tag{2}$$

The tuple $Diff_j$ (i) captures the amount of change in freq (f_i, op_k) f a specific file f_i after applying the obfuscation method obm_j. For instance, let us assume that N = 2 and K = 3. For obfuscation method obm_2 and file f_i, let us assume that (1, 2, 3) for $freq_i$ before obfuscation and (10, 0, 20) for $freqobm_i^j$ after obfuscation. In this case, $Diff_j$ (i) is converted into (9, 2, 17) for op_0, op_1 and op_2.

The vectorized sum of $Diff_j$ (i) over $i = 0 \dots N$-1 refers to the sum of the amounts of changes over all the files. Each entry of this summation by the opcode may indicate the dominance of the opcodes. For instance, for obm_j, let us assume that N is 2, K = 3, $Diff_j$ (0) = (9, 2, 17) for file f_0, and $Diff_j$ (1) = (5, 1, 12) for file f_1. The vectorized sum of $Diff_j$ is (14, 3, 29), which implies that op_2 imposes the most significant effect among the three opcodes, whereas op_1 imposes the least. For file f_i and an obfuscation method obm_j, when a hyperparameter α is provided,

$$DomOp_j = \sigma_{\text{select top a elements}} \left(\sum_{i=1}^{n} Diff_j(i) \right), \tag{3}$$

which indicates that the top α appears primarily as an opcode in the vectorized sum of $Diff_j$. Among the opcodes used in the files, the elements of $DomOp_j$ are the most closely related to the effects of obfuscation method obm_j. From the experiment, for bcf, $DomOp_3$ with $\alpha = 10$ was "mov," "cmp," "jmpq," "test," "jne," "sub," "and," "or," "sete," "setl." Hence, we used O*, the union of the dominant opcodes $DomOp_j$, to classify all the obfuscation methods.

3.3   Opcode Histogram-Based Obfuscation Technique Classification Model

In Sect. 3.2, changes in opcodes based on the obfuscation technique applied are presented. To transform the information regarding these opcodes, each program is converted into a histogram that represents the frequencies of the opcodes. The histogram can fully represent the types and frequencies of the opcodes based on the program. Figure 2 shows the entire process of the proposed approach.

The process comprises two steps. The learning and testing steps are the training and classification processes of the test dataset, respectively. In the training process, the dataset is first disassembled and preprocessed to obtain the opcodes. Next, histograms are extracted after selecting the meaningful ones among the opcodes. In this case, the opcodes included in the histogram are the O*-selected ones based on the procedure proposed in Sect. 3.2. Subsequently, these histograms are input into the model. During the testing step the target program is disassembled and preprocessed and then the obfuscation technique is classified by the model. In our process, the model was implemented based on a deep neural network (DNN). A DNN comprises two or more hidden layers between an input layer and an output layer. Each layer is composed of nodes, and a model that performs the desired task can be created by learning the input data. Our model stacks 2 hidden layers, and we adopted a rectified linear unit function as an activation function.

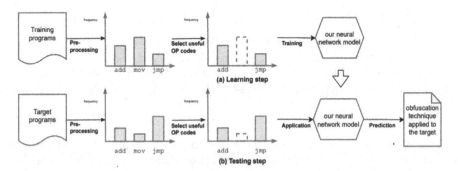

Fig. 2. Process flow of our approach

The input data of our model is an opcode histogram, and several models with different dimensions of the input data were implemented based on the design parameter α. The model classifies the obfuscation technique applied to the file by feeding only the opcode histograms.

4   Configuration of Experiments

This section describes the datasets used in the experiment. Another model is described as well to compare the performance of our models.

Obtaining an obfuscated dataset is extremely difficult. To obtain data that are similar to those in the real world [8], the source code of the *Linux gcc-7.4.0 compiler* was used as the dataset. To build a dataset, each gcc source code was compiled with *OLLVM* [9] and obfuscated simultaneously to create an object file. Finally, the dataset was segregated into a training set and a test set at a ratio of 70:30. The details of the dataset are shown in Table 2.

Three obfuscation options were applied to the dataset: fla, bcf, and sub. In addition, the sub and fla, fla and bcf, and sub and bcf techniques, which are multiple obfuscation techniques, were applied to the program to verify whether multiple applied obfuscation was identified. Moreover, the tigress-generated programs of [17] were used as a test set to evaluate the model to verify whether our models generalized well. In [17], 5037 original programs were acquired and applied to each obfuscation technique. Table 3 lists the details of the dataset. However, not all programs changed when obfuscation was applied. When an opcode histogram (not using O*) was extracted from an obfuscated file, the program that did not change compared with the original file was excluded from the dataset.

Table 2. Details of our dataset (gcc-7.4.0)

	Original	Sub	Fla	Bcf	Sub-fla	Fla-bcf	Sub-bcf	Sum
Train set	5514	5765	5149	8739	6675	8795	9510	50147
Test set	2363	2470	2206	3746	2861	3770	4076	21492

Table 3. Details of our dataset (tigress generated program)

	Original	Sub	Fla	Bcf	Sub-fla	Fla-bcf	Sub-bcf	Sum
Test set	5037	5037	5037	5037	5037	5037	5037	35259

In addition, random-forest-based feature selection was implemented and used to compare our models trained with the proposed opcode histogram. We trained a random forest model using an opcode histogram to classify the obfuscation technique. This model selects the opcodes that are important for classification. In this study, another model, RF-DNN, was trained with an opcode histogram that contained opcodes selected from the random forest. RF-DNN has the same structure as our proposed model. Subsequently, the results were compared with those of our models.

5   Experiments

For the experiment, we used the framework with PyTorch, and the NVIDIA GeForce RTX 3090 GPU. The results of the two opcode selection methods implemented in this study and the performances of our models are provided in this section.

First, the O* returned by setting the design parameter α to all, 10, 15, and 20 is described and compared with the random forest-based feature selection. Next, the performance comparison of five models trained with each O* and RF-DNN is provided. Furthermore, we show that obfuscation can be classified by only certain types of opcode frequencies. Finally, we present the efficacy of our proposed model in generalizing new datasets.

5.1   Instruction Selection

Table 4 shows the number of opcodes in O*, which was returned based on the opcode selection formula and the design parameter α.

In this study, O* was used for our proposed opcode histogram. The opcodes in O* varied based on the design parameter α. When O* was obtained by setting α from 10 to 20, the number of opcodes was reduced from 403 to 21. In other words, the required information was minimized by excluding the opcode, which did not change significantly even when obfuscation was applied. Moreover, because we can only select the changed opcode, we can improve the histogram implemented based on the unselected opcode, as shown in Fig. 1. However, in the case of opcode "mov," a peculiar frequency was indicated depending on all obfuscation techniques and was included in the selected opcode set O*. However, the "mov" increased with the program size. Therefore, "mov" was excluded to ensure the robustness of the model with respect to the program size.

Table 4. Opcodes selected based on α (O*)

α	O*	|O*|
α=10	add,sub,pop,jmpq,and,cmovne,jne,cmovl,cmove,or,mov,xor,setl,sete,mov abs,cmp,push,movl,test,jge,je	21
α=15	jmpq,sub,or,nopw,mov,sete,jne,setl,cmp,imul,movups,cmovne,test,movab s,callq,pop,add,xor,cmovl,je,nopl,setne,and,jge,movl,cmove,push,xchg	28
α=20	cmp,movl,setp,add,test,je,imul,cmovne,jp,movsd,cvtsi2sd,jae,xor,movaps ,or,push,movups,cmove,callq,dec,jne,cmovl,nopl,mov,setl,sub,lea,cvtsi2s dl,jmpq,pop,and,nopw,setne,sete,movabs ,xchg,jge	37

Finally, the opcode histogram was implemented based on each O* from which the "mov" opcode was removed; subsequently, it was input to the obfuscation classification model.

5.2 Evaluation: Single Obfuscation Techniques

In this experiment, the training set shown in Table 2 was input to the model and evaluated using the test set. The performance metrics were accuracy and true positive rate (TPR). The accuracy was evaluated as $(TP + TN)/(TP + FN + FP + TN)$ for all the data. The TPR is a classification evaluation indicator named recall, and it is the ratio of data perceived as true by the model among of the actual true data. $TP/(TP + FP)$ is the calculation result of recall. In this study, TPR indicates the rate at which the model correctly predicts the obfuscation technique applied to the obfuscated file. As shown in Table 5, we trained and evaluated the model using only the dataset for the single obfuscation techniques shown in Table 2.

Among the models trained on O*, the highest accuracy was indicated when α was 15, and no significant differences were observed in all cases, including both the models (α = all), which were trained without selection and the RF-DNN. An obfuscated classifier with high performance can be implemented using only a few opcode frequencies. Furthermore, we confirmed that the algorithm implemented by *OLLVM* obfuscation is an easy problem that can be determined using the frequency of a specific opcode. The RF-DNN shown in Table 5 was implemented for comparison with the proposed model, as mentioned above. The following 28 opcodes were selected: cpuid, xchg, movslq, movabs, lea, retq, cmpl, pop, callq, cmovl, push, jge, imul, movl, cmp, add, mov, jmpq, sete, test, setl, or, and, je, cmovne, sub, jne, and xor, and the mov instruction was excluded. The RF-DNN exhibited a similar or slightly worse performance than the proposed model when similar opcodes were selected; however, the RF-DNN required approximately 17.76 s to perform feature selection, which was longer compared with the time required by the proposed model, i.e., 3.16s. In addition, our proposed formula yielded more consistent results compared with random-forest-based instruction code selection, which may yield different results each time it is trained.

Table 5. Performance of models (single obfuscation technique)

TPR					
	Original	sub	fla	bcf	ACC
Model 0 (α = all)	0.90	0.84	0.96	0.97	92.82
Model 1 (α = 10)	0.87	0.85	0.99	0.97	92.24
Model 2 (α = 15)	0.92	0.86	0.99	0.92	93.65
Model 3 (α = 20)	0.90	0.82	0.98	0.97	92.16
RF- DNN	0.85	0.86	0.99	0.96	92.09

5.3 Evaluation: Multiple Obfuscation Techniques

To evaluate the case where the two obfuscation techniques are applied, the dataset shown in Table 2 and the evaluation metrics presented in Sect. 5.2 were used.

Table 6. Performances of models (multiple obfuscation technique)

TPR								
	original	sub	fla	bcf	sub-fla	fla-bcf	sub-bcf	ACC
Model 0 (α = all)	0.79	0.79	0.91	0.92	0.62	0.97	0.91	85.37
Model 1 (α = 10)	0.84	0.76	0.82	0.94	0.62	0.98	0.93	85.79
Model 2 (α = 15)	0.83	0.83	0.79	0.94	0.71	0.97	0.93	87.21
Model 3 (α = 20)	0.80	0.87	0.79	0.94	0.62	0.97	0.93	86.04
RF- DNN	0.85	0.78	0.86	0.94	0.61	0.97	0.94	86.16

Table 6 shows the results of training and evaluating the model with all the datasets shown in Table 2. The results presented in Table 6 shows that when classifying multiple obfuscation techniques simultaneously, the obfuscation classification model trained with the selected opcode histogram performed better than the model trained with the histogram comprising 403 opcodes prior to opcode selection. The TPR for classifying the obfuscation technique is generally high; however, the TPR is not high for files to which fla and sub obfuscation are applied simultaneously. For files with multiple sub-fla obfuscation applied, the most typical FPs were misclassification as fla obfuscation applied as a single class. It can be inferred that this is because sub obfuscation changes the frequency of a specific instruction code only slightly compared with other obfuscation techniques.

5.4 Model Performance on Unseen Data

Table 7 shows the performance of the model, which was evaluated using the data shown in Table 3. We compared Model 2, which demonstrated the best performance, as shown in Tables 5 and 6, with the obfuscation detection model OBFEYE implemented in [8]. OBFEYE was trained using gcc-7.4.0 and evaluated using tigress-generated programs; therefore, it can be compared with our proposed model. In this experiment, we demonstrated that our model generalized well. As shown in Table 7, both models demonstrated extremely high recall and accuracy values. Consequently, the lightweight model based on the opcode histogram proposed herein performed well for unseen data, which implies that it is not inferior to the existing complex model [8].

Table 7. Performance of models (unseen data)

TPR								
	original	Sub	Fla	Bcf	Sub-fla	Fla-bcf	sub-bcf	ACC
Model 2 ($\alpha = 15$)	0.99	0.99	1.00	1.00	0.99	1.00	0.99	0.9954
OBFEYE	0.98	0.99	1.00	0.99	0.99	0.99	0.99	0.9966

Notably, the performance of Model 2 differed significantly from that shown in the experiments on the gcc compiler dataset presented in Sects. 5.2 and 5.3. The model implemented in this study is robust even for unseen data and is well generalized.

6 Conclusion

Herein, we proposed a neural network model with high accuracy for classifying obfuscation techniques based on opcode histograms. Motivated by the difference in opcodes between the original programs and their corresponding programs, our opcode histogram was extracted by selecting opcodes that were associated highly with obfuscation techniques. The obfuscation technique was classified by learning the histograms of the opcodes. We discovered that the obfuscation technique can be classified with only opcodes, and that the performance of the proposed model was comparable to that of the existing complicated model. In addition, we confirmed that our proposed model classified obfuscation techniques of a different obfuscation tool as accurately as they did our test dataset, which implies that the proposed opcode histogram is an effective feature for classifying obfuscation techniques supported by various obfuscation tools. We plan to develop a large-scale obfuscation dataset that encompasses various obfuscation techniques and combinations thereof involving different obfuscation tools, and subsequently improve the model using them.

Acknowledgement. This work was supported by Institute for Information & communications Technology Planning & Evaluation (IITP) grant funded by the Korea government (MSIT) (No.2019–0-01343, Training Key Talents in Industrial Convergence Security).

References

1. Xu, D., Ming, J., Fu, Y., Wu, D.: VMHunt: a verifiable approach to partially-virtualized binary code simplification. The 2018 ACM SIGSAC Conference on Computer and Communication Security (CCS 2018), pp. 442–458 (2018)
2. Mok, S.-K., et al.: Program slicing for binary code deobfuscation. J. Korea Inst. Inf. Secur. Cryptology **27**(1), 59–66 (2017)
3. Kaplan, S., Livshits, B., Zorn, B., Siefert, C., Cursinger, C.: NOFUS: Automatically Detecting' String.fromCharCode(32) 'ObFuSCateD '. toLowerCase()' JavaScript Code. Technical Report Microsoft Research (2011)
4. Likarish, P., Jung, E., Jo, I.: Obfuscated Malicious JavaScript Detection Using Classification Techniques. In: 4th International Conference on Malicious and Unwanted Software (MALWARE), pp. 47–54, (2009)
5. Jodavi, M., Abadi, M., Parhizkar, E.: JSObfusDetector: a binary PSO-based One-class classifier ensemble to detect obfuscated JavaScript Code. The International Symposium on Artificial Intelligence and Signal Processing (AISP), pp. 322–327 (2015)
6. Kan, Z., Wang, H., Wu, L., Guo, Y., Xu, G.: Deobfuscating android native binary code. In: 2019 IEEE/ACM 41st International Conference on Software Engineering: Companion Proceedings (ICSE-Companion), pp. 322–323 (2019)
7. Yadegari, B., Debray, S.: Symbolic execution of obfuscated code. In: Proceedings of the 22nd ACM SIGSAC Conference on Computer and Communications Security (CCS 2015). Association for Computing Machinery, New York, NY, USA, pp. 732–744 (2015)
8. Zhao, Y., et al.: Semantics-aware obfuscation scheme prediction for binary. Comput. Secur. **99**, 102072 (2020)
9. Junod, P., Rinaldini, J., Wehrli, J., Michielin, J.: Obfuscator-LLVM -- software protection for the masses. In: IEEE/ACM 1st International Workshop on Software Protection, pp. 3–9 (2015)
10. Kang, S.Y., et al.: OBFUS: an obfuscation tool for software and vulnerability protection. In: Proceedings of the Eleventh ACM Conference on Data and Application Security and Privacy (CODASPY 2021) Association for Computing Machinery, New York, NY, USA, pp. 309–311 (2021)
11. Lim, H.-I.: Applying code vectors for presenting software features in machine learning. In: IEEE 42nd Annual Computer Software and Applications Conference (COMPSAC), vol. 01, pp. 803–804 (2018)

12. Rad, B.B., Masrom, M., Ibrahim, S.: Opcodes histogram for classifying metamorphic portable executables Malware. In: International Conference on E-Learning and E-Technologies in Education, ICEEE (2012)
13. Saxe, J., Berlin, K.: deep neural network based malware detection using two-dimensional binary program features. In: 10th International Conference on Malicious and Unwanted Software (MALWARE), pp. 11–20 (2015)
14. Rad, B.B., et al.: Metamorphic virus variants classification using opcode frequency histogram. In: Proceedings of the 14th WSEAS international conference on Computers: part of the 14th WSEAS CSCC Multiconference, Volume I WSEAS, Stevens Point, WI, USA, pp. 147–155 (ICCOMP 2010) (2010)
15. Kim, D., et al.: Revisiting Binary Code Similarity Analysis using Interpretable Feature Engineering and Lessons Learned. ArXiv abs/2011.10749 (2020)
16. Opcode and Instruction Reference Homepage. http://ref.x86asm.net/coder32.html
17. Obfuscation-Benchmarks (2018). https://github.com/tum-i22/obfuscation-benchmarks

A Method for Collecting Vehicular Network Data for Enhanced Anomaly Detection

Samuel De La Motte and Jin B. Hong[✉]

University of Western Australia, Perth, Australia
`jin.hong@uwa.edu.au`

Abstract. Advances in anomaly and intrusion detection systems (IDS) for vehicle networks can enable attacks to be stealthier, such as mimicking the behaviours of aggressive driving to disrupt normal vehicle operations. Moreover, data collection, classification and evaluation has been challenging due to vehicle manufacturers deploying proprietary encoding schemes for sensor communications. This paper proposes a method for vehicle network data collection and processing to provide naturalistic datasets for identifying different driving behaviours. Firstly, we provide a guide for the assembly of an Arduino Uno R3 with a Sparkfun CAN bus shield for connection to the on-board diagnostics (OBD) port to collect the vehicle data. Secondly, we offer baseline metrics for labelling passive and aggressive driving behaviours through the analysis of a vehicle's CAN bus data. Finally, a state-of-the-art deep learning model that combines the convolutional neural network (CNN) and recurrent neural network (RNN) architectures is implemented to evaluate the fitness of the data collected using the proposed method. The collected naturalistic dataset was used to train this model in-order to recognise driver behaviour patterns that are otherwise unobservable to humans and that can be used to identify passive and aggressive driver events. Our experiment shows a 0.98 F1 score, indicating our data collection method and metrics used for selecting features can provide quality datasets for intrusion detection against attacks mimicking aggressive driving.

Keywords: Driver profiling · Arduino · LSTM · Self-Attention mechanism

1 Introduction

Electronic controller units (ECUs) are now integral components in CAN bus networks and their measurements they provide are becoming increasingly complex. But as the CAN bus is a shared multi-master network that does not authenticate connected nodes, any device can intercept the transmissions between ECUs or potentially inject malicious messages that aim to reduce or disable vehicle functionalities by physically connecting to it. Additionally, the CAN protocol does not implement any complex security measures such as encryption or verification of messages, making it prone to intrusion attacks. Impaired vehicle functionalities could pose significant risks to both the driver and other individuals on the road.

© Springer Nature Switzerland AG 2021
H. Kim (Ed.): WISA 2021, LNCS 13009, pp. 16–27, 2021.
https://doi.org/10.1007/978-3-030-89432-0_2

Anomalies in CAN bus telemetries could be caused by attacking the vehicle network, including a change in the driver's behaviours. Various drivers of the same vehicle will generate unique ECU telemetry patterns which they refer to as an individual's driving fingerprint [6]. This provides an attack vector which could be exploited to inject more advanced attacks, such as inducing the behaviour of the vehicle to be aggressive, which potentially bypass anomaly and intrusion detection systems (IDSs). Data collection from the vehicle network for such attacks can be challenging for many researchers due to the inaccessibility of appropriate vehicles or hardware for data collection. Although most recent vehicles have an OBD port, where a vehicle's OBD port can be accessed using an OBD-II standard [10] (SAE J1979/ISO 15031–5) adapter (i.e., ECU telemetries trans-mitted on a vehicle's CAN bus can be seen via the OBD-II port), it is not trivial to collect and export such data easily. Further, although the OBD port is now a standard, different vehicle manufacturers often utilise their own encoding scheme for ECU messages (e.g., messages for acceleration will be different across vehicle models, even from the same manufacturer), requiring reverse engineering or additional steps for data cleansing before being able to conduct the analysis. Finally, it is difficult to extract useful features when classifying driver behaviours for anomaly detection, due to hundreds of ECU message types and their potential combinations. The lack of naturalistic vehicle network datasets along with the described research limitations significantly impede the enhancement of IDSs to thwart advanced attacks.

This paper describes a method to collect naturalistic vehicle telemetry data using "off-the-shelf" electronics, and verifies that deep learning can be used on raw/encoded CAN bus data to identify passive and aggressive driving (i.e., anomalies caused by driver behaviour changes). The collected datasets can then be used to further refine IDSs to be more robust against such attacks. The contributions of this paper are as follows:

- An "off-the-shelf" hardware and software configuration for collecting CAN bus telemetries from vehicle networks via an OBD-II port.
- Identify useful features from the data for identifying individual's driving behaviours as either passive or aggressive, relative to their own person.
- Implement an IDS, a deep learning model, to identify driving behaviours from the collected dataset in-order verify the effectiveness when used on raw/encoded telemetries.
- Evaluate the goodness of the collected naturalistic data using the proposed method by measuring the performance of the implemented IDS.
- Provide foundational work for future research that aims to improve state-of-the-art IDSs in detecting truly stealthy intrusion attacks.

2 Literature Review

2.1 Driver Profiling

Existing methods can detect the theft of a vehicle by analysing unique driver behaviours that are reflected in the vehicle's CAN bus telemetries [17]. Specific driving events during a trip have been successfully classified in [18] and the detection of driver fatigue in [19], all by using combinations of sensor measurements from a vehicle's CAN bus and smart phone sensor measurements. Hallac et al. [8] identified a unique driver from a pool of 64 drivers by only looking at CAN bus data collected from a single turn, a random forest classifier was used, and the authors achieved an average accuracy of 76.9%. Furthermore, Enev et al. [6] implemented four ML algorithms (SVM, Random Forrest, Naïve Bayes and K-nearest neighbour) to determine the top sensor measurements that are most significant when identifying a driver. The dataset collection did not include any collection of data that was not already present (i.e., smart phone sensors) on the OBD-II port in the vehicle. They found that the brake pedal, max engine torque, steering wheel angle and lateral acceleration sensor data were most significant in-order to differentiate between drivers. Wahab et al. [3] ascertained that the accelerator and brake pedal pressures were critical in accurately profiling a driver. Kwak et al. [17] found that pre-processing your feature set to include statistical features could drastically improve classification accuracy in driver profiling applications. Regarding deep learning specific approaches, a review of driver profiling studies [9] identified the high prediction accuracy of neural networks as they are capable in learning sequential input and output relationships. The authors state that there is a lack of driver profiling studies prior to 2018 that adopt Long Short-term Memory Recurrent Neural Networks (LSTMs) for driver profiling applications. In recent years, Klusek et al. [5] used an LSTM with 'Kalman Filtering' and Mekki et al. [4] used a hybrid LSTM with a fully convolutional network (FCN). Both studies additionally boast prediction accuracies that encourage the use of LSTMs in driver profiling applications.

Thus far, the studies mentioned do not take into consideration vehicle telemetry anomalies that occur when attacks are used to mimic aggressive driving (i.e., caused by an attack, not the driver). However, such attacks are mentioned in [17], highlighting the importance of identifying and intercepting intrusion attacks mimicking different driving behaviours that could affect the safety of passengers.

2.2 Naturalistic Datasets

For the ability to conduct research for driver profiling applications and even investigating intrusion attacks on a vehicle CAN bus, a dataset is required. Past studies in these areas have seen the collection of small and large CAN bus telemetry datasets with and without intrusion attacks. However, the datasets in [13–15] had been collected in controlled environments (i.e., closed roads). Thus, they do not reflect real-world CAN bus telemetries that would be present in a naturalistic dataset collection and additionally are not publicly available. The Osclab dataset provided by the Hacking and Countermeasure Research Lab (HCRL) is a publicly available naturalistic driving dataset that was collected for the 2018 Information and Security Research and Development event held in South Korea. The raw CAN bus data from a Kia vehicle was collected from 10 individuals during two-round trips between Korea University and SANGAM World Cup Stadium around 8 pm–11 pm. It contains 51 unique features with a total of 94,401 samples which have been decoded into human readable form [1]. The AEGIS Big Data Repository dataset is another publicly available naturalistic driving dataset which contains raw CAN bus data in its decoded form. It contains 19 unique features with a total of 158,659 samples collected during trips from 3 individuals driving the same vehicle in Austria [2]. To the best of our knowledge, the Osclab and the AEGIS CAN bus datasets are the only publicly available naturalistic CAN bus telemetry datasets. Even then, no such datasets are available that contain intrusion attacks with the aim to mimic different driving behaviours.

3 Materials and Methods

First, we describe metrics to classify passive and aggressive driving behaviours in Sect. 3.1. Then, we provide an overview of the naturalistic dataset collection pipeline used to obtain real-word CAN bus telemetries in Sect. 3.2. Next, we describe the dataset cleaning process in Sect. 3.3, and lastly, we describe the IDS for evaluating the goodness of our collected dataset in Sect. 3.4.

3.1 Passive vs. Aggressive Metrics

It is difficult to provide a "one-size-fits-all" approach to identify an individual's passive driver behaviours from their aggressive ones. Martinez et al. [11] surveyed driving style recognition studies and concluded that there is no unique definition or measure to categorise a person's unique driving style. This is due to the large combination of vehicle telemetries and driver features that could affect driving style identification metric results between different individuals. What could be considered a passive or aggressive driving behaviour, is ultimately relative to that specific individual. Fugiglando et al. [12] presented the first ever concept of "Driver DNA" as a way of comparing individualistic driver behaviour profiles by calculating a driver profile score that combines the driver's braking, turning, speeding and fuel efficiency. CAN bus signals were collected from 53 different drivers of the same vehicle. The authors then extracted CAN bus signals including frontal acceleration (braking), lateral acceleration (turning), vehicle speed (speeding) and engine revolutions per minute (fuel efficiency). This information was then used in real-time to visualise a driver profile score to aid the driver to practice safe driver behaviours. Insight from [11] shows that combinations of vehicle types and driver behaviour features ultimately affect ones driving style, and in conjunction with the successful outcome from [12], this paper will utilise engine RPM readings as a metric to compare passive Vs. aggressive driver behaviours. Through visual analysis of the RPM curves for the passive and aggressive dataset collections provided in this paper, we will be able to verify that our passive Vs. aggressive collections have produced noticeably different curve characteristics.

For example, consider 2 drivers (A and B) of the same vehicle that have been instructed to only perform passive driving actions during an experiment. Driver B might exert more force on the accelerator when taking off from a set of lights as opposed to Driver A. This would result in the revolutions per minute (RPM) curve of the vehicle's engine during that time period for Driver B to be largely exponential at first, which would abruptly decrease and plateau, where it will stay relatively constant once the designated speed limit is reached. Driver A's RPM curve for that time period would be more linear in nature as it gradually increases until they have also reached the speed limit, at which point the curve will begin to plateau. Figure 1(a) and 1(b) below depicts the engine RPM curves for the 2 drivers in this example. Additionally, Driver B would reach the maximum speed limit significantly faster in comparison to Driver A. We can assume that this event occurs at timestep (t) when the RPM value starts to decrease for each driver. Thus, Driver A reached the speed limit at t = 25 and Driver B reached the speed limit at t = 17.

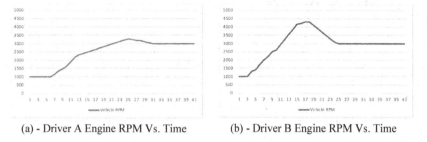

(a) - Driver A Engine RPM Vs. Time   (b) - Driver B Engine RPM Vs. Time

Fig. 1. Engine RPM vs. time for two different drivers

Now if a third-party were asked to identify which of the drivers was practicing an aggressive driving style, it would be reasonable for them to state that Driver B appears to be a more aggressive driver compared to Driver A. However, both Driver A and Driver B stated that they were practicing passive driving behaviours. The point alluded to here is that there is no definitive metric for identifying passive Vs. aggressive driving behaviours as it is a relative measure corresponding to that individual's underlying driving style. Thus, when referring to the passive and aggressive driving behaviours used during the collection of the naturalistic driving dataset presented in this paper, it is a subjective comparison that forms what we consider to be our unique passive and aggressive driving styles. Figures 2(a) and 2(b) below depict the vehicle's engine RPM during a passive data collection and an aggressive data collection for the naturalistic dataset presented in this paper. Figure 2(a) shows that the readings centre around~1500 rpm with peaks between 2000–2700 rpm. Figure 2(b) readings with a centre around~2000 rpm with peaks between 2700–5000 rpm. It is important to note that both RPM curves result from the same driver.

Similarly, using the Osclab dataset [1], the decoded CAN bus signals for the engine RPM of the Kia vehicle used in this data collection for 4 of the 10 unique drivers are shown in Fig. 4. Figures 3(a), 3(b), 3(c) and 3(d) correspond to Drivers A, B, C and D respectively. Despite the RPM values for these curves differing from Figs. 3(a) and 3(b) due to the different vehicles used, it is evident that all 4 drivers in this dataset have produced RPM curves with readings that mostly lay within the range of ~ 500–2500 rpm.

Thus, it could be stated that all drivers have similar underlying driving styles, but it does not provide sufficient evidence to state that any particular driver was practicing passive or aggressive driving behaviours relative to their own person. A similar trend can also be observed when analysing the AEGIS dataset [2].

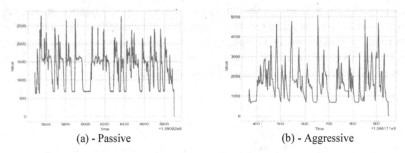

(a) - Passive   (b) - Aggressive

Fig. 2. Passive and aggressive engine RPM from the collected dataset

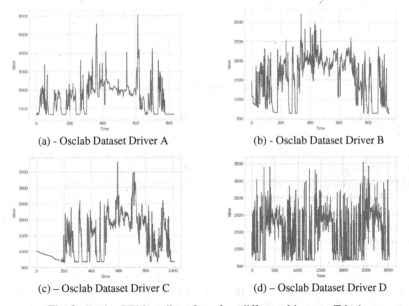

(a) - Osclab Dataset Driver A   (b) - Osclab Dataset Driver B

(c) – Osclab Dataset Driver C   (d) – Osclab Dataset Driver D

Fig. 3. Engine RPM readings from four different drivers on Trip 1

Based on the observations above, the following generalisations are derived to give justification for categorising an individual's driving behaviours as either passive or aggressive, relative to their person:

1. There is a reasonable shift in the range where most of the peaks in engine RPM readings lay, when comparing passive and aggressive data collections.
2. Underlying driving style for the individual ultimately determines their resulting passive or aggressive driving behaviours.

3. Vehicle engine RPM readings for a unique vehicle will centre roughly around the same value despite practicing passive or aggressive driving behaviours.

3.2 Dataset Collection Pipeline

Figure 4 provides an overview for the naturalistic dataset collection pipeline. The vehicle used to perform the passive and aggressive data collection was a 2014 model Hyundai i30, but other makes/models can also be used instead. Due to the intricacies of successfully setting up the necessary hardware and software within this pipeline, a more in-depth report is publicly available on this paper's GitHub repository[1].

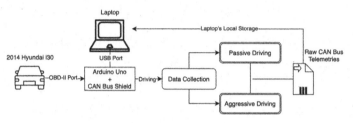

Fig. 4. Dataset collection pipeline overview

Table 1. Required hardware and software

Hardware requirements	Software requirements
• (1x) Linux or MacOS capable laptop • (2x) Sparkfun's CAN-BUS Shield • (2x) Arduino Uno R3 • (1x) DB9 to OBD2(RS232) Cable • (32x) 2.54 cm Breakable Pin Headers • (2x) USB 2.0 Type A to Type B Cable • (4x) Female to Female Jumper Wires • (1x) 1000 Ω Resistor	• Arduino IDE • Seeed studio's CAN Bus Shield Arduino Library • Anaconda or Miniconda

The hardware components listed in Table 1 include the parts for a receiver node and a sender node. In the dataset collection pipeline, the receiver node defines the Arduino and CAN bus shield that is used to intercept the vehicles raw CAN bus telemetries via its OBD-II port. It is also responsible for transferring these signals via USB serial bus to the laptop, where it is stored locally. The sender node can be used for injecting custom intrusion attacks onto the vehicle's CAN bus to include attack packets during the data collection process. An example flood network intrusion attack implementation, written in the Arduino programming language has also been included in the GitHub repository. If an intrusion attack were to be performed by the sender node, the receiver will additionally intercept the injected packets alongside the CAN bus telemetries. Once the receiver

---

[1] https://github.com/samueldelamotte/intrusion-ai-CANsniffer-v2.

and sender nodes have been wired together accordingly, the "CAN-Reader.ino" and the "CAN-Sender-Flooder.ino" Arduino scripts need to be flashed to the receiver and sender nodes respectively via the Arduino IDE. The receiver node needs to be connected to the vehicles OBD-II port with the DB9 to OBD2 (RS232) cable, this port also outputs 12V and will power both the receiver and sender nodes together. Lastly, the USB Type B serial bus port on the receiver node's Arduino needs to be connected to the laptop's USB Type A serial bus port.

When collecting the CAN bus telemetries for both the passive and aggressive driving styles, it was vital that the collections would ensure the data reflected real-world CAN bus telemetries as closely as possible. Certain aggressive behaviours were performed frequently throughout the course of the aggressive data collection. These included behaviours such as randomly braking when it wasn't necessary and then speeding up to reach the speed limit again, frequent changing of lanes when not necessary and even random acceleration periods. The most notable differences regarding the actions performed during aggressive data collections were - every take-off after a complete stop, rapid acceleration was performed in-order to reach the speed limit as quickly as possible, and the force exerted on the brake pedal during deceleration events was greater. The data collection was carried out over a period of 3 months, including a freeway trip and a wet weather condition trip for both styles of driving at various times of the day and included different routes and distances. This was done to enable the ability for the driver profiling framework presented in this paper to generalise on CAN bus telemetry patterns it had never seen before. The full details of the trips made to collect these datasets are available on the GitHub repository[2].

3.3 Dataset Preparation

The resulting dataset collected for this paper contains 411 features with 2,641,117 passive samples and 1,770,912 aggressive samples. The dataset first needs to be normalised so that all features share a common scale to prevent the anomaly detection model from assigning higher feature importance to larger scaled features. Message payloads communicated on a typical CAN bus by the various ECUs are in hexadecimal encoding, thus, we converted these payloads into their equivalent decimal representations. All passive CAN messages are assigned a class label of "0", and all aggressive CAN messages are assigned a class label of "1".

CAN bus telemetries are transmitted on a vehicle's CAN bus in a continuous and sequential manner. They are by nature, a form of time-series data. This needs to be considered before splitting the dataset into training and testing sub-sets. Thus, the separated passive and aggressive log files are then concatenated into a singular array-like structure. Next, we need to extract the class labels for both the passive and aggressive data. A windowing technique is then employed so the data can be split into sequential segments (i.e., windows), where each window has the same user specified window size (W). The number of sequential CAN messages that reside within each window is equivalent to W. After splitting the dataset into windows, any leftover samples (message and class labels) are simply discarded. Figure 5 depicts what the sliding window process looks like.

---

[2] https://github.com/samueldelamotte/intrusion-ai-CANsniffer-v2.

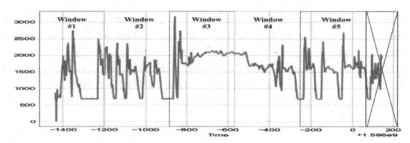

Fig. 5. Sliding Window Process

3.4 Driver Profiling Framework

This paper implements a similar variation of the DeepConvLSTM-Self-Attention architecture from [7]. Their architecture is comprised of two convolutional layers, a pooling
layer and a LSTM layer with two stacked self-attention units. The authors utilise the
Osclab dataset [1] to perform driver identification predictions and they demonstrate an
accuracy of 97.86% and an F1 score of 97.87%. They also demonstrate that decoded CAN
bus data does not require any form of feature engineering or feature extraction before
using it in any sort of driving profiling application. The large number of features that
are intrinsic to CAN bus telemetry datasets tend to handicap the performance of architectures without self-attention units as they are less capable of learning the importance
of features.

3.4.1 Decoding CAN bus Telemetries

Decoding raw CAN bus telemetries into human readable form is a tedious manual process
of reverse engineering the bytecode via trial and error. But this process is still necessary
due to the inaccessible and proprietary translations used by each car manufacturer to
define what message IDs correspond to which ECU on the vehicle's CAN bus, as well
as the meanings for each of the message payload byte values. There has been recent
push from the open-source community for allowing these proprietary translations to be
released by car manufacturers in-order to maximise technology advancements in the
autonomous vehicle space. A public repository has been established by CommaAI [16]
that hosts a database of reversed engineered CAN bus messages for a selection of vehicles
from many car manufacturers, but the list is still limited.

3.4.2 Driver Behaviour Framework

The DeepConvLSTM-Self-Attention implementation is layered as follows. Firstly, three
1D convolution layers with ReLu activation are used to extract key features to allow the
model to capture local dependencies along the temporal dimension. Secondly, an LSTM
that uses a single self-attention unit to allow the model to self-learn the most important
features. Both use the Tanh activation function and employ dropout to prevent the model
from overfitting. Thirdly, a dense layer using ReLu activation is used to help reduce the
dimensionality from the outputs of the previous layer. Lastly, a fully connected layer

is used with a Sigmoid activation function, outputting a singular value. The resulting architecture has 632,762 total and trainable parameters.

Figure 6 shows the pipeline used to train DeepConvLSTM-Self-Attention model. The processed naturalistic dataset collected for this paper was used to train the model to learn patterns in the data by feeding it sequential fragments (windows) of the time-series data. Once trained, the model then performs predictions on the test set and the total sum of the predicted passive Vs. aggressive CAN bus messages that reside in that window are then calculated to determine if that window is passive or aggressive with the threshold value of 0.5. For validating our result we used validation through comparison of the decoded predictions and actual values, by utilising the DBC translation file for the Hyundai i30 from [16] for converting values into human readable form and analysing the average RPM for the passive Vs. aggressive frames. The complete code base for dataset processing, model training, model testing, model evaluation and the saved model used in this paper are also available on the GitHub repository[3].

Fig. 6. Driver behaviour framework pipeline

4   Results

The DeepConvLSTM-Self-Attention architecture described above was used to predict on the naturalistic dataset collected in this paper, to classify sequential windows of CAN bus telemetries as either passive or aggressive[4]. The loss function used was binary cross entropy and the Adam optimiser was used. The window size was set to 60 timesteps and the dataset was split into sub-sets of 80% used for training, and 20% used for testing. Table 2 describes each layer and their hyper-parameters.

The actual and predicted passive and aggressive windows were then decoded into human readable form using the.DBC translation file for the Hyundai i30. Further analysis of these windows was performed, and the average RPM values were obtained for validation. An accuracy of 0.9868 was observed, a F1 score of 0.9836 with a loss of 0.032, a precision of 0.989 and a recall of 0.9787. The average RPM values for the actual passive and aggressive windows within the test set were calculated to be 1567.62 and 1631.55. This verifies our justifications presented in Sect. 3.1 as it can be observed that aggressive driving behaviours would produce a shift in the range of where most of the RPM peaks would lay. Thus, resulting in an increased average RPM across the time period. The model predicted the average RPM values for the passive Vs. aggressive windows to be 1563.17 and 1641.94 respectively.

The results described above solidify that the DeepConvLSTM-Self-Attention architecture is capable for classifying passive Vs. aggressive driver behaviours with an

---

[3]. https://github.com/samueldelamotte/intrusion-ai-CANsniffer-v2.
[4]. Hyperparameters were tuned as recommended in [7].

Table 2. DeepConvLSTM-self-attention hyper-parameters

Layer	Output shape	Dropout	Activation	Optimiser
1D Convolution	(128, 60, 64)*	n/a	ReLu	Adam
1D Convolution	(128, 60, 64)*	n/a	ReLu	Adam
1D Convolution	(128, 60, 64)*	n/a	ReLu	Adam
LSTM	(128, 60, 256)*	0.3	Tanh	Adam
Attention unit	(128, 60, 256)*	n/a	Tanh	Adam
Dense	(128, 60, 1024)*	n/a	ReLu	Adam
Dense	(128, 60, 1)*	n/a	Sigmoid	Adam

1. *Note: Output shapes of each layer i.e., (x, y, z), where x = batch-size, y = Window size, z(1D Convolution) = Number of filters, z(LSTM) = Number of LSTM units, z(Attention Unit) = Number of Attention units and z(Dense) = Number of neurons.*

F1 score and accuracy that is comparable to the work presented by Zhang et al. [7]. Although they used the Osclab dataset [1] to classify between individual drivers of the same vehicle, this paper shows that the same methodology can be used for classifying passive and aggressive driver behaviours for an individual with a similar performance. Furthermore, our proposed methodology can be used to enhance the state-of-the-art intrusion detection systems (IDSs). For example, the results obtained from the DeepConvLSTM-Self-Attention architecture allows for investigation into how malicious adversaries could implement CAN bus intrusion attacks that are truly stealthy. Considering an IDS deployed on a CAN bus that had learned to ignore CAN bus telemetry anomalies produced from the driver operating the vehicle in an aggressive way. If an intrusion attack were used that was capable of learning both the passive and aggressive driver behaviours of an individual, it could potentially mimic the complex telemetry patterns resulting from this driver behaviour. Consequently, the IDS assumes that the telemetry anomalies are simply the result of the driver's behaviour, and the intrusion attack could go undetected.

5   Conclusion

This paper presented an end-to-end methodology for the classification of driver behaviours for anomaly detection. A naturalistic dataset containing passive and aggressive driving behaviours for an individual driving a 2014 model, Hyundai i30 was collected in-order to implement a state-of-the-art framework for driver behaviour classification. A complete and detailed guide is provided demonstrating how to collect, process and decode CAN bus telemetries using "off-the-shelf" electronics in the hopes to improve vehicular security in CAN bus networks. The results showed accuracy and F1 scores over 0.98, indicating the goodness of the data collection method proposed and metrics to identify useful features. Hence, a wider adoption of naturalistic dataset collection using our method that include custom intrusion attacks can be harnessed to evaluate and enhance anomaly and intrusion detection systems for vehicle networks.

References

1. Byung-Il, K.: Driving Dataset (2016). http://ocslab.hksecurity.net/Datasets/driving-dataset. Accessed 30 June 2021
2. Kaiser, C., Stocker, A., Festl, A.: Automotive CAN bus data: an example dataset from the AEGIS big data project. Zenodo (2019). https://doi.org/10.5281/zenodo.3267184
3. Wahab, Q.: Driving profile modeling and recognition based on soft computing approach. IEEE Trans. Neural Networks **20**(4), 563–582 (2009)
4. Mekki, B.: Improving driver identification for the next-generation of in-vehicle software systems. IEEE Trans. Veh. Technol. **68**(8), 7406–7415 (2019)
5. Klusek, K.: Driver profiling by using LSTM networks with Kalman filtering. In: Proceedings of IEEE Intelligent Vehicle Symposium (IV 2018) (2018)
6. Enev, T.: Automobile driver fingerprinting. Proc. Priv. Enhancing Technol. **2016**(1), 34–50 (2016). https://doi.org/10.1515/popets-2015-0029
7. Zhang, W.: A deep learning framework for driving behavior identification on in-vehicle CAN-BUS sensor data. Sensors **19**(6), 1356 (2019)
8. Hallac, S.: Driver identification using automobile sensor data from a single turn. In: proceedings of 19th IEEE International Conference on Intelligent Transportation Systems (ITSC) (2016)
9. Alluhaibi, S., Al-Din, M., Moyaid, A., A. : Driver behavior detection techniques: a survey. Int. J. Appl. Eng. Res **13**(11), 8856–8861 (2018)
10. ISO. Road vehicles—Communication between vehicle and external equipment for emissions-related diagnostics—Part 5: Emissions-related diagnostic services (2015). https://www.iso.org/standard/66368.html. Accessed Jun 30 2021
11. Martinez, C.M., et al.: Driving style recognition for intelligent vehicle control and advanced driver assistance: a survey. IEEE Trans. Intell. Transp. Syst. (2017)
12. Fugiglando, S., et al.: Characterizing the 'Driver DNA' through CAN bus data analysis. In: Proceedings of the 2nd ACM International Workshop on Smart, Autonomous, and Connected Vehicular Systems and Services (2017)
13. Miyajima, C., et al.: Driver modeling based on driving behavior and its evaluation in driver identification. Proc. IEEE **95**(2), 427–437 (2007)
14. Carmona, G.: Data fusion for driver behaviour analysis. Sensors **15**(10), 25968–25991 (2015). https://doi.org/10.3390/s151025968
15. Castignani, G., et al.: Driver behavior profiling using smartphones: A low-cost platform for driver monitoring. IEEE Intell. Transp. Syst. Mag. **7**(1), 91–102 (2015)
16. Commaai: Opendbc: democratize access to car decoder rings (2020). https://github.com/commaai/opendbc. Accessed 30 June 2021
17. Kwak, B., Woo, J., Kim, H.: Know your master: driver profiling-based anti-theft method. In: Proceedings of 14th IEEE Annual Conference on Privacy, Security and Trust (PST) (2016)
18. Johnson, D., Trivedi, M.: Driving style recognition using a smartphone as a sensor platform. In: Proceedings of IEEE International Conference on Intelligent Transportation Systems (ITSC) (2011)
19. Grace, R., et al.: A drowsy driver detection system for heavy vehicles. In: Proceedings of 17th DASC. AIAA/IEEE/SAE. Digital Avionics Systems Conference (1998)

Unsupervised Driver Behavior Profiling Leveraging Recurrent Neural Networks

Young Ah Choi[1], Kyung Ho Park[2], Eunji Park[1], and Huy Kang Kim[1(✉)]

[1] School of Cybersecurity, Korea University, Seoul, Republic of Korea
{choiya3168,epark911,cenda}@korea.ac.kr
[2] SOCAR, Seoul, Republic of Korea
kp@socar.kr

Abstract. In the era of intelligent transportation, driver behavior profiling has become a beneficial technology as it provides knowledge regarding the driver's aggressiveness. Previous approaches achieved promising driver behavior profiling performance through establishing statistical heuristics rules or supervised learning-based models. Still, there exist limits that the practitioner should prepare a labeled dataset, and prior approaches could not classify aggressive behaviors which are not known a priori. In pursuit of improving the aforementioned drawbacks, we propose a novel approach to driver behavior profiling leveraging an unsupervised learning paradigm. First, we cast the driver behavior profiling problem as anomaly detection. Second, we established recurrent neural networks that predict the next feature vector given a sequence of feature vectors. We trained the model with normal driver data only. As a result, our model yields high regression error given a sequence of aggressive driver behavior and low error given at a sequence of normal driver behavior. We figured this difference of error between normal and aggressive driver behavior can be an adequate flag for driver behavior profiling and accomplished a precise performance in experiments. Lastly, we further analyzed the optimal level of sequence length for identifying each aggressive driver behavior. We expect the proposed approach to be a useful baseline for unsupervised driver behavior profiling and contribute to the efficient, intelligent transportation ecosystem.

Keywords: Driver behavior profiling · Unsupervised learning · Recurrent neural networks

1 Introduction

Recently, driver behavior profiling has become a significant technology in the era of intelligent transportation. Driver behavior profiling implies a sequence of operations that collects driving data, analyzes the driving pattern, and provides appropriate actions to the driver to achieve the benefit of safety and energy-aware driving [7]. For example, if the driver behavior profiling can detect sudden

---

Y.A. Choi, K.H. Park—Equal Contribution.

© Springer Nature Switzerland AG 2021
H. Kim (Ed.): WISA 2021, LNCS 13009, pp. 28–38, 2021.
https://doi.org/10.1007/978-3-030-89432-0_3

driving pattern changes (in the cases that aggressive driving or car-theft), it can contribute to the road-safety highly. To collect the data from the vehicle, prior works leveraged various sensors such as a telematics system or Controller Area Network (CAN) embedded in a car. As drivers in these days always carry their smartphones to the car, several studies utilized sensor measurements extracted from mobile devices, analyzed driver behaviors, and commercialized industrial applications such as Pay-How-You-Drive [3]. Early approaches to driver behavior profiling started with statistical analyses. Previous studies scrutinized the driving data and figured our particular heuristic rules to identify aggressive driver behaviors. While statistical approaches were easy to implement and deploy in the wild, there exist several limits. First, the practitioners should establish detection rules on each aggressive driver behavior, and it creates a particular amount of resource consumption in the real world. Second, heuristic rules necessitated frequent updates if the pattern of driver behavior changes [5,10,18].

Along with the development of machine learning algorithms, recent approaches started to resolve the aforementioned limits by training a large amount of driving data to the learning-based models. As machine learning algorithms could effectively analyze the unique characteristics of aggressive driver behaviors, prior learning-based methods achieved an improved driver behavior profiling performance. Nevertheless, there exist several hurdles to deploy learning-based driver behavior profiling approaches. As learning-based approaches trained the model under the supervised learning paradigm, the practitioner must prepare a finely-labeled dataset, which consumes a particular amount of resource consumption in the real world. Furthermore, the trained model could only identify aggressive driver behaviors known a priori. If an unseen aggressive driver behavior happens in the wild, the model trained under the supervised learning paradigm could not classify it as aggressive driver behavior [3,12,17]. In pursuit of resolving these limits of the supervised learning paradigm, several works cast the driver behavior profiling task as an anomaly detection paradigm. They provided normal driving data only to the model and let the model identify any other patterns distinct from the trained normal patterns as anomalies (i.e., aggressive driver behaviors). Previous studies employed an unsupervised learning paradigm to scrutinize the normal driving data and achieved a promising driver behavior profiling performance.

Following the motivation of the aforementioned unsupervised paradigm, our study proposes a novel approach to driver behavior profiling that only requires normal driving data during the model training. An overview of our approach is illustrated in Fig. 1. First, our approach establishes a sequence of feature vectors from the log-level driving data. Second, we trained the model to regress the feature vector right after the sequence given a sequence of feature vectors. Suppose that we set a single sequence consisting of 10 feature vectors recorded from the timestamp 1 to 10. In this case, we designed the model to predict the feature vector at timestamp 11, given the sequence of feature vectors. After the model analyzes a particular amount of normal driving data, we expected it would learn the pattern of normal driver behaviors during the training phase.

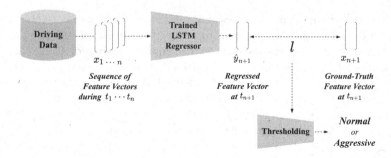

Fig. 1. The architecture of the proposed driver behavior profiling approach

Note that we designed the model with recurrent neural networks to capture the pattern of time-series characteristics of driving data. Third, we measured the error between the predicted feature vector and the ground-truth feature vector. If the given sequence was originated from normal driver behaviors, the error would be small as the trained model already learned the normal driver behaviors' patterns. On the other hand, the error would be large if the given sequence illustrates aggressive driver behavior. As aggressive driver behaviors' characteristics are not trained during the training phase, the trained model presumably fails to predict the feature vectors of aggressive driver behaviors. Lastly, we analyzed this error as an adequate flag to identify aggressive driver behaviors from normal driver behaviors; therefore, we classified a particular sequence as an anomaly (*i.e.*, aggressive driver behavior) if the error goes larger than a particular threshold level.

The contributions of our study are as follows:

- We designed a novel approach to driver behavior profiling under the unsupervised learning paradigm.
- We examined our approach effectively identifies 6 types of aggressive driver behavior types unless the model is only trained with normal driving data.
- We experimentally discovered the optimal size of sequence length varies along with aggressive driver behavior types.

2   Literature Review

In this section, we briefly scrutinized prior studies on driver behavior profiling in three categories: statistical approaches, supervised approaches, and unsupervised approaches.

2.1   Statistical Approaches

The statistical approach includes driving data analysis and statistic-based driving events classification. Berndt *et al.* conducted a study to infer the driver's intention for lane change and rotation. With data from internal sensors, the feature signals got generated for identifying the driver's intention. Through pattern matching using Hidden Markov Models (HMMs), they proposed a method to determine whether upcoming action is dangerous and provide feedback [2]. Choi et al. conducted the study with three objectives: classifying the actions of driving, detecting distractions, and identifying a driver. First, they used HMMs to classify actions and detect distractions by capturing dynamic driving features. Subsequently, they identified drivers while modeling features by a driver with the Gaussian Mixture Model (GMM) [5]. SafeDrive, a proposed system by Zhang et al., performed real-time detection of abnormal drivings. It created state graphs on the behavior model of driving data and compared them to the online behavior streams. If the comparison showed a significant difference, they classified the case as abnormal driving [18]. Eren et al. proposed a methodology that analyzed driving behavior and informed how to reduce fuel consumption. They established three modules: an action detecting module with a linear model, a fuzzy module for evaluating fuel consumption, a proposing module. The last one suggested more efficient driving patterns under eight rules [7]. Dai et al. focused on detecting dangerous driving related to drunk drivers. They used data from the horizontal accelerometer using sensors from smartphones. The predefined pattern of drunk driving went through multiple matching rounds with collected data for efficient detection [6]. The studies above achieved reliable performance of classification. Most of them solved the problem in a way that used predefined rules or patterns. However, they have a limitation that the statistical approach could not detect abnormal driving of unknown types.

2.2   Supervised Approaches

Approaches using supervised learning models have been studied to detect more diverse driving behaviors. Zhang et al. researched driving behavior classification through high-dimensional data from multi-sensors. They extracted features using a convolutional neural network (CNN) after modeling features by exploring correlations between data points. The classification model was designed with two types of Attention-based recurrent neural networks (RNN) [17]. Amata et al. proposed a prediction model, depending on two factors: the driving styles and traffic conditions. For action prediction with only driving styles, they constructed a linear regression model. They also used a Bayesian network to predict if the driver would decelerate in a given situation considering both factors [1]. Similarly, Olaviyi et al. also conducted a study to predict driving behavior. A system using a deep bidirectional recurrent neural network (DBRNN) recognized traffic conditions and current driving styles and then predicted driving actions ahead [14]. Wu et al. established learning models for classifying driving behaviors such as accelerating, braking, and turning, rather than just identifying normal/abnormal drivings. Their study went through a data processing process that separated segments based on a time window and managed models using various machine learning techniques such as support vector machine (SVM), logistic regression, and K-nearest neighbors (KNN) [16]. Chen et al. proposed a system called Driving Behavior Detection and iDentification System

(3D). Similar to [16], they classified abnormal drivings as six behaviors. The proposed system classified incoming data streams in real-time, using SVM [4]. These methods surpassed the boundaries of statistical methods and showed high detection performance as a result of research. Most of the data used in these studies were collected under experimental environments; thus, the label they had were accurate. However, in reality, the accessibility to unlabeled data is much higher, which can be seen as a limitation of the supervised approach.

2.3   Unsupervised Approaches

The prior studies identified driving behaviors and styles with unlabeled data for better application to the real world. Fugiglando *et al.* researched to classify multiple drivers by driving styles using unlabeled data. The features related to drivers' similarities were selected to cluster them with similar driving styles. Then they successfully classified drivers by proceeding to K-means clustering [9]. Van Ly *et al.* conducted a similar study and further sought to provide feedback based on driving styles. They first utilized K-means clustering to profile the drivers' styles using collected data such as accelerating, braking, and turning from inertial sensors. After the profiling, the feedback-providing process was implemented with a model using SVM [15]. Mitrovic *et al.* worked on driving style classification and prediction of driving actions. For short-term prediction, they trained a multilayer perceptron (MLP) model using 10 min of data. Moreover, they proposed long-term prediction through K-means clustering, and it used data with more divergence of driving actions than the short-term prediction [13]. Mantouka *et al.* studied to detect unsafe driving styles separately with an unsupervised approach. The proposed methodology had a two-stage clustering architecture, in which the first stage was to detect unsafe driving, and the second stage classified unsafe driving into six classes [11].

3   Proposed Methodology

3.1   Dataset Acquisition

In this study, we utilized a publicly-distributed dataset illustrate in [3] and [8]. The dataset includes driving data of two experienced drivers who drove the car for more than 15 years. The drivers drove the paved road on a sunny day. The IMU measurements embedded in the smartphone are established while two drivers drove the route with Honda Civic four times during near 13 min. To minimize the influence from the hardware installation, the smartphone was fixed to the vehicle's windshield and never moved or manipulated while data was being accumulated. The features of the collected driving data are composed of acceleration, linear acceleration, magnetometer, and gyroscope. Each feature includes three values at the axis x, y, z, the total number of features goes 12. Note the detailed explanation of the data collection environment is illustrated in [3] and [8]. The dataset includes seven types of driver behaviors: 1 normal driver behavior and six aggressive driver behaviors of aggressive brake, aggressive acceleration, aggressive left turn, aggressive right turn, aggressive lane change to the right, and aggressive lane change to the left.

3.2   Feature Engineering

After we acquired the dataset, we extracted feature vectors from the raw log-level driving data. We aim to transform raw driving data into feature vectors and establish pairs of (sequence of feature vectors, feature vector right after the sequence), which becomes an input and output of the model, respectively. The feature engineering process consists of three steps: timestamp calibration, scaling, and window sliding.

Timestamp Calibration. The acceleration, linear acceleration, magnetometer, and gyroscope sensor measurements are recorded in different frequencies in raw data. Since each feature's number of data points is different for a particular period, it is necessary to apply a frequency calibration to create a fixed shape of the feature vector. We performed the frequency calibration process by designing a scheme that downsampled the data of features with high frequency and upsampled features with low frequency. First and foremost, following the prior approaches illustrated in [8] and [3], we set the target frequency 50 Hz and integrated the frequencies of all features 50 Hz. For features with a frequency higher 50 Hz, the first value during an initial period is selected as a representative value to be downsampled for the sake of computation convenience. Note that we experimentally verified that the index of representative values did not show any meaningful difference in driver behavior learning patterns. Upsampling uses a zero-order-hole scheme to extract an approximation from the first value of the initial period in feature data with a frequency less than the target frequency. Zero-order-hold is a scheme commonly used in signal processing, and it creates continuous data by duplicating constant values approximating values between them from given data. In a nutshell, the upsampling and downsampling approach is chosen following the target frequency (50 Hz); therefore, we could have established fixed-shape feature vectors.

Scaling. After we resolved an obstacle of frequency differences, we should have to manage the scale differences among features. We mitigated this difference by applying a MinMax scaler as we expected different scales of each feature to hinder the model training. We established a MinMax scaler following the definition described in Eq. 1.

$$X_{scaling} = \frac{X_i - X_{min}}{X_{max} - X_{min}}.$$
(1)

We established a MinMax scaler, since our approach only utilizes normal driving data during the model training. Note the scaler established from normal driving data is also utilized during the inference stage. Therefore, we could have unified the scale of each feature under the particular range by applying the scaler.

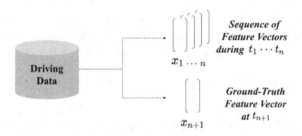

Fig. 2. Pairs of data consists of the feature vector sequences and the ground-truth feature vector

Window Sliding. We set a particular window size and slid along with the timestamps to generate a pair of data consists of (feature vector sequence, single feature vector right after the sequence). The aforementioned pair becomes an input to the model and the ground truth for the model's prediction, respectively. Suppose that we set the window size as 25. In this case, the shape of the feature vector sequence (input) becomes (25, 12) as there exist 12 feature types, and the ground truth value's shape becomes (1, 25). Therefore, we established the dataset composed of feature vector sequences and its target ground truth. The composition is illustrated in Fig. 2. Note that we fully acknowledge different window sizes would influence the effectiveness of learning the pattern of driving data; thus, we processed the window sliding with window sizes of 25, 50, 100, and 200 and examined the driver behavior profiling performance in the later section.

3.3 Training Stage

During the training stage, we trained the model to learn unique characteristics of the normal driving data. As prior researches analyzed in [17], we expected the driving data to have temporal dynamics in feature space; therefore, we employed recurrent form of neural networks to scrutinize the time-series pattern of driving data effectively. Among various forms of recurrent neural networks, we utilized Long Short Term Memory (LSTM) neural networks as a model. We implemented the LSTM layers and added fully connected layers at the end of recurrent layers to regress the target value. We designed the model to sequence feature vectors as input and predicted the feature vector recorded right after the given input sequence. We set the earning objective to minimize the difference (error) between the predicted feature vector and the ground truth by employing the loss function as Mean Squared Error (MSE). Moreover, we utilized $l1$ and $l2$ regularizers to evade the risk of overfitting and optimized the model with Adam optimizer.

3.4 Inference Stage

During the inference stage, the key takeaway is classifying whether a given sequence of feature vectors illustrates aggressive driver behaviors or normal driver behaviors. Suppose the given sequence of feature vectors represents a normal driver behavior. In this case, the regression loss during the inference stage would be small as the pattern of normal driver behaviors is already trained during the training stage. On the other hand, the regression loss would become large when the given sequence implies aggressive driver behaviors. As the characteristics of aggressive driver behaviors are not trained a priori, the model would not be able to precisely regress the target feature vector of aggressive driver behaviors. Following the aforementioned analogies, we provided validation sequences into the trained model, calculate the loss between the predicted value and the target value, and classified the sequence as an aggressive driver behavior if the loss goes larger than a particular threshold level. Note that we acknowledged the threshold level can influence the classification performance; thus, we employed adequate evaluation metrics to validate our approach's effectiveness, which will be further elaborated in the following section.

4   Experiments

4.1   Experiment Setup

During the training stage, we sampled a particular number of normal driving data to train the model. During the inference stage, we utilized both normal driving data and 6 types of driving data to perform a binary classification; therefore, we conducted 6 types of test sets to measure our approach's effectiveness: aggressive right turn, left turn, right lane change, left lane change, brake, and acceleration. Throughout experiments, we employed the evaluation metric as Receiver Operating Characteristic - Area Under Curve (ROC-AUC). As our approach's driver behavior profiling performance varies along with threshold levels, we aimed to measure overall effectiveness at numerous thresholds; thus, ROC-AUC was an adequate metric to validate the performance. Suppose the difference between regression losses from normal driving data and aggressive driving data is large. In this case, the ROC-AUC would go large, and it implies our approach successfully discriminated normal driver behaviors and aggressive driver behaviors. Experiment results are shown in Table 1.

4.2   Experiment Result

Experimental results can be checked by window size and aggressive driving pattern type. Among the four windows in Table 1, the models with a window size of 200 showed the highest performance (0.89), while the model with a window size is 100 or 50 showed 0.88, and the 25 window model showed a slight difference with 0.87.

By aggressive driving pattern type, **Aggressive Turn** showed the best detection rate with an average value of 0.97 and 0.93. The **Aggressive Brake** showed the result of 0.9, slightly better than the **Aggressive Lane Change** of 0.89. Since the degree of variation in the lane change was smaller than that of right and left turns; there was also a slight difference in the detection rate.

Table 1. Experiment result on our approach. Our approach precisely achieved driver behavior profiling performance in general but failed to identify aggressive acceleration.

		Window				Avg of AUC by label
		200	100	50	25	
Label	Aggressive Right Turn	0.9648	0.9722	**0.9725**	0.9647	0.9686
	Aggressive Left Turn	0.9213	0.9409	**0.9421**	0.9202	0.9311
	Aggressive Right Lane Change	**0.9028**	0.8872	0.8979	0.8691	0.8892
	Aggressive Left Lane Change	0.8962	0.8855	**0.9026**	0.8747	0.8897
	Aggressive Brake	**0.9057**	0.8889	0.8954	0.8936	0.8959
	Aggressive Acceleration	**0.7326**	0.7012	0.6769	0.7241	0.7087
Average of AUC by window		**0.8872**	0.8793	0.8812	0.8744	
Average of AUC						**0.8805**

In the case of **Aggressive Acceleration**, it is difficult to distinguish it from the normal driver. In fact, this label showed significantly less difference than the other aggressive labels. Five other aggressive drivings show the high precision with 0.8 to 0.9; However, in the case of the **Aggressive Acceleration**, all windows showed low performance with about 0.677 to 0.724.

For other labels, the inertia value measured with IMU sensors was used as a feature. This feature is useful to detect significant value changes when drivers do right turn, left turn, brake, and lane change. That means this feature is sensitive to detect the aggressive driving pattern. Likewise, our model showed a good performance for **Aggressive right and left turns**, **Aggressive brake**, and **Aggressive lane change**.

Aggressive Acceleration and Brake representative events that provide plentiful information about the aggressive driving pattern. For **Aggressive Acceleration and Brake**, the window size of 200 showed a good performance.

In case of the **Aggressive turn and lane change**, the window size of 50 showed a good performance in the experiment.

To summarize, our proposed model trained with only normal driving patterns can successfully detect aggressive driving patterns. Also, we present the window sizes which show a good performance for each labeled event as shown in the experiment result.

5   Conclusions

Throughout the study, we propose a novel approach to driver behavior profiling by leveraging recurrent neural networks under an unsupervised learning paradigm. First, we extracted fixed-shape feature vectors from raw log-level smartphone sensor measurements. Second, we designed LSTM regressors that predict the next feature vectors given a sequence of feature vectors and trained the model with normal driving data only to learn time-series characteristics of normal driver behaviors. During the inference stage, we figured out the trained model results in high regression error given a sequence of feature vectors derived from aggressive driver behaviors. As the trained model only understands the pattern of normal driver behaviors, it fails to precisely predict the next feature vector followed by the given sequence. On the other hand, the model provides low regression error given normal sequences as their patterns are already trained during the training stage. By thresholding the aforementioned regression error, our approach can effectively classify aggressive driver behaviors from normal behaviors. Although we showed a concrete baseline of unsupervised driver behavior profiling, we fully acknowledge there should be further improvements and strict validations on our work for real-world deployment. We shall perform further external validations of our approach with various drivers, different types of cars, different routes, and several types of smartphones. Along with the aforementioned validations and experiments, we expect the proposed driver behavior profiling approach can provide various benefits to society.

Acknowledgement. This work was supported by Institute of Information & communications Technology Planning & Evaluation (IITP) grant funded by the Korea government (MSIT) (No.2021-0-00624, Development of Intelligence Cyber Attack and Defense Analysis Framework for Increasing Security Level of C-ITS).

References

1. Amata, H., Miyajima, C., Nishino, T., Kitaoka, N., Takeda, K.: Prediction model of driving behavior based on traffic conditions and driver types. In: 2009 12th International IEEE Conference on Intelligent Transportation Systems, pp. 1–6. IEEE (2009)
2. Berndt, H., Dietmayer, K.: Driver intention inference with vehicle onboard sensors. In: 2009 IEEE International Conference on Vehicular Electronics and Safety (ICVES), pp. 102–107. IEEE (2009)
3. Carvalho, E., et al.: Exploiting the use of recurrent neural networks for driver behavior profiling. In: 2017 International Joint Conference on Neural Networks (IJCNN), pp. 3016–3021. IEEE (2017)
4. Chen, Z., Yu, J., Zhu, Y., Chen, Y., Li, M.: D 3: abnormal driving behaviors detection and identification using smartphone sensors. In: 2015 12th Annual IEEE International Conference on Sensing, Communication, and Networking (SECON), pp. 524–532. IEEE (2015)
5. Choi, S., Kim, J., Kwak, D., Angkititrakul, P., Hansen, J.: Analysis and classification of driver behavior using in-vehicle can-bus information. In: Biennial Workshop on DSP for In-vehicle and Mobile Systems, pp. 17–19 (2007)
6. Dai, J., Teng, J., Bai, X., Shen, Z., Xuan, D.: Mobile phone based drunk driving detection. In: 2010 4th International Conference on Pervasive Computing Technologies for Healthcare, pp. 1–8. IEEE (2010)
7. Eren, H., Makinist, S., Akin, E., Yilmaz, A.: Estimating driving behavior by a smartphone. In: 2012 IEEE Intelligent Vehicles Symposium, pp. 234–239. IEEE (2012)
8. Ferreira, J., et al.: Driver behavior profiling: an investigation with different smartphone sensors and machine learning. PLoS ONE **12**(4), e0174959 (2017)
9. Fugiglando, U., et al.: Driving behavior analysis through can bus data in an uncontrolled environment. IEEE Trans. Intell. Transp. Syst. **20**(2), 737–748 (2018)

10. Hu, J., Xu, L., He, X., Meng, W.: Abnormal driving detection based on normalized driving behavior. IEEE Trans. Veh. Technol. **66**(8), 6645–6652 (2017)
11. Mantouka, E.G., Barmpounakis, E.N., Vlahogianni, E.I.: Identifying driving safety profiles from smartphone data using unsupervised learning. Saf. Sci. **119**, 84–90 (2019)
12. Martínez, M., Echanobe, J., del Campo, I.: Driver identification and impostor detection based on driving behavior signals. In: 2016 IEEE 19th International Conference on Intelligent Transportation Systems (ITSC), pp. 372–378. IEEE (2016)
13. Mitrovic, D.: Machine learning for car navigation. In: Monostori, L., Váncza, J., Ali, M. (eds.) IEA/AIE 2001. LNCS (LNAI), vol. 2070, pp. 670–675. Springer, Heidelberg (2001). https://doi.org/10.1007/3-540-45517-5_74
14. Olabiyi, O., Martinson, E., Chintalapudi, V., Guo, R.: Driver action prediction using deep (bidirectional) recurrent neural network. arXiv preprint arXiv:1706.02257 (2017)
15. Van Ly, M., Martin, S., Trivedi, M.M.: Driver classification and driving style recognition using inertial sensors. In: 2013 IEEE Intelligent Vehicles Symposium (IV), pp. 1040–1045. IEEE (2013)
16. Wu, M., Zhang, S., Dong, Y.: A novel model-based driving behavior recognition system using motion sensors. Sensors **16**(10), 1746 (2016)
17. Zhang, J., et al.: A deep learning framework for driving behavior identification on in-vehicle can-bus sensor data. Sensors **19**(6), 1356 (2019)
18. Zhang, M., Chen, C., Wo, T., Xie, T., Bhuiyan, M.Z.A., Lin, X.: Safedrive: online driving anomaly detection from large-scale vehicle data. IEEE Trans. Ind. Inf. **13**(4), 2087–2096 (2017)

On the Robustness of Intrusion Detection Systems for Vehicles Against Adversarial Attacks

Jeongseok Choi and Hyoungshick Kim[✉]

Sungkyunkwan University, Suwon, Republic of Korea
{wjdtjr123,hyoung}@skku.edu

Abstract. Because connected cars typically have several communication capabilities (through 5G, WiFi, and Bluetooth), and third-party applications can be installed on the cars, it would be essential to deploy intrusion detection systems (IDS) to prevent attacks from external attackers or malicious applications. Therefore, many IDS proposals have been presented to protect the controller area network (CAN) in a vehicle. Some studies showed that deep neural network models could be effectively used to detect various attacks on the CAN bus. However, it is still questionable whether such an IDS is sufficiently robust against adversarial attacks that are crafted aiming to target the IDS. In this paper, we present a genetic algorithm to generate adversarial CAN attack messages for Denial-of-Service (DoS), fuzzy, and spoofing attacks to target the state-of-the-art deep learning-based IDS for CAN. The experimental results demonstrate that the state-of-the-art IDS is not effective in detecting the generated adversarial CAN attack messages. The detection rates of the IDS were significantly decreased from 99.27%, 96.40%, and 99.63% to 2.24%, 11.59%, and 0.01% for DoS, fuzzy, and spoofing attacks, respectively.

Keywords: Controller area network (CAN) · Adversarial attack · Intrusion detection system

1 Introduction

Recent advances in the automobile industry make our cars more intelligent and more connected. Therefore, a typical vehicle is composed of about 150 electronic control units (ECU), and each ECU communicates with other ECUs using a bus system [11,18]. Controller area network (CAN) is a representative bus system for in-vehicle networks and supports efficient communication between ECUs [3]. However, because CAN basically uses a broadcast-based communication mechanism without applying authentication and encryption schemes, it is known to be vulnerable to fabricated messages injected through the on-board diagnostic (OBD-II) port [1], and remote network channels [10].

It is essential to prevent cyber attacks over CAN because such attacks could severely threaten drivers' safety. Therefore, many intrusion detection systems

© Springer Nature Switzerland AG 2021
H. Kim (Ed.): WISA 2021, LNCS 13009, pp. 39–50, 2021.
https://doi.org/10.1007/978-3-030-89432-0_4

(IDS) [8] have been introduced to detect suspicious messages on CAN. Furthermore, in recent years, as deep learning technologies have achieved remarkable success in various domains, some researchers have tried to build deep learning-based models achieving a high detection rate [6,7,12,13,17]. The DNN-based IDSs have been primarily designed to mitigate three types of cyber attacks: Denial-of-Service (DoS), fuzzy, and spoofing attacks. To launch a DoS attack, an attacker typically generates dummy messages with the highest priority and then exhaustively injects those messages to take over the CAN bus so that normal messages are not delivered on time. To launch a fuzzy attack, an attacker generates attack messages with random ID values and then injects those messages to induce faults in a victim's vehicle. To launch a spoofing attack, an attacker generates attack messages with specific ECU ID values to perform her desired functions.

However, recent studies (e.g., [5]) showed that deep learning models could be vulnerable to adversarial attacks, which are crafted by adding intentionally generated distortions onto normal inputs in a sophisticated manner. Therefore, we are motivated to analyze the robustness of DNN-based IDS against adversarial attacks. To achieve this goal, we evaluate the robustness of the state-of-the-art DNN-based IDS [13] against adversarial attacks based on a genetic algorithm. The chosen model [13] is known as one of the most advanced DNN-based IDSs, achieving detection rates of 99.27%, 96.40%, and 99.63% for each attack of DoS, fuzzy, spoofing attacks.

We aim to generate a sequence of attack messages that the IDS [13] cannot easily detect by modifying only a few bits of original attack messages that are contained in the public dataset. To demonstrate the feasibility of our adversarial attacks, we performed experiments under the same settings of the previous work [13]. The experimental results show that the detection rates of the DNN model were significantly decreased from 99.27%, 96.40%, and 99.63% to 2.24%, 11.59%, and 0.01% for DoS, fuzzy, and spoofing attacks, respectively, when we can generate effective attack messages by modifying only 1, 1, and a few bits for each of the DoS, fuzzy, and spoofing attacks. The main contributions of this work can be summarized below:

- We propose a genetic algorithm-based framework that generates DoS, fuzzy, and spoofing attacks to evade a target IDS for CAN (see Sect. 3);
- We evaluated the robustness of the state-of-the-art IDS [13] against adversarial attacks and showed that the model's performance could be significantly degraded with such adversarial attacks (see Sect. 4);
- We publicly release our tool and dataset for adversarial attacks (see https://github.com/jschoi0126/adversarial-attack-on-CAN-IDS).

2   Target IDS

Recently, there were many proposals to develop an IDS to detect suspicious sequences of CAN messages. In this paper, we specifically chose the model [13] as our target model because it is one of the most advanced DNN-based IDSs, achieving detection rates of 99.27%, 96.40%, and 99.63% for each attack of DoS, fuzzy, spoofing attacks, and its dataset is publicly available online, which is helpful to reimplement the original model proposed in [13]. To detect suspicious attack messages, Song et al. suggested a reduced Inception-ResNet, as shown in Fig. 1, which was built by reducing the number of parameters and simplifying the structure of a layer of the Inception-ResNet [15].

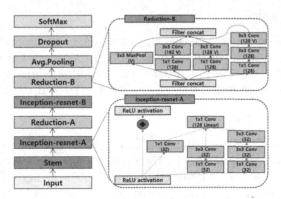

Fig. 1. Reduced Inception-ResNet architecture in [13].

Because the Inception-ResNet is a model which was initially implemented as an image classifier, the model in [13] first transforms a sequence of CAN messages into an image and then processes it. To represent each CAN message, we use the 29-bit message identifier (ID) only consisting of the regular 11-bit base identifier and an 18-bit identifier extension (see Fig. 2).

Fig. 2. Structure of the CAN message ID.

Figure 3 shows the transformation process of a sequence of 29 CAN messages to create the input of the deep learning model. With 29 CAN messages, we generate a 29 × 29 image where each message is mapped to a 29-bit binary sequence.

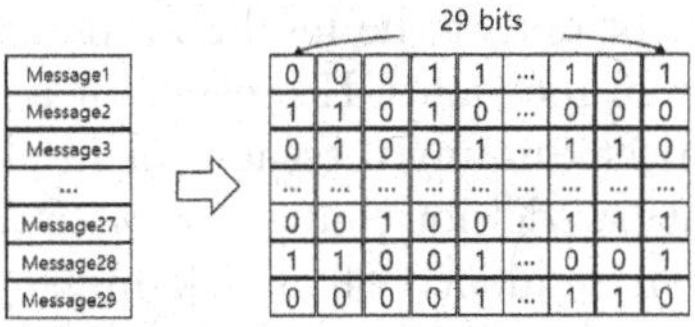

Fig. 3. Transformation of CAN messages into an image.

3   Methodology

In this section, we first explain our threat model and provide an overview of the proposed framework to generate adversarial attacks that cannot be detected by the target IDS for CAN.

3.1   Threat Model

In our threat model, we assume that the attacker can monitor all network messages over CAN because there is no encryption process in CAN. In addition, since the CAN bus does not require an additional authentication process, the attacker can inject the message with an arbitrary ID and modify the message payload if it is needed.

DoS Attack. The CAN bus selects the message to be transmitted depending on the priority of ECU when several ECUs transmit their messages simultaneously. The priority of a message transmitted from an ECU is higher when its ECU ID is smaller. An attacker abuses this priority scheme for CAN by setting the ECU ID of attack messages as 0. The DoS attack aims to transmit a massive number of attack messages having the highest priority for preventing the transmissions of normal messages over CAN.

Fuzzy Attack. A fuzzy attack injects a message with a random ID. The purpose of this attack is to cause some anomaly in the target vehicle. For example, some warning messages could be displayed on the target vehicle's dashboard due to a fuzzy attack.

Spoofing Attack. The spoofing attack is performed by targeting the specific ECU ID of the vehicle. An attacker injects a CAN message targeting a specific ECU ID to perform the attacker's desired function in the spoofing attack.

3.2   Overall Framework

Figure 4 shows the proposed framework to generate adversarial CAN messages. Our framework is designed to modify existing attack messages in feature space so that the target IDS cannot detect the modified messages. That is, our framework does not change normal messages. However, for a given sequence of attack messages, attackers can inject dummy messages or modify some parts of attack messages if those modifications do not change the attack effects. Our framework iteratively modifies a given sequence of attack messages using perturbations selected by a genetic algorithm. Perhaps, the modifications applied would be insufficient to bypass the IDS. To validate the effectiveness of attack messages, we rerun the target IDS with the modified attack messages. When the target IDS

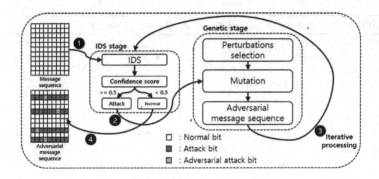

Fig. 4. Proposed framework to generate attack messages.

does not detect them, the modifications by our framework would be practical to bypass the target IDS.

The process of generating attack messages is presented in Algorithm 1. We use a genetic algorithm to generate modified attack messages with effective perturbations. Algorithm 1 has $Attack_{origin}$, P_{size}, and G_{max} as the input, and produces $Attack_{adv}$ as the output where $Attack_{origin}$ represents the sequence of attack messages; P_{size} represents the population size; and G_{max} represents the maximum number of generation. This process begins by initializing the population with P_{size} copies generated from the original sequence of attack messages with mutations. The $Mutate$ operation selects a random bit and flips it with some probability. We use POP_i to represent the ith population. POP_0 represents the initial population.

For the ith generation, we calculate the confidence score of each individual in POP_i using the target IDS. Suppose there exists an individual with a confidence score is less than 0.5. In that case, the algorithm produces the individual as the sequence of attack messages ($Attack_{adv}$) because in the current target IDS, if the confidence score of a given sequence of attack messages is less than 0.5, the IDS classifies it as a benign sequence of CAN messages. Consequently, $Attack_{adv}$ would become an effective sequence of attack messages to evade the target IDS. However, if the confidence score is higher than 0.5, the IDS classifies it as a sequence of attack messages. Therefore, in this case, we need to continue the message sequence modification process. We select two individuals x and y from POP_i with probability inversely proportional to their confidence scores. We first perform the $Crossover$ operation with x and y to generate z by choosing each bit in z from either x or y with equal probability. Next, we perform the $Mutate$ operation to update z by flipping a random bit in z with some probability.

3.3 Adversarial DoS Attack

For an adversarial DoS attack, attack messages should have the highest priority of ECU ID. In each CAN message, the 3 bits are used to represent its priority. Therefore, attackers can only modify the other remaining bits in the message to preserve the same effect of the original DoS attack.

Algorithm 1: Generation of adversarial attack messages

Input: $Attack_{origin}, P_{size}, G_{max}$
Output: $Attack_{adv}$
for ($i = 0$; $i < P_{size}$; $i++$) {
　　$Attack_{copy} \leftarrow Mutate(Attack_{origin})$;
　　Add $Attack_{copy}$ to POP_0;
for ($j = 0$; $j < G_{max}$; $j++$) {
　　Calculate the confidence score of each individual in POP_i using the IDS;
　　if *There exists an individual with a confidence score* < 0.5 **then**
　　　　Output the individual as $Attack_{adv}$;
　　　　Terminate the attack message generation process;
　　for ($i = 0$; $i < P_{size}$; $i++$) {
　　　　Select x from POP_i with probability inversely proportional to its
　　　　　confidence score;
　　　　Select y from POP_i with probability inversely proportional to its
　　　　　confidence score;
　　　　$z \leftarrow Crossover(x, y)$;
　　　　$z \leftarrow Mutate(z)$;
　　　　Add z to POP_{i+1};

Print "We failed to produce attack messages.";

Figure 5 shows an example of a sequence of DoS attack messages where the left figure represents the sequence of original attack messages (detected by the target IDS) and the right figure the sequence of adversarial attack messages generated from the original attack messages. In each figure, the ith row represents the ith message where the bit '0' is mapped to black and the bit '1' is mapped to white – the lines of all zero bits represent the dummy messages generated explicitly for the DoS attack. Interestingly, we can see that a sequence of adversarial attack messages can effectively be generated, which is not detected by the target IDS, by setting '1' at a bit in each dummy message consisting of all zero bits from the sequence of original attack messages.

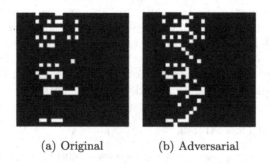

(a) Original　　　　　(b) Adversarial

Fig. 5. Example of adversarial DoS attacks.

3.4   Adversarial Fuzzy Attack

We can modify any bits randomly for each message used for a fuzzy attack because it still has a random ECU ID. Therefore, we can try to generate a sequence of adversarial attack messages without any restriction. Figure 6 shows that setting a single '1' bit is sufficient to generate an effective sequence of adversarial attack messages, which is not detected by the target IDS.

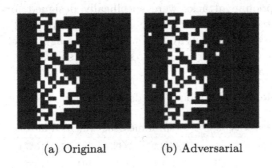

(a) Original   (b) Adversarial

Fig. 6. Example of adversarial fuzzy attacks.

3.5   Adversarial Spoofing Attack

For adversarial spoofing attacks, attack messages are divided into two types of messages: dummy messages and ECU-control messages. For dummy messages, an attacker arbitrarily modifies all 29 bits. However, for ECU-control messages, we cannot modify any bits to preserve the attack effects. Therefore, our adversarial attacks should be performed by modifying dummy messages only. Figure 7 shows that a large number of bits are newly set to '1' to generate an effective sequence of adversarial attack messages, which is not detected by the target IDS.

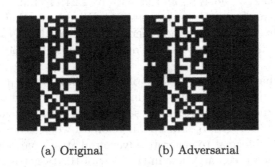

(a) Original   (b) Adversarial

Fig. 7. Example of adversarial spoofing attacks.

4   Experiments

4.1   Experiment Setup

Datasets. We use the same dataset and data configuration used in our target IDS [12,13]. In the dataset, the CAN messages (consisting of 26 CAN IDs) were collected from the ECUs in a real vehicle while the vehicle is running. The dataset is divided into normal and three attack types (DoS, fuzzy, and spoofing) of CAN messages. The spoofing attacks were specifically designed for RPM spoofing attacks. Those attack messages were generated by injecting attack messages periodically in a controlled environment. Each message injection process was performed during a period from 3 to 5 s. Table 1 shows the number of CAN messages for each attack type.

Table 1. Description of the dataset used in experiments.

Attack type	Nomral messgae	Injected message
DoS attack	3,078,250 (84%)	587,521 (16%)
Fuzzy attack	3,347,013 (87%)	491,847 (13%)
Spoofing attack	2,290,185 (78%)	654,897 (22%)

Implementation Details. The target IDS was implemented by using TensorFlow https://www.tensorflow.org/. The model was trained with the total epochs of 10, the batch size of 128. The model with the best performance was saved for our experiments. For the genetic algorithm, we set the population size $P_{size} = 100$, and the maximum number of generations $G_{max} = 75$.

4.2   Detection Rate

Table 2 shows that the detection rates of the target IDS [13] against original attacks and adversarial attacks. The detection rates of the IDS were significantly decreased from 99.27%, 96.40%, and 99.63% to 2.24%, 11.59%, and 0.01% for DoS, fuzzy, and spoofing attacks, respectively. We can see that the target IDS would be ineffective in detecting the generated adversarial CAN attack messages even though the model achieved high detection rates for the original attack message sequences.

We surmise that the characteristics of the original attack messages used to train the target model may explain this inferiority in the detection performance. We can see that the original attack messages used only 11-bit identifiers in the standard format (see Fig. 5, 6, and 7). Therefore, if we use the other remaining bits in the extended format to generate adversarial attack messages, such attack messages would be unseen and new in the view of the target model.

Interestingly, it seems relatively harder to generate adversarial attack messages for fuzzy attacks compared with other attacks. The detection rate of the target IDS for fuzzy attacks is 11.59%, whereas the detection rate of the target

Table 2. Detection rates of the target IDS [13] against original attacks and adversarial attacks.

Attack type	Original attacks	Adversarial attacks
DoS attack	99.27 %	**2.24 %**
Fuzzy attack	96.40 %	**11.59 %**
Spoofing attack	99.63 %	**0.01 %**

IDS for spoofing attacks is 0.01%. The structure of the attack messages for a fuzzy attack is not fixed and relatively dynamic because attack messages have random IDs. For adversarial fuzzy attacks, the attack messages are still generated with random IDs, which may hold similar characteristics to the original fuzzy attack messages having random IDs. In contrast, spoofing attacks have a predictable specific pattern that can effectively be trained by a DNN model. Therefore, attackers would easily generate adversarial attack messages that seem unseen and new in the view of the DNN model.

4.3   Number of Generations

To show the efficiency of the proposed genetic algorithm, we count the number of generations taken to generate successful attack messages that can evade the detection of the target IDS. Table 3 shows the mean number of generations taken to effective attack messages for each attack type. Surprisingly, we could generate effective attack messages for all attack types within eight generations on average. In particular, it can generate an effective sequence of attack messages with the mean generations of 1.016, indicating that the target IDS would be overfitted and lack generalization capabilities.

Table 3. Average iteration for each attack.

Attack type	DoS attack	Fuzzy attack	Spoofing attack
# of iterations	5.831	7.674	1.016

5   Related Work

5.1   IDS Proposals for CAN

In the CAN, ECUs need to communicate with each other. However, the existing CAN communication mechanism has no security features such as encryption and authentication. Therefore, several defense mechanisms have been proposed to prevent cyber attacks over CAN. Furthermore, with the recent advancement of deep learning technology, a research trend is to develop a deep learning-based IDS.

Kang et al. [7] presented a classifier using a deep belief network structure and conducted experiments with a synthetic dataset that was created through open car tested and network experiments (OCTANE) [2]. Taylor et al. [17] proposed an IDS using a long-short term memory (LSTM) based model to detect attack messages over CAN. They constructed an individual model for every ECU ID with the 64-bits CAN data field as the input. Seo et al. [12] proposed an IDS using a generative adversarial network. They tried to build a one-class classification model to detect unseen attacks using only normal data. The proposed model was trained with the dataset generated from a real vehicle's CAN messages. Song et al. [13] introduced an IDS using a deep convolutional neural network (DCNN). They used a simple data assembly module that efficiently converts the CAN bus data into a grid-like structure fitted to the DCNN.

5.2   Adversarial Attacks

Many recent studies demonstrated that deep learning models are vulnerable to adversarial attacks. The traditional idea of an adversarial attack is to add a small amount of well-tuned additive perturbation to the input. This attack causes the target classifier to label the modified input as a different class. Szegedy et al.'s pioneer work [16] showed that artificial perturbations, which can be manipulated by several gradient-based algorithms using backpropagation, can trick deep learning models into erroneous outcomes. Goodfellow et al. [4] showed that misclassification for adversarial examples could be originated from the linear nature of neural networks and a high dimensional input space called gradient sign method (FGSM). Mardy et al. [9] demonstrated that the projected gradient descent (PGD), a multi-step variant of FGSM, can make the adversarial attack more effective.

However, it is still unclear how we can generate adversarial attacks to evade the detection of a target IDS. It would be challenging to apply gradient-based adversarial attack generation methods to the IDSs over CAN because the confidence score functions of the IDS would generally not be differentiable.

Su et al. [14] presented a method modifying only a few pixels of the input image to fool deep neural networks with a differential evolution algorithm. They showed that a target classifier could be tricked into recognizing the modified input image as a different class. We extend their work into the CAN IDS area. We introduce a framework using a genetic algorithm to generate adversarial attack messages in order to evade the detection of a target IDS for CAN. We believe that the proposed framework could be used to evaluate the robustness of a given IDS by generating adversarial attacks against the target IDS and evaluating its detection performance with the generated adversarial attacks.

6   Limitations

In the proposed framework, adversarial attack samples are created by conducting perturbations directly on the vector of ECU ID fields in feature space rather than generating actual attack messages. Thus, our framework does not check the correctness and validity of adversarial attack samples generated. Perhaps, changes in the ECU ID values of CAN messages can affect the attack results. In future work, we will check the correctness and validity of adversarial attack samples in the real CAN in a vehicle and then transform attacks in feature space to actual attack messages that can be transmitted to the CAN in a real-world vehicle.

In this paper, we considered only one representative IDS [13] as a testbed for experiments. In future work, we will consider more IDSs to generalize our observations.

7   Conclusion

In this paper, we present a framework to generate adversarial attack messages for DoS, fuzzy, and spoofing attacks to evade the detection of the state-of-the-art DNN-based IDSs for CAN. We found that effective adversarial attacks can be generated by modifying only a few bits of the original attack messages that remain ineffective against the IDS.

The experimental results show that the adversarial attacks could significantly decrease the detection rate of the IDS [13] tested while preserving the same attack effects of original attack messages. We observed that the target IDS is highly ineffective for detecting the attack messages generated by our framework. The attack detection rates of the target IDS are 2.24%, 11.59%, and 0.01% for DoS, fuzzy, and spoofing attacks, respectively.

In future work, we plan to evaluate the robustness of other DNN-based IDS proposals. Based on our evaluation results, we will also develop an IDS robust to such adversarial attacks. In addition to genetic algorithms, several techniques can be used to generate adversarial examples. We will consider such techniques to generate more effective adversarial attacks against various IDSs.

Acknowledgement. This research was supported by the IITP grant (IITP-2019-0-01343), the High-Potential Individuals Global Training Program (2020-0-01550), and the National Research Foundation of Korea (NRF) grant (No. 2019R1C1C1007118) funded by the Korea government.

References

1. Checkoway, S., et al.: Comprehensive experimental analyses of automotive attack surfaces. In: Proceedings of the USENIX Conference on Security. USENIX Association (2011)

2. Everett, C.E., McCoy, D.: OCTANE (open car testbed and network experiments): bringing cyber-physical security research to researchers and students. In: Workshop on Cyber Security Experimentation and Test (CSET). USENIX Association (2013)
3. Farsi, M., Ratcliff, K., Barbosa, M.: An overview of controller area network. Comput. Control Eng. J. **10**(3), 113–120 (1999)
4. Goodfellow, I.J., Shlens, J., Szegedy, C.: Explaining and harnessing adversarial examples. arXiv preprint arXiv:1412.6572 (2014)
5. Ibitoye, O., Abou-Khamis, R., Matrawy, A., Shafiq, M.O.: The threat of adversarial attacks on machine learning in network security-a survey. arXiv preprint arXiv:1911.02621 (2019)
6. Kalutarage, H.K., Al-Kadri, M.O., Cheah, M., Madzudzo, G.: Context-aware anomaly detector for monitoring cyber attacks on automotive CAN bus. In: Proceedings of the ACM Computer Science in Cars Symposium (2019)
7. Kang, M.J., Kang, J.W.: Intrusion detection system using deep neural network for in-vehicle network security. PloS one **11**(6), e0155781 (2016)
8. Kemmerer, R., Vigna, G.: Intrusion detection: a brief history and overview. Computer **35**(4), 27–30 (2002)
9. Madry, A., Makelov, A., Schmidt, L., Tsipras, D., Vladu, A.: Towards deep learning models resistant to adversarial attacks. arXiv preprint arXiv:1706.06083 (2017)
10. Miller, C., Valasek, C.: Remote exploitation of an unaltered passenger vehicle (2015)
11. Park, T.J., Han, C.S., Lee, S.H.: Development of the electronic control unit for the rack-actuating steer-by-wire using the hardware-in-the-loop simulation system. Mechatronics **15**(8), 899–918 (2005)
12. Seo, E., Song, H.M., Kim, H.K.: GIDS: Gan based intrusion detection system for in-vehicle network. In: Annual Conference on Privacy, Security and Trust (PST) (2018)
13. Song, H.M., Woo, J., Kim, H.K.: In-vehicle network intrusion detection using deep convolutional neural network. Veh. Commun. **21**, 100198 (2020)
14. Su, J., Vargas, D.V., Sakurai, K.: One pixel attack for fooling deep neural networks. IEEE Trans. Evol. Comput. **23**(5), 828–841 (2019)
15. Szegedy, C., Ioffe, S., Vanhoucke, V., Alemi, A.A.: Inception-v4, inception-resnet and the impact of residual connections on learning. In: AAAI conference on artificial intelligence (2017)
16. Szegedy, C., et al.: Intriguing properties of neural networks. arXiv preprint arXiv:1312.6199 (2013)
17. Taylor, A., Leblanc, S., Japkowicz, N.: Anomaly detection in automobile control network data with long short-term memory networks. In: Proceedings of the IEEE International Conference on Data Science and Advanced Analytics (DSAA) (2016)
18. Yu, F., Li, D.F., Crolla, D.: Integrated vehicle dynamics control—state-of-the art review. In: Proceedings of the Vehicle Power and Propulsion Conference. IEEE (2008)

A Framework for Generating Evasion Attacks for Machine Learning Based Network Intrusion Detection Systems

Raymond Mogg[1], Simon Yusuf Enoch[1,2], and Dong Seong Kim[1]

[1] The University of Queensland, St Lucia QLD 4072, Australia
dan.kim@uq.edu.au
[2] Federal University, Kashere, Gombe State, Nigeria

Abstract. Intrusion Detection System (IDS) plays a vital role in detecting anomalies and cyber-attacks in networked systems. However, sophisticated attackers can manipulate the IDS' attacks samples to evade possible detection. In this paper, we present a network-based IDS and investigate the viability of generating interpretable evasion attacks against the IDS through the application of a machine learning technique and an evolutionary algorithm. We employ a genetic algorithm to generate optimal attack features for certain attack categories, which are evaluated against a decision tree-based IDS in terms of their fitness measurements. To demonstrate the feasibility of our approach, we perform experiments based on the NSL-KDD dataset and analyze the algorithm performance.

Keywords: Adversarial machine learning · Evasion attacks · Genetic algorithms · Intrusion detection

1 Introduction

In the past few years, cyber-criminals have become more skilled and organized, as attackers use sophisticated means to frequently evade state-of-the-art security defenses on networked systems [8]. Consequently, the attackers can gain authorized access, exploit security vulnerabilities, and control a victim machine without being detected. An *evasion* is any technique used by the cyber-criminals that modifies a detectable attack to avoid possible detection. Intrusion Detection Systems (IDSes) play a critical role in the security of networked systems by monitoring and detecting malicious attacks against systems [3]. Machine Learning (ML) algorithms can assists an IDS to continuously learn and adapt to changes based on known attacks and to improve detection accuracy [9,10,13,19]. However, despite the benefits offered by the ML approaches, attackers with knowledge about the type of the model or the working/design of the system, can exploit weaknesses in the algorithm and evade the defense mechanism put in place. In this paper, we focus on the practicability of generating interpretable evasive attacks based on IDSes' benign samples. In particular, we investigate the

© Springer Nature Switzerland AG 2021
H. Kim (Ed.): WISA 2021, LNCS 13009, pp. 51–63, 2021.
https://doi.org/10.1007/978-3-030-89432-0_5

feasibility of generating interpretable teardrop attack and probe attack against IDSes, and also we develop an approach to generate the new attacks from benign samples (which were considered normal but have characteristics of real attacks). We achieved this by generating possible samples that are similar to known seed attacks while still ensuring that the IDS classified them as benign. Moreover, we developed a decision tree (DT) based IDS which can be trained based on a dataset using behavior-based detection and network-based audit. We design a Genetic Algorithm (GA) [4,21] that uses the output of the decision tree-based IDS as a feedback loop to compute the fitness measurement that produces samples that are similar in structure (to a known attack), but were incorrectly classified as benign. Furthermore, in order to demonstrate the feasibility of our approach, we utilize the NSL-KDD dataset to conduct experiments.

- We investigate the possibility of generating interpretable evasion attacks against IDSes from benign samples;
- We develop a decision tree-based IDS with behavior-based detection and a network-based audit source;
- We propose a technique that generalized attack pipeline to allow the generation of interpretable evasion attacks against any black box IDS using Genetic Algorithms;
- We perform a comparative analysis of attack performance via experiments on the NSL-KDD dataset.

The rest of the paper is organized as follows. Section 2 summarizes the related work on attacks and machine learning-based IDS. Section 3 introduces our proposed approach. In Sect. 4, we present the experiments including evaluation, numerical results, and discussions. Finally, Sect. 5 concludes the paper.

2   Related Work

Pawlicki et al. [7] proposed an approach for evasion attack detection for IDS based on Neural Networks. In their work, they developed a four-phase IDS training/testing process which is capable of attacks binary classification (i.e., attacks or benign) based on a dataset. Vigneswaran et al. [20], proposed an approach to predict attacks on network IDS using Deep Neural Networks based on KDDCup-'99' dataset. Furthermore, they compared the results of the deep learning methods with other classical ML algorithms (e.g., Linear Regression, Random Forest, Linear Regression, Linear Regression), and then showed that the deep learning methods are more promising for cybersecurity tasks.

Roopak et al. [11] presented a deep learning IDS model for attack detection and security of Internet of Things networks, where they compared the deep learning models, machine learning models, and a hybrid model. Their results showed that the hybrid model performed better than the other models. Karatas et al. [6] used the Neural Network approach to identify new attacks for dynamic IDS and to improve attack detection. Chapaneri et al. [2] presented an approach to detect malicious network traffic based on deep convolution Neural Networks using UNSW-NB15 dataset. Sabeel *et al.* [12] compared the performance of two techniques; deep neural network and Long Short Term Memory, in terms of their binary prediction of unknown Denial of Service (DoS) and Distributed Dos attacks using CICIDS2017 dataset. Their results showed that both models failed to accurately detect unknown (new) attacks as a result of the attacker's action of varying his profile slightly. In [15], the author presented a methodology for the automatic generations of rules for classifying network connections for IDS using genetic algorithms and DTs. Sarker *et al.* [14] presented a machine learning-based IDS model named IntruDTree for detecting cyber-attacks and anomalies in a network. In this work, they consider the ranking of security features according to their importance and based on the ranking a tree-based IDS is constructed. In [1], Bayesian Network, Naive Bayes classifier, DT, Random Decision Forest, Random Tree, Decision Table, and Artificial Neural Network was used to detect inconsistency and attacks in a computer network based on datasets. In the work, they showed that Random Decision Forest and DT outperformed their counterpart, respectively in terms of accuracy in their classifiers. Motivated by this work, we adopt the DT approach for our work. Sindhu *et al.* [16] proposed a lightweight IDS to detect anomalies in networks using on DT, where they removed redundant instance that they think may influence the algorithm decision. Stein *et al.* [17] presented a technique using a genetic algorithm and DT to increase the detection rate and decrease false alarm for IDS by selecting features based on DT classifiers. They used the KDDCUP 99 dataset to train and evaluate the DT classifier. Their results showed that the GA and DT combined were able to outperform the DT algorithm without feature selection. Ingre *et al.* [5] proposed a DT-based IDS that uses the CART (Classification and Regression Tree) algorithm with Gini index as splitting criteria for pattern classification and correlation-based feature selection for dimensionality reduction in order to improve the performance of IDS with respect to time and space.

3   Proposed Approach

Figure 1 summarizes the model, and we describe it as follows. We design the model based on a network traffics dataset. First, the dataset is extracted and analyzed based on relevant fields or features (such as protocol type, service, flag, src_bytes). After that, the fields' information that is extracted is pre-processed and transformed by encoding and normalization, then storing the results. We use both the training data traffic and testing traffic which contains labels indicating malicious or normal, where the labels in the testing traffic are used to check accuracy. We consider only evasion attacks; probe and teardrop attack. Afterward, the training data are pass to the training algorithm for training, which is used to construct decision tree IDS.

The attack ML pipeline is shown in Fig. 1. It contains the individual components required to generate sample evasion attacks.

Intrusion Detection System: We choose to use a DT-based IDS, the choice of using a DT for the IDS is because they are highly interpretable, and as such,

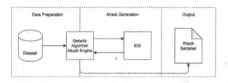

Fig. 1. The proposed approach and the stage of the training pipeline

results can easily be analyzed. In the model, the DT-based IDS provides the core function of classifying the traffic samples. Moreover, it is used in the attack generation pipeline as a feedback loop to gauge the fitness of individual samples. To train and test the model, we used a regular train test split. In particular, we test and load the datasets into Pandas Dataframe. We create an attack label based on a binary column with regards to whether the sample is an attack that is being trained on. So, if the sample is an attack other than the attack being investigated, the column's value will be 0. We drop the protocol type, service, and flag columns in both the training and testing sets and also the column for attacks from the training dataset. We use only the attack label column for the training. Furthermore, we take the processed data from the training traffic into the DT model for training.

Genetic Algorithm: The GA is the second key component used in the attack generation pipeline. It is responsible for producing the final attack samples. Based on GA, we design chromosome representation, a decoding procedure, genetic operators, constraints, and genetic representation of the solution space. In particular, in order to represent the solutions, we consider each feature variable within a dataset as a single gene.

In order to ensure that a sample is not changed in excess, causing it to no longer be a valid attack of the type being investigated, we added restrictions to limit which parameters can be mutated during the mutation phase. This ensures that the algorithm does not change fields that should not be changed for an attack type. The fields constrained were protocol type, service, and flag. These will ensure that the attack remains consistent with the attack type being generated. We use a fitness function to evaluate the quality of individual samples based on a specific goal. Specifically, our goal is to produce samples that were classified as benign by the DT-based IDS, but the characteristics of their data show that they are attacks. Hence, we achieve this by generating benign samples that are as similar to a known attack as possible, while still ensuring that they are classified as benign by the IDS.

$$f = \begin{cases} 2*(1/d), & \text{If the sample is classified as benign} \\ \\ (1/d), & \text{If the sample is classified as an attack} \end{cases} \tag{1}$$

The deviation is defined as the sum of the difference in each feature variable from the given sample to the attack sample that seeded the algorithm. It is calculated by Eq. (2), where s represents the attack sample that seeded the attack, g is the given sample that deviation is being calculated for, and n is index of the feature variable.

$$d = \sum_{n=1}^{41} abs(s_n - g_n) \tag{2}$$

The scalar value used as part of the benign sample fitness function is present to ensure that benign samples are more favored by the algorithm than attack samples. The inverse of deviation is used to ensures that deviation is minimized. Furthermore, we produce the initial population of the algorithm by taking the seed attack and breeding it with itself to produce the initial population of the required population size of 120. In order to breed each generation, we use the breeding function. This function takes in two samples, chosen randomly from the current population, and produces a new sample base on the following steps:

- With equal probability, produce a new sample by picking each feature variable from either parent 1, or parent 2 and using it as part of the new sample.
- Add genetic mutation on a gene by gene bases by sampling a number between 0 and 100 for each gene (feature variable) of the sample. If this number is less than the genetic mutation percentage, then mutate the gene.
- Mutate each gene as required by picking a new value for that gene that is within the maximum and minimum value for that feature variable. This new value is chosen randomly with equal distribution across the maximum and minimum value.

4   Experiments and Analysis

Dataset and Data Processing: We choose to use the NSL-KDD dataset [18] which is publicly available for researchers (and, it is also well labeled).

Attack Generation: We summarize the steps taken by the attack pipeline as follows and then discuss them afterward.

- Train a DT based IDS on the provided attack types.
- From the dataset, select a seed attack to be used by the algorithm. The seed attack is a random sample from the dataset which is the specific attack type being investigated.
- Start the genetic algorithm using the produced IDS and seed attack.
- Run the genetic algorithm for 20 generations. Each generation contains 120 samples, with the fittest 30 of those samples (As evaluated by the algorithms fitness function) moving to the next generation.
- Final 30 fittest samples are collected and classified. Here, the fittest sample is considered the best candidate for an evasion attack sample as it is most similar to the seed attack.

4.1   Analysis of Results

To generate quality results on the NSL-KDD dataset, we conduct hyper-parameter tuning to find the optimal operating conditions for the algorithm. We explain each of them as follows:

In order to evaluate the sensitivity and effect of the genetic mutation variable on the produced attacks, we vary the genetic mutation variable from values 0% to 50%, but kept other parameter fixed. For each mutation value used in the experiment, we record the maximum and minimum fitness function values, as well as the number of attack samples and benign samples produced when we run the algorithm. The results are shown in Table 1.

Table 1. Genetic mutation testing results

Mutation Percentage	Max fitness value	Min fitness value	Samples classified as an attack	Samples classified as benign
0	79.985	79.985	10	0
5	38.366	37.579	10	0
10	44.574	3.160	9	1
15	3.869	0.947	7	3
20	1.013	0.528	4	6
25	0.608	0.406	1	9
30	0.454	0.330	0	10
35	0.427	0.285	2	8
40	0.348	0.240	0	10
45	0.373	0.217	1	9
50	0.301	0.195	0	10

As can be seen from the results, the genetic mutation percent variable has a linear effect on the number of benign samples produced as well as the minimum and maximum value for fitness. However, we see that the fitness value later converges (with minimum deviation) for any given seed attack, where there is a maximum fitness value which depends on the attack seed used in the algorithm. Furthermore, the results show that higher mutation percentages produces more benign samples (which we consider a form of over-fitting). This is due to the fact that a high mutation percentage means each sample mutates very frequently, leading which lead it to differ from the original attack sample vastly. Therefore, it is best to keep the mutation values low. Thus, we reasonable choose to use 18% percent, as it sits between the 15% and 20% values which is where the optimal performance of the algorithm appears to occur.

The iterations parameter defines how many generations the GA runs for. In this section, we increase the number of generations/iterations from 10 to 100 in steps of 10, to observe their effect on the final output generated. To do this, we kept the genetic mutation percent, samples per iteration, and offspring number fixed at 20%, 20, and 10 respectively.

We observed that it is better to use a low number of generations. And we choose to use 20 generations to maximize time when running the algorithm in the performance analysis.

The number of offspring and fittest offspring parameters define how many offspring to breed in each generation and how many of those bred move onto the next generation for breeding, respectively. To verify the effect of these two parameters and their interaction with each other, we conduct two different experiments. First, we fix the ratio between the two parameters, and then incrementally change the values. we set and use the ratio using Eq. (3). Where n is the total number of offspring produced in each round, and f is the fittest offspring that moved through to the next round. In summary, in each generation, half of the offspring are killed off and half move through to be breed.

$$n = 2 * f \tag{3}$$

Furthermore, we verify the effect of the ratio between the two values. To do this, we fix the number of fittest offspring as 30, and then increase the total number of offspring per generation incrementally using Eq. (4). From the equation, n is the total number of offspring produced, while the value i ranges from 2 to 10. We show the results in Table 2.

$$n = i * 30 \tag{4}$$

Table 2. Ratio between offspring produced and fittest offspring testing results

Ratio (i)	Max fitness value	Min fitness value	Samples classified as an attack	Samples classified as benign
2	1.715	0.567	12	18
3	1.470	0.641	12	18
4	50.0	0.908	20	10
5	50.0	0.938	21	9
6	8.377	0.987	18	12
7	6.538	1.037	18	12
8	2.174	1.0	21	9
9	5.009	1.218	20	10

Table 2 shows that the ratio in terms of the number of generated offspring and fittest offspring vs samples classified as attacks. The results show that samples classified as attacks slightly increase with the ratios, but the sample classified as benign did not show any effect in terms of the ratio. Similarly, the maximum fitness value did not show any relationship with changes in the ratios used. However, the minimum fitness value increases with an increase in the ratio used.

4.2   Algorithm Performance

Based on the experiments conducted from the previous section, we use the following hyperparameter values to analyze the algorithm performance.

- Mutation Percentage - the percent chance that an individual feature variable mutates in any given offspring: 18%
- Iterations/Generations - The number of iterations the algorithm is run: 20
- Offspring - The total number of offspring to produce at each iteration: 120
- Fittest Offspring - the total number of offspring to live and breed the next generation: 30

The results in Fig. 2 provide a high-level view of the performance of the GA for different attacks in terms of the number of attack samples, the number of benign samples, and the evasion rate. It is noted that the evasion rate is still a potential evasion rate as the benign samples have not been validated in real attacks, and only the fittest sample has been analyzed in a later section for the individual analyses.

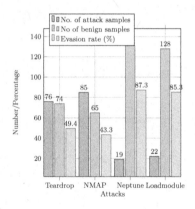

Fig. 2. Algorithm performance

In Fig. 2, we included the analysis of other attack types as well to provide a general view on the performance of the algorithm with respect to the other attack types, which the hyperparameters were not tuned for. From the results, we may see that there is a lower evasion rate (i.e., 49.4% and 43.3%) for the Teardrop and Nmap attacks respectively, compared to 87.3% and 85.3% for Neptune and Loadmodule. However, upon analysis of the generated results for the other attacks (i.e., Neptune and Loadmodule), we observed that the higher evasion rate occurs as a result of the overfitting of the produced samples. This means that while the samples produced are benign, the algorithm has produced samples that differ significantly from the actual seed attack used. Whereas, in the teardrop and Nmap attacks, we observe that the samples that are generated are strong candidates for evasion attacks (this is shown in the next section), though they have a less number of benign samples produced. However, this can be reduced by tuning the hyperparameters for the specific attack sample being considered.

4.3   Attack Samples

In order to generate a more accurate result for the teardrop and Nmap attack, we perform experiments based on only one attack per time (i.e., only a single attack generation pipeline run is being considered for each experiment). This will allows more detailed analysis as only a single generated sample with a single seed sample and IDS is being analyzed. In each experiment, we run the algorithm many times to select the single pipeline run data that was to be used as part of the analysis, Then the average sample is computed and selected. This *average sample* is not a statistical average but it is based purely on the observation of the types of samples seen over the testing of the algorithm, and by picking a suitable average sample. Another approach that could have been taken would have been to run the algorithm N times and select the best result of the N algorithm runs - with best being defined as picking the run that produced the overall fittest sample, however, this does not accurately reflect the algorithms usual output and as such, this method was avoided for this analysis.

Teardrop Attack. Figure 3 show the DT for the teardrop attack. From the decision tree classifier, it can be seen that the algorithm has successfully altered the values that the decision tree uses as part of its boundary decisions in order to produce a sample similar to the seed attack, but instead of being classified as an attack, it is classified as benign. This process can be seen from the following differences between the seed sample and the generated sample:

- The wrong fragments flag in the produced sample has a value of 2, which is equal to the value at that decision boundary, and as such the left node is selected.
- The wrong fragments value is still greater than the 0.5 value at this decision boundary and as such the right node is selected.
- At the final node, the number of source bytes used in the generated sample is analyzed. The cutoff value at this node is 754, and as such the right node is again selected resulting in a benign classification.

One of the advantages of having a highly interpretable IDS is the fact that analysis along the decision boundaries of the IDS can be observed and inspected. This interpretability also allows a comparison of the generated sample to the ideal sample for a single path taken along the IDS. The ideal sample is one that has values exactly corresponding to the decision boundary of the IDS. This

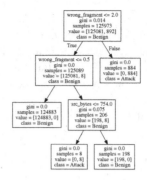

Fig. 3. Decision Tree for teardrop attack classification

is considered an ideal sample as it will give a value closest to where the IDS considers the cutoff for an attack, which means that the sample may still be an attack itself as it will be very similar to a sample classified as an attack, but simply deviates enough to avoid attack classification.

For this produced sample, it can be seen that it correctly alters the wrong fragment feature variable to be in line with the ideal sample value of 2. In the context of a teardrop attack, this value is quite sensible as the aim of the teardrop attack is to send lots of wrong fragments to a host system. Any less than 2 wrong fragments and by definition the attack is no longer a teardrop attack as only a single wrong fragment is sent. The other value used to classify this generated simple is the source bytes feature variable. The source bytes feature variable is not in line with the ideal sample value of 745 and deviates substantially from this value with a value of 155268078 bytes. In the context of a teardrop attack, this could make logical sense as sending lots of bytes leads to many packets being sent. The validation of these generated samples and their values in the context of specific attacks is however out of scope for this paper.

NMAP Attack. Using the same process as the teardrop attack, we analyze the benign samples. We discuss the decision steps that classify the samples as benign as follows.

- dst host srv diff host rate error for the produced sample is equal to zero, so move left at the first decision boundary as this is less than 0.245.
- dst host same src port rate is equal to 1 which is greater than the 0.785 value for the current decision node, so move right.
- dst host serror rate is equal to 1 which is greater than 0.73, so again move right.
- Finally, dst host same srv rate is equal to 1 which is again greater than the decision value of 0.525, leading to a classification of benign.

On the DT, we observed that the first feature variable is altered (the dst host srv diff host rate error) and its optimal value for benign classification was 0.245, while the sample is having a value of 0, giving a difference of 0.245. Applying this same logic to all other variables, we get a total deviation sum of 1.25 out of a max possible deviation sum of 2.795, giving approx a difference of 44% from the optimal value. This is only a deviation percentage for the feature variables that were used to classify the sample, and by looking at the produced sample across the rest of the feature variables, it can be seen it is quite similar to the seed sample. In the context of the attack itself, it can be seen that the produced sample is still viable as an attack. The feature variable in the classification of the sample is the fact that the dst host same srv rate value of the produced sample is 1, compared to the seed attacks value of 0.06. This leads to the sample being classified as benign. Since the dst host same srv rate feature variable identifies the percent of connections that were too different services, this means that all the connections to the dest server, identified by the feature variable dst host count, were too different services. This is logically sound in a probe where an attacker is attempting to identify what services are running on a given server, and as such the sample seems viable.

Also, the measure of deviation and use of a single seed sample can be considered a limitation of the GA pipeline. Since a single seed sample is used as part of the fitness function, all samples are limited to attempting to minimize the deviation from this sample. However, this may not be the most optimal way of producing samples as attacks in themselves can differ substantially across a single attack type. By using some aggregated method to seed the algorithm, improved attack samples may be able to be produced.

In the future, we will address these limitations and also implement real-time online IDS detection. We will also compare the DT and other machine learning approaches based on the GA.

5 Conclusion

In this paper, we have developed a DT-based-IDS. Based on the IDS and NSL-KDD dataset, we have investigated the practicability of generating interpretable evasion attacks against IDSes using genetic algorithms. In addition, we have proposed a generalized attack pipeline that allows the generation of evasion samples from a dataset. We demonstrated the feasibility of the proposed scheme and the results showed that the new genetic-based feature selection algorithm proposed is helpful in identifying important features needed to classify attacks from incorrectly classified benign samples. Besides, our experimental results showed attacks that similar to a given seed attack that has been classified as benign for both the teardrop and Nmap attack types.

References

1. Alqahtani, H., Sarker, I.H., Kalim, A., Minhaz Hossain, S.M., Ikhlaq, S., Hossain, S.: Cyber intrusion detection using machine learning classification techniques. In: Chaubey, N., Parikh, S., Amin, K. (eds.) COMS2 2020. CCIS, vol. 1235, pp. 121–131. Springer, Singapore (2020). https://doi.org/10.1007/978-981-15-6648-6_10

2. Chapaneri, R., Shah, S.: Detection of malicious network traffic using convolutional neural networks. In: 2019 ICCCNT, pp. 1–6. IEEE (2019)
3. Debar, H., Dacier, M., Wespi, A.: Towards a taxonomy of intrusion-detection systems. Comput. Netw. **31**(8), 805–822 (1999)
4. Harik, G.R., Lobo, F.G., Goldberg, D.E.: The compact genetic algorithm. IEEE Trans. Evol. Comput. **3**(4), 287–297 (1999)
5. Ingre, B., Yadav, A., Soni, A.K.: Decision tree based intrusion detection system for NSL-KDD dataset. In: Satapathy, S.C., Joshi, A. (eds.) ICTIS 2017. SIST, vol. 84, pp. 207–218. Springer, Cham (2018). https://doi.org/10.1007/978-3-319-63645-0_23
6. Karatas, G., Demir, O., Sahingoz, O.K.: A deep learning based intrusion detection system on GPUs. In: 2019 11th International Conference on Electronics, Computers and Artificial Intelligence (ECAI), pp. 1–6. IEEE (2019)
7. Pawlicki, M., Choraś, M., Kozik, R.: Defending network intrusion detection systems against adversarial evasion attacks. Future Gener. Comput. Syst. **110**, 148–154 (2020)
8. Porras, P.: Directions in network-based security monitoring. IEEE Secur. Priv. **7**(1), 82–85 (2009)
9. Quiring, E., Klein, D., Arp, D., Johns, M., Rieck, K.: Adversarial preprocessing: understanding and preventing image-scaling attacks in machine learning. In: USENIX Security 20 (2020)
10. Ren, Y., Zhou, Q., Wang, Z., Wu, T., Wu, G., Choo, K.-K.R.: Query-efficient label-only attacks against black-box machine learning models. Comput. Secur. **90**, 101698 (2020)
11. Roopak, M., Tian, G.Y., Chambers, J.: Deep learning models for cyber security in iot networks. In: 2019 IEEE 9th Annual Computing and Communication Workshop and Conference (CCWC), pp. 0452–0457. IEEE (2019)
12. Sabeel, U., Heydari, S.S., Mohanka, H., Bendhaou, Y., Elgazzar, K., El-Khatib, K.: Evaluation of deep learning in detecting unknown network attacks. In: 2019 SmartNets, pp. 1–6. IEEE (2019)
13. Saranya, T., Sridevi, S., Deisy, C., Chung, T.D., Khan, M.A.: Performance analysis of machine learning algorithms in intrusion detection system: a review. Procedia Comput. Sci. **171**, 1251–1260 (2020)
14. Sarker, I.H., Abushark, Y.B., Alsolami, F., Khan, A.I.: Intrudtree: a machine learning based cyber security intrusion detection model. Symmetry **12**(5), 754 (2020)
15. Sinclair, C., Pierce, L., Matzner, S.: An application of machine learning to network intrusion detection. In: Proceedings 15th Annual Computer Security Applications Conference (ACSAC 1999), pp. 371–377. IEEE (1999)
16. Sindhu, S.S.S., Geetha, S., Kannan, A.: Decision tree based light weight intrusion detection using a wrapper approach. Expert Syst. Appl. **39**(1), 129–141 (2012)
17. Stein, G., Chen, B., Wu, A.S., Hua, K.A.: Decision tree classifier for network intrusion detection with ga-based feature selection. In: Proceedings of the 43rd Annual Southeast Regional Conference-Volume 2, pp. 136–141 (2005)
18. Tavallaee, M., Bagheri, E., Lu, W., Ghorbani, A.A.: A detailed analysis of the KDD cup 99 data set. In: IEEE CISDA (2009)
19. Ullah, K., Rashid, I., Afzal, H., Iqbal, M.M.W., Bangash, Y.A., Abbas, H.: Ss7 vulnerabilities–a survey and implementation of machine learning vs rule based filtering for detection of ss7 network attacks. IEEE Commun. Surv. Tutor. **22**(2), 1337–1371 (2020)

20. Vigneswaran, R.K., Vinayakumar, R., Soman, K.P., Poornachandran, P.: Evaluating shallow and deep neural networks for network intrusion detection systems in cyber security. In: ICCCNT, pp. 1–6. IEEE (2018)
21. Yang, J., Honavar, V.: Feature subset selection using a genetic algorithm. In: Liu, H., Motoda, H. (eds.) Feature Extraction, Construction and Selection. The Springer International Series in Engineering and Computer Science, vol. 453, pp. 117–136. Springer, Boston, MA (1998). https://doi.org/10.1007/978-1-4615-5725-8_8

Echo-Guard: Acoustic-Based Anomaly Detection System for Smart Manufacturing Environments

Chang-Bae Seo[1] , Gyuseop Lee[2] , Yeonjoon Lee[3](✉) ,
and Seung-Hyun Seo[1,2](✉)

[1] The Department of Electronic and Electrical Engineering, Graduate School,
Hanyang University, Seoul 04763, Korea
cbseook@hanyang.ac.kr
[2] The Division of Electrical Engineering, Hanyang University (ERICA),
Ansan 15588, Korea
{r22jiw0n,seosh77}@hanyang.ac.kr
[3] The Department of Computer Science and Engineering,
Hanyang University (ERICA), Ansan 15588, Korea
yeonjoonlee@hanyang.ac.kr

Abstract. The Industrial Internet of Things (IIoT) provides intelligence to industrial systems by linking sensors and devices with computer systems and software. However, it also increases the attack surface and exposes industrial systems to various types of IIoT threats. Smart manufacturing environments, built based on IIoT, are also automated and unattended and must respond to physical threats (e.g., vandalism, destruction, theft, etc.) and cybersecurity threats (e.g., DoS, DDOS, backdoor, etc.). In this paper, we propose ECHO-GUARD, an acoustic-based anomaly detection system to protect smart manufacturing environments. The ECHO-GUARD records acoustic signals coming from machines in the smart manufacturing environment and converts them into spectrogram images. The spectrogram images are further classified using CNN to detect anomalies in machine motion sounds. Our evaluation, conducted in a smart factory environment, shows that Echo-Guard is effective, achieving 99.44% accuracy, confirming the possibility that machine motion sounds can be utilized to detect anomalies.

Keywords: IIoT · Anomaly detection · Smart manufacturing ·
Monitoring · Physical threats · Signal processing · CNN · Intrusion
detection

This work was supported by Electronics and Telecommunications Research Institute(ETRI) grant funded by the Korean government [2018-0-00230, Development on Autonomous Trust Enhancement Technology of IoT Device and Study on Adaptive IoT Security Open Architecture based on Global Standardization].

This research was supported by the MSIT(Ministry of Science and ICT), Korea, under the ITRC(Information Technology Research Center) support program(IITP-2021-2018-0-01417) supervised by the IITP(Institute for Information & Communi-cations Technology Planning & Evaluation).

© Springer Nature Switzerland AG 2021
H. Kim (Ed.): WISA 2021, LNCS 13009, pp. 64–75, 2021.
https://doi.org/10.1007/978-3-030-89432-0_6

1   Introduction

The Industrial Internet of Things (IIoT) offers intelligence to industrial systems by interconnecting devices such as sensors and actuators with computer systems and software. Such intelligence of IIoT provides a higher degree of automation and optimization through data collection, exchange, and analysis, enhancing industrial processes (e.g., manufacturing) in terms of productivity and efficiency [6]. With such benefits, the use of IIoT in manufacturing (i.e., smart factory) is rapidly growing: the global smart factory market is expected to grow at a compound annual growth rate (CAGR) of 9.6% to reach around 244.8 billion U.S. dollars by 2024 [1]. However, security is a critical concern for IIoT adoption as consequences can be serious once they are attacked.

Threats to Smart Manufacturing. The threats of IIoT in manufacturing (i.e., smart manufacturing) include not only physical threats such as vandalism, sabotage, and theft, but also additional cybersecurity threats such as DoS, DDoS, and backdoor [25]. More specifically, the interconnection provided by IIoT enables more efficient processes but also exposes industrial systems to threats; as numerous devices are connected to each other, the attack surface of the industrial systems significantly increases. Also, as traditional industrial systems are not meant to be interconnected, they tend to be more vulnerable against attacks [9]. Such threats can lead to severe consequences. For example, Tuptuk et al. show that attackers can subtly alter the quality or consistency of the final product through eavesdropping or man-in-the-middle attacks based on denial of service [25]. Furthermore, [9] demonstrate that attackers can cause catastrophic losses or accidents such as damaged products and injured workers by shutting down the entire production line through forced malfunctions.

To mitigate such threats, recent studies check device operations and detect abnormal signs (e.g., manufacturing defects, malfunctioning of actuators) from the actuators based on sensors (e.g., accelerometer, pressure sensor) and machine learning techniques [4,8,13,15,20,24,26]; they focus on detecting *small errors* (e.g., change of angle or movement) from a *single actuator* that can cause damage to the machines or final products. To detect small errors, such sensors are closely positioned or attached to the actuators. While such approaches are effective in detecting attacks that make subtle changes to a specific device (i.e., actuator or machine), they are less suitable for detecting physical threats or attacks that target the manufacturing process; e.g., attackers can physically intrude on the environment and replace networking or monitoring devices with malicious ones or damage the system, and also, modify configurations of controller software and make changes to the process [21,28]. Attacking the manufacturing process, including timing and sequence, could cause serious consequences to the smart factory as steps of the automated process are tightly coupled to each other. Note that some threats such as configuration changes can be detected with previous approaches as those sensors attached to the actuators would notice the difference made by the attacker. However, they cannot prevent such attacks from happening.

Acoustic-Based Anomaly Detection. We propose ECHO-GUARD, an acoustic-based anomaly detection system, which aims to protect smart manufacturing environments. The ECHO-GUARD particularly focuses on defending against attacks that physically intrude the smart factory or target the manufacturing process by analyzing acoustic signals coming from the environment and the actuators. The ECHO-GUARD continuously monitors the environment using multiple microphones and then uses deep learning for anomaly detection. We utilize acoustic signals as they could effectively detect anomalies at a low cost. More specifically, the entire manufacturing process, which consists of multiple states, can be monitored by analyzing the acoustic coming from the machines (i.e., actuators). Furthermore, the ECHO-GUARD can be built with ordinary MEMS microphones, which come at a low cost; the cost is an important factor as many sensors would be needed to cover the entire smart factory.

In this paper, we present a proof of concept of ECHO-GUARD by demonstrating that acoustic signals can be used for detecting anomalies in smart factory environments. We can further build upon this idea to come up with stronger defense mechanisms by combining with other security measures such as security event logs, surveillance systems, and individual device monitoring systems to deter sophisticated attacks. The ECHO-GUARD would provide security equivalent to the two-factor authentication without making significant changes to the existing system as they are small. The system can also be adding with minimal cost as acoustic sensors are cheap.

In our proof of concept experiment, we set up a prototype ECHO-GUARD to record acoustic signals in a real smart factory environment (see Fig. 3 in Sect. 4) and exploit machine learning classification with relevant features to detect anomalies. We conduct a series of experiments and find that ECHO-GUARD can detect anomalies with an accuracy of 99.44%. The high accuracy of ECHO-GUARD confirms the possibility that machine motion sounds can be utilized to detect anomalies.

The rest of this paper is composed as follows. Section 2 introduces techniques for monitoring and diagnosing device behavior in an IIoT environment. Section 3 describes the learning model proposed in this paper. Section 4 presents and analyzes the experimental results of applying the proposed model in a smart manufacturing environment. Section 5 describes the discussion and future works. Finally, Sect. 6 concludes this paper.

2   Related Work

Smart factories are becoming popular and is a milestone for the manufacturing industry. Thus, ensuring the security of the manufacturing process in smart factories leads to an active research area.

Anomaly Detection for IIoT Attacks. Latif et al. [11] proposed an novel lightweight random neural network (RaNN)-based prediction model to predict cybersecurity attacks in IIoT environments. This model is lightweight and easy to deploy on single-board computers. For DS2OS dataset, the (RaNN)-based prediction model predicted cybersecurity attacks more effectively than other machine learning classifiers (e.g., SVM, DT, ANN). Li et al. [14] proposed an adaptive long and short-term memory network with multi-feature layer (B-MLSTM), which allows adaptive selection of an attack interval and a retraining period for detection model in IIoT. Furthermore, B-MLSTM is designed based on MLSTM, enabling low frequency and multi-stage attacks detection on IIoT. They studied NN-based models using datasets from IIoT to predict cybersecurity attacks such as DoS and DDoS.

Anomaly Detection for Sensor Devices. Otoum et al. [19] proposed a hybrid architecture to detect intrusive behavior of sensors for both unknown and known intruders. This architecture is identify an anomaly or possible misbehavior at any sensor in the networks by using Random Forest (RF) algorithm and E-DBSCAN. Saeed et al. [23] proposed a Context-Aware Fault Diagnostic (CAFD) scheme based on Extra-Trees for lightweight machine learning-based fault detection and diagnosis in wireless sensor networks (WSNs). CAFD scheme successfully detected and diagnosed six sensor failures (e.g., drift, hardover, spike, data-loss, etc.) in a realistic WSN scenario consisting of humidity sensors and temperature sensors. Xiao et al. [27] proposed a system that leverages Nonlinear Polynomial Graph Filter to analyze temperature sensors to identify the presence of abnormal data in IoT environments while also locating failed sensors. They studied sensor monitoring techniques to analyze and learn sensor data from IIoT.

Anomaly Detection for Machines. Replacing aging machines with IoT machines at factories is not easy because it costs a lot of money and time. For these reasons, technologies are being developed to remotely monitor the status of a device using various methods, such as visual/sound/heat/power consumption [10,12]. Liang et al. [16] proposed a three-layer fog and cloud model that detects anomalies by applying Convolutional Neural Network (CNN) to power signals that are easier to deploy and lower data sampling rate than vibration or acoustic sensors. Yun et al. [29] proposed a deep learning-based intrusion detection system by applying STFT and CNN to acoustic sensor data obtained from robot arms. The system uses stethoscope microphones for efficient noise reduction and cost, and can detect DDoS attacks via an estimating rotating point. Kim et al. [10] proposed a multi-device operation monitoring system by analyzing sound. In order to monitor the state of multiple devices in real time in the manufacturing process, acoustic signals are collected with Mic array, and STFT and CNN are utilized.

While these studies may provide more secure cybersecurity or manufacturing systems, they were not considered physical threats or attacks aimed at the manufacturing process. Roux et al. [22] proposed an extended system to monitor radio signals at the physical layer via radio signal display (RSSI). This system could detect physical localization, but had limitations that it could not determine what physical threats posed.

The main goal of this study is to introduce deep learning-based models for the detection of anomaly (e.g., physical threats or attacks) arising from the manufacturing process. Here, we propose a CNN-based model that enables anomaly detection of surrounding machines using multiple microphones.

3   Methodology

The ECHO-GUARD detects anomalies in smart factory environments and their manufacturing process by analyzing the recorded acoustic signals of the machines and the workers with the help of a CNN model. In this section, we elaborate on how the ECHO-GUARD is designed and implemented.

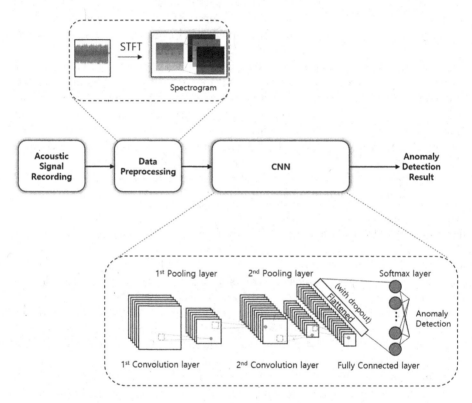

Fig. 1. CNN model for anomaly detection

Approach Overview. The design of the ECHO-GUARD shown in Fig. 1, consists of three modules: *Acoustic Signal Recording, Signal Preprocessing*, and *CNN*. First, the *Acoustic Signal Recording* module records the acoustic signals from the smart manufacturing environment with a microphone array. Second, the *Signal Preprocessing* module converts the recorded signals to spectrogram images via STFT. Lastly, given the spectrogram images as an input, the *CNN* module detects anomalies in the smart factory environment. The prototype of our idea, ECHO-GUARD, is built using a raspberry pi 4b [3] and a matrix voice [2] as shown in Fig. 3. A detailed description of each step is described below.

3.1 Acoustic Signal Recording

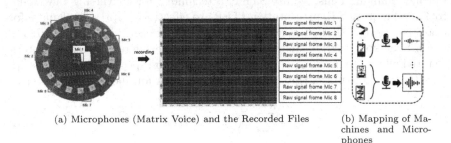

(a) Microphones (Matrix Voice) and the Recorded Files

(b) Mapping of Machines and Microphones

Fig. 2. How to record acoustic signal from machine in manufacturing process: (a) The composition of the microphone and recorded files, (b) the noise range around which the microphone records.

The *Acoustic Signal Recording* module records acoustic signals from the smart factory environment; Fig. 2(a) illustrates the microphone array (i.e., matrix voice) used for ECHO-GUARD. The microphone array consists of eight microphones, and each of them independently records acoustic signals from the environment; using such a microphone array makes efficient data collection possible. While we use a single microphone array for our prototype, multiple microphone arrays can be used together to cover a larger area. As shown in Fig. 2(b), each microphone array should be mapped to multiple machines and the microphone arrays should be placed between the machines; the positioning of the microphone array and the mapping (microphone array and machines) can be determined by considering the operation cycle of the machine and the amplitude of the noise that is generated by the machine. If the microphone array is too close to a machine that is too loud, the noise may mask the acoustic signals coming from other machines.

3.2 Signal Preprocessing

The key functionality of the *Signal Preprocessing* module is to process the recorded acoustic signals to a proper format for the *CNN* module. For that purpose, we STFT and convert the acoustic signals to spectrogram images.

More specifically, interpreting an acoustic signal at time domain allows analyzing the strength of a signal that changes over time. However, if the signal is a mixed signal with various frequency components, it becomes difficult to analyze the signal characteristics. To analyze the frequency components of a signal, it is necessary to convert the signal to frequency domain through Fourier transform (e.g., FFT or DFT) [17].

$$f_j = \sum_{k=0}^{n-1} x_k e^{-\frac{2\pi i}{n} jk}, j = 0, ..., n-1 \tag{1}$$

However, such a technique is not suitable for real-time analysis or detection techniques; changes in signals that occur over time cannot be analyzed in the frequency domain. Thus, we use STFT, a technique for converting raw signals into Time-Frequency Representation (TFR) to effectively represent signal information [5]; using STFT, the acoustic signals are transformed to spectrogram images. Such spectrogram images allow us to verify different spectral patterns generated while the machine operates. We analyze the spectral patterns as they reflect the machine movements and further use them for anomaly detection.

$$X(l, k) = \sum_{n=0}^{N-1} w(x)x(n + lH)e^{\frac{-2\pi kn}{N}} \tag{2}$$

Once the acoustic signals are transformed to spectrogram images, they are given as an input data to the *CNN* module. Figure 2 illustrates how the *Signal Preprocessing* module works; applies STFT to acoustic signals recorded from machines and generates spectrogram images. Note that as STFT is TFR transformation, we can obtain a spectrogram image for a specific time or frequency range.

3.3   CNN

What we have done so far is to transform the recorded acoustic signals into a suitable data format (i.e., spectrogram images) for detecting anomalies. The spectrogram images created from the previous modules are used as an input for the *CNN* module, which is built based on Convolutional Neural Network (CNN), a deep learning approach commonly used for image classification. The structure of CNNs used in this paper consists of a convolutional layer, a pooling layer, a fully connected layer, and a softmax layer, as shown in the CNN process of Fig. 1.

CNN uses a mathematical operation called convolution and is a deep learning model mainly used for visual image analysis. CNN consists of steps to extract features and steps to classify images. The steps to extract features consist of convolution layer and pooling layer. The convolution layer is able to extract features of input data using many convolution filters, and the pooling layer is able to extract local features by compressing the information to reduce the size of the intermediate image. The steps for classifying images consist of a fully connected layer and a softmax layer. The fully connected layer flattens the feature data extracted through convolution layers and pooling layers into one-dimensional arrays, and the softmax layer uses the softmax function to classify the probability values calculated for each category.

4   Evaluation

In this section, we evaluate our prototype ECHO-GUARD which is built based on a raspberry pi 4b and matrix voice. The experiment was conducted in a smart manufacturing environment (see Fig. 3) made for research which has various types of industrial machines; e.g., Assembly W/UR-3, Vision Inspection (VI), industrial robots, etc. As shown in Fig. 3, the ECHO-GUARD is placed between the industrial robot, Assembly W/UR-3, and the Vision Inspection. The machine cycle of assembly W/UR-3 is 14 s, and the machine cycle of Vision Inspection is 55 s; a cycle refers to the length of time a machine operates.

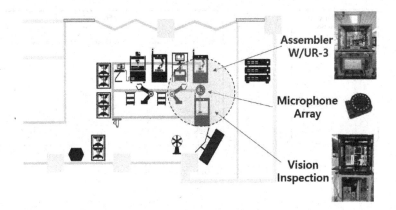

Fig. 3. Smart manufacturing environment settings

Table 1. Experimental cases considering anomalies

Experiment case	Detail situation (acoustic)
Machine malfunction	(1) Machine collision
	(2) Mechanical parts drop
Physical intrusion	(3) Keyboard typing
	(4) Footsteps
	(5) Ringtone
	(6) Conversation
	(7) Jumping
	(8) Card tag

As shown in Table 1, our evaluation answers the following research questions: (1) Could ECHO-GUARD detect machine malfunction?; (2) Could ECHO-GUARD detect physical intrusion? The experimental case for machine malfunction consists of two scenarios: a collision between machines and dropping parts while being moved. The experimental case for intrusion of a malicious attacker consists of six cases: footsteps, ringtone, conversation, card tagging, keyboard typing, and jumping from 50 cm (e.g., attackers may go over a fence or a wall to sneak into the smart factory). Figure 4 illustrates the spectrograms of each case. As shown in the figure, while analyzing the signals in the time domain only allows us to check the amplitude change of the signal, analyzing the signals using the spectrogram images allows us to check the frequency components; the spectral patterns that appears in the spectrogram images makes anomaly detection possible.

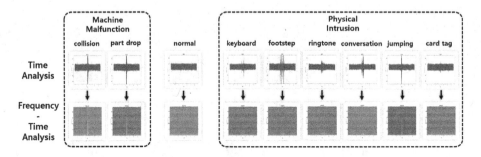

Fig. 4. STFT transform of acoustic signals

The acoustic signals are recorded as WAV file format by a program coded with pyaudio of python. The acoustic signals are recorded in 48 kHz 16-bit poly WAV format. The raw acoustic signals are converted to spectrogram images using pyplot module supported by python's matplotlib. The frequency of the output spectrogram image ranges from 0–24 kHz.

Table 2. CNN model

Layer (type)	Output shape
conv2d (Conv2D)	(None, 124, 124, 32)
max_pooling2d (MaxPooling2D)	(None, 62, 62, 32)
conv2d_1 (Conv2D)	(None, 58, 58, 64)
max_pooling2d_1 (MaxPooling2D)	(None, 29, 29, 64)
flatten (Flatten)	(None, 53824)
dense (Dense)	(None, 1024)
dense_1 (Dense)	(None, 18)

The acoustic signals are stored as a spectrogram image; a jpg of 128×128 pixels. The design of the CNN is shown in Table 2. In the first convolution layer, #32 5×5 convolution filters are applied. In the first pooling layer, 2 $\times$ 2 max pooling filter is applied. In the second convolution layer, #64 5×5 convolution filters are applied. In the second pooling layer, 2×2 max pooling filter is applied. Finally, we softmax 18 outputs for classification of 8 anomalies and 1 normal for 2 machines. We trained 1,080 training data and 360 test data with 120 batch sized and 30 epochs, resulting in 98.80% training accuracy and 99.44% test accuracy. The classification results show that the ECHO-GUARD is effective, with a precision of 99.44%. The high accuracy of ECHO-GUARD confirms the possibility that machine motion sounds can be utilized to detect anomalies.

5 Discussion

Limitations. In this paper, we presented an acoustic-based proof of concept anomaly detection system, which aims to protect smart manufacturing environments; the system specifically focuses on defending against attacks that physically intrude into the smart factory or target the manufacturing process. In order to monitor the process and physical threats, our approach places the acoustic sensors in the smart manufacturing environment, such as between machines. Because of the location of the acoustic sensors, our system cannot handle problems and threats that are caused by small issues (e.g., errors, inaccuracy) of the actuators and the machine; e.g., defects in actuators, machine deterioration, and attacks that make subtle configuration (e.g., angle, temperature) change to actuators. Such cases can be tackled by monitoring the data collected from individual machines or sensors that are attached to them. Commonly used approaches include power signals of machines, acoustic or vibration sensors attached to the machine, and stethoscope microphones. We believe that our ECHO-GUARD can be used with such approaches to make a more robust defense mechanism.

Future Work. In this work, we apply STFT and CNN to acoustic signals generated by the machine to build ECHO-GUARD. However, anomaly situations arising from actual smart manufacturing have not been formulated. Therefore, for unlabeled real-world anomaly cases, unsupervised machine learning algorithms can be more suitable than supervised learning such as CNN [7,18]. In addition, there are many other Time-Frequency Representation (TFR) transformation techniques besides STFT; e.g., Mel-Frequency Cepstral Coefficient (MFCC), Linear-Frequency Cepstral Coefficient (LFCC), Wavelet Transform (WT), and Wavelet Packet Decomposition (WPD). Therefore, we plan to explore other TFR techniques to understand the appropriate approach for detecting anomalies in smart manufacturing environments. Note that the approach should be suitable for showing the characteristic of the sound and motion of the machine.

6 Conclusion

The Industrial Internet of Things (IIoT) provides intelligence to industrial systems. With such benefits, IIoT in Manufacturing, smart manufacturing, is becoming popular. However, IIoT increases the attack surface and exposes manufacturing to various types of IIoT threats. In this work, we propose ECHO-GUARD, which uses acoustic sensors and deep learning to detect anomalies in smart manufacturing environments. Unlike previous studies that conduct research on detecting attacks that subtly alter a particular device (i.e., actuator or system) in a machine, we focus on a model that detects physical threats or attacks targeting the manufacturing process. We generate spectrogram images by applying STFT to acoustic signals recorded from machine motions and were able to detect anomalies with a precision of 99.44%, confirming the possibility that machine motion sounds can be utilized to detect anomalies.

References

1. Global size of the smart factory market. https://www.statista.com/statistics/872289/worldwide-smart-factory-market-size/
2. Matrix voice. https://www.matrix.one/products/voice/
3. Raspberry pi 4 model b. https://www.raspberrypi.org/products/raspberry-pi-4-model-b/
4. Al-Ghamd, A.M., Mba, D.: A comparative experimental study on the use of acoustic emission and vibration analysis for bearing defect identification and estimation of defect size. Mech. Syst. Signal Process. **20**(7), 1537–1571 (2006)
5. Allen, J.: Short term spectral analysis, synthesis, and modification by discrete fourier transform. IEEE Trans. Acoust. Speech Signal Process. **25**(3), 235–238 (1977)
6. Boyes, H., Hallaq, B., Cunningham, J., Watson, T.: The industrial internet of things (IIoT): an analysis framework. Comput. Ind. **101**, 1–12 (2018)
7. Duman, T.B., Bayram, B., İnce, G.: Acoustic anomaly detection using convolutional autoencoders in industrial processes. In: Martínez Álvarez, F., Troncoso Lora, A., Sáez Muñoz, J.A., Quintián, H., Corchado, E. (eds.) SOCO 2019. AISC, vol. 950, pp. 432–442. Springer, Cham (2020). https://doi.org/10.1007/978-3-030-20055-8_41
8. Elforjani, M., Mba, D.: Accelerated natural fault diagnosis in slow speed bearings with acoustic emission. Eng. Fract. Mech. **77**(1), 112–127 (2010)
9. Huh, J., Pham Van, H., Han, S., Choi, H.-J., Choi, S.-K.: A data-driven approach for the diagnosis of mechanical systems using trained subtracted signal spectrograms. Sensors **19**(5), 1055 (2019)
10. Kim, J., Lee, H., Jeong, S., Ahn, S.-H.: Sound-based remote real-time multi-device operational monitoring system using a convolutional neural network (CNN). J. Manuf. Syst. **58**, 431–441 (2021)
11. Latif, S., Zou, Z., Idrees, Z., Ahmad, J.: A novel attack detection scheme for the industrial internet of things using a lightweight random neural network. IEEE Access **8**, 89337–89350 (2020)
12. Lee, G.-Y., et al.: Machine health management in smart factory: a review. J. Mech. Sci. Technol. **32**(3), 987–1009 (2018). https://doi.org/10.1007/s12206-018-0201-1
13. Lee, J., Wu, F., Zhao, W., Ghaffari, M., Liao, L., Siegel, D.: Prognostics and health management design for rotary machinery systems–reviews, methodology and applications. Mech. Syst. Signal Process. **42**(1–2), 314–334 (2014)
14. Li, X., Xu, M., Vijayakumar, P., Kumar, N., Liu, X.: Detection of low-frequency and multi-stage attacks in industrial internet of things. IEEE Trans. Veh. Technol. **69**(8), 8820–8831 (2020)

15. Li, Y., Li, G., Yang, Y., Liang, X., Xu, M.: A fault diagnosis scheme for planetary gearboxes using adaptive multi-scale morphology filter and modified hierarchical permutation entropy. Mech. Syst. Signal Process. **105**, 319–337 (2018)
16. Liang, Y., Li, W., Lu, X., Wang, S.: Fog computing and convolutional neural network enabled prognosis for machining process optimization. J. Manuf. Syst. **52**, 32–42 (2019)
17. Nussbaumer, H.J.: The fast fourier transform. In: Nussbaumer, H.J. (ed.) Fast Fourier Transform and Convolution Algorithms. Springer Series in Information Sciences, vol. 2, pp. 80–111. Springer, Heidelberg (1981). https://doi.org/10.1007/978-3-662-00551-4_4
18. Oh, D.Y., Yun, I.D.: Residual error based anomaly detection using auto-encoder in SMD machine sound. Sensors **18**(5), 1308 (2018)
19. Otoum, S., Kantarci, B., Mouftah, H.T.: Detection of known and unknown intrusive sensor behavior in critical applications. IEEE Sens. Lett. **1**(5), 1–4 (2017)
20. Qian, J., Kim, D.-S., Lee, D.-W.: On-vehicle triboelectric nanogenerator enabled self-powered sensor for tire pressure monitoring. Nano Energy **49**, 126–136 (2018)
21. Riedel, C., Fu, G., Beyette, D., Liu, J.-C.: Measurement system timing integrity in the presence of faults and malicious attacks. In: 2019 International Conference on Smart Grid Synchronized Measurements and Analytics (SGSMA), pp. 1–8. IEEE (2019)
22. Roux, J., Alata, E., Auriol, G., Nicomette, V., Kaâniche, M.: Toward an intrusion detection approach for IoT based on radio communications profiling. In: 2017 13th European dependable computing conference (EDCC), pp. 147–150. IEEE (2017)
23. Saeed, U., Lee, Y.-D., Jan, S.U., Koo, I.: CAFD: context-aware fault diagnostic scheme towards sensor faults utilizing machine learning. Sensors **21**(2), 617 (2021)
24. Santos, P., Villa, L.F., Reñones, A., Bustillo, A., Maudes, J.: An SVM-based solution for fault detection in wind turbines. Sensors **15**(3), 5627–5648 (2015)
25. Tuptuk, N., Hailes, S.: Security of smart manufacturing systems. J. Manuf. Syst. **47**, 93–106 (2018)
26. Vichare, N.M., Pecht, M.G.: Prognostics and health management of electronics. IEEE Trans. Compon. Packag. Technol. **29**(1), 222–229 (2006)
27. Xiao, Z., Fang, H., Wang, X.: Nonlinear polynomial graph filter for anomalous IoT sensor detection and localization. IEEE Internet Things J. **7**(6), 4839–4848 (2020)
28. Xie, J., Liu, C.-C., Sforna, M., Bilek, M., Hamza, R.: On-line physical security monitoring of power substations. Int. Trans. Electr. Energy Syst. **26**(6), 1148–1170 (2016)
29. Yun, H., Kim, H., Kim, E., Jun, M.B.: Development of internal sound sensor using stethoscope and its applications for machine monitoring. Proc. Manuf. **48**, 1072–1078 (2020)

Research on Improvement of Anomaly Detection Performance in Industrial Control Systems

Sungho Bae, Chanwoong Hwang, and Taejin Lee[✉]

Department of Information Security, Hoseo University, Asan-si 31499, South Korea
baesungho21@naver.com

Abstract. In the automated Industrial Control System (ICS) where advanced technology is being integrated with core infrastructure, technology development is ahead of the application of security solutions. Our city, power, and transportation control systems are getting smarter and more efficient, but new connectivity and interoperability are making them more vulnerable than ever before. Accordingly, various studies have been conducted for anomaly detection in ICS. In this paper, we propose an unsupervised stacked bidirectional Long Short-Term Memory (LSTM) model for automated anomaly detection in large-scale ICS and introduce a method for performance improvement. In addition, it was written based on participation in HAICon2020, an ICS security threat detection contest hosted by the National Security Research Institute. We use the HAI 2.0 dataset published at HAICon2020 and use Time-series Aware Precision and Recall (TaPR), which is suitable for anomaly detection evaluation in ICS. As a result of submission of test data, we were awarded 2nd place at HAICon2020. We have detected anomalies in ICS. As a follow-up work, we will do further research to identify the sensor and actuator that caused the anomaly and to quickly respond and recover.

Keywords: Industrial Control System · Anomaly detection · Unsupervised stacked bidirectional LSTM · HAI dataset · TaPR

1 Introduction

Industrial Control System (ICS) refers to systems that monitors and controls important national infrastructure and industrial processes such as power, gas, water and sewage, nuclear power, transportation, and manufacturing. Early ICS is isolated systems to ensure availability and differed from traditional Information Technology (IT) systems. Programmable Logic Controller (PLC), the main element of the control system, was not connected to the network, so there were few threats other than physical disturbances or natural disasters. Therefore, ICS manufacturers were able to operate the systems without considering security at all when designing systems operating in a closed network. However, as the ICS, which used to be a safe closed network, is converted to an open network with the development of information and communication technology, security vulnerabilities are exposed [1, 2]. In order to prevent and respond to such security incidents, systematic security technology for ICS is required [3].

H. Kim (Ed.): WISA 2021, LNCS 13009, pp. 76–87, 2021.
https://doi.org/10.1007/978-3-030-89432-0_7

Attacks on ICS has been continuously occurring since the past, and the frequency of these attacks has been increasing recently. A representative security incident targeting ICS is Stuxnet. It was discovered in June 2010 by infecting Microsoft Windows and then monitoring and destroying industrial facilities, targeting PLCs. This sparked interest in ICS security [4]. In December 2015, a cyberattack on Ukrainian utilities resulted in a massive blackout, affecting more than 80,000 people [5]. In December 2017, it was detected while preparing for an attack using the zero-day vulnerability of the firmware through the EWS (Engineering WorkStation) of a chemical plant in Saudi Arabia. This case was not detected for more than 3 years after it penetrated the IT network in 2014. Such ICS security accidents may cause not only economic loss but also supply chain problems due to discontinuation of product launches, as well as human casualties due to explosions. In this paper, we introduce an anomaly detection method using a Recurrent Neural Network (RNN) and a time series analysis technique in an ICS environment. The contributions of this paper are as follows:

- An anomaly detection method for multivariate industrial process time series data;
- Attempts of various approaches to reduce false positives in anomaly detection model;
- A higher TaPR score for anomaly detection on the HAI dataset when using our method (Result of HAICon2020);

The rest of this paper is organized as follows. Section 2 describes the ICS operating structure and HAICon2020, and summarizes related research on anomaly detection. Section 3 describes the proposed model for anomaly detection in ICS and approaches to improve performance. Section 4 describes the dataset used, HAICon2020 results, and anomaly detection results. Finally, Sect. 5 describes the conclusions of this study and future work.

2 Related Work

2.1 Industrial Control System Operation Structure

ICS components are controller, HMI, actuator, sensor, and can be managed by various industrial protocols (see Fig. 1). The ICS consists of multiple PLCs. PLCs are used in both Supervisory Control and Data Acquisition (SCADA) and Distributed Control Systems (DCS) as the control component of full hierarchical systems to provide local management of processes through feedback control. Each PLC component consists of Process Variable (PV), Set Point (SP), and Control Variable (CV). In the process, the controller generates CV by interpreting PV, which is the value collected through sensors such as pressure, temperature, and speed, and flows to actuators such as valves and motors. HMI for integrated ICS control monitors multiple PLCs and has a structure that can change SPs suitable for process procedures [6].

2.2 ICS Security Threat Detection AI Contest (HAICon2020)

Cybersecurity threats to the control systems of national infrastructure and industrial facilities are on the increase. Cyber-attacks on critical national facilities can cause enormous and irreparable damage to society. Consequently, countries around the world are

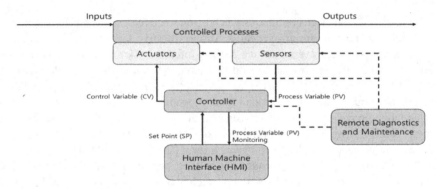

Fig. 1. Industrial control system operation structure.

focusing on developing security technologies. In this context, a dataset that accurately reflects the characteristics of the on-site control systems and sets out various types of control systems cyberattacks is an essential element for AI-based security technology research. The National Security Research Institute built a control system testbed using industrial control devices, sensors, and actuators built by General Electric, Emerson, and Siemens. This was then used to develop a HIL-based Augmented ICS (HAI) dataset. The first version of the HAI dataset, HAI 1.0, was made available on GitHub and Kaggle in February 2020. This dataset included ICS operational data from normal and anomalous situations for 38 attacks [7, 8]. The improved HAI 2.0 dataset was released at HAICon2020. HAICon2020 is the first competition in Korea for machine learning and deep learning models that can detect attacks and abnormal situations by learning only normal data using HAI 2.0 datasets created for ICS security research. Performance evaluation is measured by TaPR evaluation, specialized in time series anomaly detection [9]. The public score is scored at about 30% of the total test data and is posted on the leaderboard during the competition. The private score is scored with the rest of the test data and released immediately after the competition ends. The model is ranked by the final private score. A total of 928 teams, including the authors, participated in this competition.

2.3 Research on Anomaly Detection

Anomaly detection, a type of intrusion detection system (IDS), is an important data analysis task that detects anomalies or abnormalities in a given dataset. Anomaly detection has been extensively studied in statistics, and AI technologies are increasingly being used to automate anomaly detection. Anomalies are defined as deviations from normal patterns. However, defining the anomaly is still difficult. Anomalies are rare, and we do not have prior knowledge of all types of anomalies. Classical approaches to anomaly detection include OC-SVM, SVDD, and KDE. What these methods have in common is that they are all unsupervised and constitute a single approach to anomaly detection. A single approach is not sufficient to apply on time series data [10]. Currently, deep learning approaches are mainly used for anomaly detection, and open Secure Water

Treatment (SWaT) datasets have been used for ICS research, and the use of recently published HAI data sets is increasing.

A study using the HAI dataset [11] proposes a supervised machine learning model using SMOTE (Synthetic Minority Oversampling Technique) to solve the problem of data imbalance in anomaly detection. They chose KNN, DT, and RF for machine learning to compare their performance. Experimental results show that RF performs better than other classifier algorithms. Another study proposes Autoencoder and SVDD approaches based on deep learning with the same dataset [12]. They calculate the difference between predicted and actual values and apply Cumulative Distribution Function (CDF)-based statistical methods to predict the top 2% of data as anomalies. As a result, the SAE model showed a higher detection rate than the SVDD model.

There are also studies using Autoencoder in combination with other models [13]. They propose an LSTM Autoencoder model using the SWaT dataset. They compare the typical LSTM model predictions with the LSTM model reconstruction results. It shows improved performance with 88.5% recall and 87.0% f1-score, unlike typical Autoencoder neural networks that predict or reconstruct data individually. The anomaly detection method does not change what is considered an anomaly by calculating the error between the predicted value and the actual value. However, performance varies greatly depending on the threshold. There are also studies that propose anomaly detection methods based on statistical deviation calculations for anomaly detection [14]. Most statistical methods use the mean and standard deviation to calculate the z-score. Based on the z-score, you can set which top percentage of the entire test dataset is considered an anomaly.

It is important to accurately identify various attacks in sequential data, such as ICS and networks. There are also studies on intrusion detection using suitable RNN in a sequential data environment [15]. They use sequential NSL-KDD datasets to compare RNN with other machine learning methods. Experimental results show that RNNs are well suited for modeling sequential data with high accuracy and outperform conventional machine learning classification methods. Another study [16] proposes a new algorithm based on SR (Spectral Residual) and CNN for time series anomaly detection, as well as RNN. The CNN algorithm automatically extracts a fixed size of features from time series data. Then, SR subtracts the predictable value from the actual value and obtains a new value. This value has a small value if there is no difference in the residuals, and a large value otherwise. Therefore, if it is greater than the preset threshold, it is considered abnormal [17]. There are also studies comparing the performance of different combinations of DNN architectures, including different variants of CNNs and RNNs. This study was performed on the SwaT dataset and successfully detected 31 attacks with 3 false positives out of a total of 36 different cyberattacks. Therefore, they prove that CNNs and RNNs are effective in time series prediction tasks.

3　Proposed Model

3.1　Overview

We propose a stacked Bi-LSTM model of a family of Recurrent Neural Networks (RNNs) to detect anomalies in ICS. Training datasets consist of unlabeled normal data and require unsupervised learning. Normalize data before model learning so that certain features are not dependent on others. The RNN model designs three-dimensional data (Samples, Time Step, Features) that predict the following data as input. Anomaly detection is based on an anomaly score calculated as the difference between the actual and predicted values. We also applied three methods to improve performance: Finally, we evaluate our model using Time-Series Awareness Precision and Recall (TaPR), which is suitable for time series evaluation. The following shows a suggested model for improving performance in anomaly detection (see Fig. 2).

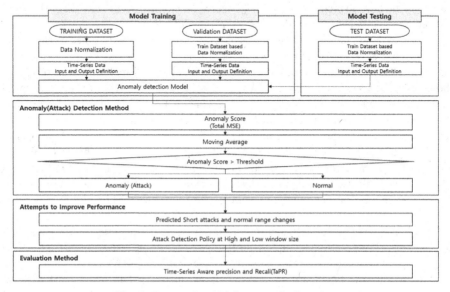

Fig. 2. Proposed model for anomaly detection

3.2 Data Preprocessing

Data Normalization. There are two reasons why normalization is necessary before input features are supplied to neural networks. First, if the features of the dataset are large compared to other features, large features take precedence. As a result, the prediction of neural networks is inaccurate. Second, Front Propagation of neural networks contains inner-product of the weight with input properties. Therefore, very high values (for image and non-image data) take a lot of time and memory to calculate the output. The same is true of Back Propagation. As a result, the model converges slowly if the input is not normalized. To solve this, we use the Min-Max scaling technique to normalize each feature to enter a scale of 0 to 1. For fields that do not change values, set all values to zero. Subsequently, exponential smoothing is used to minimize noise from sensors and actuators. Finally, verify that the normalized data has values less than zero or greater than one.

Time-Series Data Input and Output Definition. An RNN is a sequence model that processes inputs and outputs based on sequences. In general, time series data have features sequentially, so you need to generate samples of the same size through a sliding window, which is called sampling. Setting the sliding window size too large or too small when learning time series data on RNNs makes it difficult to derive appropriate predictions. Assuming that an RNN model predicts the next t + 1 based on the current point t, the size of the range predicted by the attack will be similar to the sliding window size. On the other hand, if the sliding window size is set small, assume that you cannot detect various attacks because each sequence is not unique.

3.3 Proposed Anomaly Detection Model Design

We compared various algorithms for processing time series data. Algorithms such as AutoEncoder, KNN, and DNN are point anomaly detection methods that are outside the scope of normal data. This was excluded because it could not reflect temporal information in time series. We also considered using CNN to extract local features and then combine them with other algorithms. Existing work combined CNN with LSTM and AutoEncoder to provide superior performance, but not with HAI datasets. CNN is suitable for images and uses many pixels as features. The HAI dataset consists of 79 features that are less than the image features, which is interpreted as having a large loss of information to extract meaningful features. RNN families are suitable for time series because they can predict the present through previously displayed sequences. We compared the performance of RNN, GRU, and LSTM on the HAI 2.0 dataset. As a result, we chose LSTM because GRU and LSTM are similar, but LSTM outperforms GRU. The results of the RNN were poor due to the vanishing gradient problem, in which the weight gradient decreases during the back propagation process.

We propose a stacked bidirectional LSTM model. Although unidirectional LSTM is available, but sometimes we expect that using bidirectional LSTM is more powerful. We chose bidirectional LSTM over unidirectional LSTM. Stacked LSTM is a method of increasing the complexity of the model by stacking LSTM in multiple layers, allowing them to train complex and large amounts of data. This approach can enable more sophisticated learning than increasing the number of cells in LSTM. However, stacking many layers does not continue to improve performance. We apply Skip connections to three bidirectional LSTM models. This minimizes the loss of information that occurs as the input goes through multiple layers, and uses the first value of the input sequence and the output of the model as an output to prevent the weight from becoming too large or too small. In order to avoid overload during the training process, we applied the callback function, which is an early stop and model selection feature, instead of dropout that randomly deletes nodes. An anomaly score is the error between the actual value and the predicted value. If the Anomaly score is greater than or equal to the threshold, it is considered an attack. Anomaly score is calculated by MAE, a typical measurement method.

3.4 Attempts to Improve Performance

Anomaly Score Moving Average. We expect the anomaly score to increase when an attack starts and decrease when an attack ends, but there are cases where it does not, so we smooth through the moving average. In statistics, Moving Average is a calculation that analyzes data elements by generating sets of means for different subsets of the entire data set. It is suitable for detecting trends or variations in data and is also used for stock price prediction analysis. However, in anomaly detection, the mean of the anomaly score is close to zero due to the data imbalance problem, which has more normal data than the anomaly data. So we apply it to the anomaly score described in Sect. 3.4 by slightly modifying the moving average without considering the average of the overall data. Calculates the anomaly score at the prediction point and the average of the most recent N sequence means. The final anomaly score is considered an attack if it is above the threshold. Otherwise, it is considered normal. We can visualize the anomaly score to set an appropriate threshold (see Fig. 3). Due to the nature of time series data, anomalies that occurred after the time of prediction are not considered. However, if the moving average is considered as the average of the anomaly score before and after the prediction time, the performance is higher than that using only the previously occurring anomaly score.

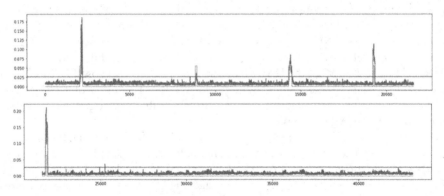

Fig. 3. Visualization of anomaly score on the validation dataset.

Predicted Short Attacks and Normal Range Changes. Even if you apply the moving average to anomaly score, false positive can occur close to certain thresholds. At this time, the anomaly score repeatedly crosses the boundary of the threshold, and the data is considered as an attack and a normal one. This increases false positive and degrades the performance of the anomaly detection model. We consider normal and attack labels predicted below a certain level to be prior to changing to minimize false positive. Therefore, a slight difference in the anomaly score prevents the attack from being considered normal, and prevents the attack from being considered normal. This method can reduce false positive and false negative by considering the time series properties.

Attack Detection Policy at High and Low Window Size. We compared the results by changing the sliding window size. If you set the window size to high, the type of attack with a higher anomaly score is considered to be an attack more broadly than the actual range of attacks. Conversely, setting a lower window size reduces attacks that are considered more broadly than the actual range of attacks, but certain types of attacks are not detected due to low anomaly score. The figure below shows anomaly scores at window sizes of 60 or 10 for five attack types in the labeled validation data set (see Fig. 4). Overall, attack types were well detected, but Type 4 and 5 were considered to be more attacks than the actual attack range due to their high window size. The reason is that the high window size affected the next input sequence. In order to reduce false positive, attack is detected by combining results from high and low window sizes. In this study, the window size was set to 60 for high and 10 for low under the same conditions. The high-window-size model detects the starting point of the attack, and the low-window-size model detects the ending point of the attack. This is only for attack types with an anomaly score of 0.1 or more.

3.5 Evaluation Method (TaPR)

In general, precision, recall, and f1-score are commonly used to classify normal and abnormal conditions. However, various abnormal sections need to be accurately detected in terms of the operation of the ICS. Also, if the process stops for false positive, availability guarantees are difficult, so there should be a difference in the evaluation index of precision and recall. Therefore, it is recommended to evaluate performance with TaPR when using HA datasets. Key elements of the TaPR assessment as follows.

- Does the prediction result detect anomaly without false positive?
- How diverse a range can be found?

In the scoring method according to the main evaluation factors of TaPR, a high score is given even if only a part of the attack range is found, and even a small amount of false positive is a factor of large deductions. In this paper, the performance of the detection model was evaluated through TaPR reflecting the characteristics of the ICS.

4 Experimental Result

For experiments, the programming language used Python 3.7 and the neural network framework for deep learning and reasoning used the Keras 2.4.3 and TensorFlow 2.3 libraries. Jupyterbook 6.2.0 was used for application and Tesla T4 GPU from NVIDIA was used for learning.

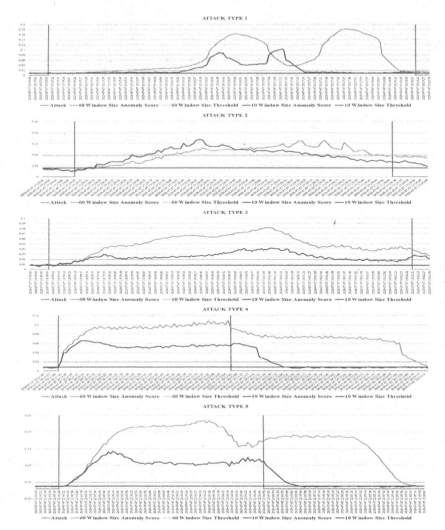

Fig. 4. Anomaly score graph at high and low window size

4.1 Dataset

In this paper, we used the HAI 2.0 dataset released by HAICon2020. The training dataset is normal data collected every second for a total of 3 collection periods, and there is no label. The validation dataset has labels for predicting attacks and anomalies, and contain five attack situations. The test dataset consists of 358,804 data generated during 4 collection periods, and the goal is to design an appropriate model to detect unknown attacks and anomalies contained in the test data set. The composition of the HAI 2.0 dataset is shown in the table below (see Table 1). All dataset consists of 79 features. There is a time field indicating time, and the remaining features are values of sensors and actuators that have been de-identified.

Table 1. HAI 2.0 dataset configuration.

Dataset	Data collection period	Total	Normal	Attack
Training	20200711–20200713	216,001	216,001	–
	20200731–20200803	226,801	226,801	–
	20200804–20200810	478,801	478,801	–
Validation	20200707–20200708	43,201	42,572	629
Test	20200709–20200711	118,801	–	–
	20200713–20200714	108,001	–	–
	20200728–20200728	39,601	–	–

4.2 Anomaly Detection Result

Based on the training dataset, we normalized the validation and test dataset using a min-max scaling technique. The proposed model sets the sliding window size to 60 and the stride parameter to 1. This is a model that predicts the 60th second with a sequence from 1 s to 59 s as input. The model configuration is a 3-stacked bidirectional LSTM, the size of the hidden cell is 100, no dropout is used, and a callback function is used. The callback function calculates the loss value based on the validation dataset at every epoch while the model is training, and saves the model if the loss value is lower than the previous epoch. Otherwise, the next epoch proceeds. Also, if the loss value does not decrease for 4 epochs, we end training to avoid overfitting. The loss function uses MSE and the optimizer uses Adam. Batch size is 512, epoch is 32. We used the skip-connection technique to make predictions by summing the first values in the input window and the output of the Bi-LSTM model. The initial anomaly score is calculated from the difference between the actual and predicted values. The final anomaly score is an average of the following two: Score at the time of prediction and average score over the previous 10 s. The threshold for anomaly score is set to 0.019 through the validation dataset. Exceeding the threshold is considered an attack. Because of the threshold, the short-predicted normal and attack range labels are considered old labels. We then train another low sliding window model by setting it to a low sliding window size of 10 and similarly detect attacks. At this point, the threshold is 0.008. The final attack is considered as an attack endpoint with a low sliding window model result for the attack range, where the proposed model result yields a score of 0.1 or higher. We placed second out of 931 teams at HAICon2020, where we submitted our test data, with a public score of 0.98031 and a personal score of 0.93614. To improve the anomaly detection performance, we reflected the features of the time series data, and we confirm that the TaPR score increases. The verification data set results (see Table 2 and 3) and test data results (see Table 4) are as follows.

Table 3. TaPR results on validation dataset.

Approach	f1-score	TaP	TaR	Detection
Bi-LSTM	0.922	0.976	0.873	5/5
Moving average	0.959	0.973	0.946	5/5
Short predicted label range change	0.971	0.995	0.948	5/5

Table 4. TaPR results on test dataset.

Approach	Public Score	Private Score
Bi-LSTM	0.9538	0.8773
Moving average	0.9682	0.9207
Short predicted label range change	0.9792	0.9373
Attack detection policy	0.9803	0.9361

Table 2. Classification evaluation metrics results from validation dataset.

Approach	Accuracy	Precision	Recall	f1-score
Bi-LSTM	0.993	0.784	0.717	0.749
Moving average	0.993	0.763	0.841	0.8
Short predicted label range change	0.993	0.765	0.842	0.802

5   Conclusion

As the ICS is a closed network environment, security is not considered at all. However, the transition of ICS, which used to be considered safe, to open networks reveals a variety of security vulnerabilities. In order to prevent and respond to such security incidents, systematic security technology for ICS is required. In this paper, we participated in HAICon2020 and proposed a Bi-LSTM-based anomaly detection model using the HAI 2.0 dataset published here. We made various attempts to improve performance considering the features of time series data, and confirmed that the TaPR score increased. The proposed model ranked second among the 931 teams participating in HAICon2020. Therefore, the proposed model can be said to be a proven model for detecting anomalies in time series ICS. However, it is interpreted that it is necessary to extract new features that can detect anomalies or add components. Because there are parts where it is difficult to detect anomalies in the industry due to lack of learning data and features. In addition, we plan to conduct additional research to characterize the device that caused the abnormal process because we have detected whether there is an abnormality in the entire industrial process. It is expected that faster response and recovery will be possible by notifying the security administrator of the result.

Acknowledgement. This work was supported by Institute for Information & communication Technology Planning & Evaluation (IITP) grant funded by the Korea government (MSIT) (No. 2019–0-00026, ICT infra-structure protection against intelligent malware threats).

References

1. Sakhnini, J., Karimipour, H., Dehghantanha, A., Parizi, R.M., Srivastava, G.: Security aspects of Internet of Things aided smart grids: a bibliometric survey. Internet Things, 1–15 (2019)
2. HaddadPajouh, H., Dehghantanha, A., Parizi, R.M., Aledhari, M., Karimipour, H.: A survey on Internet of Things security: requirements, challenges, and solutions. Internet Things, 1–19 (2019)
3. Karimipour, H., Dinavahi, V.: Robust massively parallel dynamic state estimation of power systems against cyber-attack. IEEE Access **6**, 2984–2995 (2018)
4. Zhang, F., Kodituwakku, H.A.D.E., Hines, J.W., Coble, J.: Multilayer data-driven cyber-attack detection system for industrial control systems based on network, system, and process data. IEEE Trans. Ind. Informat. **15**(7), 4362–4369 (2019)
5. CISA. Cyber-Attack Against Ukrainian Critical Infrastructure (2016). https://www.us-cert.gov/ics/alerts/IR-ALERT-H-16-056-01
6. Stouffer, K., Pillitteri, V., Lightman, S., Abrams, M., Hahn, A.: Guide to Industrial Control System Security, NIST SP 800–82 (2015)
7. Shin, H.-K., Lee, W., Yun, J.-H., Kim, H.C.: {HAI} 1.0: HIL-based Augmented {ICS} Security Dataset. In: 13th {USENIX} Workshop on Cyber Security Experimentation and Test ({CSET} 20) (2020)
8. Zaroosin. HIL-based Augmented ICS (HAI) Security Dataset (2020). https://github.com/ics dataset/hai
9. Hwang, W.-S., Yun, J.-H., Kim, J., Kim, H.C.: Time-series aware precision and recall for anomaly detection: considering variety of detection result and addressing ambiguous labeling. In: Proceedings of the 28th ACM International Machine Learning and Artificial Intelligence for Data Communication Networks, pp. 22–28 (2019)
10. Ruff, L., et al.: A unifying review of deep and shallow anomaly detection. Proc. IEEE (2021)
11. Mokhtari, S., et al.: A machine learning approach for anomaly detection in industrial control systems based on measurement data. Electronics **10**(4), 407 (2021)
12. Kim, D., Hwang, C., Lee, T.: Stacked-autoencoder based anomaly detection with industrial control system. In: Lee, R., Kim, J.B. (eds.) SNPD 2021. SCI, vol. 951, pp. 181–191. Springer, Cham (2021). https://doi.org/10.1007/978-3-030-67008-5_15
13. Wang, C., et al.: Anomaly detection for industrial control system based on autoencoder neural network. Wireless Communications and Mobile Computing 2020 (2020)
14. Xie, X., et al.: Multivariate abnormal detection for industrial control systems using 1D CNN and GRU. IEEE Access **8**, 88348–88359 (2020)
15. Yin, C., et al.: A deep learning approach for intrusion detection using recurrent neural networks. IEEE Access **5**, 21954–21961 (2017)
16. Ren, H., et al.: Time-series anomaly detection service at microsoft. In: Proceedings of the 25th ACM SIGKDD International Conference on Knowledge Discovery and Data Mining (2019)
17. Kravchik, M., Shabtai, A.: Detecting cyber attacks in industrial control systems using convolutional neural networks. In: Proceedings of the 2018 Workshop on Cyber-Physical Systems Security and Privacy (2018)

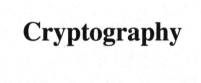

Cryptography

Quantum Cryptanalysis Landscape of Shor's Algorithm for Elliptic Curve Discrete Logarithm Problem

Harashta Tatimma Larasati[1,2] and Howon Kim[1(✉)]

[1] School of Computer Science and Engineering, Pusan National University,
Busan 609735, Republic of Korea
{harashta,howonkim}@pusan.ac.kr
[2] School of Electrical Engineering and Informatics, Institut Teknologi Bandung,
Bandung 40116, Indonesia

Abstract. Shor's algorithm is recognized as one of the most influential algorithms that shape the research interest in quantum computation and quantum cryptanalysis today. In particular, the algorithm is one of the firsts to show clear applicability of quantum computation to solve classically intractable problems underpinning the widely used public-key cryptosystems (i.e., RSA and ECC), igniting an ever-growing research interest in the respective fields. However, of the two algorithms introduced by Peter Shor in 1994, i.e., Shor's quantum factoring algorithm and Shor's discrete logarithm problem, the latter is not discussed as often. In this paper, we discuss the works done on Shor's algorithm to solve the elliptic curve discrete logarithm problem. In particular, we introduce the methods and optimizations proposed by researchers from the early era to the most recent ones and map them to obtain a comprehensive overview of the existing works. From our mapping, we analyze some of the trends in optimizations that help carve the research direction in Shor's algorithm for the elliptic curve discrete logarithm problem.

Keywords: Shor's algorithm · Elliptic curve discrete logarithm problem · Quantum cryptanalysis · Review

1 Introduction

Since its introduction in 1994, Shor's algorithm [18,19] has played a pivotal role in escalating the research interest in quantum computation and quantum

This work was supported by Institute for Information & Communications Technology Planning & Evaluation (IITP) grant funded by the Korea government (MSIT) (No. 2019-0-00033, Study on Quantum Security Evaluation of Cryptography based on Computational Quantum Complexity, 50%) and this work was also supported by Institute of Information & Communications Technology Planning & Evaluation (IITP) grant funded by the Korea government (MSIT) (2019-0-01343, Regional strategic industry convergence security core talent training business).

© Springer Nature Switzerland AG 2021
H. Kim (Ed.): WISA 2021, LNCS 13009, pp. 91–104, 2021.
https://doi.org/10.1007/978-3-030-89432-0_8

cryptanalysis. Specifically, the algorithm demonstrates the evident applicability of quantum computation to address two problems underpinning the widely used public-key cryptosystems (e.g., RSA and ECC family), which were classically believed to be intractable, i.e., no efficient algorithm can solve them in polynomial time. As a result, these cryptosystems are no longer guaranteed secure, given that a full-fledged quantum computer exists.

Following the discovery, research in the area of quantum cryptanalysis and quantum computing in general has started to proliferate and continued to flourish. In relation to Shor's algorithm, various studies have been conducted to pursue the most optimized quantum circuit subroutines, which may translate to the most efficient implementation in the quantum computer. Furthermore, the quantum resource requirement of Shor's algorithm is also of great interest because it provides an estimate of when in fact the current cryptosystems need to be replaced with quantum-resistant cryptographic schemes.

Regarding the Shor's algorithm itself, there are two problems addressed by Peter Shor in his 1994 seminal work: to factor a large integer into its prime factors and to find the discrete logarithms over finite groups [15,18], in which the first is the problem underlying the security of RSA cryptosystem, whereas the latter builds the foundation of Diffie-Hellman and DSA schemes, and its extension to the elliptic curve is the basis of ECC security. Despite the importance of both algorithms, Shor's algorithm for Integer Factorization Problem (IFP), sometimes referred to as Quantum Factoring Algorithm (QFA), seems to be studied more extensively than the Shor's algorithm for Elliptic Curve Discrete Logarithm Problem (ECDLP)—perhaps due to its less complex circuit construction—yielding a clearer research landscape of the former. In contrast, the works on Shor's ECDLP have not been clearly mapped. This is unfortunate considering the verdict that elliptic curve-based cryptosystem is likely to be crackable earlier than RSA due to its shorter key length [15]. Even though there have not been many papers specifically addressing Shor's ECDLP, a compilation of the findings and approach taken by researchers on this topic would be beneficial for future research on Shor's ECDLP and for the readers who start delving from classical into quantum cryptanalysis.

In this paper, we provide an overview[1] of the works on Shor's ECDLP performed by researchers over the years. Specifically, we describe approaches and optimizations of the algorithms utilized by researchers in the existing literature, then perform a mapping of the approaches (i.e., elliptic curve type, underlying finite field, point addition technique used, etc.) to obtain a comprehensive landscape of the existing works. The mapping enables us to analyze some of the trends in optimizations that help carve the research direction in Shor's ECDLP. Note that even though research fields are undoubtedly intercorrelated, and quantum circuits proposed for different areas (e.g., for Shor's QFA, or for cracking the symmetric cryptography such as AES) also influence and contribute to the

---

[1] Due to space constraints, we have removed the preliminary section (i.e., the theoretical background of ECDLP, Shor's ECDLP, and hierarchy of ECC operations). Those passages can be found in the extended version of this paper.

development in this field, for this study we focus on papers that specifically aim for the use in the Shor's ECDLP.

2   Research Landscape of Shor's ECDLP

To provide a clearer analysis of the research landscape of Shor's ECDLP, we will first describe the chronological overview of the existing proposals—from which we have derived the general research trends over the years—before mapping the proposed techniques and going into the detail of each existing proposal. In our study, we have observed that the research focus and approaches in Shor's ECDLP papers have changed over the years, most likely following the development in the field of quantum computation itself, including the emergence of quantum computer simulators. For instance, the proposed quantum circuits have generally become more detailed, i.e., more into the gate-level implementation with a clear description of each step. Also, the metrics used and resource counted have eventually been more geared towards the fault-tolerant quantum computation (FTQC) implementation.

2.1   Chronological Overview

Based on our study, we find that early publications had focused on adapting the original Shor's DLP algorithm for the case of the elliptic curve. In other words, they proposed the description of Shor's ECDLP, such as in [8,15]. Thus, the proposals were mainly into the relatively high-level algorithm, including replacing the standard inverse quantum Fourier transform (IQFT) with the semiclassical version, as in [15]. Nevertheless, [15] also presented notable efforts to describe the underlying quantum circuits and estimate the resource counts, which has been of great influence to the later proposals even to this day.

Subsequently, succeeding papers started to explore the lower level, examining alternative ways to yield a more efficient gate-level implementation of the quantum circuits for Shor's ECDLP, primarily for the point addition and the underlying finite field operations. In particular, various papers adopted well-known techniques in classical computation (e.g., Itoh-Tsujii inversion in [2], Mastrovito multiplier in [13], or different point addition techniques in [2,6]), adjusting them for use in the quantum area. Another notable approach was proposing the use of projective coordinates to eliminate the particularly expensive inversion operation, as in [1,2,17]. Unfortunately, since quantum simulators were not available during those times, a finer yet important detail, e.g., the cost of conversion for projective coordinates, had often been overlooked in their resource estimates.

Nevertheless, the emergence of quantum computer simulators with relatively decent functionalities only less than five years ago has arguably been a game-changer. This is because researchers can now perform simulations to verify their methods down to the smaller details, such as the implementation of Kaliski's almost inverse circuit in [16], whose circuit is later improved in [12]. Moreover, heuristic optimizations tailored to specific logical implementations can also be performed, yielding more precise resource estimates, as in [3,12,16]. Additionally, simulators also open the possibilities to address or experiment on finer details previously left out.

Still, there are many open possibilities for improvement, particularly in the scalar multiplication circuit. Furthermore, to the best of our knowledge, despite the advantages of quantum simulators, a complete simulation of Shor's ECDLP (including the QFT components) for a meaningful scale has not yet to be performed due to the enormous resource required for a full-scale quantum simulation. More importantly, implementing the logical circuit on real quantum hardware would require a far greater number of qubits, and many other considerations will need to be taken into account, such as the quantum error correction and mapping from logical to physical qubits.

2.2 Mapping of Techniques

From the examined papers, we list the techniques proposed in each of the papers to obtain the research trends over the years. Specifically, we categorize the techniques according to the hierarchy of ECC operations (which can be found in the extended version of this paper). Level 1, i.e., the bottom part of the hierarchy, includes the type of finite field (i.e., $GF(p)$ or $GF(2^m)$) and the proposed quantum circuits for realizing the corresponding finite field arithmetic (if applicable), notably the resource-expensive inversion operation. Moving on to Level 2, we map the curve choice, coordinates used, as well as methods to realize point addition. Next, if applicable, we also take notes of the point multiplication proposed for the mapping in Level 3. Note that in the classical hardware implementation, the description generally starts from the higher level, i.e., defining from Level 4 downwards. The mapping of existing proposals is presented in Table 1.

3 Review of Proposed Techniques for Shor's ECDLP

For ease of discussion, we group the proposals on Shor's ECDLP into three categories in chronological order based on their time of publication, following the general description in Sect. 2.1: (1) early proposals; (2) prior to quantum simulator's emergence; and (3) after quantum simulator's emergence. The first category refers to the pioneering papers, i.e., one of the firsts to translate Shor's DLP for use in the elliptic curve case. Meanwhile, the second one refers to the papers in the more recent time, but when the quantum computer simulators were not available. In contrast, the last category points to the papers at the time when significant research efforts on quantum computer simulators have commenced. Furthermore, for each group, we discuss the proposals on elliptic curve over a prime field (i.e., $GF(p)$) and a binary field (i.e., $GF(2^m)$) separately.

Table 1. Mapping of techniques for realizing Shor's algorithm for Elliptic Curve Discrete Logarithm Problem (ECDLP)

No.	Authors	Year	Main/Notable contribution	ECC level	Finite field	Field basis	Curve choice	Coord.	Algorithm for arithmetic circuit	Metrics	Platf. (Lang.)	QC provided?
1	Eicher & Opoku[8]	1997	- Algorithm-level analysis and description on how Shor's ECDLP works / -Provide example of Shor's ECDLP on Massey-Omura cryptosystem / -Provide walkthrough example of Shor's algorithm ran four times	on whole Shor's ECDLP	$GF(2^m)$ (example purpose)	-	SW	-			-	-
2	Proos & Zalka[15]	2003	- First detailed description of PM and PA + simplify addition rule + replace QFT with semiclassical QFT (baseline for recent methods) / - Rough resource estimates / - First to show that ECC is crackable sooner than RSA	Level 1-3	$GF(p)$	B	SW	A	- PM: R-L Double-and-Add using classically precomputed points / - FI: standard Euclidean algorithm / - FM: multiplication by doubling + conditional addition	#qubits, time (depth) in "1-qubit addition" unit	-	Description only
3	Kaye [13]	2004	- Adopt PZ for binary curves / - Describe naïve and optimized implementation of extended Euclidean algorithm	Level 1-2	$GF(2^m)$	P	SW	A	- PM, PA: follow PZ / - FI: extended Euclidean algorithm for Ps, also describe long division circuit	#qubit	-	Yes, figures + description
4	Cheung et al. [7]	2008	- Propose linear-depth FM using adopted classical Mastrovito multiplier in projective coordinate	Level 1	$GF(2^m)$	P	SW	SP	- PM: Double-and-Add / -PA: Not specified / - FM: Adopted classical Mastrovito multiplier	Toffoli + CNOT gates	-	Yes, example figures + description
5	Maslov et al. [14]	2009	- Description of FM for Linear Nearest Neighbor architecture (lower than logical-level implementation)	Level 2	$GF(2^m)$	P	SW	SP	- PM: Double-and-Add / - PA: Not specified / - FM: follow Cheung	Circuit depth	-	Yes
6	Amento et al. [1]	2012	- FI using different basis representations to reduce depth / - Resource estimates	Level 1	$GF(2^m)$	GH, GNB	-	-	- FM: Ghost-bit basis, Gaussian normal basis-based multiplier / - FI: Itoh-Tsujii	Rough circuit depth and gate count (Toffoli + CNOT gates)	-	Yes, figures + description

(continued)

Table 1. (*continued*)

No.	Authors	Year	Main/Notable contribution	ECC level	Finite field	Field basis	Curve choice	Coord.	Algorithm for arithmetic circuit	Metrics	Platf. (Lang.)	QC provided?
7	Amento et al [2]	2012	- Use Higuchi-Takagi's mixed PA to reduce T-gate complexity	Level 2	$GF(2^m)$	P	SW, CBE	LD	- PA: Higuchi-Takagi, mixed addition (Lopez-Dahab projective coordinate, added to A point) - FI: Itoh-Tsujii	Rough circuit depth, T depth, #T, and #gates	–	Description only
8	Roetteler & Steinwandt [17]	2013	- Parallelization of FM and PM -Multiplication and inversion circuit with lower depth than Kaye and Maslov -Derivation of unique A from projective representation	Level 1, 3	$GF(2^m)$	P	CBE	SP	- FM: Parallelized L-R Double-and-Add - FM: Mastrovito multiplier - PA: follow Amento T gate - Conversion from projective to A coordinate: FI using Itoh-Tsujii	Circuit depth	–	Partially yes + description
9	Budhathoki & Steinwandt [6]	2015	- Propose classical Al-Daoud's PA for reducing #T and T-depth - Heuristic optimization using edge colorings of certain bipartite graphs	Level 1-2	$GF(2^m)$	P	SW	LD	- PA: adapt classical Al-Daoud et al., mixed addition (Lopez-Dahab projective coordinate, added to a fixed A point) -FM: black box - Constant multiplication, squaring: heuristic optimization using edge colorings	#T, T-depth, #qubits	Python	Partially yes
10	Roetteler et al [16]	2017	- First detailed resource estimates - Detailed whole circuit subroutines and optimization, - PA implementation in F# (not publicly available)	Level 1-3	$GF(p)$	B	SW	A	- PM, PA: follow PZ - FM: Montgomery multiplier, also present quantum circuit realization from description in PZ - FI: B GCD algorithm (Kaliski's almost inverse) Squaring: black box	#qubits, #Toffoli gates, Toffoli depth	LIQUi|⟩ (F#)	Yes, figures + some description

(*continued*)

Table 1. (*continued*)

No.	Authors	Year	Main/Notable contribution	ECC level	Finite field	Field basis	Curve choice	Coord.	Algorithm for arithmetic circuit	Metrics	Platf. (Lang.)	QC provided?
11	Haner et al. [12]	2020	- Improved PM circuits from RNSL (fewer T gates), - Detailed resource estimates, - Full PA implementation in Q# (publicly available), - Resource estimates for NIST P256, P384, P521 point addition	Level 1-3	$GF(p)$	B	SW	A	- PM: adapted from Gidney (fixed-window) Double-and-Add using classically precomputed points - PA: follow PZ - FI: RNSL's version, improved using swap operations - FM: (windowed) Montgomery multiplier from RNSL	#gates (T + total), depth (T + total), #qubits (aux + total, each for case of low width, low T-depth, and low T-count)	QDK (Q#)	Yes, figures + description
12	Banegas et al. [3]	2021	- Detailed resource estimates - Detailed whole circuit subroutines and optimization - Full PA implementation in Q# (partly publicly available)	Level 1-3	$GF(2^m)$	P	SW	A	- PM: (fixed-window) adopted from PZ - PA: adapted for B curves from RNSL - FI: Euclidean algorithm, Itoh-Tsujii - FM: Van Hoof's Karatsuba	#Toffoli, bound for #CNOT, #T, and T-depth	QDK (Q#)	Yes, figures + description

Note: "ECC Level" column refers to the main area addressed according to the ECC hierarchy. "Finite Field" column refers to the underlying finite field of the curve. "Field Basis" refers to the basis representation employed by the finite field, with B: Binary (standard) basis, P: Polynomial basis, GH: Ghost-bit basis, GNB: Gaussian normal basis. For curve choice, SW: Short Weierstrass curve, CBE: Complete Binary Edwards curve. "Coord." refers to the coordinate representation, with A: Affine coordinate, SP: Standard projective, LD: Lopez-Dahab projective coordinate. "Algorithm for Arithmetic Circuit" column refers to the algorithm used, presented, or proposed in the paper, with PM: Point Multiplication, PA: Point Addition, FM: Finite Field Multiplication, FI: Field Inversion.

3.1   Early Research Proposals' Focus: Algorithmic Level Modification

High-Level Algorithm Modification. To the best of our knowledge, one of the first papers to describe Shor's DLP for cracking elliptic curve-based cryptosystem was by Eicher and Opoku [8] in 1997. In particular, they first describe the original Shor's DLP, primarily on how to recover the discrete log r from the good pairs (c, d), i.e., the output of measurement on the quantum computer, and the necessary condition. Subsequently, they describe the steps for the use in the elliptic curve, modifying the condition that needs to be met in order to determine whether the measurement output is a "good pair". Furthermore, the authors also elaborate on the example of applying the algorithm for breaking the Massey-Omura cryptosystem, providing step by step process with a numerical example to aid explanation. Namely, they use the binary elliptic curve $y^2 + y = x^3$ over $GF(2^5)$, run four times to describe different results from a quantum computer, and determine whether the condition constitutes it a "good pair" is satisfied each time. Note that in their paper, since their focus is on the algorithmic level, the whole scalar multiplication circuit is treated as a black box, and there is no discussion on resource estimates.

Works over $GF(p)$. Not limited to the prime field case, the paper by Proos and Zalka [15] is also often considered as the first to give a relatively detailed discussion on Shor's ECDLP implementation on a quantum computer. Rather than treating the function as a black box, the authors elaborate on how to perform point addition (which is the base for point multiplication) in a quantum computer, for the case of an elliptic curve over a prime field. In the paper, they also specify the underlying finite field arithmetic and how to implement it reversibly, mentioning the process of uncomputation that needs to be performed on each step. Additionally, the authors initially approach Shor's DLP problem from Shor's QFA viewpoint, i.e., that Shor's DLP can be thought of as a two-dimensional version of the QFA.

In detail, the authors' methods to implement Shor's ECDLP include using the Double-and-Add technique for the point multiplication, simplifying the point addition rule by restricting to the generic case (i.e., $P + R$ where $P, R \neq \mathcal{O}$ and $P \neq \pm R$), and fixing one of the points. Furthermore, they detail the steps of a more space-efficient reversible point addition by computing one part while uncomputing the slope (i.e., λ) in the group shift operation. The steps to implement (modular) multiplication, doubling, and addition are also explained. Moreover, they describe in detail on how to perform the modular inversion, which is arguably the most resource-expensive part of point addition, adapting the extended Euclidean algorithm (EEA) for the quantum case.

Besides point multiplication subroutines, the authors of [15] also propose a modification to the (inverse) Quantum Fourier Transform (QFT) part. In particular, they suggest the use of semiclassical QFT first described by Griffiths and Niu [11], which basically argued that a QFT directly followed by measurement could be simplified by measuring each qubit on the appropriate basis based on the preceding measurement outcomes [15]. By employing this method, the need of two input registers can be eliminated, thus reducing the overall qubit size.

Remarkably, this paper is considered the first to give a quite detailed resource estimate for implementing the whole of Shor's ECDLP. Specifically, the metric is in terms of qubit size (around $6n$) and running time. The paper shows that even though Shor's ECDLP requires larger resources than Shor's QFA for the same key length, the elliptic curve-based cryptosystem may be cracked sooner than RSA due to its lower key length in real-world applications. Due to their detailed discussions, the approach taken by this paper serves as a standard reference which is often followed, even by the latest proposals to date.

Works over $GF(2^m)$. Later, Kaye [13] extends the work on the curves over a prime field in [15] to a binary field. The focus of [13] is the description of modular inversion implementation for the binary field, adjusting the previously discussed extended Euclidean algorithm for use on a polynomial basis. Similar to the classical computation, operations in the binary field are generally simpler than that of the prime field in terms of the circuit implementation, such as an exact same circuit for performing addition and subtraction, and a multiplication that can be performed independently for each bit. Therefore, the implementation can be optimized. Compared to the work in [15], this paper present a more detailed circuit implementation, based on the multiplication circuit by [5] and controlled gates by [4]. For this paper, the metric for the resource estimates is focused on qubit count, whereas the detailed runtime is not specified.

3.2 More Recent Proposals' Focus: Gate-Level Optimization

As research has expanded on various aspects of quantum computation, more recent proposals in general have started to take into account implementation considerations such as T-depth for fault-tolerant quantum computation (FTQC), or the circuit construction for near intermediate-scale quantum computation (NISQ). In terms of the development for Shor's ECDLP, later proposals can be divided into two phases: the era before and after the development of quantum computer simulators. Prior to the emergence of simulators, researchers mostly analyzed through mathematical analysis; improvements such as parallelization and other design optimizations mostly gave rather rough resource estimates. More importantly, tracking the required auxiliary qubits was not very straightforward, contributing to the difficulty in compiling a more comprehensive resource estimate. Fortunately, the emergence of quantum simulators has allowed for more precise resource estimates; researchers can now account for what was previously sketched only on paper-and-pencil: control qubits or registers, depth reduction when using certain methods, qubit reuse, etc. Also, researchers can verify the workings and the correctness of their proposed algorithm more easily.

Prior to Quantum Simulators Emergence: Mostly on $GF(2^m)$. In summary, prior to the emergence of quantum simulators, most works (except [15]) on Shor's ECDLP are into the binary elliptic curves. Additionally, the focus is mostly drawn into the scalar multiplication (or the underlying operations, whereas the (inverse) QFT part seems well established on the standard QFT, the semiclassical QFT, or outside the scope of the work. Furthermore, there seems to be in favor of projective coordinate (except the early works, i.e., [13, 15]) for point representation due to the advantage of eliminating division operation, despite its challenge of a non-unique point representation. Such works are given by [2, 6, 7, 14, 17]. However, since the emergence of quantum simulators —and thus, the ability to verify the proposed methods on a quantum computer simulator - recent works (i.e., [3, 12, 16]) have shifted back to affine coordinates. As later pointed out in the appendix of [12], the use of projective coordinates for the elliptic curve in quantum computation still poses particular challenges that need to be addressed beforehand. Mainly, a unique representation of each point is arguably required in Shor's algorithm to guarantee history independence, which relates to a proper interference of the superposed states. Consequently, if one wishes to use the projective coordinate, achieving a unique representation may indeed be essential, which in the standard classical method is accomplished via division by Z coordinate. However, this also comes with a tradeoff of expensive division. Additionally, an in-place addition to save space may also require a unique representation in order to uncompute it for "re-use" in the succeeding computation. Therefore, alternative methods to achieve efficient, division-free arithmetic while maintaining a unique projective representation would still need to be explored.

Works over $GF(2^m)$. In [7], Cheung et al. improved the work of Kaye [13] by utilizing a more efficient multiplication circuit for the binary field. Precisely, they adapted the classical Mastrovito multiplier for use in quantum, which resulted in a linear-depth circuit. Additionally, the authors also opened the discussion of utilizing a projective coordinate for representing points on the curve. As classically understood, they argue that the projective coordinate would also be advantageous in quantum since group operation can be executed without division, and it provides a simple representation of the point of infinity $\mathcal{O}$. However, the drawback of this approach, as acknowledged by the authors, is that more than one representation exists for any particular point [7], making it unsuitable for the case of reversible (and thus, quantum) computing. Unfortunately, this challenge is not well discussed and addressed in the paper.

Subsequently, extending the work of [7], Maslov et al. [14] detailed the implementation of the multiplier in the Linear Nearest Neighbor (LNN) architecture. An illustration of the quantum multiplier circuit utilizing this architecture, along with the permutation stages, is also provided. In the case of the projective coordinates used, the authors mention that a multiplicative inversion is indeed required to transform back the points to affine coordinate, but the method or the issue in the previous work is not addressed. Nevertheless, the authors derive a quadratic depth circuit for implementing the Shor's ECDLP [17], which is lower than the bound described earlier by Proos and Zalka [15].

In [1], Amento et al. explored the possibility of improvements in the binary field inversion circuit by changing the basis representation to the Gaussian normal basis or to the 'ghost-bit' basis, which maps the polynomial one to a new basis that appends an extra zero bit to the coefficient vector. They adapt the Itoh-Tsujii classical binary inversion algorithm using each of the proposed basis, which in their paper shows lower asymptotic circuit depth and the number of gates in subquadratic units. Subsequently, the work was then extended for the implementation in Shor's ECDLP in [2]. Going back to the polynomial basis, Amento et al. described the steps to implement a point addition circuit by following the classical Higuchi-Takagi method. Projective coordinates are still used for this case, with a complete binary Edwards curve as the curve choice.

Roetteler and Steinwandt [17] enhanced the work of Cheung et al. [7] by parallelization to reduce the circuit depth in the computation of the scalar products $kP + lQ$ as well as in the underlying binary field multiplications. Also, several circuits of relevant sub-operations, such as multiplication and copy in logarithmic instead of linear depth, are provided. Working with a complete binary Edwards curve as in [2], the authors also present a subquadratic depth, polynomial-size circuit. Notably, as they work in a projective coordinate, they specify the methods to transform the projective points to unique affine points.

In [6], Budhathoki and Steinwandt continued the work of [2], in which they focused on point addition circuit generation and optimization by utilizing their own Python-based program, providing an automated and optimized circuit description compared to [2]. Following the previous work, the authors also employ a short Weierstrass curve with Lopez-Dahab projective coordinate but now adopt the classical point addition formula by Al-Daoud et al. rather than that of Higuchi-Takagi since it is considered more efficient [6]. Furthermore, the focus is to reduce the number of T-gates without increasing the T-depth by making use of the concept in graph theory, i.e., the edge colorings of certain bipartite graphs. Also, they provide explanations and show examples of the resulting quantum circuit from this optimization. For the point addition circuit, the authors describe the steps and the required resource for each step, along with an example of the quantum point addition circuit for adding a point in Lopez-Dahab coordinates on $E_{1,1}(\mathbb{F}_2)$ with the fixed affine point $(1,1)$. Unfortunately, the underlying binary field multiplier is treated as a black box, and their code seems to be not readily available.

3.3 Post-simulator Emergence Proposals' Focus: Finer Gate-Level Detail & Optimization, More Precise Resource Estimation

As the development of quantum computer simulators has emerged, researchers now have a more comprehensive tool for assessing and verifying their work on quantum computation, enabling them to go into the lower-level detail of the circuit, therefore yielding more precise resource estimates. To the best of our knowledge, there have only been three works focusing on Shor's ECDLP in this phase, i.e., [3,12,16]. Nevertheless, they are considered much more comprehensive since the authors acquire their resource estimates of point addition from real simulation. Still, for large numbers, the resource counts are obtained from interpolation due to the enormous computing power required to handle those operations.

In all three works, we notice that all of them prefer the use of affine as opposed to the projective coordinate frequently proposed in the era before the emergence of quantum simulators. Additionally, a short Weierstrass curve is used in all three papers. The main reason is that projective coordinate for quantum point addition is argued to incur a high indirect cost for the conversion and uncomputation. As elaborated on [3], projective coordinates have a much larger space requirement for storing the intermediate addition results since the naive addition of $-P_2$ to the output $P_1 + P_2$ do not necessarily uncompute P_1. Furthermore, the authors of [12] argue that unique representation, which is not the case for projective coordinate, is required in Shor's algorithm to ensure history independence, which is vital to establish proper interference of states in superposition. Another similarity of all three papers is that they restrict their implementation to the generic case of point addition. Note that these techniques follow the approach by Proos and Zalka [15], which is the reason why we consider [15] as the groundwork in Shor's ECDLP.

Works over $GF(p)$. One of the revolutionary works utilizing a quantum simulator was by Roetteler et al. [16], which simulated the point addition circuit and provided the first concrete resource estimates, utilizing LIQU$i|\rangle$ quantum computer simulator. Referring primarily to [15], the authors provide a reversible elliptic curve point addition over $GF(p)$ along with the circuit implementations for reversible modular arithmetic, including modular addition, multiplication, as well as inversion. For their finite field multiplication, they also provide the quantum circuit of the multiplier described in [15], but proposed their own multiplier based on the classical Montgomery multiplier. To implement the inversion, they also proposed their own technique based on binary GCD algorithm, namely the Kaliski's almost inverse since they did not find an efficient method to realize the Euclidean-based inversion as proposed in [15]. Additionally, they simulate the case from various bit sizes, including the NIST standard curves of P-192, P-224, P-256, P-384, and P-521, and compare the results with Shor's QFA. Their conclusion is in accordance with [15] which suggests that ECC is indeed crackable sooner than RSA. Note that their simulation is only for point addition while the resource for the whole of Shor's ECDLP is obtained from interpolation.

Improving the work in [16], Haner et al. [12] adopted the work by Gidney [9,10], using a more efficient adder and incorporating the classically-inspired windowing technique. Furthermore, the authors propose a modification to the inversion algorithm, now using swaps as opposed to conditional logic in [16] to achieve a lower cost. Additionally, the squaring is still treated as a black box as in [16], but a more efficient scheme is provided. Other mechanisms that they discussed include pebbling and the use of signed point addition. Implemented in Q# with the code readily available, they provide comprehensive resource estimates for the circuit subroutines in terms of various metrics.

Works over $GF(2^m)$. Banegas et al. [3] described the quantum circuit and resource estimates for binary elliptic curves. Adopting the work of [16], they provide the scalar multiplication and the underlying subroutines, along with optimizations tailored for the binary curve case. In particular, the Karatsuba polynomial multiplier from [20] is utilized, and the squaring circuit using LUP decomposition is described. Notably, the authors also examine and simulate two different algorithms for inversion: extended GCD (i.e., Euclidean algorithm) and Fermat's little theorem (FLT)-based Itoh Tsujii, highlighting the strength and weakness of each algorithm. Additionally, the weakness of previous proposals on binary curves is also investigated.

4   Conclusion and Future Work

In this paper, we have described the research landscape of Shor's ECDLP. From our observation, we find that early publications focused on translating Shor's DLP for the elliptic curve case on the high-level algorithm, such as utilizing the semiclassical QFT to replace the standard IQFT. Nevertheless, there have also been notable achievements in describing the underlying quantum circuits and calculating the resource estimates, which serve as a baseline for the later proposals to date. Another note is that adapting the classically efficient circuits to their quantum counterpart has been one of the favored methods from more recent proposals. Furthermore, quantum computer simulators have played a significant role in transforming the research approach, allowing to investigate and verify the finer detail of implementations and provide more precise resource estimates. For future work, we plan to extend our scope to include the works that are influential to, but not specifically targeted for Shor's ECDLP, expand our observations into a discussion, and provide the recent adoption of Shor's algorithm to other cases. Finally, we need to note that the field of quantum computation is highly active and not matured yet; our report is not conclusive since the landscape may shift again according to new findings in the future. Therefore, further studies would be beneficial to see which approach is actually the most appropriate and efficient for the implementation in a real quantum computer.

References

1. Amento, B., Rötteler, M., Steinwandt, R.: Quantum binary field inversion: improved circuit depth via choice of basis representation. In: arXiv preprint arXiv:1209.5491 (2012)
2. Amento, B., Steinwandt, R., Roetteler, M.: Efficient quantum circuits for binary elliptic curve arithmetic: reducing T-gate complexity. arXiv preprint arXiv:1209.6348 (2012)
3. Banegas, G., Bernstein, D.J., van Hoof, I., Lange, T.: Concrete quantum cryptanalysis of binary elliptic curves. IACR Trans. Cryptogr. Hardw. Embed. Syst. **2021**(1), 451–472 (2020). https://doi.org/10.46586/tches.v2021.i1.451-472, https://tches.iacr.org/index.php/TCHES/article/view/8741
4. Barenco, A., et al.: Elementary gates for quantum computation. Phys. Rev. A **52**(5), 3457 (1995)
5. Beauregard, S., Brassard, G., Fernandez, J.M.: Quantum arithmetic on Galois fields. arXiv preprint quant-ph/0301163 (2003)

6. Budhathoki, P., Steinwandt, R.: Automatic synthesis of quantum circuits for point addition on ordinary binary elliptic curves. Quantum Inf. Process. **14**(1), 201–216 (2014). https://doi.org/10.1007/s11128-014-0851-6

7. Cheung, D., Maslov, D., Mathew, J., Pradhan, D.K.: On the design and optimization of a quantum polynomial-time attack on elliptic curve cryptography. In: Kawano, Y., Mosca, M. (eds.) TQC 2008. LNCS, vol. 5106, pp. 96–104. Springer, Heidelberg (2008). https://doi.org/10.1007/978-3-540-89304-2_9

8. Eicher, J., Opoku, Y.: Using the quantum computer to break elliptic curve cryptosystems (1997)

9. Gidney, C.: Halving the cost of quantum addition. Quantum **2**, 74 (2018)

10. Gidney, C.: Windowed quantum arithmetic. arXiv preprint arXiv:1905.07682 (2019)

11. Griffiths, R.B., Niu, C.-S.: Semiclassical fourier transform for quantum computation. Phys. Rev. Lett. **76**, 3228–3231 (1996). https://doi.org/10.1103/PhysRevLett.76.3228

12. Häner, T., Jaques, S., Naehrig, M., Roetteler, M., Soeken, M.: Improved quantum circuits for elliptic curve discrete logarithms. In: Ding, J., Tillich, J.-P. (eds.) PQCrypto 2020. LNCS, vol. 12100, pp. 425–444. Springer, Cham (2020). https://doi.org/10.1007/978-3-030-44223-1_23

13. Kaye, P.: Optimized quantum implementation of elliptic curve arithmetic over binary fields. Quantum Inf. Comput. **5**(6), 474–491 (2005). ISSN 1533–7146

14. Maslov, D., et al.: An O(m2)-depth quantum algorithm for the elliptic curve discrete logarithm problem over GF(2)a. Quantum Info. Comput. **9**(7), 610–621 (2009). https://doi.org/10.5555/2011814.2011818. ISSN 1533-7146

15. Proos, J., Zalka, C.: Shor's discrete logarithm quantum algorithm for elliptic curves. arXiv preprint quant-ph/0301141 (2003)

16. Roetteler, M., Naehrig, M., Svore, K.M., Lauter, K.: Quantum resource estimates for computing elliptic curve discrete logarithms. In: Takagi, T., Peyrin, T. (eds.) ASIACRYPT 2017. LNCS, vol. 10625, pp. 241–270. Springer, Cham (2017). https://doi.org/10.1007/978-3-319-70697-9_9

17. Rötteler, M., Steinwandt, R.: A quantum circuit to find discrete logarithms on ordinary binary elliptic curves in depth O (log⁀ 2 n). arXiv preprint arXiv:1306.1161 (2013)

18. Shor, P.W.: Algorithms for quantum computation: discrete logarithms and factoring. In: Proceedings 35th Annual Symposium on Foundations of Computer Science, pp. 124–134. IEEE (1994)

19. Shor, P.W.: Polynomial-time algorithms for prime factorization and discrete logarithms on a quantum computer. SIAM Rev. **41**(2), 303–332 (1999)

20. Van Hoof, I.: Space-efficient quantum multiplication of polynomials for binary finite fields with sub-quadratic Toffoli gate count. arXiv preprint arXiv:1910.02849 (2019)

Anonymous IBE from PEKS: A Generic Construction

Hyun Sook Rhee[1] and Dong Hoon Lee[2(✉)]

[1] Global Privacy Office, Samsung Electronics Co. Ltd., Suwon-si, Gyeonggi-do, Korea
[2] Graduate School of Information Security, CIST, Korea University, Seoul, Korea
donghlee@korea.ac.kr

Abstract. Abdalla et al.[1,6] proposed a transform of an *anonymous* IBE (A-IBE) scheme to a PEKS (Public key encryption with keyword search) scheme. Boneh et al. proposed a transform of a PEKS scheme to an A-IBE scheme for only one-bit message. A transform for constructing an A-IBE scheme for polynomially many-bit message by using a PEKS scheme has not been proposed yet. To construct a transform from any PEKS scheme to an A-IBE scheme for a polynomially many-bit message, we firstly define a multiple PEKS (mPEKS) scheme and show that a mPEKS scheme can be constructed from a PEKS scheme. We also prove that if a PEKS scheme is confidential, so is the resulting mPEKS scheme. We then provide a transform from a mPEKS scheme to an A-IBE scheme for a polynomially many-bit message.

Keywords: Searchable encryption · Anonymous identity-based encryption · Public key encryption with keyword search

1 Introduction

An identity-based encryption (IBE) scheme is a public-key encryption scheme in which the public-key of a user is an identity of the user. Recently, there has been much interest in *anonymous* IBE (A-IBE) schemes with increasing applicability in various privacy preserving settings such as private broadcast encryption, encrypted email system and hidden credentials [4,6,9,11,13,15,16]. (An IBE scheme is said to be anonymous if a ciphertext does not reveal the identity of the intended recipient.) A study of identifying the relationships among cryptographic primitives greatly clarifies our understanding of the primitives themselves and is considered to be one of the promising approaches in cryptography. Once the relationship between two primitives is identified, a secure and customized primitive can be inexpensively constructed by exploiting the relationship and utilizing firm results of the other primitive.

Along the line of the approach above, an effort to identify the relation between A-IBE and PEKS has been continued. A PEKS is a variant of searchable encryption which provides a privacy of data and a retrievability on encrypted data.

Prior results have shown that a PEKS scheme can be constructed from any A-IBE scheme [1,6] and an A-IBE scheme for one-bit message can be constructed

© Springer Nature Switzerland AG 2021
H. Kim (Ed.): WISA 2021, LNCS 13009, pp. 105–118, 2021.
https://doi.org/10.1007/978-3-030-89432-0_9

from any PEKS scheme [6]. However, it has not yet been known to construct an A-IBE scheme for a polynomially many-bit message from an IBE scheme. Based on these results, the construction of an A-IBE scheme has been considered to be harder and more challenging than the construction of a PEKS scheme.

1.1 PEKS

The notion of PEKS firstly was suggested by Boneh et al. [6] and has received a lot of attention in the field of searchable encryption [20–23]. A PEKS scheme is a searchable encryption scheme over a store-and-forward system. A PEKS scheme enables an email server to correctly test whether or not a given keyword ndis present in an encrypted email without revealing any information on the email. In PEKS, a sender generates a *PEKS ciphertext* CT_w of a keyword w user the public key of a receiver and sends the PEKS ciphertext CT_w along with an encrypted email message to a server. To retrieve from the server the email messages containing a keyword w', a receiver provides the server with a *trapdoor* $T_{w'}$ (generated under the receiver's secret key). The server then runs a test function with CT_w and $T_{w'}$ to identify whether or not $w = w'$, and forwards the corresponding email messages to the receiver. In PEKS, an adversary (or the server) without the trapdoor T_w should not be able to learn anything about the corresponding keyword w from given PEKS ciphertext CT_w. The corresponding formal notion is denoted indistinguishability under a chosen-plaintext attack (IND-CPA) in PEKS. It should also be infeasible to find distinct keywords w and w' such that the result of the test function with CT_w and $T_{w'}$ is to indicate $w = w'$. This notion is called consistency and was firstly defined in [1]. If a PEKS does not meet the consistency then email messages will be incorrectly routed. The IND-CPA and the consistency have been considered as the security conditions PEKS should provide [1,6].

1.2 IBE

Shamir [17] firstly introduced the concept of IBE. An IBE scheme is a public-key encryption in which a public key is a public identifier (i.e. a user's email address). In set-up, a trusted third party, called the Private Key Generator (PKG), generates master public/secret keys. To send a message, a sender encrypts the message by using the master public key and the identifier ID of a intended recipient. To decrypt the message, the recipient obtains the private key d_{ID} corresponding ID from the PKG.

In IBE, indistinguishability under a chosen-plaintext attack (IND-CPA), i.e. privacy of the encrypted data, as well as anonymity under a chosen-plaintext attack (ANO-CPA) have been considered as important security requirements [7,8,18].

1.3   Contribution

Table 1. The relations among A-IBE, PEKS and mPEKS.

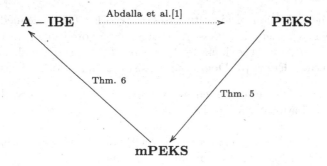

In this paper, we show that an A-IBE scheme for a polynomially many-bit message can be constructed from any PEKS scheme. We first define a multiple PEKS (mPEKS) scheme, which encrypts multiple keywords instead of one keyword with the same public key, and prove that a confidential mPEKS scheme can be derived from any confidential PEKS scheme. Next, we provide a transform of a confidential mPEKS scheme to an anonymous IBE scheme for a polynomially many-bit message. Table 1 shows the relationships among A-IBE, PEKS, and mPEKS. In the proposed transform, we prove that (1) if a PEKS scheme is IND-CPA then the resulting IBE scheme is ANO-CPA and IND-CPA (2) if a PEKS scheme provides consistency (which requires that email messages should be correctly routed) then the A-IBE scheme satisfies a correctness (which requires that the result of decrypting of any valid ciphertext should be an original message). To verify the correctness of the resulting A-IBE scheme, we newly define a computational relaxation of the notion of correctness as the same manner in [1]. The crux of our technical contribution is to provide one direction of constructing an A-IBE scheme from a PEKS scheme. Providing anonymity to IBE is an challenging problem as noted in [8,18]. In fact, a number of IBE schemes [2,3,7,8,10,18,19] have been proposed, but only few of them are anonymous [7,8,18,19].

1.4   Paper Organization

The remainder of this paper is organized as follows. We review several primitives that are necessary for our transforms, such as the IBE and PEKS schemes in Sect. 2. In Sect. 3, we define a multiple PEKS (mPEKS) scheme and its security model. We then a confidential mPEKS scheme can be constructed from a confidential PEKS scheme. In Sect. 4, we propose a transform of a confidential mPEKS scheme to a A-PEKS scheme. Finally, Sect. 5 concludes the paper.

2   Preliminaries

2.1   Identity-Based Encryption

We follow the definition of identity-based encryption (IBE) defined by Boneh and Franklin [7]. Let the message space be denoted by $\mathcal{M}$, the ciphertext space by $\mathcal{C}$, and the identity space by $\mathcal{ID}$. An IBE scheme **IBE** = (**Setup, Extract, Encrypt, Decrypt**) consists of four algorithms as follows.

- **Setup**(k) takes as input a security parameter k, and outputs public parameters PP and a master secret key msk.
- **Extract**(msk, ID) takes as input a master secret key msk and an identity ID $\in \mathcal{ID}$. It outputs a private key d_{ID} corresponding to an identity ID.
- **Encrypt**(PP, ID, M) takes as input PP, ID, and $M \in \mathcal{M}$ where $\mathcal{M}$ is a finite message space. It outputs a ciphertext C.
- **Decrypt**(C, d_{ID}) takes as input C $\in \mathcal{C}$ and a private key d_{ID}, where $\mathcal{C}$ is a ciphertext space. It outputs either $M \in \mathcal{M}$ or a symbol $\perp$ indicating failure.

Correctness. For all ID $\in \mathcal{ID}$, all $M \in \mathcal{M}$, if C is the output of **Encrypt** with input (PP, ID, M) and d_{ID} is a valid private-key about ID, then M is the result of applying **Decrypt** with input (C, d_{ID}). That is, for the given PP we have

$$\Pr[\mathbf{Decrypt}(\mathbf{Encrypt}(\mathsf{PP}, \mathsf{ID}, M), d_{\mathsf{ID}}) = M] = 1 - \epsilon(k),$$

where $\epsilon(k)$ is a negligible function (Table 2).

Table 2. The confidentiality (IND-CPA) and the anonymity (ANO-CPA) of IBE

$\mathbf{Exp}_{\mathbf{IBE},\mathcal{A}}^{\text{ibe-ind-cpa-}b}(k)$	$\mathbf{Exp}_{\mathbf{IBE},\mathcal{A}}^{\text{ibe-ano-cpa-}b}(k)$
SetID $\leftarrow \emptyset$; (PP, msk) $\leftarrow$ **Setup**(k)	SetID $\leftarrow \emptyset$; (PP, msk) $\leftarrow$ **Setup**(k)
(ID, M_0, M_1, s) $\leftarrow \mathcal{A}^{\mathbf{Extract}(\cdot)}(\texttt{find}, \mathsf{PP})$	($\mathsf{ID}_0, \mathsf{ID}_1, M, s$) $\leftarrow \mathcal{A}^{\mathbf{Extract}(\cdot)}(\texttt{find}, \mathsf{PP})$
if $\{M_0, M_1\} \not\subseteq \mathcal{M}$ then return 0	if $\{M\} \not\subseteq \mathcal{M}$ then return 0
$b \leftarrow \{0, 1\}$; C $\leftarrow$ **Encrypt**(PP, ID, M_b)	$b \leftarrow \{0, 1\}$; C $\leftarrow$ **Encrypt**(PP, ID_b, M)
$b' \leftarrow \mathcal{A}^{\mathbf{Extract}(\cdot)}(\texttt{guess}, \mathsf{C}, s)$	$b' \leftarrow \mathcal{A}^{\mathbf{Extract}(\cdot)}(\texttt{guess}, \mathsf{C}, s)$
if ID $\notin$ SetID and $|M_0| = |M_1|$	if $\{\mathsf{ID}_0, \mathsf{ID}_1\} \cap$ SetID $= \emptyset$
then return b' else return 0	then return b' else return 0

2.2   Security for A-IBE

Let **IBE** = (**Setup, Extract, Encrypt, Decrypt**) be an IBE scheme and $\mathcal{A}$ be an adversary. The confidentiality (IND-CPA-security) and anonymity (ANO-CPA-security) of IBE scheme against adaptive chosen-plaintext attacks follows [1,5], as shown in Table 1. The oracle **Extract**$(\cdot)$ is defined as: when ID is queried by $\mathcal{A}$

SetID $\leftarrow$ SetID $\cup$ {ID} ;   Return $d_{\mathsf{ID}} \leftarrow$ KeyDer(msk, ID).

The advantage of $\mathcal{A}$ in the corresponding experiment as

$$\mathbf{Adv}_{\mathbf{IBE},\mathcal{A}}^{ibe\text{-}ind\text{-}cpa}(k) = \Pr[\mathbf{Exp}_{\mathbf{IBE},\mathcal{A}}^{ibe\text{-}ind\text{-}cpa\text{-}1}(k) = 1] - \Pr[\mathbf{Exp}_{\mathbf{IBE},\mathcal{A}}^{ibe\text{-}ind\text{-}cpa\text{-}0}(k) = 1],$$

$$\mathbf{Adv}_{\mathbf{IBE},\mathcal{A}}^{ibe\text{-}ano\text{-}cpa}(k) = \Pr[\mathbf{Exp}_{\mathbf{IBE},\mathcal{A}}^{ibe\text{-}ano\text{-}cpa\text{-}1}(k) = 1] - \Pr[\mathbf{Exp}_{\mathbf{IBE},\mathcal{A}}^{ibe\text{-}ano\text{-}cpa\text{-}0}(k) = 1].$$

Definition 1. *We say that an* **IBE** *is IND-CPA-secure (resp., ANO-CPA-secure) if for any probabilistic polynomial-time (PTT) adversary $\mathcal{A}$ attacking* **IBE** *scheme the advantage* $\mathbf{Adv}_{\mathbf{IBE},\mathcal{A}}^{ibe\text{-}ind\text{-}cpa}(k)$ *(resp.,* $\mathbf{Adv}_{\mathbf{IBE},\mathcal{A}}^{ibe\text{-}ano\text{-}cpa}(k)$*) is negligible.*

2.3   Public-Key Encryption with Keyword Search

A public key encryption with keyword search (PEKS) scheme [6] **PEKS** = (**KG**, **PEKS**, **Td**, **Test**) defined by Boneh *et al.* consists of four polynomial time randomized algorithms as follows.

- **KG**(k) takes as input a security parameter k, and outputs a pair of public and private keys (PK, SK).
- **PEKS**(PK, w) takes as input the public key PK and a keyword $w \in \mathcal{KW}$, where $\mathcal{KW}$ is a keyword space. It returns a ciphertext CT.
- **Td**(SK, w) takes as input the secret key SK and a keyword w. It returns a trapdoor T_w.
- **Test**(CT, $T_{w'}$) takes as input a ciphertext CT and a trapdoor T_w. It outputs '1' if $w = w'$ and '0' otherwise, where CT = **PEKS**(PK, w) and $T_{w'} \leftarrow$ **Td**(SK, w').

Correctness. For all $w \in \mathcal{KW}$, CT $\leftarrow$ **PEKS**(PK, w), and $T_w \leftarrow$ **Td**(SK, w), then **Test**(CT, T_w) always accepts. That is, for all $w \in \mathcal{KW}$ we have

$$\Pr[\mathbf{Test}(\mathbf{Td}(SK, w), \mathbf{PEKS}(PK, w)) = 1] = 1 - \epsilon(k),$$

where the probability is taken over the choice of $(PK, SK) \leftarrow$ **KG**(k) and $\epsilon(k)$ is a negligible function.

2.4   Security for PEKS

A PEKS system [1,6] requires a confidentiality (IND-CPA security), it should be infeasible for an adversary to decide which keyword is used in generating the ciphertext, and a consistency, email messages should be correctly routed. Let **PEKS** = (**KG**, **PEKS**, **Td**, **Test**) be a PEKS scheme and let $\mathcal{A}$ be a PPT adversary. We review a confidentiality and a computational consistency for PEKS scheme as follows.

Confidentiality of PEKS. The confidentiality (IND-CAP-secure) for a PEKS scheme was defined using an experiment in the Table 3 [1,6].

The advantage of $\mathcal{A}$ is defined as follows.

$$\mathbf{Adv}_{\mathbf{PEKS},\ \mathcal{A}}^{peks\text{-}ind\text{-}cpa}(k) = \Pr[\mathbf{Exp}_{\mathbf{PEKS},\mathcal{A}}^{peks\text{-}ind\text{-}cpa\text{-}1}(k) = 1] - \Pr[\mathbf{Exp}_{\mathbf{PEKS},\mathcal{A}}^{peks\text{-}ind\text{-}cpa\text{-}0}(k) = 1] .$$

Table 3. The security (IND-CPA) of PEKS.

$\mathbf{Exp}_{\mathbf{PEKS},\,\mathcal{A}}^{peks\text{-}ind\text{-}cpa\text{-}b}(k)$	Oracle $\mathbf{Td}(w)$
$\quad$ SetTrap $\leftarrow \emptyset$	$\quad$ SetTrap $\leftarrow$ SetTrap$(k) \cup \{w\}$
$\quad (PK, SK) \leftarrow \mathbf{KG}(k)$	$\quad T_w \leftarrow \mathbf{Td}(SK, w)$
$\quad (w_0, w_1, s) \leftarrow \mathcal{A}^{\mathbf{Td}(\cdot)}(PK)$	$\quad$ Return T_w
$\quad b \leftarrow \{0, 1\}$; $\;$ CT $\leftarrow \mathbf{PEKS}(\mathtt{find}, PK, w_b)$	
$\quad b' \leftarrow \mathcal{A}^{\mathbf{Td}(\cdot)}(\mathtt{guess}, \mathsf{CT}, s)$	
$\quad$ If $\{w_0, w_1\} \cap$ SetTrap$(k) = \emptyset$	
$\quad$ then return b' else return 0	

Table 4. Computational consistency of PEKS.

$\mathbf{Exp}_{\mathbf{PEKS},\mathcal{A}}^{peks\text{-}cons}(k)$
$\quad (PK, SK) \leftarrow \mathbf{KG}(k)$
$\quad (w, w') \leftarrow \mathcal{A}(PK)$
$\quad$ CT $\leftarrow \mathbf{PEKS}(PK, w)$; $T_{w'} \leftarrow \mathbf{Td}(SK, w')$
$\quad$ If $w \neq w'$ and $\mathbf{Test}(\mathsf{CT}, T_{w'}) = 1$ then return 1 else return 0

Definition 2. *We say that a* **PEKS** *is IND-CPA-secure if for any PPT adversary $\mathcal{A}$ attacking PEKS scheme the advantage $\mathbf{Adv}_{\mathbf{PEKS},\,\mathcal{A}}^{peks\text{-}ind\text{-}cpa}(k)$ is negligible.*

Consistency of PEKS. In [1], Abdalla *et al.* defined a computational consistency for PEKS scheme. Suppose there exists an adversary $\mathcal{A}$ that wants to make consistency fail. A computational consistency for a mPEKS scheme is defined using an experiment in the Table 4.

The advantage of $\mathcal{A}$ is defined as follows.

$$\mathbf{Adv}_{\mathbf{PEKS},\mathcal{A}}^{peks\text{-}cons}(k) = \Pr[\mathbf{Exp}_{\mathbf{PEKS},\mathcal{A}}^{peks\text{-}cons}(k) = 1],$$

where the probability is taken over all possible coin flips of all the algorithms involved.

Definition 3. *We say that a* **PEKS** *is "computationally consistent" if for any PPT adversary $\mathcal{A}$ attacking PEKS scheme the advantage $\mathbf{Adv}_{\mathbf{PEKS},\mathcal{A}}^{peks\text{-}cons}(k)$ is negligible.*

3 Multiple PEKS

In this section, we firstly define a notion of multiple PEKS (mPEKS) and the security for mPEKS. We then prove that any PEKS scheme having an IND-CPA security is secure even when used to encrypt multiple messages.

3.1 Definition of Multiple PEKS

A multiple public key encryption with keyword search (mPEKS) scheme **mPEKS** = (**KG**, **mPEKS**, **Td**, **mTest**) for encrypting multiple keywords is as follows.

- **KG**(k) takes as input a security parameter k and outputs a pair of public and private keys (PK, SK).
- **mPEKS**$(PK, \overrightarrow{w})$ takes as input the public key PK and a vector of keywords $\overrightarrow{w} = (w_1, ..., w_t)$. For every i $(1 \leq i \leq t)$, it computes $c_i = \textbf{PEKS}(PK, w_i)$ and returns a ciphertext $\mathsf{CT} = [c_1, ..., c_t]$ of $\overrightarrow{w}$.
- **Td**(SK, w_i) takes as inputs the secret key SK and a keyword w_i. It computes $T_{w_i} = \textbf{Td}(PK, w_i)$.
- **mTest**$(\mathsf{CT}, T_{\overrightarrow{w}})$ takes as inputs a ciphertext $\mathsf{CT} = [c_1, ..., c_t]$ and a vector of trapdoors $T_{\overrightarrow{w}} = [T_{w_1}, ..., T_{w_t}]$. For every i $(1 \leq i \leq t)$, it computes $res_i = \textbf{Test}(c_i, T_{w_i})$ and outputs $[res_1, ..., res_t]$.

Correctness. For all vector of t keywords $\overrightarrow{w} = (w_1, ..., w_t) \in \mathcal{KW}^t$, $\mathsf{CT} \leftarrow$ **mPEKS**$(PK, \overrightarrow{w})$, $T_{w_i} \leftarrow \textbf{Td}(PK, w_i)$, and let a vector of trapdoors $T_{\overrightarrow{w}} = [T_{w_1}, ..., T_{w_t}]$, then **mTest**$(\mathsf{CT}, T_{\overrightarrow{w}})$ always outputs $\overrightarrow{1}$. That is, for all $\overrightarrow{w} = (w_1, ..., w_t) \in (\mathcal{KW})^t$ we have

$$\Pr[\textbf{mTest}(\textbf{mPEKS}(PK, (w_1, ..., w_t)), [\textbf{Td}(SK, w_1), ..., \textbf{Td}(SK, w_t)]) = \overrightarrow{1}] = 1 - \epsilon(k),$$

where the probability is taken over the choice of $(PK, SK) \leftarrow \textbf{KG}(k)$ and $\epsilon(k)$ is a negligible function.

3.2 Security for mPEKS

In this subsection, we firstly define a confidentiality and a computational consistency for mPEKS. Let **mPEKS** = (**KG**, **mPEKS**, **Td**, **mTest**) be a mPEKS scheme and $\mathcal{A}$ be a PPT adversary. We suppose that $\overrightarrow{w}_0 = (w_0^1, ..., w_0^t)$ and $\overrightarrow{w}_1 = (w_1^1, ..., w_1^t)$ are vectors of $t(k)$ keywords. We let that $D = \{j \mid w_0^j \neq w_1^j, 1 \leq j \leq t\}$.

The definitions of securities are as follows.

Confidentiality of mPEKS. The confidentiality (IND-CAP-secure) for a mPEKS scheme is defined using an experiment in the Table 5. The advantage of $\mathcal{A}$ is defined as follows.

$$\textbf{Adv}_{\mathsf{mPEKS}, \mathcal{A}}^{\mathsf{mpeks\text{-}ind\text{-}cpa}}(k) = \Pr[\textbf{Exp}_{\mathsf{mPEKS},\mathcal{A}}^{\mathsf{mpeks\text{-}ind\text{-}cpa\text{-}1}}(k) = 1] - \Pr[\textbf{Exp}_{\mathsf{mPEKS},\mathcal{A}}^{\mathsf{mpeks\text{-}ind\text{-}cpa\text{-}0}}(k) = 1].$$

Definition 4. *We say that a mPEKS scheme* **mPEKS** *is IND-CPA-secure if for any PPT adversary $\mathcal{A}$ attacking* mPEKS *scheme the advantage* $Adv_{\mathsf{mPEKS}, \mathcal{A}}^{\mathsf{mpeks\text{-}ind\text{-}cpa}}(k)$ *is negligible.*

Table 5. IND-CPA-security of mPEKS.

$\mathbf{Exp}_{\mathbf{mPEKS},\ \mathcal{A}}^{\text{mpeks-ind-cpa-}b}(k)$	Oracle $\mathsf{Td}(w)$
$\quad$ SetTrap $\leftarrow \emptyset$	$\quad$ SetTrap $\leftarrow$ SetTrap$(k) \cup \{w\}$
$\quad (PK, SK) \leftarrow \mathbf{KG}(k)$	$\quad T_w \leftarrow \mathbf{Td}(SK, w)$
$\quad (\vec{w}_0, \vec{w}_1, s) \leftarrow \mathcal{A}^{\mathsf{Td}(\cdot)}(PK)\ (|\vec{w}_0| = |\vec{w}_1| = t(k))$	$\quad$ Return T_w
$\quad b \leftarrow \{0,1\}\ ;\ \mathsf{CT} \leftarrow \mathsf{mPEKS}(\mathtt{find}, PK, \vec{w}_b)$	
$\quad b' \leftarrow \mathcal{A}^{\mathsf{Td}(\cdot)}(\mathbf{guess}, \mathsf{CT}, s)$	
$\quad$ If $\{w_0^j, w_1^j \mid j \in D\} \cap$ SetTrap$(k) = \emptyset$	
$\quad$ then return b' else return 0	

Table 6. Computational consistency of mPEKS.

$\mathbf{Exp}_{\mathbf{mPEKS},\mathcal{A}}^{\text{mpeks-cons}}(k)$
$\quad (PK, SK) \leftarrow \mathbf{KG}(k)$
$\quad (\vec{w}_0 = (w_0^1, ..., w_0^t), \vec{w}_1 = (w_1^1, ..., w_1^t)) \leftarrow \mathcal{A}(PK)$
$\quad \mathsf{CT} \leftarrow \mathbf{PEKS}(PK, w_j)\ ;\ T_{w_j'} \leftarrow \mathbf{Td}(SK, w_j')$
$\quad$ If there exists $j \in \{1, ..., t\}$ such that $w_j \neq w_j'$ and $\mathbf{Test}(\mathsf{CT}, T_{w_j'}) = 1$
$\quad$ then return 1 else return 0

Consistency of mPEKS. Suppose there exists an adversary $\mathcal{A}$ that wants to make consistency fail. A computational consistency for a mPEKS scheme is defined using an experiment in the Table 6.

The advantage of $\mathcal{A}$ is defined as follows.

$$\mathbf{Adv}_{\mathbf{mPEKS},\mathcal{A}}^{\text{mpeks-cons}}(k) = \Pr[\mathbf{Exp}_{\mathbf{mPEKS},\mathcal{A}}^{\text{mpeks-cons}}(k) = 1],$$

where the probability is taken over all possible coin flips of all the algorithms involved.

Definition 5. *We say that a **mPEKS** is "computationally consistent" if for any PPT adversary $\mathcal{A}$ attacking* mPEKS *scheme the advantage* $\mathbf{Adv}_{\mathbf{mPEKS},\mathcal{A}}^{\text{mpeks-cons}}(k)$ *is negligible.*

3.3   Relation Between PEKS and mPEKS

We show here that, if a PEKS scheme **PEKS** is IND-CPA-secure, then a multiple PEKS scheme **mPEKS** is IND-CPA-secure. To prove this, we consider the following hybrid games which differs on what challenge ciphertext CT_i is given by the challenger to the adversary.

$$\mathsf{CT}_0 = (\mathsf{PEKS}(PK, w_1^1), \mathsf{PEKS}(PK, w_1^2), ..., \mathsf{PEKS}(PK, w_1^i)), ..., \mathsf{PEKS}(PK, w_1^t))$$
$$\mathsf{CT}_1 = (\mathsf{PEKS}(PK, w_0^1), \mathsf{PEKS}(PK, w_1^2), ..., \mathsf{PEKS}(PK, w_1^i), ..., \mathsf{PEKS}(PK, w_1^t))$$

$$\vdots \qquad\qquad \vdots$$

$$\mathsf{CT}_i = (\mathsf{PEKS}(PK, w_0^1), ..., \mathsf{PEKS}(PK, w_0^i), \mathsf{PEKS}(PK, w_1^{i+1}), ..., \mathsf{PEKS}(PK, w_1^t))$$
$$\mathsf{CT}_{i+1} = (\mathsf{PEKS}(PK, w_0^1), ..., \mathsf{PEKS}(PK, w_0^{i+1}), \mathsf{PEKS}(PK, w_0^{i+2}), ..., \mathsf{PEKS}(PK, w_1^t))$$

$$\vdots \qquad\qquad \vdots$$

$$\mathsf{CT}_t = (\mathsf{PEKS}(PK, w_0^1), ..., \mathsf{PEKS}(PK, w_0^i), ..., \mathsf{PEKS}(PK, w_0^{t-1}), \mathsf{PEKS}(PK, w_0^t)).$$

CT_0 is the challenge ciphertext given to the adversary when $b = 0$ is chosen and CT_t is the challenge ciphertext given to the adversary when $b = 1$ is chosen. Since the above PEKS ciphertexts are always performed using independent random coins, and so the above one actually represents a distribution over vectors containing t PEKS ciphertexts. We show that no polynomially-bounded adversary is able to distinguish between CT_0 and CT_t by proving that CT_i and CT_{i+1} ($1 \leq i \leq t-1$) are computationally indistinguishable. We note that the proof idea follows from the work of Katz and Lindell [12].

Theorem 1. *If* **PEKS** *is IND-CPA-secure, then* **mPEKS** *is IND-CPA-secure.*

Proof. Let $\mathcal{A}$ be any PPT adversary who distinguishes between CT_0 and CT_t. We construct an algorithm $\mathcal{B}$ which uses $\mathcal{A}$ to attack the IND-CPA-security in **PEKS**. Let $t = t(k)$ be an upper-bound on the number keywords in each of the two vectors output by $\mathcal{A}$.

Given a public key PK, an adversary $\mathcal{B}$ runs $\mathcal{A}(\mathtt{find}, pk)$ to get challenge vectors of keywords $\overrightarrow{w}_0 = (w_0^1, ..., w_0^t)$ and $\overrightarrow{w}_1 = (w_1^1, ..., w_1^t)$ with $t = t(k)$. Without loss of generality, $D = \{j \mid w_0^j \neq w_1^j, \ 1 \leq j \leq t\} \neq \emptyset$ and we let that $|D| = d$ and $D = \{j_1, ..., j_d\}$. $\mathcal{B}$ chooses a random $j_\xi \in D$ (for some $1 \leq \xi \leq d$) then there exists $i(1 \leq i \leq t)$ such that $i = j_\xi$. $\mathcal{B}$ gives a challenge query (w_0^i, w_1^i) to $\mathcal{C}$ to obtain $c_b = \mathsf{PEKS}(PK, w_b^i)$ from $\mathcal{C}$ and $\mathcal{B}$ sets $c_i = c_b$ and computes $c_j = \mathsf{PEKS}(PK, w_0^j)$ $(1 \leq j < i)$ and $c_j = \mathsf{PEKS}(PK, w_1^j)$ $(i < j \leq t)$. Then $\mathcal{B}$ gives $\mathsf{CT}^* = [c_1, ..., c_t]$ back to $\mathcal{A}$. $\mathcal{B}$ outputs the bit b' that is output by $\mathcal{A}$. Using the above notation, we have
$$\Pr\nolimits_{\mathcal{A},\mathbf{mPEKS}}^{\mathsf{mpeks\text{-}ind\text{-}cpa}}[\mathsf{Succ}] = \tfrac{1}{2} \cdot \Pr[\mathcal{A}(\mathsf{CT}_t) = 0] + \tfrac{1}{2} \cdot \Pr[\mathcal{A}(\mathsf{CT}_0) = 1]$$
For every index $i \in \{0, ..., t-1\}$, if $\mathcal{A}$ distinguishes between CT_i and CT_{i+1} this means that it distinguishes between an encryption w_0^i and an encryption of w_1^i. Hence,

$$\Pr[\mathcal{B} \text{ outputs } 0 \mid b = 0] = \sum_{j=1}^{t} \Pr[\mathcal{B} \text{ outputs } 0 \mid b = 0 \wedge i = j] \cdot \Pr[i = j]$$

$$= \sum_{j=1}^{t} \frac{1}{t} \cdot \Pr[\mathcal{A}(\mathsf{CT}_j) = 0],$$

$$\Pr[\mathcal{B} \text{ outputs } 1 \mid b = 1] = \sum_{j=1}^{t} \Pr[\mathcal{B} \text{ outputs } 1 \mid b = 1 \wedge i = j] \cdot \Pr[i = j]$$

$$= \sum_{j=1}^{t} \frac{1}{t} \cdot \Pr[\mathcal{A}(\mathsf{CT}_{j-1}) = 1] = \sum_{j=0}^{t-1} \frac{1}{t} \cdot \Pr[\mathcal{A}(\mathsf{CT}_j) = 1].$$

By the assumption of IND-CPA security of PEKS scheme, there exists a negligible function $\epsilon(n)$ such that $\mathbf{Adv}_{\mathbf{PEKS},\,\mathcal{A}}^{\text{peks-ind-cpa}}(k) = |\Pr_{\mathcal{A},\mathbf{PEKS}}^{\text{peks-ind-cpa}}[\mathsf{Succ}] - 1/2| \le \epsilon(k)$. And

$$\frac{1}{2} + \epsilon(n) \ge \Pr_{\mathcal{A},\mathbf{PEKS}}^{\text{peks-ind-cpa}}[\mathsf{Succ}]$$

$$= \frac{1}{2} \cdot \Pr[\mathcal{A}(\mathsf{CT}_t) = 0] + \frac{1}{2} \cdot \Pr[\mathcal{A}(\mathsf{CT}_0) = 1] = \sum_{j=1}^{t} \frac{1}{2t} \cdot \Pr[\mathcal{A}(\mathsf{CT}_j) = 0] + \sum_{j=0}^{t-1} \frac{1}{t2} \cdot \Pr[\mathcal{A}(\mathsf{CT}_j) = 1]$$

$$= \frac{1}{2t} \cdot \sum_{j=1}^{t-1} (\Pr[\mathcal{A}(\mathsf{CT}_j) = 0] + \Pr[\mathcal{A}(\mathsf{CT}_j) = 1]) + \frac{1}{2t} \cdot (\Pr[\mathcal{A}(\mathsf{CT}_t) = 0] + \Pr[\mathcal{A}(\mathsf{CT}_0) = 1])$$

$$= \frac{t-1}{2t} + \frac{1}{t} \cdot \Pr_{\mathcal{B},\mathbf{mPEKS}}^{\text{mpeks-ind-cpa}}[\mathsf{Succ}].$$

Hence, there exists a negligible function $\epsilon'(k) = t(k) \cdot \epsilon(k)$ such that $\frac{1}{2} + t(k) \cdot \epsilon(k) \ge \Pr_{\mathcal{B},\mathbf{mPEKS}}^{\text{mpeks-ind-cpa}}[\mathsf{Succ}]$. ∎

4   Relation Between mPEKS and A-IBE

We investigate the relation between PEKS and A-IBE scheme. In [1], Abdalla et al. provided a transform of an A-IBE scheme for only one-bit message from a confidential and consistent PEKS scheme. The transform sketched by Boneh et al. [6] is as follows.

- Setup(k): This algorithm runs $\mathbf{KG}(k)$ to obtain (PK, SK). The public parameter is $\mathsf{PP} = PK$ and the master secret key is $\mathsf{mk} = SK$. It outputs $(\mathsf{PP}, \mathsf{mk}) = (PK, SK)$.
- Extract(mk, ID): Let $\mathsf{ID} \in \mathcal{ID}$ be a set of identities. To generate a private key $d_{\mathsf{ID}} = [T_{\mathsf{ID}\|0}, T_{\mathsf{ID}\|1}]$ of ID, the key extraction algorithm runs $T_{\mathsf{ID}\|0} \leftarrow \mathbf{Td}(SK, \mathsf{ID} \| 0)$ and $T_{\mathsf{ID}\|1} \leftarrow \mathbf{Td}(SK, \mathsf{ID} \| 1)$. The private key is $d_{\mathsf{ID}} = [T_{\mathsf{ID}\|0}, T_{\mathsf{ID}\|1}]$.
- Encrypt(PK, ID, b): To encrypt a message $b \in \{0,1\}$ under the identity ID, this algorithm runs $\mathsf{CT} \leftarrow \mathbf{PEKS}(PK, \mathsf{ID} \| b)$ to obtain a ciphertext CT.
- Decrypt($\mathsf{CT}, d_{\mathsf{ID}}$): Let $d_{\mathsf{ID}} = [d_0 \| d_1]$. Output 0 if $\mathbf{Test}(\mathsf{CT}, d_0) = \text{'1'}$ and output 1 if $\mathbf{Test}(\mathsf{CT}, d_1) = \text{'1'}$.

In their resulting IBE scheme, there is a property which is not identical to a general IBE scheme as for the standard definition of the latter [7]. In their construction, (1) an encryption of only one-bit message was considered and (2) to decrypt the ciphertext about one-bit message $b \in \{0, 1\}$, a receiver should obtain private keys about two pairs of his identity and message, (ID $\|$ 0) and (ID $\|$ 1), from a key generation center (KGC). Also, their construction has not given an extension method from the above encryption for a one-bit message to an encryption for an arbitrary length message.

Table 7. Computational correctness of IBE. Here, $\mathcal{ID}$ is a set of identities and ID $\in \mathcal{ID}$ and $R, R' \in \{0, 1\}^{t(k)} \subseteq \mathcal{M}$ are binary messages.

$\mathbf{Exp}_{\mathbf{IBE}, \mathcal{A}}^{\text{ibe-correct}}(k)$
  $(\mathsf{PP}, \mathsf{msk}) \leftarrow \mathbf{Setup}(k)$
  $(R, R', \mathsf{ID}) \leftarrow \mathcal{A}(\mathsf{PP})\ (|R| = |R'| = t(k))$
  $\mathsf{C} \leftarrow \mathbf{Encrypt}(\mathsf{PP}, \mathsf{ID}, R)\ ;\ d_{\mathsf{ID}} \leftarrow \mathbf{Extract}(\mathsf{msk}, \mathsf{ID})$
  If $R \neq R'$ and $\mathbf{Decrypt}(\mathsf{C}, d_{\mathsf{ID}}) = R'$ then return 1 else return 0

4.1   The New Transform mpeks-2-ibe from mPEKS to A-IBE

To obtain an A-IBE scheme from mPEKS scheme with a transform mpeks-2-ibe, we need to consider inputs of **mPEKS** algorithm which consist of a public key PK and a vector of keywords $\overrightarrow{w}$. To encrypt a t-bit binary message $(m_1, ..., m_t)$ by using the **mPEKS** algorithm, we convert the message $(m_1, ..., m_t)$ to the vector of keywords $\overrightarrow{w}$. Here, a receiver having his private key d_{ID} should obtain the valid result of decryption from decryption process by using **mTest** algorithm.

To guarantee a correctness of A-IBE, we can convert the message $(m_1, ..., m_t)$ to the vector of keywords $\overrightarrow{w}$ as follows. If $m_i = 1$ $(1 \leq i \leq t)$ then we set $w_i = \mathsf{ID}$; otherwise, we choose a random identity $\mathsf{ID}' \in \mathcal{ID}$ $(\mathsf{ID}' \neq \mathsf{ID})$ and set $w_i = \mathsf{ID}'$. Then $\mathsf{CT} \leftarrow \mathbf{mPEKS}(PK, \overrightarrow{w})$ and $\mathbf{mTest}(\mathsf{CT}, \overrightarrow{d}_{\mathsf{ID}})$ are satisfied, where $\overrightarrow{d}_{\mathsf{ID}} = (d_{\mathsf{ID}}, ..., d_{\mathsf{ID}})$. However, if we choose a random identity $\mathsf{ID}' \in \mathcal{ID}$ $(\mathsf{ID}' \neq \mathsf{ID})$ then the private key of the selected identity ID' cannot be extracted and it is a contradict to the security model of A-IBE scheme. (Generally, the private key of any identity $\mathsf{ID}' \in \mathcal{ID}$ $(\mathsf{ID}' \neq \mathsf{ID})$ except the target identity ID should be extracted in the security model of A-IBE scheme.) The key idea of our transform is to solve this problem as follows. In **Encrypt** algorithm, if $m_i = 1$ $(1 \leq i \leq t)$ then we set $w_i = (1\|\mathsf{ID})$; otherwise, we set $w_i = (0\|\mathsf{ID})$. Then we obtain a ciphertext $\mathsf{CT} \leftarrow \mathbf{mPEKS}(PK, \overrightarrow{w})$ of a message $(m_1, ..., m_t)$. The receiver obtaining his private key $d_{\mathsf{ID}} = T_{(1\|\mathsf{ID})}$ of a keyword $(1\|\mathsf{ID})$ by running $T_{(1\|\mathsf{ID})} \leftarrow \mathbf{Td}(SK, 1\|\mathsf{ID})$ can decrypt a ciphertext $\mathsf{CT} = (c_1, ..., c_t)$ by running $\mathbf{mTest}(\mathsf{CT}, \overrightarrow{d}_{\mathsf{ID}})$ to obtain $(m_1, ..., m_t)$. Also, in A-IBE scheme $\mathbf{IBE} = $ mpeks-2-ibe($\mathbf{mPEKS}$), the private key of any identity $\mathsf{ID}' \in \mathcal{ID}$ $(\mathsf{ID}' \neq \mathsf{ID})$ can be extracted.

Our transform mpeks-2-ibe works as follows.

- Setup(k): This algorithm runs $\mathbf{KG}(k)$ to obtain (PK, SK). The public parameter is PP = PK and the master secret key is mk = SK. It outputs $(\mathsf{PP}, \mathsf{mk}) = (PK, SK)$.
- **Extract**(mk, ID): Let ID $\in \mathcal{ID}$ be a set of identities. To generate a private key $d_{\mathsf{ID}} = T_{(1\|\mathsf{ID})}$ of ID, the key extraction algorithm runs $T_{(1\|\mathsf{ID})} \leftarrow \mathbf{Td}(SK, 1\|\mathsf{ID})$. The private key is $d_{\mathsf{ID}} = T_{(1\|\mathsf{ID})}$.
- **Encrypt**(PP, ID, M): To encrypt a message $M = (m_1, ..., m_t) \in \{0,1\}^t$ (with $t = |M|$) under the identity ID, this algorithm first sets $\vec{w} = (w_1, ..., w_t)$ and runs CT $\leftarrow \mathbf{mPEKS}(\mathsf{PP}, \vec{w})$ to obtain a PEKS ciphertext CT. Here, the t-bit message $M = (m_1, ..., m_t)$ is mapped to the vector of keywords $\vec{w} = (w_1, ..., w_t)$ as follows. For $i \in \{1, ..., t\}$, if $m_i = 1$ then sets $w_i = (1\|\mathsf{ID})$; otherwise, sets $w_i = (0\|\mathsf{ID})$.
- **Decrypt**(CT, d_{ID}): To decrypt CT with a private key d_{ID}, this algorithm sets $\vec{d}_{\mathsf{ID}} = (d_{\mathsf{ID}}, ..., d_{\mathsf{ID}})$ and runs $(m_1, ..., m_t) \leftarrow \mathbf{mTest}(\mathsf{CT}, \vec{d}_{\mathsf{ID}})$ to obtain a message $(m_1, ..., m_t)$.

When assuming the ciphertext is well-formed, the correctness of the resulting IBE scheme in our transform is verified in the following subsection. To verify the correctness of the resulting IBE scheme in our transform, we define a correctness of IBE scheme using an experiment in the Table 7 as follows.

Correctness of IBE. Suppose there exists an adversary $\mathcal{A}$ that wants to make correctness fail. A correctness for an IBE scheme is defined using an experiment in the Table 7.

The advantage of $\mathcal{A}$ is defined as follows.

$$\mathbf{Adv}_{\mathbf{IBE}, \mathcal{A}}^{\text{ibe-correct}}(k) = \Pr[\mathbf{Exp}_{\mathbf{IBE}, \mathcal{A}}^{\text{ibe-correct}}(k) = 1],$$

where the probability is taken over all possible coin flips of all the algorithms involved.

Definition 6. *We say that an **IBE** satisfies "computationally correctness" if for any PPT adversary $\mathcal{A}$ attacking IBE scheme the advantage $\mathbf{Adv}_{\mathbf{IBE}, \mathcal{A}}^{\text{ibe-correct}}(k)$ is negligible.*

We showed the following results. Let **mPEKS** be a mPEKS scheme and let **IBE** be an IBE scheme derived from **mPEKS** via a new transform mpeks-2-ibe.

Theorem 7. *If **mPEKS** is IND-CPA-secure, then **IBE** is ANO-CPA-secure.*

Theorem 8. *If **mPEKS** is IND-CPA-secure, then **IBE** is IND-CPA-secure.*

Theorem 9. *If **mPEKS** is computationally consistent, then **IBE** satisfies the correctness.*

5   Conclusions

We have examined the necessary properties of a PEKS and mPEKS scheme in producing secure (anonymous and confidential) A-IBE scheme for polynomially many-bit message. It turned out that both an anonymity and a confidentiality for an IBE scheme can be derived from the confidentiality for a PEKS scheme. Also, we have identified that the computational consistency of a PEKS scheme gives rise to the correctness of an IBE scheme. Our result has shown that an A-IBE scheme for polynomially many-bit message can be constructed by using a PEKS scheme.

References

1. Abdalla, M., et al.: Searchable encryption revisited: consistency properties, relation to anonymous IBE, and extensions. J. Cryptol. **21**(3), 350–391 (2008)
2. Boneh, D., Boyen, X.: Secure identity based encryption without random oracles. In: Franklin, M. (ed.) CRYPTO 2004. LNCS, vol. 3152, pp. 443–459. Springer, Heidelberg (2004). https://doi.org/10.1007/978-3-540-28628-8_27
3. Boneh, D., Boyen, X., Goh, E.-J.: Hierarchical identity based encryption with constant size ciphertext. In: Cramer, R. (ed.) EUROCRYPT 2005. LNCS, vol. 3494, pp. 440–456. Springer, Heidelberg (2005). https://doi.org/10.1007/11426639_26
4. Barth, A., Boneh, D., Waters, B.: Privacy in encrypted content distribution using private broadcast encryption. In: Di Crescenzo, G., Rubin, A. (eds.) FC 2006. LNCS, vol. 4107, pp. 52–64. Springer, Heidelberg (2006). https://doi.org/10.1007/11889663_4
5. Bellare, M., Boldyreva, A., Desai, A., Pointcheval, D.: Key-privacy in public-key encryption. In: Boyd, C. (ed.) ASIACRYPT 2001. LNCS, vol. 2248, pp. 566–582. Springer, Heidelberg (2001). https://doi.org/10.1007/3-540-45682-1_33
6. Boneh, D., Di Crescenzo, G., Ostrovsky, R., Persiano, G.: Public key encryption with keyword search. In: Cachin, C., Camenisch, J.L. (eds.) EUROCRYPT 2004. LNCS, vol. 3027, pp. 506–522. Springer, Heidelberg (2004). https://doi.org/10.1007/978-3-540-24676-3_30
7. Boneh, D., Franklin, M.: Identity-based encryption from the Weil pairing. SIAM J. Comput. **32**(3), 586–615 (2003)
8. Boyen, X., Waters, B.: Anonymous hierarchical identity-based encryption (without random oracles). In: Dwork, C. (ed.) CRYPTO 2006. LNCS, vol. 4117, pp. 290–307. Springer, Heidelberg (2006). https://doi.org/10.1007/11818175_17
9. Boneh, D., Waters, B.: Conjunctive, subset, and range queries on encrypted data. In: Vadhan, S.P. (ed.) TCC 2007. LNCS, vol. 4392, pp. 535–554. Springer, Heidelberg (2007). https://doi.org/10.1007/978-3-540-70936-7_29
10. Gentry, C., Silverberg, A.: Hierarchical ID-based cryptography. In: Zheng, Y. (ed.) ASIACRYPT 2002. LNCS, vol. 2501, pp. 548–566. Springer, Heidelberg (2002). https://doi.org/10.1007/3-540-36178-2_34
11. Holt, J.E., Bradshaw, R., Seamoms, K.E., Oeman, H.: Hidden credentials. In: Proceedings of WPES 2003, pp. 1–8 (2003)
12. Katz, J., Lindell, Y.: Introduction to Modern Cryptography. Chapman & Hall/CRC Press (2007)

13. Katz, J., Sahai, A., Waters, B.: Predicate encryption supporting disjunctions, polynomial equations, and inner products. In: Smart, N. (ed.) EUROCRYPT 2008. LNCS, vol. 4965, pp. 146–162. Springer, Heidelberg (2008). https://doi.org/10.1007/978-3-540-78967-3_9

14. Park, D.J., Kim, K., Lee, P.J.: Public key encryption with conjunctive field keyword search. In: Lim, C.H., Yung, M. (eds.) WISA 2004. LNCS, vol. 3325, pp. 73–86. Springer, Heidelberg (2005). https://doi.org/10.1007/978-3-540-31815-6_7

15. Rhee, H.S., Park, J.H., Susilo, W., Lee, D.H.: Improved searchable public key encryption with designated tester. In: Proceedings of ASIACCS 2009, pp. 376–379 (2009)

16. Rhee, H.S., Susilo, W., Kim, H.J.: Secure searchable public-key encrytion against keyword guessing attacks. IEICE Electron. Express **6**(5), 237–243 (2009)

17. Shamir, A.: Identity-based cryptosystems and signature schemes. In: Blakley, G.R., Chaum, D. (eds.) CRYPTO 1984. LNCS, vol. 196, pp. 47–53. Springer, Heidelberg (1985). https://doi.org/10.1007/3-540-39568-7_5

18. Seo, J.H., Kobayashi, T., Ohkubo, M., Suzuki, K.: Anonymous hierarchical identity-based encryption with constant size ciphertexts. In: Jarecki, S., Tsudik, G. (eds.) PKC 2009. LNCS, vol. 5443, pp. 215–234. Springer, Heidelberg (2009). https://doi.org/10.1007/978-3-642-00468-1_13

19. Waters, B.: Efficient identity-based encryption without random oracles. In: Cramer, R. (ed.) EUROCRYPT 2005. LNCS, vol. 3494, pp. 114–127. Springer, Heidelberg (2005). https://doi.org/10.1007/11426639_7

20. Byun, J.W., Rhee, H.S., Park, H.-A., Lee, D.H.: Off-line keyword guessing attacks on recent keyword search schemes over encrypted data. In: Jonker, W., Petković, M. (eds.) SDM 2006. LNCS, vol. 4165, pp. 75–83. Springer, Heidelberg (2006). https://doi.org/10.1007/11844662_6

21. Fang, L., Susilo, W., Ge, C., Wang, J.: Public key encryption with keyword search secure against keyword guessing attacks without random oracle. Inf. Sci. **238**, 221–241 (2013)

22. Huang, Q., Li, H.: An efficient public-key searchable encryption scheme secure against inside keyword guessing attacks. Inf. Sci. **403**, 1–14 (2017)

23. Lu, Y., Wang, G., Li, J.: Keyword guessing attacks on a public key encryption with keyword search scheme without random oracle and its improvement. Inf. Sci. **479**, 270–276 (2019)

Secure Computation of Shared Secrets and Its Applications

Xin Liu[✉], Willy Susilo, and Joonsang Baek

Institute of Cybersecurity and Cryptology, School of Computing and Information
Technology, University of Wollongong, Wollongong, Australia
xl879@uowmail.edu.au, {wsusilo,baek}@uow.edu.au

Abstract. There has been renewed attention to threshold signature in
recent years as the threshold version of the ECDSA and SM2 Elliptic
Curve Cryptographic Algorithm (SM2) could be used in Bitcoin as an
underlying digital signature scheme to protect users' private keys that
guarantees transactions. A (t, n) threshold signature scheme means in
a set of n parties, at least t players can exercise the right of generating signatures on behalf of the group, and any less than t of the players'
cooperation cannot generate a valid signature for the message nor obtain
any information about the shared secret key. Thus, it is meaningful to
construct a purely (t, n) threshold SM2 signature scheme (purely (t, n)
means in the whole signature scheme, the threshold value is fixed to t).
We propose a robust multiplication protocol of shared secrets to resolve
the "multiplication of shared secrets" problem in existing threshold signature schemes. Using the proposed multiplication protocol, we improve
the existing secret reciprocal computation protocol and show how to get
a purely (t, n) threshold SM2 signature scheme.

Keywords: Threshold signature · SM2 · Secure computation of
shared secrets

1 Introduction

Threshold cryptography [1, 2, 9, 26] was first introduced in the 80s and has drawn
renewed interest in recent years when technologies such as distributed computing
and blockchain continue to develop and have been widely used on the Internet.
With the development of these technologies, preservation, legal recovery and utilization of the essential and sensitive information including private key material
in these systems have now become an important subject in cryptography. The
most effective way to solve such problems is to utilize secret sharing [2, 26] and
derivative threshold systems. These systems mainly include threshold encryption and threshold signature schemes where the key is secretly shared among a
group of players in such a way that only certain parts of the players can sign or
encrypt messages without recovering the secret key.

Digital signatures schemes (especially in SM2 [17] and ECDSA [18]) are a
basic tool for network and system authentication. To be more specific, SM2

© Springer Nature Switzerland AG 2021
H. Kim (Ed.): WISA 2021, LNCS 13009, pp. 119–131, 2021.
https://doi.org/10.1007/978-3-030-89432-0_10

signature scheme played an important role in the construction of Chinese information security system. Due to the use of ECDSA and SM2 in Bitcoin to ensure the security of the user's private signing key that authorizes transactions, we can observe the growing need for threshold versions of ECDSA and SM2 because a threshold signature can satisfy the requirements of those applications.

It is worth mentioning that an effective (t, n) threshold SM2 elliptic curve signature scheme can replace ECDSA in most applications (especially some confidential applications), however, unlike the threshold signature schemes for ECDSA, there are still few researches on secure SM2 threshold signature scheme.

1.1 Related Work

The threshold signature was first proposed by Boyd [4] and Desmedt [10].

Gennaro *et al.* proposed the most classic yet important threshold DSS system in 1996 [14,19]. It is noticeable that the distributed key generation of the scheme requires the cooperation of n players to generate a DSS public and private key pair with a (t, n) threshold, but in the threshold signature or threshold decryption phase, $(2t-1)$ honest players not t are required to generate a valid signature or complete the correct decryption. Meanwhile, in the distributed key generation algorithm, this scheme needs to use Pedersen's verifiable secret sharing scheme [25] as a sub-protocol.

To address this issue, in 2001 Mackenzie et al.[22] designed a $(1, 2)$ threshold signature scheme, which was further improved in [23]. Gennaro et al. [3,13] later enabled the ECDSA scheme to allow more than two players under the case of a dishonest majority, i.e., with the full threshold $t = n - 1$.

Lindell and others [6,11,20] improved the ECDSA scheme in the two-party condition. And recent works [5,8,12,21] have delivered full threshold ECDSA signature scheme for multiparty players. Most proposed threshold ECDSA protocols, however, rely on computationally heavy primitives such as Paillier encryption and zero-knowledge (ZK) proofs.

In 2014, Shang et al. [27] proposed the first threshold implementation of the SM2 elliptic curve cryptographic algorithm[17]. Yan et al. [28] designed another SM2 threshold signature algorithm based on the Joint-Shamir-RSS algorithm [24]. However, in the threshold signature or threshold decryption algorithms of their schemes, the problem that the threshold value of the entire system will raise from t to $(2t - 1)$ still has not been resolved.

1.2 Our Contributions

Our contributions can be summarized as follows.

- Coming up with a new multiplication protocol for shared secrets based on Gennaro et al.'s protocol [14,15] to avoid additional cryptographic assumptions. Our protocol can solve the following problem and avoid the ZK proof: When two secrets α and β are distributed among n players in (t, n) way at the same time, each player needs to compute its own share of the product of two secrets $\alpha\beta$ without recovering α and β, and at least t players can jointly recover the secret $\alpha\beta$.

- Improving the existing secret reciprocal computation protocol and obtaining a reciprocal computation protocol for shared secret without increasing the threshold value so as to ensure that at least t players can cooperate to compute their own shares of k^{-1} without obtaining the secret k with the proposed multiplication protocol.
- Producing a new purely (t, n) threshold SM2 signature scheme based on the two proposed protocols. – Our proposed (t, n) threshold SM2 signature scheme not only avoids zero-knowledge (ZK) proof but also ensures the value of the threshold t is fixed.

2   A Robust Secure Multiplication Protocol of Shared Secrets

2.1   Preliminaries

Joint Random Secret Sharing. Assume a secret sharing scheme that is not performed by a single dealer, each player can be considered as a dealer instead and none of the players can know the secret exactly. A more detailed joint random sharing scheme can be found in [24] and [25].

Adversary. We assume that an adversary $\mathcal{A}$ has the ability to corrupt at most t of n players in the network and define three kinds of adversaries here:

- An *Eavesdropping Adversary*: It can know all information stored in the damaged network nodes (players) and hear all broadcast messages in the network.
- A *Halting Adversary*: While having all the characteristics of an *Eavesdropping Adversary*, it may also cause corrupted players to stop sending messages during the processing step of the designated protocol.
- A *Malicious Adversary*: While having all the characteristics of a *Halting Adversary*, it is also possible to derail those corrupted players from the designated protocol in any (even malicious) manner.

2.2   Gennaro's Simplified Multiplication Protocol

We first recall Gennaro's Simplified Multiplication Protocol [16], which we will utilize in our protocol. The following computations in the protocol are made under the assumption that all players can perform secret sharing and transmission steps correctly. $f_\alpha(i)$ and $f_\beta(i)$ are to represent the shares of α and β which P_i obtained after a round of dealer D's distribution, and the corresponding secret sharing polynomials are $f_\alpha(x)$ and $f_\beta(x)$. We multiply the two polynomials to get the polynomial (1):

$$f_\alpha(x)f_\beta(x) = r_{2(t-1)}x^{2(t-1)} + \cdots + r_1 x + \alpha\beta \overset{\text{def}}{=} f_{\alpha\beta}(x) \qquad (1)$$

We assign values to the new polynomial $f_{\alpha\beta}(i) = f_\alpha(i)f_\beta(i)$, for $1 \leq i \leq 2t - 1$, and obtain the following Eq. (2):

$$A \begin{bmatrix} \alpha\beta \\ r_1 \\ \vdots \\ r_{2(t-1)} \end{bmatrix} = \begin{bmatrix} f_{\alpha\beta}(1) \\ f_{\alpha\beta}(2) \\ \vdots \\ f_{\alpha\beta}(2t-1) \end{bmatrix} = \begin{bmatrix} f_\alpha(1)f_\beta(1) \\ f_\alpha(2)f_\beta(2) \\ \vdots \\ f_\alpha(2t-1)f_\beta(2t-1) \end{bmatrix} \tag{2}$$

Where matrix $A = (a_{ij})$ is a $(2t-1)$ by $(2t-1)$ **Van der Monde Matrix** defined by $a_{ij} = i^{j-i}$. It is obvious that A is non-singular and has an inverse. Let the first row of the inverse matrix A^{-1} be $(\lambda_1, \ldots, \lambda_{2t-1})$, and $\lambda_1, \ldots, \lambda_{2t-1}$ are known constants. Then we can get an Eq. (3) as:

$$\begin{bmatrix} \alpha\beta \\ r_1 \\ \vdots \\ r_{2(t-1)} \end{bmatrix} = A^{-1} \begin{bmatrix} f_{\alpha\beta}(1) \\ f_{\alpha\beta}(2) \\ \vdots \\ f_{\alpha\beta}(2t-1) \end{bmatrix} \tag{3}$$

From the above Eq. (3) can easily get: $\alpha\beta = \lambda_1 f_{\alpha\beta}(1) + \cdots + \lambda_{2t-1}f_{\alpha\beta}(2t-1)$. Players P_i then choose a $(t-1)$-degree random polynomial $h_i(x)$, for $1 \leq i \leq 2t-1$ respectively, where $h_i(0) = f_{\alpha\beta}(i)$. Define $H(x) \stackrel{\text{def}}{=} \sum_{i=1}^{2t-1} \lambda_i h_i(x)$, and $H(0) = \lambda_1 f_{\alpha\beta}(1) + \cdots + \lambda_{2t-1}f_{\alpha\beta}(2t-1) = \alpha\beta$.

And each player's share of secret $\alpha\beta$ is $H(j) = \sum_{i=1}^{2t-1} \lambda_i h_i(j)$, for $1 \leq j \leq 2t-1$. Thus, if $(2t-1)$ players P_i shares his share using a $(t-1)$-degree polynomial $h_i(x)$ with the proper steps as defined above, then the polynomial $H(x)$, used for the sharing of secret $\alpha\beta$ is automatically of degree $(t-1)$.

Theorem 1. *Gennaro's Simplified Multiplication Protocol is a secure multiplication protocol against an Eavesdropping Adversary with no restriction on computation power.*

In this protocol, the secret $\alpha\beta$ obtained after performing the multiplication computation is: $\alpha\beta = \lambda_1 f_{\alpha\beta}(1) + \cdots + \lambda_{2t-1}f_{\alpha\beta}(2t-1)$. It is easy to recognize that this solution seems to solve the problem of increasing threshold value in the multiplication protocol, but in the actual process when constructing the final random secret sharing polynomial $H(x)$, only constants $(\lambda_1, ..., \lambda_{2t-1})$ are fixedly used. That means, in the (t, n) threshold secret sharing scheme, there are a total of n players, while only $(2t-1)$ players can participate in the process of sharing secret $\alpha\beta$.

2.3 Secure Multiplication Protocol of Shared Secrets

To solve the problem in Gennaro's Simplified Multiplication Protocol, we propose a robust secure multiplication protocol of shared secrets. In our multiplication protocol, we still use $f_\alpha(i)$ and $f_\beta(i)$ to represent the shares of secret α and β

that the player P_i obtained after a round of dealer D's distribution, and the secret sharing polynomials are still $f_\alpha(x)$ and $f_\beta(x)$.

In order to ensure the robustness of the scheme, we require that the relationship between the number of players n and the threshold value t in the initial secret sharing scheme must follow $2t - 1 \leq n$. Under this condition, according to the relationship between t and n, we divide our protocol into the following three cases:

Case A where $2t - 1 = n$: When the number of players and threshold value in the scheme satisfy $2t - 1 = n$, it is obvious that the simple protocol given in Sect. 2.2 meets the requirements of reducing the threshold to (t, n) in this case.

Case B where $2t - 1 < n$ **for odd** n: When the number of players and threshold value in the scheme satisfy $2t - 1 < n$, n is odd, we deal with this case as follows: we first need to expand the threshold value of the scheme from t to t', and make $2t' - 1 = n$.

We now use $f'_\alpha(i)$ and $f'_\beta(i)$ to represent the shares of secret α and β that the player P_i obtained after a round of dealer D's distribution, and the $(t'-1)$-degree secret sharing polynomials are $f'_\alpha(x)$ and $f'_\beta(x)$. In this case, in order to reduce the threshold of the scheme to t again, the dealer have to publish $2(t'-t)$ shares after finish a round of distribution: $\{f'_\alpha(k), f'_\beta(k) | k = (n+1, n+2, \ldots, n+t'-t)\}$ in the system when performing a round of distribution, when t players in the system need to recover the secret α or β, using the players' own t shares and the system's $(t'-t)$ public shares, any group of t players can use the Lagrange polynomial interpolation to recover α or β.

Case C where $2t - 1 < n$ **for even** n
Expand the Number of Players: from n to n', $n' - 1 = n$
Expand the Threshold Value: from t to t', $2t' - 1 = n$

1. Dealer D uses two $(t'-1)$-degree polynomials $f'_\alpha(x)$ and $f'_\alpha(x)$ to compute the share of secrets α and β that player P_i will obtain after a round of distribution;
2. Dealer D publishes $2(t'-t)$ shares: $\{f'_\alpha(k), f'_\beta(k) | k = (n', n'+1, \ldots, n'+t'-t-1)\}$.

Input of Player P_i: the values $f'_\alpha(i)$ and $f'_\beta(i)$

1. Player P_i shares the value $f'_\alpha(i) f'_\beta(i)$ by choosing a random polynomial $h'_i(x)$ of degree $(t-1)$. He gives player P_j the value $h'_i(j)$ for $1 \leq j \leq n, j \neq i$.
2. Each player P_i computes his share of $\alpha\beta$ via a random polynomial H', i.e. the value $H'(j)$, by locally computing the linear combination: $H'(j) = \lambda'_{n'} f'_\alpha(n') f'_\beta(n') + \sum_{i=1}^{n} \lambda'_i h'_i(j)$.

Fig. 1. Secure multiplication protocol of shared secrets in case C

Case C where $2t - 1 < n$ **for even** n: When the number of players and threshold value in the (t, n)- threshold secret sharing scheme satisfy $2t - 1 < n$, n is even, we deal with this case as follows: we first need to expand the number of players from n to n', $n' = n + 1$. That is, we assume that there is a virtual player in the scheme at this time. And, we still need to expand threshold value of the scheme from t to t', and make $2t' - 1 = n'$.

In Case C, the share of $\alpha\beta$ which each player obtains can be achieved directly following protocol in Fig. 1.

Theorem 2. *Secure Multiplication Protocol of Shared Secrets in Case B and C is a secure multiplication protocol against an Eavesdropping Adversary with no restriction on computation power.*

We still need to discuss another condition that if the adversary is a Halting Adversary or even a Malicious Adversary, note that there are dishonest players can send wrong messages to other players. For the scheme to have the ability to tolerate the two adversarial models we defined in Sect. 1.2, it is necessary to verify the actions of the players. To solve this problem, we can introduce Verifiable Secret Sharing (VSS) Scheme which is proposed by Chor B., Goldwasser S. in [7]. In a verifiable secret sharing scheme with a (t, n) threshold, each player can verify whether the share they received is correct or not.

3   Our Reciprocal Computation Protocol

In the SM2 digital signature scheme, a round of reciprocal computation is performed. Thus, players need to follow a process of Joint Random Secret Sharing algorithm (Joint-RSS) to share a secret k in (t, n) threshold way. The $(t - 1)$-degree secret sharing polynomial formed by the Joint-RSS is denoted as $f_k(x)$. The share u_i is the share of k^{-1}, which is the multiplicative inverse of secret k, and it needs to be computed without revealing any information about secret k, k^{-1}. The common solution is generating a random sharing a first, then multiply a_i and k_i and get $\mu = ka$, $u_i = \mu^{-1}a_i = k^{-1}a^{-1}a_i$.

We can notice that when reconstructing the secret $\mu = ka$, the threshold value of the whole scheme has increased from t to $2(t-1)$ due to the implementation of a round of secure multiplication of two shared secrets k and a. We use the robust secure multiplication protocol of shared secrets we proposed in Sect. 2. The improved secret reciprocal computation protocol with a fixed threshold value, short as (t, n)-Reciprocal Protocol is shown below.

We still divide the improved protocol into three cases according to the relationship between the number of players n and threshold value t, $2t - 1 = n$ for Case A, $2t - 1 < n$ where n is odd for Case B, and $2t - 1 < n$ where n is even for Case C. Now we list the secret reciprocal computation protocol in Case C as the most complicated one:

1. Players follow the process of joint random secret sharing and share a secret k in (t', n') threshold way. The $(t' - 1)$-degree secret sharing polynomial formed by Joint-RSS is denoted as $f'_k(x)$, and player P_i obtains its share as $k'_i = f'_k(i)$;

2. Players continue to compute $(t'-t)$ shares and make it public, and get $(t'-t)$ public shares about secret k: $\{f'_k(j)|j = (n', n'+1, \cdots, n'+t'-t-1)\}$;

3. Players follow the process of joint random secret sharing and share a secret a in (t', n') threshold way. The $(t'-1)$-degree secret sharing polynomial formed by Joint-RSS is denoted as $f'_a(x)$, and player P_i obtains its share as $a'_i = f'_a(i)$;

4. Players continue to compute $(t'-t)$ shares and make it public, and get $(t'-t)$ public shares about secret a: $\{f'_a(j)|j = (n', n'+1, \cdots, n+t'-t-1)\}$;

5. Player P_i chooses a random polynomial $h'_i(x)$ of degree $(t-1)$, and the constant term of $h'_i(x)$ is $h'_i(0) = f'_k(i)f'_a(i)$. Then $h'_i(j)$ is broadcast to the remaining players P_j, $1 \le j \le n$;

6. Player P_i computes his secret share $k_i a_i$ about ka through the constructed $(t-1)$-degree random polynomial $H'(x) \overset{\text{def}}{=} \lambda'_{n'} f'_k(n')f'_a(n') + \sum_{i=1}^{n} \lambda'_i h'_i(x)$;

7. The secret share of player P_j is computed as follows: $H'(j) = \lambda'_{n'} f'_k(n')f'_a(n') + \sum_{i=1}^{n} \lambda'_i h'_i(j)$, for $1 \le j \le n$;

8. t or more than t players broadcast their $H'(i)$ in the system, and reconstructing the secret $\mu = ka$;

9. Player P_i gets u_i as a share of the multiplicative inverse of secret k: $u_i = \mu^{-1} a_i = k^{-1} a^{-1} a_i$.

Theorem 3. *Secret Reciprocal Computation Protocol is a secure computation protocol against an Eavesdropping Adversary with no restriction on computation power.*

Proof. We have discussed the correctness and security of the robust and secure multiplication protocol of shared secrets which we proposed in Sect. 2. It is evident that we have not changed the protocol we proposed in Sect. 2 but just embed it in the reciprocal computation protocol. So we can draw a conclusion as that any active adversary cannot gain any information about the two shared secrets k and a, nor can gain ka or k^{-1} according to the security model of Shamir's secret sharing scheme.

Lemma 1. *Our (t,n)-Reciprocal Protocol holds that $\{u_1, u_2, \cdots, u_n\} \overset{(t,n)}{\longleftrightarrow} k^{-1}$. There exists a simulator $\mathcal{SIM}$ such that for any adversary $\mathcal{A}$ with access to $(t-1)$ shares $\{k_1, k_2, \cdots, k_{t-1}\}$, $\mathcal{VIEW}_{\mathcal{A}}\big((t,n)\text{-Reciprocal Protocol }(k_1, k_2, \cdots, k_n)\big)$ is computationally indistinguishable from $\mathcal{SIM}(k_1, k_2, \cdots, k_{t-1})$.*

Proof. Indeed it holds that $\{u_1, u_2, \cdots, u_n\} \overset{(t,n)}{\longleftrightarrow} k^{-1}$, since the interpolation polynomial has degree $d = (t-1)$ and there can be at most $t-1$ wrong points $H'(i), i = 1, \cdots, t-1$. We have mentioned that Shamir's secret sharing scheme works if one has at least t points to interpolate the polynomial. Since $2t-1 \le n$ by hypothesis, the protocol is correct.

The protocol also achieves privacy. Indeed we describe a simulator for the protocol. We give the simulation in Case C as an example, since the adversary is static we assume that $\mathcal{SIM}$ receives the inputs $k_i, i = 1, \cdots, t-1$ of the corrupted players right at the start of the simulation.

The simulation proceeds as follows:

- $\mathcal{SIM}$ runs a (t', n') secret sharing protocol on a random secret for each good player to simulate the execution of Joint-RSS, and continues to compute $(t'-t)$ shares and make it public. $\mathcal{SIM}$ also receives the shares of the sharings done by the adversary for the corrupted players. Notice that this implies that $\mathcal{SIM}$ knows the values $a_i, i = 1, \cdots, t-1$ of the corrupted players.
- $\mathcal{SIM}$ chooses random $H'(i)$ for the good players such that all the values $H'(i)$ can interpolate a polynomial of degree $(t-1)$. $\mathcal{SIM}$ can do this because he knows the values $H'(i)$ for the corrupted players.

Through Theorem 3 and Lemma 1, we can draw a conclusion that our protocol can tolerate at most $(t-1)$ players are corrupted or even destroyed by an Eavesdropping Adversary as every one executes it correctly.

4 A Purely (t, n) Threshold SM2 Signature Scheme

4.1 Our Purely (t, n) Threshold SM2 Signature Scheme

Our purely (t, n) SM2 elliptic curve threshold signature scheme is divided into four algorithms: system parameter generation, threshold key generation, threshold signing algorithm, and the verification algorithm.

System Parameter Generation. The system parameter generation algorithm takes as input a security parameter λ, then returns the system parameters $SP = (F_p, E(F_p), G, p, q, H)$. F_p is a finite field, $a, b \in F_p$ define an equation of the elliptic curves $E(F_p)$, $G = (x, y)$ $(G \neq O)$ is a base point over $E(F_p)$ where x and y are two elements of F_p, q is the degree of G, H is a Hash function.

Threshold Key Generation. Given the threshold value t, we first suppose that the set of the players is $\mathcal{P} = \{P_1, P_2, \cdots P_n\}$, and $2t - 1 \leq n$.

To reduce the computational complexity, we perform the following equivalent deformation on the s computational equation in the SM2 signature scheme:

$$s = (d+1)^{-1}(k - rd) = \left((d+1)^{-1}(k+r) - r\right) \bmod q.$$

According to our (t, n)-Reciprocal Protocol, the algorithm can be divided into three cases by the relationship between the number of players n and threshold value t: $2t - 1 = n$ for Case A, $2t - 1 < n$ where n is odd for Case B, and $2t - 1 < n$ where n is even for Case C. The detailed process of the threshold key generation algorithm in Case C is as follows:

1. Players follow the process of joint random secret sharing and share a secret d as private key in (t', n') threshold way, $n' = n + 1$, $2t' - 1 = n'$. The $(t' - 1)$-degree secret sharing polynomial formed by Joint-RSS is denoted as $f'_d(x)$, and player P_i obtains its share as $d_i = f'_d(i)$;
2. Players continues to compute $(t'-t)$ shares and make it public, and get $(t'-t)$ public shares about secret d: $\{f'_d(j)|j = (n', n'+1, \cdots, n'+t'-t-1)\}$;

3. Players follow the process of joint random secret sharing and share a secret a in (t', n') threshold way, $n' = n + 1$, $2t' - 1 = n'$. The $(t' - 1)$-degree secret sharing polynomial formed by Joint-RSS is denoted as $f'_a(x)$, player P_i obtains its share as $a_i = f'_a(i)$ and need to publish $Q_i = [a_i^{-1}]G$ for the partial signature verification algorithm;

4. Players continues to compute $(t' - t)$ shares and make it public, and get $(t' - t)$ public shares about secret a: $\{f'_a(j)|j = (n', n' + 1, \cdots, n' + t' - t - 1)\}$;

5. Player P_i chooses a random polynomial $h'_i(x)$ of degree $(t - 1)$, and the constant term of $h'_i(x)$ is $h'_i(0) = f'_d(i)f'_a(i)$. Then $h'_i(j)$ is broadcast to the remaining players P_j, $1 \leq j \leq n$;

6. Player P_i calculates his secret share $d_i a_i$ about da through the constructed $(t - 1)$-degree random polynomial $N_3(x) \overset{\text{def}}{=} \lambda'_{n'} f'_d(n') f'_a(n') + \sum_{i=1}^{n} \lambda'_i h'_i(x)$;

7. The secret share of player P_j get about $(d + 1)a$ is calculated as follows: $R(j) = a_j + N_3(j)$, for $1 \leq j \leq n$;

8. t or more than t players broadcast their $R(i)$ in the system, and reconstructing the secret $\mu = da + a = (d + 1)a$;

9. Player P_i gets d'_i as a share of the multiplicative inverse of secret $d' = (d + 1)^{-1}$: $d'_i = D(i) = \mu^{-1}a_i = \left((d + 1)a\right)^{-1}a_i = (d + 1)^{-1}a^{-1}a_i = d'a_i$.

Threshold Signing Algorithm. The signing algorithm takes as input a message m, the partial private key d_i, d'_i as the share of d', public parameters in threshold key generation phase and the system parameters SP. The detailed process of signature (r, s) in (t, n) way in case C is described as follows.

At least t players P_i performs the following process to sign the message m, with system public parameters: $n' = n_1$, $2t' - 1 = n'$, $\{f'_d(j)|j = (n', n' + 1, \cdots, n + t' - t - 1)\}$, $\{a_j = f'_a(j)|j = (n', n' + 1, \cdots, n + t' - t - 1)\}$, $\mu = \left((d + 1)a\right)^{-1}$. Meanwhile, $d'_i = D(i) = \mu a_i, 1 \leq i \leq n'$:

1. Players follow the process of joint random secret sharing and share a secret k in (t', n') threshold way, $n' = n + 1$, $2t' - 1 = n'$. The $(t' - 1)$-degree secret sharing polynomial formed by Joint-RSS is denoted as $f'_k(x)$, and player P_i obtains its share as $k_i = f'_k(i)$;

2. Players continues to compute $(t' - t)$ shares and make it public, and get $(t' - t)$ public shares about secret k: $\{f'_k(j)|j = (n', n' + 1, \cdots, n' + t' - t - 1)\}$;

3. Player P_i get the point multiply $[k_i]G = (x_{1i}, y_{1i})$, and computes $e = H(m)$ to get $r_i = (H(m) + x_{1i}) \bmod q$. Meanwhile, $[k_{n'}]G = (x_{n'i}, y_{n'i})$, and $r_{n'} = (H(m) + x_{n'i}) \bmod q$;

4. Player P_i chooses a random polynomial $g'_i(x)$ of degree $(t - 1)$, and the constant term of $g'_i(x)$ is $g'_i(0) = D(i)f'_k(i)$. Then $g'_i(j)$ is broadcast to the remaining players P_j, $1 \leq j \leq n$;

5. Player P_i calculates his secret share $d'_i k_i$ about $d'k$ through the constructed $(t - 1)$-degree random polynomial $M_3(x) \overset{\text{def}}{=} \lambda'_{n'} D(n') f'_k(n') + \sum_{i=1}^{n} \lambda'_i g'_i(x)$;

6. Player P_i chooses a random polynomial $c'_i(x)$ of degree $(t-1)$, and the constant term of $c'_i(x)$ is $c'_i(0) = r_i D(i)$. Then $c'_i(j)$ is broadcast to the remaining players P_j, $1 \leq j \leq n$;

7. Player P_i calculates his secret share $d_i' r_i$ about $d'r$ through the constructed $(t-1)$-degree random polynomial $M_3'(x) \stackrel{\text{def}}{=} \lambda_{n'}' r_{n'} D(n') + \sum_{i=1}^{n} \lambda_i' c_i'(x)$;

8. Player P_i computes:

$$s_i = d_i'(k_i + r_i) - r_i \triangleq M_3(i) + M_3'(i) - r_i \qquad (4)$$

and gets s_i as the share of signature s. The partial signature of player P_i is $\sigma_{mi} = (r_i, s_i)$;

9. At least t players broadcast their partial signatures, and get the signed result (r, s) by performing interpolation formula and PM-SS. If $r = 0$ or $s = 0$, then $\mathcal{P}$ has to generate a new k and computes (r, s) again.

Verification Algorithm. The verification algorithm consists of two parts: the partial signature verification algorithm and the threshold signature verification algorithm.

Partial-Verify: The partial signature verification algorithm takes as input a message-partial signature pair (m', σ_{mi}'), $\sigma_{mi} = (r_i', s_i')$, the partial public key $P_i = [d_i]G$, the system public parameter $Q_i = [a_i^{-1}]G$, $\mu' = (d+1)a$, and the system parameters SP.

First, it computes $e' = H(m')$, $(x_{1i}', y_{1i}') = [\mu' s_i']Q_i + [r_i']P_i$ and accepts the partial signature if $(e' + x_{1i}') = r_i'$.

Verify: The verification algorithm takes as input a message-signature pair (m', σ_m'), $\sigma_m' = (r', s')$, the public key pk, and the system parameters SP.

It needs to verify whether $r' \in [1, q-1]$ and $s' \in [1, q-1]$ holds first, if not, the verifier outputs reject. Then, computes $t = (r' + s') \bmod q$ and verify whether $t \neq 0$ holds, if not, the verifier outputs reject. Last, it computes $e' = H(m')$, $(x_1', y_1') = [s']G + [t]P$ and accepts the signature if $(e' + x_1') = r'$.

Lemma 2. *If the SM2 signature scheme is unforgeable and the threshold SM2 signature scheme is simulable, then this threshold SM2 signature scheme is also unforgeable.*

Table 1. The traffic contrast between purely (t, n) threshold SM2/ECDSA signature scheme under Case C.

Process		Broadcast (bit)	Secret transmission (bit)
Key generation	SM2	$4\|p\| + (2t' - 2t + 1)\|q\|$	$3(n-1)\|q\|$
	ECDSA	$2\|p\| + (t' - t)\|q\|$	$(n-1)\|q\|$
Signing	SM2	$2\|p\| + 2(t' - t + 1)\|q\|$	$3(T-1)\|q\|$
	ECDSA	$2\|p\| + (2(t' - t + 1))\|q\|$	$4(T-1)\|q\|$

q: a player performs one round (t, n) Joint-RSS, $\|q\|$ bits information is sent to other $(n-1)$ players.

p: a player broadcasts an elliptic curve point, $2\|p\|$ bits information is published.

We analyze the communication efficiency of purely (t, n) threshold ECDSA signature scheme based on our purposed technology and our threshold SM2 signature scheme. Assuming that there are T ($t \leq T \leq n$) players jointly generating a signature for message m, the traffic contrast between the purely (t, n) threshold SM2/ECDSA signature scheme under Case C ($2t - 1 < n$ for even n, and $2t' - 1 = n + 1$) is shown in Table 1. We can draw a conclusion that the broadcast and secret transmission costs of threshold ECDSA signature scheme are clearly higher than our threshold SM2 signature scheme during the signature generation phase.

5 Conclusion

We proposed a secure multiplication protocol for shared secrets and proved its security. From the proposed protocol, we constructed an efficient secret reciprocal computation protocol with a fixed threshold value t. The new SM2 threshold signature scheme based on the secret reciprocal computation protocol ensures that the threshold value of the SM2 signature scheme does not change during the entire process, which makes the new threshold SM2 system practical.

An interesting future work includes constructing an efficient purely (t, n) threshold ECDSA signature scheme. Applying our SM2 threshold signature scheme to will also be our future work.

References

1. Béguin, P., Cresti, A.: General short computational secret sharing schemes. In: Guillou, L.C., Quisquater, J.-J. (eds.) EUROCRYPT 1995. LNCS, vol. 921, pp. 194–208. Springer, Heidelberg (1995). https://doi.org/10.1007/3-540-49264-X_16
2. Blakley, G.R.: Safeguarding cryptographic keys. In: 1979 International Workshop on Managing Requirements Knowledge (MARK), pp. 313–318. IEEE (1979)
3. Boneh, D., Gennaro, R., Goldfeder, S.: Using level-1 homomorphic encryption to improve threshold DSA signatures for bitcoin wallet security. In: Lange, T., Dunkelman, O. (eds.) LATINCRYPT 2017. LNCS, vol. 11368, pp. 352–377. Springer, Cham (2019). https://doi.org/10.1007/978-3-030-25283-0_19
4. Boyd, C.: Digital multisignatures. Cryptography and Coding, pp. 241–246 (1986)
5. Canetti, R., Gennaro, R., Goldfeder, S., Makriyannis, N., Peled, U.: UC non-interactive, proactive, threshold ECDSA with identifiable aborts. Cryptology ePrint Archive, Report 2021/060 (2021). https://eprint.iacr.org/2021/060
6. Castagnos, G., Catalano, D., Laguillaumie, F., Savasta, F., Tucker, I.: Two-party ECDSA from hash proof systems and efficient instantiations. In: Boldyreva, A., Micciancio, D. (eds.) CRYPTO 2019. LNCS, vol. 11694, pp. 191–221. Springer, Cham (2019). https://doi.org/10.1007/978-3-030-26954-8_7
7. Chor, B., Goldwasser, S., Micali, S., Awerbuch, B.: Verifiable secret sharing and achieving simultaneity in the presence of faults. In: 26th Annual Symposium on Foundations of Computer Science (SFCS 1985), pp. 383–395, October 1985. https://doi.org/10.1109/SFCS.1985.64

8. Damgård, I., Jakobsen, T.P., Nielsen, J.B., Pagter, J.I., Østergaard, M.B.: Fast threshold ECDSA with honest majority. In: Galdi, C., Kolesnikov, V. (eds.) SCN 2020. LNCS, vol. 12238, pp. 382–400. Springer, Cham (2020). https://doi.org/10.1007/978-3-030-57990-6_19

9. Davida, G.I., DeMillo, R.A., Lipton, R.J.: Protecting shared cryptographic keys. In: 1980 IEEE Symposium on Security and Privacy, p. 100. IEEE (1980)

10. Desmedt, Y., Frankel, Y.: Threshold cryptosystems. In: Brassard, G. (ed.) CRYPTO 1989. LNCS, vol. 435, pp. 307–315. Springer, New York (1990). https://doi.org/10.1007/0-387-34805-0_28

11. Doerner, J., Kondi, Y., Lee, E., Shelat, A.: Secure two-party threshold ECDSA from ECDSA assumptions. In: 2018 IEEE Symposium on Security and Privacy (SP), pp. 980–997. IEEE (2018)

12. Gennaro, R., Goldfeder, S.: Fast multiparty threshold ECDSA with fast trustless setup. In: Proceedings of the 2018 ACM SIGSAC Conference on Computer and Communications Security, pp. 1179–1194 (2018)

13. Gennaro, R., Goldfeder, S., Narayanan, A.: Threshold-optimal DSA/ECDSA signatures and an application to bitcoin wallet security. In: Manulis, M., Sadeghi, A.-R., Schneider, S. (eds.) ACNS 2016. LNCS, vol. 9696, pp. 156–174. Springer, Cham (2016). https://doi.org/10.1007/978-3-319-39555-5_9

14. Gennaro, R., Jarecki, S., Krawczyk, H., Rabin, T.: Robust threshold DSS signatures. In: Maurer, U. (ed.) EUROCRYPT 1996. LNCS, vol. 1070, pp. 354–371. Springer, Heidelberg (1996). https://doi.org/10.1007/3-540-68339-9_31

15. Gennaro, R., Jarecki, S., Krawczyk, H., Rabin, T.: Secure distributed key generation for discrete-log based cryptosystems. In: Stern, J. (ed.) EUROCRYPT 1999. LNCS, vol. 1592, pp. 295–310. Springer, Heidelberg (1999). https://doi.org/10.1007/3-540-48910-X_21

16. Gennaro, R., Rabin, M.O., Rabin, T.: Simplified VSS and fast-track multiparty computations with applications to threshold cryptography. In: Proceedings of the Seventeenth Annual ACM Symposium on Principles of Distributed Computing, pp. 101–111 (1998)

17. GM/T 0003–2012: Public Key Cryptographic Algorithm SM2 Based on Elliptic Curves. China's State Cryptography Administration, Beijing (2010)

18. Johnson, D., Menezes, A., Vanstone, S.: The elliptic curve digital signature algorithm (ECDSA). Int. J. Inf. Secur. 1(1), 36–63 (2001)

19. Langford, S.K.: Threshold DSS signatures without a trusted party. In: Coppersmith, D. (ed.) CRYPTO 1995. LNCS, vol. 963, pp. 397–409. Springer, Heidelberg (1995). https://doi.org/10.1007/3-540-44750-4_32

20. Lindell, Y.: Fast secure two-party ECDSA signing. In: Katz, J., Shacham, H. (eds.) CRYPTO 2017. LNCS, vol. 10402, pp. 613–644. Springer, Cham (2017). https://doi.org/10.1007/978-3-319-63715-0_21

21. Lindell, Y., Nof, A.: Fast secure multiparty ECDSA with practical distributed key generation and applications to cryptocurrency custody. In: Proceedings of the 2018 ACM SIGSAC Conference on Computer and Communications Security, pp. 1837–1854 (2018)

22. MacKenzie, P., Reiter, M.K.: Two-party generation of DSA signatures. In: Kilian, J. (ed.) CRYPTO 2001. LNCS, vol. 2139, pp. 137–154. Springer, Heidelberg (2001). https://doi.org/10.1007/3-540-44647-8_8

23. MacKenzie, P., Reiter, M.K.: Two-party generation of DSA signatures. Int. J. Inf. Secur. 2(3–4), 218–239 (2004)

24. Pedersen, T.P.: Distributed provers with applications to undeniable signatures. In: Davies, D.W. (ed.) EUROCRYPT 1991. LNCS, vol. 547, pp. 221–242. Springer, Heidelberg (1991). https://doi.org/10.1007/3-540-46416-6_20

25. Pedersen, T.P.: Non-interactive and information-theoretic secure verifiable secret sharing. In: Feigenbaum, J. (ed.) CRYPTO 1991. LNCS, vol. 576, pp. 129–140. Springer, Heidelberg (1992). https://doi.org/10.1007/3-540-46766-1_9

26. Shamir, A.: How to share a secret. Commun. ACM **22**(11), 612–613 (1979)

27. Shang, M., Ma, Y., Lin, J., Jing, J.: A threshold scheme for SM2 elliptic curve cryptographic algorithm. J. Cryptol. Res. **1**(2), 155 (2014). https://doi.org/10.13868/j.cnki.jcr.000015. http://www.jcr.cacrnet.org.cn/CN/abstract/abstract24.shtml. (in Chinese)

28. Yang, J., Lu, Y., Chen, L., Ni, W.: A SM2 elliptic curve threshold signature scheme without a trusted center. TIIS **10**, 897–913 (2016)

Pattern Matching over Encrypted Data with a Short Ciphertext

Jongkil Kim$^{(\boxtimes)}$, Willy Susilo, Yang-Wai Chow, Joonsang Baek, and Intae Kim

Institute of Cybersecurity and Cryptology, School of Computing and Information Technology, University of Wollongong, Wollongong, Australia
{jongkil,wsusilo,caseyc,baek,intaekim}@uow.edu.au

Abstract. In this paper, we propose a new searchable encryption with shiftable trapdoor (SEST) scheme to enable pattern matching over encrypted data. In the proposed scheme, data is encrypted per character and the trapdoor for searching can be shifted. This implies that the trapdoor can be created over any string, which is not necessarily pre-defined. Also, it does not require any additional data tokenization method, which will expand the ciphertext size. As ciphertext size increases with the size of data, it is imperative to reduce ciphertext size in the SEST scheme as the matching operation requires expensive pairing computations proportional to the ciphertext length. Our work reduces the ciphertext size by up to 50% of the state-of-art scheme in this research domain while maintaining the same level of search efficiency.

1 Introduction

Middlebox systems are security control systems widely adopted for organizational security. Intrusion detection systems (IDS) or exfiltration systems are typical examples of such systems. They are located in the middle of the network (i.e., between a client and a server) and moderate network packets to detect/prevent malicious attempts.

Demand for user privacy has resulted in end-to-end encryption becoming commonplace in modern Internet services. For example, the use of HTTPS has significantly increased nowadays. However, this trend makes detecting malicious attempts in middlebox systems difficult as data in network traffic can only be decrypted at each end, i.e., at the user end and the server end.

A number of techniques have been proposed to overcome this difficulty. Techniques such as interception proxies [7,8,12] or TLS subversion [1] have been proposed. However, these systems require encrypted packets to be fully decrypted in the middlebox, which does not provide user privacy.

Recently, deep packet inspection (DPI) systems [14] over encrypted traffic have been proposed to enable middleboxes to inspect packets in the middle of the network, while still preserving user privacy. In middlebox systems that use DPI techniques, encrypted user data is not decrypted in the middlebox. Instead, they encrypt detection keywords (i.e. patterns) in the same way that the data is

H. Kim (Ed.): WISA 2021, LNCS 13009, pp. 132–143, 2021.
https://doi.org/10.1007/978-3-030-89432-0_11

encrypted and match them with the encrypted data without knowing the user's encryption key. Since they do not decrypt data and only compute a limited number of search tokens, this guarantees user privacy.

In an orthogonal direction, pattern matching systems have recently been developed as a variant of searchable encryption [5,9,15]. They are proposed to detect patterns in the encrypted data stream. This allows many practical systems, such as deep packet inspection (DPI) systems over the encrypted traffic and genetic sequence search over encrypted genetic data. Besides, in those pattern matching systems, the size of encrypted data is much larger than the size of a search token, and hence, the efficiency of the systems largely depends on the ciphertext size and the search speed. Particularly, in existing DPI systems [6,10,11,13,14] and pattern matching systems [2,4], each alphabet character or tokenized data is encrypted and represented as a group element with a large number, or a point on an elliptic curve, which is unavoidable. Therefore, developing an efficient pattern matching system having a small ciphertext and a fast search mechanism is essential for practical use.

2   Contribution

In this paper, we propose a new scheme for searchable encryption with shiftable trapdoor (SEST) for matching patterns on encrypted traffic. Our system has a shorter ciphertext size while still preserving efficient decryption compared to existing SEST schemes [2,4]. As a result, compared to [4], our system reduces both the size of encrypted data and the number of pairings required for the search. Furthermore, we reduce the ciphertext size by up to 50% compared to the most efficient SEST scheme [2]. This will significantly reduce data storage and network bandwidth consumed by SEST.

In our scheme, we need to divide strings to be encrypted in multiple fragments for efficient encryption and search. In Fig. 1, we show an example to demonstrate how our fragmentation method can be set. We design two adjacent fragments share $\ell - 1$ strings where ℓ is the maximum size of a search string. This overlap is inevitable for continuous search and also similarly appears in [2]. However, in our scheme, only two elements are required to encrypt strings in the overlapped area and an element for the non-overlapped area (and an element per fragment). However, in [2], four elements are required for strings in the overlapped area and two elements are required for strings in the non-overlapped area. Therefore, even in the worst-case scenario in our fragmentation where $f = 2(\ell - 1)$ and most of the strings except a few strings in the first and the last fragment are located in the overlapped area in Fig. 1, our scheme requires only two elements for each string in the ciphertext, which still outperforms Bkakria et al.'s work [2] in terms of ciphertext size.

We provide a detailed comparison in Table 1. Matching in the table implies the number of pairings required for matching. The size of ciphertext is compared based on each fragment. Therefore, the ciphertext size of [4] is compared differently since it does not fragment an encrypted string. We mainly compare our

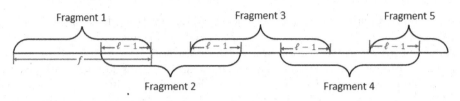

ℓ : The maximum size of a search string (i.e., a pattern)
f : The size of a fragment (a fragmentation window).

Fig. 1. Fragmentation example

scheme to [2], which is the state-of-the-art scheme in this area. Our work reduces the ciphertext size by almost half if a similar fragmentation method is applied, although we need an extra element for each fragment. In both schemes, * is used to denote the number of elements for each character located in the overlapped area. The sizes of a public key and a token are proportional to the fragment size in ours unlike those of Bkakria et al.'s scheme. However, as previously mentioned, even if we set $f = 2(\ell - 1)$ so that we make the size of a public key and a token increase with ℓ not f, our scheme still reduces the size of a ciphertext compared to Bkakria et al.'s scheme.

Table 1. Efficiency comparison with existing work (for single query)

	Public key	Token	Ciphertext	Matching
Desmoulins et al. [4]	$O(|\mathcal{S}| \cdot m_{max})$	$O(\ell_W)$	$2 \cdot m$	$2m \cdot \ell$
Bkakria et al. [2]	$O(|\mathcal{S}| \cdot \ell)$	$O(\ell_W)$	$(2 \text{ or } 4^*)f$	$2m$
Ours	$O(|\mathcal{S}| \cdot f)$	$O(f - \ell)$	$(1 \text{ or } 2^*)f + 1$	$2m$

m: The size of a string to be encrypted.
m_{max}: The maximum size of a string to be encrypted.
ℓ_W: The size of a string for a search token W.
ℓ: The maximum size of a string for a search token.
f: The size of a fragmentation window.

3   Related Work

The pattern matching system called middlebox searchable encryption was proposed by Sherry et al. [14]. BlindBox can perform fast pattern matching since its matching algorithm only requires AES encryption. However, BlindBox requires interaction between the receivers to create trapdoors (i.e. detection rules) for search before it encrypts any data. This limits usage of the system since the encryption party can only encrypt data per receiver. Also, the interaction causes a significant delay which is not suitable for network packet monitoring. Moreover, it needs to tokenize the data before it encrypts, which bloats the ciphertext size. More recently, PrivDPI [13] and P2DPI [10] were proposed. They improve the efficiency of BlindBox by many orders of magnitude. However, they still have the same restrictions that BlindBox has.

BlindIDS from Canard et al. [3] does not require any additional interaction to create a trapdoor, thus it is quite similar to SEST. However, its trapdoor is still based on tokenized words and it cannot be shifted. Therefore, its ciphertext still becomes larger and the matching is not as flexible as in proposed SEST systems [2,4].

The first SEST scheme was proposed by Desmoulins et al. [4]. It is the first encryption scheme that uses a shiftable trapdoor. Therefore, it greatly improves the flexibility and efficiency of pattern matching. More recently, Bkakria et al. [2] proposed a system that improves both efficiency and security. This achieves an anonymous trapdoor so that a string corresponding to a trapdoor is hidden. It also significantly improves the computation for matching keywords.

4 Preliminaries

4.1 Bilinear Pairing

Let set $\mathcal{G}$ be a group generator that takes a security parameter λ as input and outputs a description of a bilinear group $\mathcal{G}$. For our purposes, we will have $\mathcal{G}$ output $(p, \mathbb{G}_1, \mathbb{G}_2, \mathbb{G}_T, e)$ where p is a prime, $\mathbb{G}_1$, $\mathbb{G}_2$ and $\mathbb{G}_T$ are cyclic groups of order p, and $e : \mathbb{G}_1 \times \mathbb{G}_2 \to \mathbb{G}_T$ is an efficiently computable non-degenerate bilinear map. We assume that the group operations in $\mathbb{G}_1$, $\mathbb{G}_2$ and $\mathbb{G}_T$ as well as the bilinear map e are efficiently computable in polynomial time with respect to λ, and that the group descriptions of $\mathbb{G}_1$, $\mathbb{G}_2$ and $\mathbb{G}_T$ include generators of the respective cyclic groups. We call e an asymmetric pairing if $\mathbb{G}_1 \neq \mathbb{G}_2$ and no efficiently computable homomorphism exists between $\mathbb{G}_1$ and $\mathbb{G}_2$, in either direction.

We use the interactive General Diffie-Hellman (i-GDH) assumption [4] to prove our security, which is defined as follows:

Assumption 1 (*i-GDH Assumption*). Let r, s, t, c and k be five positive integers and $\mathsf{R} \in \mathbb{F}_p[X_1; \ldots ; X_c]^r$, $\mathsf{S} \in \mathbb{F}_p[X_1; \ldots ; X_c]^s$, and $\mathsf{T} \in \mathbb{F}_p[X_1; \ldots ; X_c]^t$ be three tuples of multivariate polynomials over $\mathbb{F}_p$.

Let $\mathcal{O}_R$ (resp. $\mathcal{O}_S$ and $\mathcal{O}_T$) be oracles that on input $\{\{a_{i_1,\ldots,i_c}^{(k)}\}_{i_j=0}^{d_k}\}_k$ add polynomials $\{\sum_{i_1;\ldots;i_c} a_{i_1,\ldots,i_c}^{(k)} \cdot \prod_j X_j^{i_j}\}_k$ to R (resp. S and T).

Let $(x_1, \ldots, x_c)$ be a secret vector and q_R (resp. q_S) (resp. q_T) be the number of queries to $\mathcal{O}_R$ (resp. $\mathcal{O}_S$) (resp. $\mathcal{O}_T$). The i-GDH assumption states that given the values $\{g^{\mathsf{R}^{(i)}(x_1,\ldots,x_c)}\}_{i=1}^{r+k\cdot q_R}$, $\{\tilde{g}^{\mathsf{S}^{(i)}(x_1,\ldots,x_c)}\}_{i=1}^{s+k\cdot q_S}$ and $\{e(g,\tilde{g})^{\mathsf{T}^{(i)}(x_1,\ldots,x_c)}\}_{i=1}^{t+k\cdot q_T}$, it is hard to decide whether $U = g^{f(x_1,\ldots,x_c)}$ or U is random if f is independent of $<\mathsf{R}, \mathsf{S}, \mathsf{T}>$.

4.2   Definitions

Searchable encryption with shiftable trapdoor is defined as follows:

A searchable encryption scheme with shiftable trapdoors is defined by five algorithms that we call **Setup, Keygen, Issue, Encrypt** and **Test**:

Setup(1^λ, ℓ): This probabilistic algorithm takes as input a security parameter k and an integer ℓ, which defines the maximum size of a string (i.e. pattern) for a token that one can use for matching. It returns public parameters pp that will be accepted as input by all the other algorithms. In the following, pp will be considered to be an implicit input to all algorithms and will thus be omitted.

Keygen($\mathcal{S}$): This probabilistic algorithm run by the receiver takes a finite set $\mathcal{S}$ as input and returns a key pair (sk, pk). The former value is secret and only known by the receiver, while the latter is public.

Issue(W, sk): This probabilistic algorithm takes as input a string W of any size $0 < \ell_W \leq \ell$, along with the receiver's secret key, and returns a trapdoor td_W.

Encrypt(S, pk): This probabilistic algorithm takes as input the receiver's public key along with a string $S = s_0 \ldots s_{m-1}$ where $m > \ell$, such that $s_i \in \mathcal{S}$ for all $i \in [0, m-1]$, and returns a ciphertext C.

Test(C, td_W): This deterministic algorithm takes as input a ciphertext C encrypting a string $S = s_0 \ldots s_{m-1}$ of size m, along with a trapdoor td_W for a string $W = w_0 \ldots w_{\ell_W - 1}$ of size ℓ_W. If $\ell_W > \ell$ or $\ell_W > m$, then the algorithm returns $\perp$. Otherwise, the algorithm returns a set (potentially empty) $\mathcal{J} \in \{0, \ldots, m - \ell_W\}$ of indexes j s.t. $s_j \ldots s_{j+\ell_W - 1} = w_0 \ldots w_{\ell_W - 1}$.

Correctness Property. For correctness, the following property must be satisfied:

Let $pp \leftarrow$ **Setup(1^k, ℓ)** and $(sk, pk) \leftarrow$ **KeyGen($\mathcal{S}$)**. For a string $W = w_0 \ldots w_{\ell_W - 1}$ of any size less than or equal to ℓ (i.e., $\ell_W \leq \ell$), $td_W \leftarrow$ Issue(W, sk) will be returned as a trapdoor. For a string $S = s_0 \ldots s_{m-1}$, a ciphertext $C \leftarrow$ **Encrypt(S, pk)** is returned. For a ciphertext C and a trapdoor td_W, the set of indexes $\mathcal{J} \in \{0, \ldots, m - \ell_W\} \leftarrow$ **Test(C, td_W)** will be returned where $\mathcal{J}$ is the set of indexes j such that $s_j \ldots s_{j+\ell_W - 1} = w_0 \ldots w_{\ell_W - 1}$.

4.3   Security Models

We define the IND-CPA security of the searchable encryption for shiftable trapdoor, namely SEST-IND-CPA security based on the security model defined in [2,4]. Let $\mathcal{O}_{\text{Issue}}$ be the oracle issuing a trapdoor td_{W_i} for a string W_i and accessible by the adversary $\mathcal{A}$.

We define SEST-IND-CPA by an experiment $\mathbf{Exp}_{\mathcal{A}}^{\text{IND-CPA-}\beta}(1^\lambda, \ell)$ where $\beta \in \{0, 1\}$ defined as follows:

- **Setup:** The challenger runs **Setup(1^λ, ℓ)** to obtain a public parameter pp. It gives $\mathcal{A}^{\mathcal{O}_{\text{Issue}}}$ the public parameter pp. The challenger also runs **KeyGen($\mathcal{S}$)**

to obtain a public key (pk). It gives $\mathcal{A}^{\mathcal{O}_{\text{Issue}}}$ the public parameter pp and a public key pk.

- **Phase I:** The adversary $\mathcal{A}^{\mathcal{O}_{\text{Issue}}}$ accesses the oracle $\mathcal{O}_{\text{Issue}}$ to query trapdoors $td_{W_1}, \ldots, td_{W_q}$ for strings $W_1, \ldots, W_q$.
- **Challenge:** If **Phase I** is over, $\mathcal{A}^{\mathcal{O}_{\text{Issue}}}$ outputs S_0 and S_1 with the restriction that there is no trivial trapdoors queried in **Phase I** to distinguish S_0 and S_1. More formally, the challenger outputs $\perp$ if $\exists W = w_0 \ldots w_{\ell_W - 1} \in \{W_1, \ldots, W_q\}$ and i, j such that

$$s_j^{(i)} \ldots s_{j+\ell_W-1}^{(i)} = w_0 \ldots w_{\ell_W-1} \neq s_j^{(i-1)} \ldots s_{j+\ell_W-1}^{(i-1)}.$$

The challenger randomly selects $\beta \in \{0, 1\}$ and runs **Encrypt** algorithm to obtain $C = \mathbf{Enc}(S_\beta, pk)$ and returns C to $\mathcal{A}^{\mathcal{O}_{\text{Issue}}}$.
- **Guess:** Finally, the adversary $\mathcal{A}^{\mathcal{O}_{\text{Issue}}}$ outputs a guess $\beta' \in \{0, 1\}$ and wins the game if $\beta = \beta'$.

We define the advantage of an adversary $\mathcal{A}$ as follows:

$$Adv_{\mathcal{A}}^{\text{IND-CPA}}(1^\lambda, \ell) = |Pr[\mathbf{Exp}_{\mathcal{A}}^{\text{IND-CPA-1}}(1^\lambda, \ell)] - Pr[\mathbf{Exp}_{\mathcal{A}}^{\text{IND-CPA-0}}(1^\lambda, \ell)]|.$$

A searchable encryption with shiftable trapdoors is SEST-IND-CPA secure if this advantage is negligible for any polynomial-time adversary.

We also define a weaker (selective) security notion SEST-sIND-CPA, in which the adversary gives S_0 and S_1 to the challenger at the beginning of the experiment before seeing any pp and pk.

5   Construction

We provide our new SEST scheme. The construction provided in this section is the simplest construction rather than the generalized construction. We set $f = 2(\ell - 1)$ to reduce the parameters used in the construction and also simplify the scheme to demonstration purpose.[1] Our scheme consists of five algorithms, **Setup, KeyGen, Issue, Encrypt** and **Test** as follows:

- **Setup**$(1^\lambda, \ell) \to pp$: The algorithm takes as input a security parameter λ, the maximum token size ℓ. It selects $g \xleftarrow{R} \mathbb{G}_1$ and $h \xleftarrow{R} \mathbb{G}_2$. Let $(\mathbb{G}_1, \mathbb{G}_2, \mathbb{G}_T, e, g, h, \ell)$ be a public parameter pp.
- **KeyGen**$(\mathcal{S}, pp) \to (sk, pk)$ The algorithm takes as input a public parameter pp which includes the description of asymmetric bilinear groups of prime order p and its generators $g \in \mathbb{G}_1$ and $h \in \mathbb{G}_2$. It selects $|\mathcal{S}| + 1$ random values z and $\{\sigma_s\}_{s \in \mathcal{S}}$ from $\mathbb{Z}_p$ and set $g_i \leftarrow g^{z^i}$. It publishes a public key $pk = (\{g_i, \{g_i^{\sigma_s}\}_{s \in \mathcal{S}}\}_{i=0}^{i=2\ell-3})$ and sets a secret key $sk = (z, h, \{\sigma_s\}_{s \in \mathcal{S}})$.

---

[1] We believe this is beneficial since 1) our scheme still has a short ciphertext compared to the existing scheme showing similar property, 2) the sizes of a public key and a search token are maintained small and 3) it is easier to understand since the complexity of the scheme is reduced, significantly.

- **Issue**$(W, sk) \to td_W$: To create a token td_W for a string $W = w_0 w_1 \ldots w_{\ell_W - 1}$ of length $\ell_W(\leq \ell)$, the algorithm generates $r_0, r_1, \ldots, r_{\ell-2}$. For $i \in \{0, \ldots, \ell - 2\}$, it sets $K_i = h^{r_i}$ and $K'_i = h^{r_i \cdot \sum_{j=0}^{\ell_W - 1} \sigma_{w_j} \cdot z^{i+j}}$. It sets the search token td_W for W as $\{K_i, K'_i\}_{i \in \{0, \ldots, \ell-2\}}$.

- **Encrypt**$(S, pk) \to CT$: To encrypt a string $S = s_0, \ldots, s_{m-1}$. It sets $n = \lfloor \frac{m-1}{\ell-1} \rfloor$ and randomly selects $\{a_i\}_{i \in \{0, \ldots, n-1\}}$ from $\mathbb{Z}_p$. For all $i \in [0, n-1]$, it sets $C_i = g_0^{a_i}$. Also, it computes the following:
  - If $i \in \{0, \ldots, n-2\}$, for all $i \in \{0, \ldots, n-2\}, j \in \{0, \ldots, 2(\ell-1) - 1)\}$, it sets $C'_{i,j} = g_j^{a_i \sigma_{s_{j+(\ell-1) \cdot i}}}$,
  - If $i = n - 1$, for all $j \in \{0, \ldots, m - (\ell - 1)(n-1) - 1\}$, it sets $C'_{n-1,j} = g_j^{a_{n-1} \sigma_{s_{j+(\ell-1)(n-1)}}}$.

It outputs the following ciphertext CT:

$$CT := (\{C_i\}_{i=0}^{i=n-1}, \{C'_{i,j}\}_{i=0,j=0}^{i=n-2,j=2(\ell-1)-1}, \{C'_{n-1,j}\}_{j=0}^{j=m-(\ell-1)(n-1)-1})$$

- **Test**$(pk, td_W, CT) \to \mathcal{J}$: The algorithm takes as inputs a public key pk, a token td_W, and a ciphertext CT. The algorithm sets $\mathcal{J} = \emptyset$. For all $j \in \{0, \ldots, m - \ell\}$, it computes $t = \lfloor \frac{j}{\ell-1} \rfloor$ and $k = j - t \cdot (\ell - 1)$. It, then, computes $C = e(C_t, K'_k)$ and $D = e(\prod_{i=0}^{\ell_W - 1} C'_{t,k+i}, K_k)$. If $C = D$, it add j to $\mathcal{J}$. Finally, it outputs the set of indexes $\mathcal{J}$.

Correctness. Let S contain W as a substring (i.e. $\exists j'$ s.t. $s_{j'} \ldots s_{j'+\ell_W-1} = w_0 \ldots w_{\ell_W-1}$). We let $t' = \lfloor \frac{j'}{\ell-1} \rfloor$ and $k' = j' - t' \cdot (\ell - 1)$. Then, one can compute C and D as follows:

$$
\begin{aligned}
C &= e(C_{t'}, K'_{k'}) \\
&= e(g_0^{a_{t'}}, h^{r_{k'} \cdot \sum_{i=0}^{\ell_W - 1} \sigma_{w_i} \cdot z^{i+k'}}) \\
&= e(g_0, h)^{a_{t'} \cdot r_{k'} \cdot \sum_{i=0}^{\ell_W - 1} \sigma_{w_i} \cdot z^{i+k'}},
\end{aligned}
$$

$$
\begin{aligned}
D &= e(\prod_{i=0}^{\ell_W - 1} C'_{t', k'+i}, K_{k'}) \\
&= e(\prod_{i=0}^{\ell_W - 1} g_{k'+i}^{a_{t'} \sigma_{s_{i+k'+t'(\ell-1)}}}, h^{r_{k'}}) \\
&= e(g_0, h)^{a_{t'} \cdot r_{k'} \cdot \sum_{i=0}^{\ell_W - 1} z^{i+k'} \cdot \sigma_{s_{i+k'+t' \cdot (\ell-1)}}} \\
&= e(g_0, h)^{a_{t'} \cdot r_{k'} \cdot \sum_{i=0}^{\ell_W - 1} z^{i+k'} \cdot \sigma_{s_{i+j'}}}.
\end{aligned}
$$

The last equality holds because $k' + t' \cdot (\ell - 1) = j'$. Therefore, $C = D$.

6   Security Analysis

Theorem 1. *Our SEST scheme in Sect. 5 is SEST-sIND-CPA secure under i-GDH assumption for R, S, and T initially set as* $R = \{(z^i, x_j \cdot z^i, a \cdot z^i)\}_{i=0,j=0}^{i=2\ell-3;j=|S|-1}$, $S = T = \emptyset$ *and* $f = a \cdot x_0 \cdot z^{2(\ell-1)}$.

Proof. Let $S^{(0)} = s_0^{(0)} \dots s_{m-1}^{(0)}$ and $S^{(1)} = s_0^{(1)} \dots s_{m-1}^{(1)}$ be the two challenge strings given by $\mathcal{A}$ at the beginning of $\mathbf{Exp}_{\mathcal{A}}^{\text{sIND-CPA-}\beta}(1^\lambda, \ell)$. First, we create substrings from $S^{(\cdot)}$

$$S_i^{(\cdot)} = s_{i \cdot (\ell-1)} \dots s_{min((i+2)(\ell-1)-1, m-1)} = s'_{(i,0)} \dots s'_{(i,\ell'_i - 1)}$$

for all $i \in \{0, \dots, n-1\}$ where $n = \lfloor \frac{m-1}{\ell-1} \rfloor$. It should be noted that, in this fragmentation, two adjacent fragments share $(\ell - 1)$ characters.

We use $I_{\neq}^{(i)}$ to denote the set of indexes k, such that $s'^{(0)}_{(i,k)} \neq s'^{(1)}_{(i,k)}$ in $S_i^{(\cdot)}$, which is $i + 1$th fragment in strings $S^{(\cdot)}$ and $I_{\neq}^{(i,j)}$ be the subset containing the first j indexes of $I_{\neq}^{(i)}$ (if $j > |I_{\neq}^{(i)}|$, then $I_{\neq}^{(i,j)} = I_{\neq}^{(i)}$). We set $\mathsf{Game}_{0,0}^{(\beta)}$ to be identical to $\mathbf{Exp}_{\mathcal{A}}^{\text{sIND-CPA-}\beta}(1^\lambda, \ell)$. We also set $\mathsf{Game}_{(i,\ell'_i)}^{(\cdot)}$ to be equivalent to $\mathsf{Game}_{(i+1,0)}^{(\cdot)}$ for all $i \in \{0, n-1\}$ by the definition where $\ell'_i = min(2\ell-3, m-i(\ell-1)-1)$. Then, in each substring $S_i^{(\cdot)}$, for all $j \in \{0, \dots, \ell'_i\}$, we define $\mathsf{Game}_{(i,j)}^{(\cdot)}$ modifies $\mathsf{Game}_{(i,0)}^{(\cdot)}$ by switching the elements $C'_{i,j}$ of the challenge ciphertext to random elements of $\mathbb{G}_1$, for $j \in I_{\neq}^{(i,j)}$. By doing this, all elements $C'_{i,j}$ in the ciphertext on $\mathsf{Game}_{(n-1,\ell'_{n-1})}^{(\cdot)}$, which is the last game in the proof, are replaced by random values if $s'^{(0)}_{(i,j)} \neq s'^{(1)}_{(i,j)}$. It means that the adversary $\mathcal{A}$ only has negligible advantage to distinguish between $\mathsf{Game}_{(n-1,\ell'_{n-1})}^{(0)}$ and $\mathsf{Game}_{(n-1,\ell'_{n-1})}^{(1)}$.

Our goal is to show that the last game, $\mathsf{Game}_{(n-1,\ell'_{n-1})}^{(\cdot)}$, is actually indistinguishable from $\mathsf{Game}_{(0,0)}^{(\cdot)}$. This can be proven by showing that for i^*th substring of $S^{(\cdot)}$ (i.e., $S_{i^*}^{(\cdot)}$), $\mathsf{Game}_{(i^*,j)}^{\beta}$ is indistinguishable from $\mathsf{Game}_{(i^*,j+1)}^{\beta}$ for all $j = \{0, \dots, \ell'_{i^*} - 1\}$. We will show this in Lemmas 1 and 2.

Lemma 1. *For all* $j \in \{0, \dots, \ell'_i\}$ *and* $\beta \in \{0, 1\}$, $\mathsf{Game}_{(i^*,j)}^{(\beta)}$ *and* $\mathsf{Game}_{(i^*,j+1)}^{(\beta)}$ *are indistinguishable.*

Proof. We will show the indistinguishablity between $\mathsf{Game}_{(i^*,j)}^{(\beta)}$ and $\mathsf{Game}_{(i^*,j+1)}^{(\beta)}$ for $j \in \{0, \dots, \ell'_i\}$ using the i-GDH assumption. The parameters of the assumption are initially set as follows: $R = \{(z^i, x_j \cdot z^i, a \cdot z^i)\}_{i=0,j=0}^{i=2(\ell-1)-1;j=|S|-1}$, $S = T = \emptyset$ and $f = a \cdot x_0 \cdot z^{2(\ell-1)}$.

First, it is straightforward that the games $\mathsf{Game}_{(i^*,j)}^{(\beta)}$ and $\mathsf{Game}_{(i^*,j+1)}^{(\beta)}$ are the same if $|I_{\neq}^{(i^*)}| < j$, because $I_{\neq}^{(i^*,j)} = I_{\neq}^{(i^*,j+1)}$ by its definition.

We show the indistinguishability in the case $I_{\neq}^{(i^*)} < j + 1$. Let k^* be the $(j + 1)$-st index of $I_{\neq}^{(i)}$. From the i-GDH assumption, $\{(g^{z^i}, g^{x_j \cdot z^i}, g^{a \cdot z^i})\}_{i=0,j=0}^{i=2(\ell-1)-1;j=|\mathcal{S}|-1}$ is given along with $U \in \mathbb{G}_1$. The simulator generates the public key pk by first defining $g_k = g^{z^{2(\ell-1)+k-k^*}}$. This results in $g_{k^*} = g^{z^{2(\ell-1)}}$. Next, it sets $g_k^{\sigma_{s'_{k^*}}} = g^{x_0 \cdot z^{2(\ell-1)+k-k^*}}$ and $g^{\sigma_s} = g^{x_{f(s)} \cdot z^{2(\ell-1)+k-k^*}}$ for all $s \in \mathcal{S} \setminus \{s'_{k^*}\}$ where a function f be a random permutation from $\forall s \in \mathcal{S} \setminus \{s'_{k^*}\}$ to $\{1, \ldots, |\mathcal{S}| - 1\}$, which is bijective (i.e. $f : \mathcal{S} \setminus \{s'_{k^*}\} \to \{1, \ldots, |\mathcal{S}| - 1\}$). This setting allows the simulator to return pk. Upon receiving a query for a trapdoor with a string $W_t = w_0 \ldots w_{\ell_t - 1}$, the simulator checks that the string complies with the restriction where $w_0 \ldots w_{\ell_t - 1} \neq s'^{(\beta)}_{k^* - j} - s'^{(\beta)}_{k^* - j + \ell_t - 1}$ for all $\beta \in \{0, 1\}$ and all $j \in [max(0; k^* - \ell + 2)), min(k^*; \ell_t - 1)]$. Finally, the simulator creates the challenge ciphertext as follows:

It sets $C_{i^*} = g^a$ (using $g^{a \cdot z^0}$) and sets $C'_{i^*, k}$ as random values from $\mathbb{G}_1$ for the first j-th indexes of $I_{\neq}^{(i^*)}$. It then uses the $\mathcal{O}_R$ oracle to get valid $C'_{i^*, k}$ for all $k \notin I_{\neq}^{(i^*, j+1)}$. It sets C'_{i^*, k^*} as U.

If $U = g^{a \cdot x_0 \cdot z^{2(\ell-1)}}$, then C'_{i^*, k^*} is a valid element and the simulator is simulating $\mathsf{Game}^{(\beta)}_{(i^*, j)}$. Otherwise, if C'_{i^*, k^*} is a random value from $\mathbb{G}_1$, it is simulating $\mathsf{Game}^{(\beta)}_{(i^*, j+1)}$.

Therefore, if an adversary $\mathcal{A}$ is able to distinguish $\mathsf{Game}^{(\beta)}_{(i^*, j)}$ from $\mathsf{Game}^{(\beta)}_{(i^*, j+1)}$, it can break the i-GDH assumption. Now, we will show that $f = a \cdot x_0 \cdot z^{2(\ell-1)}$ is independent of the sets R, S and T (after q queries to $\mathcal{O}_S$ and 1 query to $\mathcal{O}_R$) in Lemma 2.

Lemma 2. *Let R, S, and T be the sets defined above after q queries to $\mathcal{O}_S$ and one query to $\mathcal{O}_R$. If, for any $t \in [1, q]$, the string $w_{t,0} \ldots w_{t, \ell_t - 1}$ submitted to $\mathcal{O}_S$ differs for all $j \in [max(0; k^* - \ell + 2)), min(k^*; \ell_t - 1)]$, from $s'_{k^* - j} \cdots s'_{k^* - j + \ell_t - 1}$, the polynomial $a \cdot \sigma_{s_{k^*}} \cdot z^{2(\ell-1)}$ is independent of $<R, S, T>$.*

Proof. In this proof, we will show that there exists no combination of polynomials from the sets R, S and T such that

$$(a \cdot \sigma_{s_{k^*}} \cdot z^{2(\ell-1)})(\sum_{i,j} a_{i,j} S^{(j)} z^i) = \sum_{i,j} b_{i,j} R^{(i)} S^{(j)} + \sum_k C_k \cdot T^{(k)}.$$

First, because the factor a appears only in the fragment where k^* belongs to and the output of $\mathcal{O}_S$ does not include a. Therefore, the elements of R in the other fragment cannot be involved in the previous relation. Due to the same reasons, we can also ignore the elements $\{z^i, \{\sigma_s \cdot z^i\}_{s \in \Sigma}\}_{i=0}^{2\ell-3}$ in the second sum. We use V_t to denote $\sum_{j=0}^{j=\ell_t} \sigma_{w_{(t,j)}} \cdot z^j$. Also, $v_{j,t}$ represent a randomization parameter used in a token. $v_{j,t}$ denotes the j-th random value, r_j, in the token of the t-th query (to $\mathcal{O}_S$). The last sum of the above equation can also be removed as T is empty. Now, we let $\{u_i, a_{i,j,t}, b_{i,j,t}, a'_{j,t}, b'_{j,t}\}$ be the scalars such that

$$(a \cdot \sigma_{s_{k^*}} \cdot z^{2(\ell-1)})(\sum_{t=0}^{q} \sum_{j=0}^{\ell-2} (b_{k^*,j,t} \cdot v_{j,t} \cdot V_t \cdot z^j + a_{k^*,j,t} \cdot v_{j,t}))$$

$$= a \cdot (\sum_{t=0}^{q} \sum_{j=0}^{\ell-2} (b'_{j,t} \cdot v_{j,t} \cdot V_t \cdot z^j + a'_{j,t} \cdot v_{j,t}))$$

$$+ \sum_{i=0,i\neq k^*}^{2\ell-3} (a \cdot u_i \cdot \sigma_{s_i} \cdot z^{2(\ell-1)+i-k^*} \cdot (\sum_{t=0}^{q} \sum_{j=0}^{\ell-2} (b_{i,j,t} \cdot v_{j,t} \cdot V_t \cdot z^j + a_{i,j,t} \cdot v_{j,t}))).$$

As $v_{j,t}$ are variables that are generated randomly for all queries made to the $\mathcal{O}_S$ oracle, $v_{j,t} \neq v_{j',t'}$ for any $t \neq t'$ and $j \neq j'$ with overwhelming probability. Therefore, the previous equation holds only if the following equation holds for all $t \in [1,q]$, $j \in [0, \ell-2]$:

$$(a \cdot \sigma_{s_{k^*}} \cdot z^{2(\ell-1)})(b_{k^*,j,t} \cdot v_{j,t} \cdot V_t \cdot z^j + a_{k^*,j,t} \cdot v_{j,t}) = a \cdot (b'_{j,t} \cdot v_{j,t} \cdot V_t \cdot z^j + a'_{j,t} \cdot v_{j,t})$$

$$+ \sum_{i=0,i\neq k^*}^{2\ell-3} (a \cdot u_i \cdot \sigma_{s_i} \cdot z^{2\ell+i-k^*} \cdot (b_{i,j,t} \cdot v_{j,t} \cdot V_t \cdot z^j + a_{i,j,t} \cdot v_{j,t})).$$

Based on the degree of monomials, we divide the above equation as follows:

1. $a \cdot a'_{j,t} \cdot v_{j,t} = 0$
2. $a \cdot \sigma_{s_{k^*}} \cdot z^{2(\ell-1)} \cdot b_{k^*,j,t} \cdot v_{j,t} \cdot V_t \cdot z^j = a \cdot b'_{j,t} \cdot v_{j,t} \cdot V_t \cdot z^j + a \cdot \sum_{i=0,i\neq k^*}^{2\ell-3} u_i \cdot \sigma_{s_i} \cdot z^{2\ell+i-k^*} \cdot b_{i,j,t} \cdot v_{j,t} \cdot V_t \cdot z^j$
3. $(a \cdot \sigma_{s_{k^*}} \cdot z^{2(\ell-1)}) \cdot a_{k^*,j,t} \cdot v_{j,t} = a \cdot \sum_{i=0,i\neq k^*}^{2\ell-3} (u_i \cdot \sigma_{s_i} \cdot z^{2\ell+i-k^*} \cdot (a_{i,j,t} \cdot v_{j,t}))$

The first condition is only met if $a'_{j,t} = 0$, because a and $v_{j,t}$ is not zero with overwhelming probability.

For the second equation, we can simplify the equation by removing common factors in the left and right hand sides of the equation.

$$\sigma_{s_{k^*}} \cdot z^{2(\ell-1)} \cdot b_{k^*,j,t} = b'_{j,t} + \sum_{i=0,i\neq k^*}^{2\ell-3} u_i \cdot \sigma_{s_i} \cdot z^{2(\ell-1)+i-k^*} \cdot b_{i,j,t}.$$

This implies that $b'_{j,t} = 0$. Moreover, because $i \neq k^*$ in the sum of the right hand side in the above equality $b_{k^*,j,t} = b_{i,j,t} = 0$ for all $i \in \{0, \ldots, k^* - 1, k^* + 1, \ldots, 2\ell - 3\}$.

For the third equation, we can also remove common factors on the both side of the equation.

$$(\sigma_{s_{k^*}} \cdot z^{2(\ell-1)}) \cdot a_{k^*,j,t} = \sum_{i=0,i\neq k^*}^{2\ell-3} (u_i \cdot \sigma_{s_i} \cdot z^{2(\ell-1)+i-k^*} \cdot (a_{i,j,t}))$$

because $i \neq k^*$ in the sum of the right hand side in the above equality $a_{k^*,j,t} = a_{i,j,t} = 0$ for all $i \in \{0, \ldots, k^* - 1, k^* + 1, \ldots, 2\ell - 1\}$. Therefore, the equality holds *iif* all in $\{u_i, a_{i,j,t}, b_{i,j,t}, a'_{j,t}, b'_{j,t}\}$ are 0.

7   Conclusion

In this paper, we presented a new searchable encryption with shiftable trapdoor (SEST) scheme for pattern matching over encrypted data. In the proposed scheme, our work reduces the ciphertext size by up to 50% of the state-of-art scheme [2] in this domain, while maintaining the same search efficiency. The search token of our scheme has a similar structure to Bkakria *et al.* [2]. This may imply that our scheme also provides anonymity, as provided in Bkakria *et al.* [2]'s scheme. The anonymity implies that a search string W is hidden even for one who has a search token for W. This is a useful property for pattern-matching. For example, in an intrusion detection system (IDS) supporting anonymous token detection, malicious patterns can be detected over the encrypted data without revealing what the matched data are. Then, IDS executes only the defined actions (e.g., terminating a connection) assigned to the anonymous token without knowing the content of the data transmitted. Therefore, it can provide better user privacy. We leave the proof of the anonymity property as future work.

References

1. Baek, J., Kim, J., Susilo, W.: Inspecting TLS anytime anywhere: a new approach to TLS interception. In: The 15th ACM Asia Conference on Computer and Communications Security, ASIA CCS 2020, Taipei, Taiwan, 5–9 October 2020, pp. 116–126. ACM (2020)
2. Bkakria, A., Cuppens, N., Cuppens, F.: Privacy-preserving pattern matching on encrypted data. In: Moriai, S., Wang, H. (eds.) ASIACRYPT 2020, Part II. LNCS, vol. 12492, pp. 191–220. Springer, Cham (2020). https://doi.org/10.1007/978-3-030-64834-3_7
3. Canard, S., Diop, A., Kheir, N., Paindavoine, M., Sabt, M.: BlindIDS: market-compliant and privacy-friendly intrusion detection system over encrypted traffic. In: ACM AsiaCCS 2017, Abu Dhabi, United Arab Emirates, 2–6 April 2017, pp. 561–574. ACM (2017)
4. Desmoulins, N., Fouque, P.-A., Onete, C., Sanders, O.: Pattern matching on encrypted streams. In: Peyrin, T., Galbraith, S. (eds.) ASIACRYPT 2018, Part I. LNCS, vol. 11272, pp. 121–148. Springer, Cham (2018). https://doi.org/10.1007/978-3-030-03326-2_5
5. Fuhr, T., Paillier, P.: Decryptable searchable encryption. In: Susilo, W., Liu, J.K., Mu, Y. (eds.) ProvSec 2007. LNCS, vol. 4784, pp. 228–236. Springer, Heidelberg (2007). https://doi.org/10.1007/978-3-540-75670-5_17
6. Guo, Y., Wang, C., Jia, X.: Enabling secure and dynamic deep packet inspection in outsourced middleboxes. In: SCCAsiaCCS 2018, Incheon, Republic of Korea, 04–08 June 2018, pp. 49–55. ACM (2018)
7. Han, J., Kim, S.M., Ha, J., Han, D.: SGX-box: enabling visibility on encrypted traffic using a secure middlebox module. In: APNet 2017, Hong Kong, China, 3–4 August 2017, pp. 99–105. ACM (2017)
8. Huang, L.-S., Rice, A., Ellingsen, E., Jackson, C.: Analyzing forged SSL certificates in the wild. In: IEEE S&P 2014, Berkeley, CA, USA, 18–21 May 2014, pp. 83–97. IEEE Computer Society (2014)

9. Kamara, S., Papamanthou, C., Roeder, T.: Dynamic searchable symmetric encryption. In: Yu, T., Danezis, G., Gligor, V.D. (eds.) ACM CCS 2012, Raleigh, NC, USA, 16–18 October 2012, pp. 965–976. ACM (2012)

10. Kim, J., Camtepe, S., Baek, J., Susilo, W., Pieprzyk, J., Nepal, S.: P2DPI: practical and privacy-preserving deep packet inspection. In: Cao, J., Au, M.H., Lin, Z., Yung, M. (eds.) ASIA CCS 2021: ACM Asia Conference on Computer and Communications Security, Virtual Event, Hong Kong, 7–11 June 2021, pp. 135–146. ACM (2021)

11. Lan, C., Sherry, J., Popa, R.A., Ratnasamy, S., Liu, Z.: Embark: securely outsourcing middleboxes to the cloud. In: Argyraki, K.J., Isaacs, R. (eds.) USENIX NSDI 2016, Santa Clara, CA, USA, 16–18 March 2016, pp. 255–273. USENIX Association (2016)

12. Naylor, D., et al.: Multi-context TLS (MCTLS): enabling secure in-network functionality in TLS. In: Uhlig, S., Maennel, O., Karp, B., Padhye, J. (eds.) Proceedings of the 2015 ACM Conference on Special Interest Group on Data Communication, SIGCOMM 2015, London, United Kingdom, 17–21 August 2015, pp. 199–212. ACM (2015)

13. Ning, J., Poh, G.S., Loh, J.-C., Chia, J., Chang, E.-C.: PrivDPI: privacy-preserving encrypted traffic inspection with reusable obfuscated rules. In: Cavallaro, L., Kinder, J., Wang, X., Katz, J. (eds.) 2019 ACMCCS 2019, London, UK, 11–15 November 2019, pp. 1657–1670. ACM (2019)

14. Sherry, J., Lan, C., Popa, R.A., Ratnasamy, S.: BlindBox: deep packet inspection over encrypted traffic. In: ACM SIGCOMM 2015, London, United Kingdom, 17–21 August 2015, pp. 213–226. ACM (2015)

15. Song, D.X., Wagner, D.A., Perrig, A.: Practical techniques for searches on encrypted data. In: IEEE S&P 2000, Berkeley, California, USA, 14–17 May 2000, pp. 44–55. IEEE Computer Society (2000)

Efficient Adaptation of TFHE for High End-to-End Throughput

Kang Hoon Lee and Ji Won Yoon[(⊠)]

School of CyberSecurity, Korea University, Seoul, Republic of Korea
{hoot55,jiwon_yoon}@korea.ac.kr

Abstract. Homomorphic Encryption (HE) allows to process over user's encrypted data. There are various HE schemes including TFHE, which offers homomorphic binary gate operation combined with bootstrapping. In most used case of TFHE's gate operations, however, they encrypted a single bit of message in a single ciphertext, resulting in low throughput when sending ciphertexts.

In this paper, we present a simple solution for the user to increase the throughput by packing multiple bits inside a single ciphertext using a ring based message space in TFHE. With the packing method, we propose a modified gate bootstrapping procedure to operate the same binary circuits on the server. Finally, without any additional public keys, we propose a new Keyswitching algorithm that we call PackKS, which enables even the server to pack multiple messages, thereby achieving high end-to-end throughput for TFHE.

Keywords: Homomorphic Encryption · TFHE · Key switching

1 Introduction

Homomorphic Encryption (HE) is a well known solution for processing user's data in an untrusted server while keeping the user's privacy. With a homomorphic encryption function E and a function f, homomorphic encryption allows to calculate $E(f(\mu))$ from the user's ciphertext $E(\mu)$ which encrypts user's data. Different from the classic encryption schemes, HE can homomorphically evaluate $E(f(\mu))$ while the ciphertext is undecrypted, which makes untrusted server to do only the computation without knowing any information about the user's data.

Despite its usefulness, HE schemes has been pointed out to be highly impractical due to its high time and space complexity. Many works has been proposed for improving efficiency for HE schemes, which includes improving the scheme

This work was supported by Institute of Information & communications Technology Planning & Evaluation (IITP) grant funded by the Korea government (MSIT) (No. 2021-0-00558, Development of national statistical analysis system using homomorphic encryption technology).

© Springer Nature Switzerland AG 2021
H. Kim (Ed.): WISA 2021, LNCS 13009, pp. 144–156, 2021.
https://doi.org/10.1007/978-3-030-89432-0_12

itself, or packing multiple messages and operate them with Single Instruction Multiple Data (SIMD) manner, etc. One of the former improvements is the Fully Homomorphic Encryption over the Torus, TFHE [7]. With its fast bootstrapping, TFHE allowed to evaluate any circuit made up of binary gates on encrypted data with high precision and exact results, taking only 13 ms per single gate.

However, many works using the gate bootstrapping operations in TFHE [13,14,18] encrypts a single bit of a message in a single ciphertext. This results in low throughput when sending messages to the server if the user has to encrypt large amount of data. Thus, we present a method for achieving high throughput while the server and the user exchanges encrypted messages, along with a packing Keyswitch method which enables the server to repack multiple messages in public, reducing the size of the total ciphertext that will be sent back to the user.

1.1 Related Works

Packing multiple messages in a single ciphertext has widely been studied. Based on the ring variant of LWE, homomorphic encryption schemes such as BFV or CKKS allowed to pack messages in a SIMD manner with vectorial arithmetic [4,12,17], achieving speedup for each element, and reducing ciphertext expansion. In TFHE, the authors proposed a method called 'vertical' and 'horizontal' packing for leveled version of TFHE, which evaluates LUT and pack them into a single ciphertext. However, apart from other homomorphic encryption schemes, the ciphertext does not support SIMD operations for TFHE.

Keyswitching also has been worked throughout various homomorphic encryption schemes. From the classic literature of Gentry's bootstrapping [10], the authors of FHEW [9] and TFHE [5,7] presented a Keyswitching method to switch back the keys that changed during refreshing. Especially, the Keyswitching in TFHE supports Keyswitching to Ring-LWE based ciphertext. Recently, Chen et al. [3] proposed a various Keyswitching methods for converting ciphertexts that can be used to switch between various HE schemes.

1.2 Our Contributions

We present a user-friendly adaptation of the fully homomorphic encryption (FHE) scheme, TFHE. First, we suggest using a ring based TRLWE encryption scheme to pack multiple messages inside a single ciphertext. Compared to the classical TLWE encryption of a bitwise message, we observe that we can save up to maximal 314.7 times of storage for packing bits in TFHE with our parameters with 127 bit of security. Corresponding to the packing method, we also suggest a modification in the gate bootstrapping operations in TFHE.

Finally, using the CMux operation in TFHE, we present a packing Keyswitch method PackKS for the server to pack multiple TLWE ciphertexts into a single TRLWE ciphertext. Compared to the Keyswitching methods presented for TFHE, our PackKS algorithm does not require additional Keyswitching Key, but reuses the Bootstrapping Key and achieves low latency for Keyswitch.

2 Background

2.1 Notation

Throughout this paper, we denote the set $\{0,1\}$ as $\mathbb{B}$, and the real torus $\mathbb{R}/\mathbb{Z}$ as $\mathbb{T}$, the set of real numbers modulo 1. Let $\left[-\frac{1}{2}, \frac{1}{2}\right)$ be the representation of $\mathbb{T}$, which is equivalent to $\mathbb{T}$ by taking modulo 1.

We use the notations $\mathbb{R}_N[X]$, $\mathbb{Z}_N[X]$ to denote $\mathbb{R}[X]/(X^N+1)$, $\mathbb{Z}[X]/(X^N+1)$, respectively. Also, the notation $\mathbb{T}_N[X]$ is used to denote $\mathbb{R}_N[X]$ modulo 1, where the coefficients are the elements of $\mathbb{T}$. We further denote the set of polynomials in $\mathbb{Z}_N[X]$ with binary coefficients as $\mathbb{B}_N[X]$.

For a set $\mathcal{S}$, we denote $x \xleftarrow{\$} \mathcal{S}$ to say that x is uniformly sampled from the set $\mathcal{S}$. Also for a distribution $\mathcal{D}$, we denote $x \leftarrow \mathcal{D}$ to say that x is sampled from $\mathcal{D}$. Also, for any ciphertext c, we use the notation $\mathsf{msg}(\mathsf{c})$ to denote the message encrypted in c. Furthermore, we denote $\mathsf{Var}(\mathsf{Err}(c)))$ to denote the variance of the noise of the ciphertext c.

2.2 TFHE

TFHE [5–7] is a fully homomorphic encryption (FHE) library based on the hardness of Learning with Errors (LWE) problem [16] and its ring variant (Ring-LWE) [15,19]. TFHE is based on FHEW [9] with faster bootstrapping method, and supports gate operations between ciphertexts. This allows to perform exact computations on encrypted messages, but brings higher latency compared to the homomorphic encryption schemes that support approximate arithmetic operations. TFHE library is available as an open source [8]. It works on 3 different ciphertext spaces, which we discuss them below.

TLWE. TLWE ciphertext is a tuple $(a, b) \in \mathbb{T}^{n+1}$. For a message $m \in \mathbb{T}$, the message is encrypted with a secret key $\mathfrak{K} \xleftarrow{\$} \mathbb{B}^n$ by $b = \langle a, \mathfrak{K} \rangle + m + e$ where $a \xleftarrow{\$} \mathbb{T}^n$. The noise e is sampled from a Gaussian distribution with mean 0 and a standard deviation σ which is decided depending on the security parameter λ. We now denote the TLWE encryption of a message m under the key $\mathfrak{K}$ as $\mathrm{TLWE}_{\mathfrak{K}}(m)$.

The decryption of a TLWE ciphertext $c = (a, b)$ is done by calculating the phase $\varphi_{\mathfrak{K}}(c) = b - \langle a, \mathfrak{K} \rangle = m + e$. The phase is then rounded to the nearest value of the message space, which is pre-defined.

TRLWE. TRLWE ciphertext is also a tuple $(A, B) \in \mathbb{T}_N[X]^{k+1}$ with secret key $\mathcal{K} \xleftarrow{\$} \mathbb{B}_N[X]^k$. TRLWE ciphertext encrypts a polynomial $m(x) \in \mathbb{T}_N[X]$ by $B = A \cdot \mathcal{K} + e(X)$ where $A \xleftarrow{\$} \mathbb{T}_N[X]^{k+1}$, and each coefficient of $e(X) \in \mathbb{T}_N[X]$ is sampled from a Gaussian distribution with mean 0 and a standard deviation σ'. Similarly, we denote the TRLWE encryption of a polynomial message $m(X)$ under the key $\mathcal{K}$ as $\mathrm{TRLWE}_{\mathcal{K}}(m(X))$.

Similar to TLWE, the decryption of TRLWE encryption $C = (A, B) \in \mathbb{T}_N[X]^{k+1}$ also starts with calculating is phase $\varphi_{\mathcal{K}}(C) = B - A \cdot \mathcal{K}$. The phase can be rounded into the nearest message space, or the authors of [7] suggests taking its expectations, which allows to work with infinite precision with continuous message space.

TRGSW. TRGSW comes from the generalization of the GSW construction [11]. Sharing the same key $\mathcal{K} \in \mathbb{B}_N[X]^k$ with the TRLWE ciphertext, TRGSW ciphertext is actually a row of TRLWE ciphertext. Apart from the aforementioned two ciphertext spaces, TRGSW encrypts a bounded integer polynomial in $\mathbb{Z}_N[X]$ with the help of the gadget decomposition with decomposition base B_g and decomposition length ℓ. We use the notation $\mathrm{TRGSW}_{\mathcal{K}}(\mu(X))$ to denote the TRGSW encryption of the integer polynomial $\mu(X) \in \mathbb{Z}_N[X]$ under the key $\mathcal{K}$.

We now describe the end-to-end procedure for evaluating a single binary gate on the server. We assume a user who wants to encrypt his or her data and send it to an untrusted server. The server evaluates the data of the user in an undecrypted state, and then sends back the result to the user.

Encryption. As the gate bootstrapping in TFHE works on binary messages, the user must first encode the message into binary form. For example, if the user wants to encrypt a natural number 6, the message is encoded into '$110_{(2)}$'. Each bit is then encoded into a discrete message space with $\{0, 1\} \mapsto \{-\frac{1}{8}, \frac{1}{8}\} \subset \mathbb{T}$. Each torus elements are then encrypted with the TLWE encryption aforementioned. Then the user's ciphertext and the public key are sent to the server for evaluation.

Binary Gate Evaluation. The additive homomorphism of TLWE enables us to evaluate gate operations with simple arithmetic. For example, the AND gate in TFHE is done by simply evaluating:

$$\mathsf{BootsAND}(\mathsf{ca}, \mathsf{cb}) = \mathsf{Bootstrap}\left(\left(0, -\frac{1}{8}\right) + \mathsf{ca} + \mathsf{cb}\right).$$

Other gate operations are also supported with similar operations, such as NAND, OR, etc. Operations before the Bootstrap makes the message space to change, and should be refreshed into a fresh ciphertext, which is called bootstrapping.

Bootstrapping. It is easy to observe that the message after the gate operation is bigger than 0 if the resulting bit is 1, and smaller than 0 if not. This allows to reconstruct a fresh encryption of the resulting bit via a procedure called bootstrapping. The main idea of bootstrapping is to homomorphically decrypt the ciphertext under another key, and switch it back to its original key. TFHE's gate bootstrapping algorithm allows to construct a fresh ciphertext with fixed variance of error, and allows to further operate with the refreshed ciphertext.

Decryption. After the operations, the resulting ciphertexts are sent back to the user. The user can decrypt those with the user's secret key. From the encoding procedure during the encryption phase, the user must decode the phase $\varphi_{\bar{\mathfrak{K}}}(c)$ into bitwise representation, and then turn it into its decimal representation.

3 Packing Messages in TRLWE Ciphertext

In this section, we will present a simple method to pack multiple messages in a single ciphertext using the TRLWE scheme. Due to the packing, we can't directly apply the classical gate bootstrapping, and thus we also present the method on how to operate with TRLWE-packed ciphertexts.

Throughout the paper, we use the notation $\mathfrak{K} \in \mathbb{B}^n$ to denote the TLWE key, and $\mathcal{K} \in \mathbb{B}_N[X]^k$ to denote the TRLWE and the TRGSW key. Also, we use an upper bar $\bar{\mathcal{K}} \in \mathbb{B}^{kN}$ to denote the TLWE-representation of the TRLWE key, which has the same sequence of coefficients.

3.1 Message Packing

Recall that the TLWE encryption allows to encrypt a single bit in a single TLWE ciphertext. This requires huge capacity for storing and sending ciphertexts. Thus, we employ the TRLWE encryption scheme to efficiently pack multiple messages. As TRLWE encryption scheme encrypts a polynomial in $\mathbb{T}_N[X]$, it only needs to encode each bit and pack them as the coefficients of the message polynomial. Furthermore, if the number of bits b_m to represent a single message is decided in advance, a single TRLWE ciphertext can pack up to $\lfloor \frac{N}{b_m} \rfloor$ messages. Compared to the TLWE encryption, using the packing method of TRLWE ciphertext can save up to $\frac{(n+1)p}{(k+1)N}$ times of capacity if the user needs to encrypt p bits with $p < N$. Moreover, if p is a multiple of N, we can save up to maximal $\frac{n+1}{k+1}$ times of storage. Note that the TRLWE encryption scheme does not support Single Instruction Multiple Data (SIMD) operations, like in other FHE schemes [4,17].

3.2 Modified Bootstrapping for Packed Ciphertexts

As the gate bootstrapping algorithm in TFHE is to evaluate a single binary gate for 2 TLWE ciphertexts under the key $\mathfrak{K}$ and to bootstrap it, we cannot directly adapt the gate bootstrapping procedure to our packed ciphertext. However, with the SampleExtract algorithm in TFHE and the modified bootstrapping presented in [2], we can simply bring out a modified gate bootstrapping method adequate for the packed TRLWE message.

The first building block comes from the SampleExtract algorithm, which enables to extract TLWE encryption from TRLWE encryption. From a TRLWE encryption $C = (A, B) \in \mathrm{TRLWE}_{\mathcal{K}}(\mu(X))$ with $\mu(X) = \mu_0 + \mu_1 X + \cdots + \mu_{N-1}X^{N-1}$ and a position $p \in [0, N-1]$, the $\mathrm{SampleExtract}_p(C) = (A_{(1,p)}, \cdots, A_{(k,p)}, B_p) \in \mathbb{T}^{kN+1}$ with $A_{(i,p)} = (A_{i,p}, A_{i,p-1}, \cdots, A_{p-N+1})$ for $i \in [1, k]$ with N-antiperiodic indices. It is easy to observe that the resulting sequence of $\mathsf{SampleExtract}_p(C)$ is a TLWE encryption of the p-th coefficient of $\mu(X)$ under the key $\bar{\mathcal{K}} \in \mathbb{B}^{kN}$.

The question for the second building block is on how to operate with extracted ciphertext. The answer is quite simple, as we can modify the gate bootstrapping procedure. The bootstrapping in TFHE consists of three consecutive algorithms for input TLWE ciphertext $c \in \mathsf{TLWE}_{\mathfrak{K}}(m)$:

$$\mathsf{Bootstrap}(c) = \mathsf{KeySwitch}_{\bar{\mathcal{K}} \to \mathfrak{K}} \circ \mathsf{SampleExtract}_0 \circ \mathsf{BlindRotate}_{\mathfrak{K} \to \mathcal{K}}(c)$$

where the subscript in the $\mathsf{KeySwitch}$ and the $\mathsf{BlindRotate}$ implies that the type of key changes when the algorithm is executed. Bourse et al. [2] presented that we can move around the $\mathsf{KeySwitch}$ around the bootstrapping procedure, giving us:

$$\mathsf{ModBootstrap}(C) = \mathsf{SampleExtract}_0 \circ \mathsf{BlindRotate}_{\mathfrak{K} \to \mathcal{K}} \circ \mathsf{KeySwitch}_{\bar{\mathcal{K}} \to \mathfrak{K}}(C)$$

for a TLWE encryption C under the key $\bar{\mathcal{K}}$. The main difference between these two bootstrapping methods is the type of the secret key where the input TLWE ciphertext is encrypted.

3.3 Gate Bootstrapping for Packed Ciphertexts

Mixing up two aforementioned building blocks altogether, we now describe the gate bootstrapping method with packed TRLWE ciphertext. We start with a simple homomorphic AND gate. We assume that two TLWE ciphertexts $c_1, c_2 \in \mathsf{TLWE}_{\bar{\mathcal{K}}}\left(\left\{-\frac{1}{8}, \frac{1}{8}\right\}\right)$ has been extracted from the packed TRLWE ciphertext. The homomorphic AND gate for these two ciphertexts can be written in:

$$\mathsf{HomAND}\,(c_1, c_2) = \mathsf{ModBootstrap}\left(\left(0, -\frac{1}{8}\right) + c_1 + c_2\right) \in \mathsf{TLWE}_{\bar{\mathcal{K}}}\left(\left\{-\frac{1}{8}, \frac{1}{8}\right\}\right).$$

Note that other binary gates can be written in similar way. With these gate operations, we can simply implement the circuits made with original TFHE gate bootstrapping methods with packed ciphertexts.

4 Packing TLWEs to TRLWE

By using the TRLWE packing method, we were able to increase the throughput when the user sends his or her ciphertext and the public key to the server by reducing the size of the ciphertext when multiple bits are encrypted. However, after homomorphic gate operations are performed on the server, the output comes out as TLWE encryption. Then, the server will have to return multiple TLWE ciphertexts to the user. This is highly costly, and we propose a method that allows a public server to pack multiple TLWE ciphertexts into a single TRLWE ciphertext. We first observe the external product and the CMux gate operation in TFHE.

4.1   Keyswitch Revisited

The authors of TFHE proposed a TLWE-to-TRLWE Keyswitching method that can homomorphically evaluate public morphism f, which is known as the TLWE-to-TRLWE public functional Key Switching.

Algorithm 1: TLWE-to-TRLWE public function Keyswitch [3, 8]

Input: p TLWE ciphertexts $\underline{c}^{(z)} = (\underline{a}^{(z)}, \underline{b}^{(z)}) \in \text{TLWE}_{\mathfrak{K}}(\mu_z)$, $z \in [1, p]$
Input: A public R-Lipschitz morphism $f : \mathbb{T}^p \to \mathbb{T}_N[X]$
Input: TRLWE Keyswitch Key $\text{KS}_{i,j} \in \text{TRLWE}_{\mathcal{K}}(\mathfrak{K}_i / B_{\text{KS}}^j)$ for
$\quad i \in [1, n], j \in [1, \ell_{\text{KS}}]$
Output: A TRLWE ciphertext $C = \text{TRLWE}_{\mathcal{K}}(f(\mu_1, \cdots, \mu_p))$

1 **for** $i \in [1, n]$ **do**
2 $\quad$ Let $a_i = f(\underline{a}^{(1)}, \cdots, \underline{a}^{(p)})$ Let $\tilde{a}_i$ be the closest multiple of $\frac{1}{B_{\text{KS}}^{\ell_{\text{KS}}}}$ to a_i.
3 $\quad$ Decompose each $\tilde{a}_i = \sum_{j=1}^{\ell_{\text{KS}}} \tilde{a}_{i,j} \cdot B_{\text{KS}}^{-j}$ where $\tilde{a}_{i,j} \in \mathbb{Z}_N[X]$ with coefficients
$\quad$ in $\{0, 1, \cdots, B_{\text{KS}} - 1\}$
4 **end**
5 **return** $(0, f(\underline{b}^{(1)}, \cdots, \underline{b}^{(p)})) - \sum_{i=1}^{n} \sum_{j=1}^{\ell_{\text{KS}}} \tilde{a}_{i,j} \times \text{KS}_{i,j}$

It is known that the TLWE-to-TRLWE Keyswitch algorithm outputs a TRLWE ciphertext $C \in \text{TRLWE}_{\mathcal{K}}(f(\mu_1, \cdots, \mu_p))$ with

$$\text{Var}(\text{Err}(C)) \leq R^2 \text{Var}(\text{Err}(\underline{c})) + n\ell_{\text{KS}} N V_{\text{KS}} + nN B_{\text{KS}}^{-2(\ell_{\text{KS}}+1)}$$

where V_{KS} is the variance of the error of the keyswitch key, $\text{KS}_{i,j}$. Note that in our case, we have two options to use the TLWE-to-TRLWE public Keyswitch. As the modified gate bootstrapping gives a TLWE encryption under the key $\bar{\mathcal{K}}$, we first pre-keyswitch it into a TLWE encryption of the key $\mathfrak{K}$, where the Keyswitching Key is already made for gate operations. Then with additional TRLWE Keyswitch Key, we can operate the TLWE-to-TRLWE Keyswitch algorithm. The second option is to make a TRLWE Keyswitch key that encrypts the decomposition of $\bar{\mathcal{K}}_i$ under the TRLWE key $\mathcal{K}$. Considering that $\bar{\mathcal{K}}$ is actually a TLWE representation of the key $\mathcal{K}$, the second option needs the assumption for circular security. As both options all need additional public keys, we propose a simple method to pack multiple messages without additional public keys.

4.2   CMux Gate

We first start with the external product $\boxdot$ between the TRGSW and the TRLWE ciphertext.

$$\boxdot : \text{TRGSW} \times \text{TRLWE} \to \text{TRLWE}$$

The external product allows to homomorphically multiply the message of the TRGSW ciphertext and the TRLWE ciphertext. That is, for a TRGSW encryption $\mathbf{C_G}$ of $\mu_G \in \mathbb{Z}_N[X]$ and a TRLWE encryption C_L of $\mu_L \in \mathbb{T}_N[X]$, the external product gives a TRLWE encryption of $\mu_G \cdot \mu_L$ with slightly increased noise variance.

The CMux gate is made on top of the external product, which enables to homomorphically control the selection based on the message of the input TRGSW ciphertext. CMux gate takes one TRGSW ciphertext $\mathbf{C_G}$ which message is restricted to $\{0,1\}$, and two TRLWE ciphertexts $d_0 \in \text{TRLWE}_{\mathcal{K}}(\mu_0)$ and $d_1 \in \text{TRLWE}_{\mathcal{K}}(\mu_1)$. Then the CMux gate outputs a TRLWE ciphertext encryption of μ_0 or μ_1 depending on the value of $\text{msg}(\mathbf{C_G})$:

$$\text{CMux}\,(\mathbf{C_G}, d_1, d_0) = \mathbf{C_G} \boxdot (d_1 - d_0) + d_0$$

with $\text{msg}(\text{CMux}(\mathbf{C_G}, d_1, d_0)) = \text{msg}(\mathbf{C_G})?\mu_1 : \mu_0$. The variance of error of the output TRLWE ciphertext is given as:

$$\text{Var}(\text{Err}(\text{CMux}(\mathbf{C_G}, d_1, d_0))) \leq \max(\text{Var}(\text{Err}(d_0)), \text{Var}(\text{Err}(d_1))) + V_{\text{Ext}}$$

where $\beta = B_g/2$, $\epsilon = \frac{1}{2B_g^\ell}$, and $V_{\text{Ext}} = (k+1)\ell N\beta^2\text{Var}(\text{Err}(\mathbf{C_G})) + (kN+1)\epsilon^2$, and ℓ is the decomposition length of the TRGSW ciphertext.

4.3   Packing TLWEs to TRLWE with Bootstrapping Key

With the controlled selection from the CMux gate, we can think of a method to simultaneously Keyswitch multiple TLWEs and pack them into a TRLWE ciphertext. We start from vertically packing p TLWE ciphertexts $c^{(z)} = \left(a^{(z)}, b^{(z)}\right) \in \text{TLWE}_{\mathcal{R}}(\mu_z)$ into $n+1$ torus polynomials by $b(X) = b^{(1)} + b^{(2)}X + \cdots + b^{(p)}X^{p-1}$ and $a_i(X) = a_i^{(1)} + \cdots + a_i^{(p)}X^{p-1}$. It only leaves to homomorphically calculate $b(X) - \sum_{i=1}^n \mathcal{R}_i \cdot a_i(X)$ using the CMux gate. Algorithm 2 describes our Keyswitching procedure.

Algorithm 2: TLWE-to-TRLWE PackKS with Bootstrapping Key

   Input: p TLWE ciphertexts $c^{(z)} = (a^{(z)}, b^{(z)}) \in \text{TLWE}_{\mathcal{R}}(\mu_z)$, $z \in [1,p]$
   Input: Bootstrapping Key $\text{BK}_i \in \text{TRGSW}_{\mathcal{K}}(\mathcal{R}_i)$ for $i \in [1,n]$
   Output: A TRLWE ciphertext $C = \text{TRLWE}_{\mathcal{K}}(\mu_1 + \cdots + \mu_p X^{p-1})$
1 $\text{ACC} \leftarrow (0, b(X) = b^{(1)} + b^{(2)}X + \cdots + b^{(p)}X^{p-1}) \in \text{TRLWE}_{\mathcal{K}}(b(X))$
2 **for** $i \in [1,n]$ **do**
3   Let $a_i(X) = a_i^{(1)} + \cdots + a_i^{(p)}X^{p-1}$
4 $\text{ACC} \leftarrow \text{CMux}(\text{BK}_i, \text{ACC} - a_i(X), \text{ACC})$
5 **end**
6 **return** ACC

With PackKS, the server can pack p TLWE ciphertexts in TRLWE ciphertext without additional keyswitch keys, as we can easily verify that the final accumulator ACC is a TRLWE encryption of $b(X) - \sum_{i=1}^{n} \mathfrak{K}_i \cdot a_i(X)$. Finally, we have:

$$\text{Var}(\text{Err}(\text{ACC})) \leq n(k+1)\ell N \beta^2 \text{Var}(\text{Err}(\text{BK})) + n(1+kN)\epsilon^2 + \max(\text{Var}(\text{Err}(c^{(z)}))).$$

since the PackKS is made up of n-CMux operations. Note that PackKS also takes the TLWE ciphertext under the key $\mathfrak{K}$. Thus to adapt in our case where TLWE ciphertexts are encrypted under the key $\bar{\mathcal{K}}$, we also have to pre-Keyswitch our TLWE encryptions into TLWE encryption under the key $\mathfrak{K}$, which is available using the Keyswitch procedure in gate bootstrapping. Likewise, by assuming circular security, we can pack TLWE ciphertexts directly without the pre-Keyswitch, but will need to produce additional TRGSW encryptions of $\bar{\mathcal{K}}_i$'s under the key $\mathcal{K}$, which is costly.

5   Experimental Results

In this section, we implement our proposed approach with and show experimental results. We used the computer equipped with Intel(R) i7-8700 CPU @ 3.20 GHz, 32 GB RAM, and Ubuntu 18.04 LTS (64-bit) operating system. We used the TFHE library [8] which is written in C++ language, and we did not use any parallel computing or GPU implementation. Note that the torus $\mathbb{T}$ is mapped into $\mathbb{Z}_{2^{32}}$ integer space, which we will later use to estimate the size of each ciphertext.

5.1   TFHE Parameters

We first propose the parameters used in our experiment in Table 1. The parameters assures 127-bit of security according to the lwe estimator [1]. Note that the Keyswitch Key in TFHE implementation consists of $k \cdot N \cdot \ell_{\text{KS}} \cdot B_{\text{KS}}$ TLWE samples, which takes up to 82.7 MB of storage.

Table 1. TFHE parameters and corresponding message sizes.

Name	TLWE		TRLWE			TRGSW					Bootstrap Key	KS Key	
	n	σ_{TLWE}	N	k	σ_{TRLWE}	N	k	B_g	ℓ	σ_{TRGSW}		B_{KS}	ℓ_{KS}
Value	630	2^{-15}	1024	1	2^{-25}	1024	1	$2^7 = 128$	3	2^{-25}	n TRGSWs	$2^2 = 4$	8
Size	2.52 kB		8.2 kB			43.2 kB					27.2 MB	82.7 MB	

5.2   Message Packing and Gate Operations on Public Server

We implemented the gate operations with the modified bootstrapping, and tested the efficiency of our TRLWE packing. We assumed the case in which the user encrypts $N = 1024$ bits and sending it to public server. Encrypting each bits into a single TLWE ciphertext requires $2.52 \cdot N\,\text{kB} \approx 2.58\,\text{MB}$. However, if we use the TRLWE encryption scheme instead, it only requires $8.2\,\text{kB}$, saving up to $\frac{n}{2} \approx 314.7$ times of resources.

Next, we tested the gate operations mixed up with the modified bootstrapping. We implemented several gate operations such has HomAND, HomOR, etc. The latency for a single modified gate bootstrapping is same as the original gate bootstrapping, as the total computation needed is exactly same as before. Thus, every single binary gate operations took $14.5\,\text{ms}$.

5.3 Comparison of Keyswitch Methods

We finally evaluate our Keyswitch method, PackKS, and compare with the TLWE-to-TRLWE Keyswitch algorithm from TFHE. We first assume the situation of packing p TLWE ciphertexts with $p \in [1, N]$, encrypted under the key $\bar{\mathcal{K}} \in \mathbb{B}^N$ inside the TRLWE encryption under the key $\mathcal{K}$. We describe 4 different Keyswitching scenarios for packing these ciphertexts:

- **Case I.** p-TLWE$_{\bar{\mathcal{K}}}$'s are first Keyswitched into p-TLWE$_{\mathfrak{K}}$'s, and PackKS is evaluated.
- **Case II.** p-TLWE$_{\bar{\mathcal{K}}}$'s are first Keyswitched into p-TLWE$_{\mathfrak{K}}$'s, and TLWE-to-TRLWE Keyswitch (Alg. 1) is evaluated with additional TRLWE Keyswitch Key, $\mathsf{KS}_{i,j}^{\mathfrak{K} \to \mathcal{K}} \in \text{TRLWE}_{\mathcal{K}}(\mathfrak{K}_i / B_{\mathsf{KS}}^j)$ with $i \in [1, n]$ and $j \in [1, \ell_{\mathsf{KS}}]$.
- **Case III.** With the assumption of circular security, PackKS is directly evaluated on p- TLWE$_{\bar{\mathcal{K}}}$'s with additional TRGSW Keyswitch Key (which can also be viewed as a circular Bootstrapping Key), $\mathsf{BK}_i^{\bar{\mathcal{K}} \to \mathcal{K}} \in \text{TRGSW}_{\mathcal{K}}(\bar{\mathcal{K}}_i)$ with $i \in [1, N]$.
- **Case IV.** With the assumption of circular security, TLWE-to-TRLWE Keyswitch (Alg. 1) is directly evaluated with additional TRLWE Keyswitch Key, $\mathsf{KS}_{i,j}^{\bar{\mathcal{K}} \to \mathcal{K}} \in \text{TRLWE}_{\mathcal{K}}(\bar{\mathcal{K}}_i / B_{\mathsf{KS}}^j)$ with $i \in [1, N]$ and $j \in [1, \ell_{\mathsf{KS}}]$.

With these 4 cases, we measured the latency and the additional storage needed for the Keyswitch Key for 4 different Keyswitching scenarios for various $p \in [1, N]$. Also, we now use the notation of RingKS to denote the TLWE-to-TRLWE Keyswitch. The results are presented in Table 2 and Fig. 1.

Table 2. Comparison of 4 Keyswitch scenarios with $p = 1024$. **Case III** and **IV** needs assumption for circular security.

	Case I	Case II	Case III	Case IV
Operations	p-KS + 1-PackKS	p-KS + 1-RingKS	1-PackKS$_{\bar{\mathcal{K}} \to \mathcal{K}}$	1-RingKS$_{\bar{\mathcal{K}} \to \mathcal{K}}$
Additional Storage	0	$n \cdot \ell_{\mathsf{KS}}$ TRLWE	N TRGSW	$N \cdot \ell_{\mathsf{KS}}$ TRLWE
	$+0\,\text{MB}$	$+41.32\,\text{MB}$	$+44.23\,\text{MB}$	$+67.17\,\text{MB}$
Latency (Amortized) $p = 1024$	$964.224\,\text{ms}$ ($0.94\,\text{ms}$)	$1010.37\,\text{ms}$ ($0.99\,\text{ms}$)	$27.264\,\text{ms}$ ($0.03\,\text{ms}$)	$111.872\,\text{ms}$ ($0.11\,\text{ms}$)

The total latency for $p = 1024$ and the amortized latency is presented in the third row of Table 2. For each $p \in [1, N]$, the (amortized) latency is presented in Fig. 1. Due to the p pre-Keyswitch operations in **Case I** and **II**, the latency increases with the number of pre-Keyswitch operations. From these 4 cases, we can conclude that using the PackKS is much faster than the original RingKS.

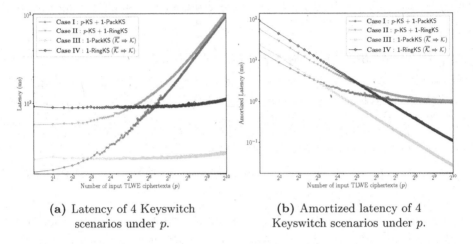

(a) Latency of 4 Keyswitch scenarios under p.

(b) Amortized latency of 4 Keyswitch scenarios under p.

Fig. 1. Comparison of latency (left) and amortized latency (right) of 4 Keyswitch scenarios. The y coordinate represents the latency in milliseconds (in logscale of base 10), and the x coordinate represents the number $p \in [1, 2^{10} = 1024]$ of TLWE ciphertexts to be Keyswitched (in logscale of base 2).

6   Conclusion

In this paper, we presented a method for achieving high end-to-end throughput in the usage of TFHE. We provided a efficient packing method for the user for reducing the size of the ciphertext using the TRLWE encryption of TFHE. Also, we suggested a modified gate bootstrapping operation which is adequate for packed ciphertext.

Finally, we presented a new Keyswitch method called PackKS, which does not require any additional public keys from the user, with better latency compared to the original TLWE-to-TRLWE Keyswitch in TFHE.

References

1. Albrecht, M.R., et al.: Estimate all the {LWE, NTRU} schemes! In: Catalano, D., De Prisco, R. (eds.) SCN 2018. LNCS, vol. 11035, pp. 351–367. Springer, Cham (2018). https://doi.org/10.1007/978-3-319-98113-0_19

2. Bourse, F., Minelli, M., Minihold, M., Paillier, P.: Fast homomorphic evaluation of deep discretized neural networks. In: Shacham, H., Boldyreva, A. (eds.) CRYPTO 2018. LNCS, vol. 10993, pp. 483–512. Springer, Cham (2018). https://doi.org/10.1007/978-3-319-96878-0_17

3. Chen, H., Dai, W., Kim, M., Song, Y.: Efficient homomorphic conversion between (ring) LWE ciphertexts. In: Sako, K., Tippenhauer, N.O. (eds.) ACNS 2021. LNCS, vol. 12726, pp. 460–479. Springer, Cham (2021). https://doi.org/10.1007/978-3-030-78372-3_18

4. Cheon, J.H., Kim, A., Kim, M., Song, Y.: Homomorphic encryption for arithmetic of approximate numbers. In: Takagi, T., Peyrin, T. (eds.) ASIACRYPT 2017. LNCS, vol. 10624, pp. 409–437. Springer, Cham (2017). https://doi.org/10.1007/978-3-319-70694-8_15

5. Chillotti, I., Gama, N., Georgieva, M., Izabachène, M.: Faster fully homomorphic encryption: bootstrapping in less than 0.1 seconds. In: Cheon, J.H., Takagi, T. (eds.) ASIACRYPT 2016. LNCS, vol. 10031, pp. 3–33. Springer, Heidelberg (2016). https://doi.org/10.1007/978-3-662-53887-6_1

6. Chillotti, I., Gama, N., Georgieva, M., Izabachène, M.: Faster packed homomorphic operations and efficient circuit bootstrapping for TFHE. In: Takagi, T., Peyrin, T. (eds.) ASIACRYPT 2017. LNCS, vol. 10624, pp. 377–408. Springer, Cham (2017). https://doi.org/10.1007/978-3-319-70694-8_14

7. Chillotti, I., Gama, N., Georgieva, M., Izabachène, M.: TFHE: fast fully homomorphic encryption over the torus. J. Cryptol. **33**(1), 34–91 (2020)

8. Chillotti, I., Gama, N., Georgieva, M., Izabachène, M.: TFHE: fast fully homomorphic encryption library, August 2016. https://tfhe.github.io/tfhe/

9. Ducas, L., Micciancio, D.: FHEW: bootstrapping homomorphic encryption in less than a second. In: Oswald, E., Fischlin, M. (eds.) EUROCRYPT 2015. LNCS, vol. 9056, pp. 617–640. Springer, Heidelberg (2015). https://doi.org/10.1007/978-3-662-46800-5_24

10. Gentry, C.: Fully homomorphic encryption using ideal lattices. In: Proceedings of the Forty-First Annual ACM Symposium on Theory of Computing, pp. 169–178 (2009)

11. Gentry, C., Sahai, A., Waters, B.: Homomorphic encryption from learning with errors: conceptually-simpler, asymptotically-faster, attribute-based. In: Canetti, R., Garay, J.A. (eds.) CRYPTO 2013. LNCS, vol. 8042, pp. 75–92. Springer, Heidelberg (2013). https://doi.org/10.1007/978-3-642-40041-4_5

12. Gilad-Bachrach, R., Dowlin, N., Laine, K., Lauter, K., Naehrig, M., Wernsing, J.: CryptoNets: applying neural networks to encrypted data with high throughput and accuracy. In: International Conference on Machine Learning, pp. 201–210. PMLR (2016)

13. Hong, M.Y., Yoo, J.S., Yoon, J.W.: Homomorphic model selection for data analysis in an encrypted domain. Appl. Sci. **10**(18), 6174 (2020)

14. Lou, Q., Feng, B., Fox, G.C., Jiang, L.: Glyph: fast and accurately training deep neural networks on encrypted data. arXiv preprint arXiv:1911.07101 (2019)

15. Lyubashevsky, V., Peikert, C., Regev, O.: On ideal lattices and learning with errors over rings. In: Gilbert, H. (ed.) EUROCRYPT 2010. LNCS, vol. 6110, pp. 1–23. Springer, Heidelberg (2010). https://doi.org/10.1007/978-3-642-13190-5_1

16. Regev, O.: On lattices, learning with errors, random linear codes, and cryptography. J. ACM (JACM) **56**(6), 1–40 (2009)

17. Smart, N.P., Vercauteren, F.: Fully homomorphic SIMD operations. Des. Codes Crypt. **71**(1), 57–81 (2014)

18. Song, B.K., Yoo, J.S., Hong, M., Yoon, J.W.: A bitwise design and implementation for privacy-preserving data mining: from atomic operations to advanced algorithms. Secur. Commun. Netw. **2019** (2019)
19. Stehlé, D., Steinfeld, R., Tanaka, K., Xagawa, K.: Efficient public key encryption based on ideal lattices. In: Matsui, M. (ed.) ASIACRYPT 2009. LNCS, vol. 5912, pp. 617–635. Springer, Heidelberg (2009). https://doi.org/10.1007/978-3-642-10366-7_36

AnyTRNG: Generic, High-Throughput, Low-Area True Random Number Generator Based on Synchronous Edge Sampling

Asep Muhamad Awaludin[ID], Derry Pratama[ID], and Howon Kim[✉][ID]

Pusan National Unviersity, Busan, South Korea
{asep.muhamad11,derry,howonkim}@pusan.ac.kr
http://infosec.pusan.ac.kr

Abstract. In this paper, we present a generic, high-throughput, and low-area true random number generator (TRNG) architecture based on synchronous edge sampling. Our approach exploits the entropy source from the jitter introduced by the clock generator with high precision sampling. The substantial gain in throughput is mainly contributed by the novel idea of using a synchronous tapped delay, ensuring the sampling is performed precisely on the signal edge. Furthermore, the jitter source can be utilized from any clock source, making our architecture generic and compatible with cloud-based field-programmable gate array (FPGA), which prohibits combinatorial loops circuits conventionally used to build a digital oscillator. We evaluate our design by implementing it on the Xilinx Artix-7 FPGA, which yields a throughput of 100 Mbps and requires only four look-up tables (LUTs) and seven flip-flops (FFs). Lastly, our proposed architecture, namely the AnyTRNG, is further validated using the NIST 800-90B entropy assessment, as well as NIST 800-22 statistical test and Dieharder, which achieves an approximate min-entropy of 0.9996 per bit.

Keywords: True random number generators · PLL · Jitter · Entropy · FPGA

1 Introduction

True Random Number Generator (TRNG) plays a crucial role in many cryptographic and security protocols. The property of unpredictability and irreproducibility of TRNG output becomes the root of security for many algorithms such

This work was supported by Institute of Information & Communications Technology Planning & Evaluation (IITP) grant funded by the Korea government (MSIT) (No. 2019-0-00097, Development of Security Chip and Real Time Control Protocol Security Technology for Smart Factory Network Infrastructure, 50%).

This work was supported by Institute of Information & Communications Technology Planning & Evaluation (IITP) grant funded by the Korea government (MSIT) (2019-0-01343, Regional strategic industry convergence security core talent training business).

H. Kim (Ed.): WISA 2021, LNCS 13009, pp. 157–168, 2021.
https://doi.org/10.1007/978-3-030-89432-0_13

as generating seed for the key generation, which requires the randomness from high entropy source [9], the random key material for one-time pad (OTP) [4], randomizing the projective blinding on ECC implementation [2], digital signature [26], and masking [1]. In the case of OTP, it strictly imposes to use the true random source with high entropy to provide perfect secrecy, where the resulting ciphertext will be impossible to break [22]. Thus, based on the information-theoretic, it is insufficient to use a pseudorandom number generator (PRNG), which can be obtained via computational methods, for providing perfect secrecy.

The randomness of TRNG can be acquired from physical phenomena such as thermal noise [5], supply voltage noise [19], clock jitter [14,17,25], metastability [18,20,23], etc. However, those physical phenomena are not easily exploited on programmable hardware since analog parameters (i.e., thermal noise and supply voltage noise) require special hardware to measure the noise. On the other hand, FPGA-based security application has been increasingly adopted, including the adoption of cloud-based FPGA and System of Chip (SoC). Additionally, more design restrictions appear on cloud-based FPGA, such as the prohibition of using combinatorial loops circuit in AWS EC2 F1, which is conventionally used to build TRNG based on Ring Oscillator (RO). The randomness of the output TRNG is typically assessed using statistical tests such as NIST [3,21] and DieHarder [6].

Several TRNG implementations on FPGA has been proposed in the literature. In 2015, Rozic et al. [17] proposed a high-throughput jitter-based TRNG that is generated from a free-running n-stage oscillator extracted with tapped delay lines. Following the similar idea with additional improvement on the compactness, Yang et al. [25] proposed ES-TRNG, which exploits timing jitter using edge sampling. They employ a high-frequency sampling rate based on a Ring Oscillator with tapped delay chain to capture the jitter, where a random output is generated when the sampling signal hits the region around the edge. Another RO-based TRNG is also presented by [14] by utilizing Programmable Delay Lines (PDLs) to generate a large variety of the oscillations while introducing jitter with high entropy. A self-timed Ring TRNG is also introduced by [7].

Other approaches that exploit circuit metastability also presented by [18,20, 23]. In particular, authors in [18] use a collection of SR latches as an entropy source, hashed using XOR gate resulting one bit output. To make SR latch in a metastable state, they provide the same input logic levels to S and R simultaneously.

However, the proposed TRNGs [14,17,18,20,23,25] are infeasible to be implemented on cloud-based FPGA due to ring oscillator usage and circuit violations. Recently, Li et al. [12] proposed cloud-based TRNG by using a time-to-digital converter (TDC) and a controllable delay line to extract the clock jitter without employing any digital oscillator.

Our Contribution: We proposed a generic, high-throughput, low-area TRNG by extracting the clock jitter using synchronous edge sampling called AnyTRNG. Our main idea is based on the fact that only the clock edge, which contains a jitter, has high entropy. Therefore, we focus on sampling techniques around the clock edge. We adopt a similar approach by [25] that uses tapped delay to extract a jitter. Nonetheless, instead of performing repetitive sampling with two asynchronous free-running oscillators to find the edge, we use a fixed and synchronized clock signal for both entropy source and extractor. As a result, higher throughput can be achieved while preserving the compactness property. Furthermore, AnyTRNG can be utilized from two independent input clocks, including the clock generated by clocking wizard on modern FPGA, making it feasible to be adopted in cloud-based FPGA. Note that although the input clock is deterministic, the jitter remains to exist.

The remainder of this paper is organized as follows. We provide the detail of AnyTRNG architecture in Sect. 2 and present the hardware implementation result and the discussions regarding its comparison to the existing methods in Sect. 3. Lastly, Sect. 4 concludes the paper.

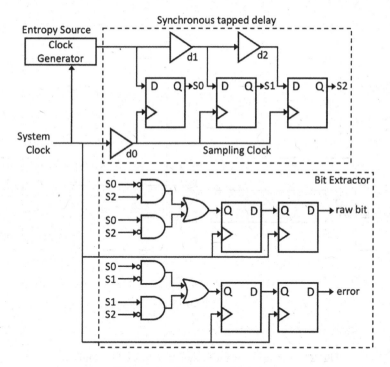

Fig. 1. AnyTRNG architecture

2   AnyTRNG Architecture

This section presents the architecture of AnyTRNG. It is constructed based on two synchronous input clocks as jitter source and extractor, and tapped delay as high precision edge sampling to assist jitter extraction. Selecting the synchronous input is considered to ensure that only the high-entropy bits around the clock edge are captured all the time with high throughput as opposed to the proposed technique by [25] which uses repetitive sampling to get a high-precision region. Moreover, the jitter source in our architecture can be utilized from any clock source, making our architecture generic and can be used even in the cloud-based FPGA with has design restrictions.

The architecture of AnyTRNG is shown in Fig. 1. The system clock signal is used as a reference to generate another clock signal, which later is utilized as an entropy source. We assume that the generated clock signal is phase-locked, aligned, and has a low jitter noise correlation with the reference clock. The jitter source is propagated through a tapped delay, resulting in shifted phase signal. These signals are later encoded at the bit extractor module.

2.1   Synchronous Edge Sampling

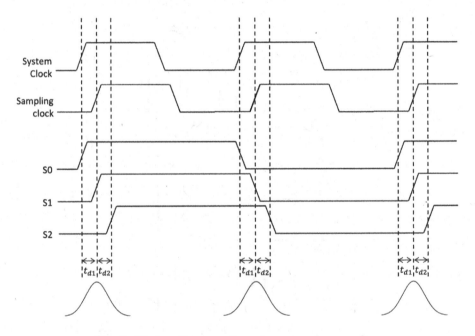

Fig. 2. Timing diagram of synchronous edge sampling

Two stages tapped delay with three FFs is utilized as a high precision sampler as shown in the top part of Fig. 1. The propagated delay are controlled with parameters t_{d1} and t_{d2}. Ideally, the amount of t_{d1} and t_{d2} have to be equal or even close. Note that the parameters t_{d1} and t_{d2} are the net delay after performing placement. Therefore, the proper placement has to be carried out carefully during implementation. The FFs are driven by the extractor signal, which also has one

Table 1. Phase encoding

Output S[2:0]	Raw bit	Error
110	1	0
001		
100	0	0
011		
111	X	1
000		
101		
010		

stage delay. The applied delay on the extractor signal aims to put the signal at the center of a Gaussian distribution. We define the frequency of the extractor signal to be half-period of the entropy source signal to maximize the entropy while preserving the high throughput. Accordingly, a phase alignment of those signals to sampling precisely at the clock edge is shown in Fig. 2. The signal $S0$, $S1$, and $S2$ are the output signal of tapped delay for 0-stage, 1-stage, and 2-stage, respectively. These three positions are expected to form a Gaussian distribution.

Note that this technique works only if the jitter correlation between entropy source and extractor must be zero or minimal. In other words, the clock generator has to reduce the jitter inherent in a reference clock while introduces owns jitter in its internal mechanism. This feature is available in modern FGPA such as Xilinx 7-series FGPA [24].

2.2 Bit Extractor with Phase Encoding

A sample is taken in three positions around the edge, resulting in three bits output (i.e., $S0$, $S1$, and $S2$). These outputs then encoded into single bit random output as shown in the bottom part of Fig. 1. We adopt the encoding technique that was introduced by [25] with some modifications as shown in Table 1. In particular, the output 111 and 000 is negligible in our design, while [25] used this value to indicates the sampling at low precision region. The error signal also is triggered when the jitter sampling is performed outside the edge region, indicated by 111 and 000.

Since one stage delay is applied to the extractor signal, the metastable signal may occur on the output signal when driving back to the system clock. This issue can be carried out by utilizing two FFs synchronizers at the output stage [8].

3   Implementation Result and Discussion

3.1   FPGA Implementation

To provide a proof of concept of our proposed design, we implemented AnyTRNG on Xilinx Zynq-7000 All Programmable SoC. We utilized clocking primitive phase-locked loop (PLL) as an entropy source. As per AnyTRNG requirement in Sect. 2, we configured the PLL to reduce the jitter on the reference clock by assigning the PLL bandwidth parameter to low [24]. On the other hand, the new output jitter is introduced by noise in Voltage Controlled Oscillators (VCO) module inside PLL primitive [10]. For a tapped delay module, we utilized $LUT1$ primitive to deliver a single unit delay. Therefore, the entire core of the AnyTRNG shown in Fig. 1 is implemented using only 1 PLL primitive, 4 LUTs, and 7 FFs. In addition to the AnyTRNG core implementation, the post-processing mechanism is implemented in the software area, which in our design uses a parity filter. We used a 100 MHz system clock in the design.

Placement. The proposed design is relatively sensitive to placement. In particular, the FFs and LUTs in the synchronous tapped delay module are required to be placed in such a way so that the total delay value of t_{d1} and t_{d2} are equal. Since our tap module design requires only 3 LUTs and 3 FFs, it can be fitted in one slice, as shown in Fig. 3. Both system clock and PLL output are routed into the global buffer (i.e., BUFG), which is commonly used for clock nets to provide the least amount of skew possible between registers that are physically located large distances apart. Meanwhile, we let the compiler manage the placement of the rest modules, including the bit extractor, since the module is not sensitive to the delay.

Throughput. Since the error bit (i.e., when jitter sampling is performed outside the edge region) has to be discarded from the output random bit, it may decrease the throughput of AnyTRNG. Yet, in our experiment, the error bit has not been found, thus achieving maximum throughput. This is due to the property of synchronization between jitter source and sampling clock (system clock), which ensures that the high entropy bit in the signal edge is sampled every single clock cycle. As a result, AnyTRNG achieved 100 Mbps throughput as high as depending on the system clock. We are aware that there is a condition that may trigger the error bit. However, we were unable to perform the test in different operating conditions (e.g., different operating temperatures). Nevertheless, suppose we consider implementing AnyTRNG on the cloud-based FPGA, which assumes that the environment is stable within normal operating conditions. In that case, we can ignore the concern on environmental setup.

3.2   Comparison with Related Work

Table 2 shows the comparison to the existing TRNG implementation on FPGA. Prior to our work, the implementation with the smallest area consumption is the proposal by Yang et al. [25] with one CARRY4 element, 10 LUTs, and 5 flip-flops, which is comparable to AnyTRNG. However, AnyTRNG has significant improvement in terms of throughput, which is 86 times higher than their design. A similar implementation approach that uses PLL as a jitter source is presented by Petura et al. [16]. They use a coherent sampling technique to extract the jitter

Fig. 3. Implemented synchronous tapped delay module in Xilinx FPGA

from output PLL. Their design utilized 34 LUTs and 14 FFs with a throughput of 0.44 Mbits/s, in which AnyTRNG still outperforms in all metrics compared to their result.

For the comparison with state-of-the-art regarding the throughput, recently, Nannipieri et al. [15] proposed Fibonacci-Galois RO-based TRNG, which outperform other similar works in terms of throughput. Although their implementation has higher throughput than AnyTRNG, it requires a relatively larger area. This is due to the fact that multiple stages of FiGaRO TRNG were placed in their design, which proportionally increases the throughput by 100 Mbits/s per stage. Thus, AnyTRNG is still comparable in terms of throughput but remarkably more compact in terms of area consumption.

3.3   Statistical Tests

In order to measure the entropy of AnyTRNG output qualitatively, three testing tools were used in this experiment. The NIST Entropy Assessment (SP800-90B) [21] is used to measure the minimum estimate of entropy, while the NIST Statistical Test Suite (SP800-22) [3] and DieHarder [6] are used to determine whether or not AnyTRNG is suitable for a particular cryptographic application. All three use the same input data bitstream from AnyTRNG with the configuration mentioned in Sect. 3.1 with a data bitstream length of 1 Gbits.

NIST Statistical Tests. NIST has designed a statistical test suite that is widely used as validation tools by previous research [11,14,15], and [12]. We used all of the 15 types of tests to evaluate the performance of our TRNG. The purpose of this test is to examine the proportion of sequences that pass

Table 2. Comparison of the proposed method with existing TRNG implementation

TRNG types	Area	Throughput (Mbits/s)	Platform	Frequency (MHz)
This work	4 LUTs 7 FFs 1 PLL	100	Zynq-7000 (Artix-7)	100
RO-Jitter [25]	10 LUTs 5 FFs 1 CARRY4	1.15	Spartan-6	100
PLL-Jitter [16]	34 LUTs 14 FFs 1 PLL	0.44	Spartan-6	200
FiGaRO [15]	288 LUTs 190 FFs	400	Stratix IV	100
Clock-Jitter [12]	791 LUTs 559 FFs	2.43	Virtex UltraScale+	–

a statistical test and the distribution of P-values to check for uniformity [3]. The majority of tests require small input data, but NIST recommends 1 Gbits of data as the minimum input for some tests, Overlapping Template Matching, Linear Complexity, and Random Excursion. The test is carried out with the recommended parameters from NIST. In the Table 3, the P-value results, the probability that a perfect random number generator would have produced a sequence less random than the sequence that was tested. When the P-value is equal to 1, it means perfect randomness, it must be greater than 0.01 in order to pass the test. The proportion column shows the proportion of sequence that has P-value > 0.01 from 100 binary sequences tested. The range of acceptable proportions determined using $\hat{p} \pm 3\sqrt{\frac{\hat{p}(1-\hat{p})}{m}}$, where $\hat{p} = 1 - \alpha$ and m is the sample size. Since the interval that we use is 100 and using significance level $\alpha = 0.01$, our confidence interval is 0.96. Therefore, the Proportion value must be more than 0.96% in order to pass the test. From the result, all of the tests are passed because both proportion and P-values are above the minimum threshold.

DieHarder. An alternative test suite for testing the quality of random generators is DieHarder [6], which is adapted from the popular "Diehard battery test" [13]. It is equipped with many test features, including those from the developed NIST Statistical Test Suite. These tools are designed to push weak generators to unambiguous failure by showing very precise failure scales. The results of the test are the same as for NIST 800.22, using a P-value. However, the P-value here is obtained from $p = F(X)$, which assumes F is the distribution of a random sample variable X. The results can be seen quite well, although there are some P-values that are quite small and less than 0.1, yet this is indeed reasonable

Table 3. NIST statistical test

No.	Test	Proportion	P-Value
1	Frequency	98%	0.262249
2	Block frequency	100%	0.534146
3	Runs	99%	0.191687
4	Longest run of ones	100%	0.275709
5	Rank	96%	0.249284
6	Spectral (FFT)	100%	0.366918
7	Non overlapping T. M.	97%	0.171867
8	Overlapping T. M.	100%	0.971699
9	Linear complexity	98%	0.657933
10	Serial	98%	0.816537
11	Approximate entropy	99%	0.514124
12	Cumulative sums	99%	0.657933
13	Universal	100%	0.213309
14	Random excursions	98%	0.468595
15	Random excursions variant	98%	0.671779

because there are a lot of tests done. This is expected even though the input is a perfectly random variable. We used the same 1 Gbit data on the previous NIST 800.22 test, and our data passed all of the reliable tests.

NIST Entropy Assessment. The expected entropy per bit is 1 for an ideal true random number generator because the proportion of '0's and '1's is ideally 0.5. To estimate the entropy rate for the generated numbers, Entropy Assessment 800-90B from NIST [21], available to test raw random numbers, is utilized in this brief. The minimum sequence of the length required for this test is 1000000 bits.

We use the Independent and Identically Distributed (IID) track to estimate the minimum entropy using Most Common Value Estimator (MCV). Given our random input $S = (S_1, ..., S_L)$, where each S_i comes from output A, $S_i \in A = \{X_1, ..., X_k\}$ and L is the sample sequence length. The proportion of the most common value is calculated as $\hat{p}$ in the dataset using 1.

$$\hat{p} = \max_i \frac{\#\{X_i \ in \ S\}}{L} \tag{1}$$

Then by using $\hat{p}$, the upper bound on the probability of the most common value p_u can be calculated as 2.

$$p_u = min\left(1, \hat{p} + 2.576\sqrt{\frac{\hat{p}(1-\hat{p})}{L-1}}\right) \tag{2}$$

Table 4. DieHarder statistical test

No.	Test	P-Value	Result
1	Birthdays	0.53612246	PASSED
2	OPERM5	0.56279960	PASSED
3	32 × 32 binary rank	0.83573000	PASSED
4	Bitstream	0.68114221	PASSED
5	Count the 1s (stream)	0.82613240	PASSED
6	Count the 1s (byte)	0.67637985	PASSED
7	Parking Lot	0.04779345	PASSED
8	Minimum distance (2d circle)	0.18184679	PASSED
9	Minimum distance (3d sphere)	0.97581053	PASSED
10	Squeeze	0.96720717	PASSED
11	Runs	0.92456822	PASSED
12	Craps	0.56419158	PASSED
13	Marsaglia and Tsang GCD	0.13250983	PASSED
14	STS monobit	0.14282980	PASSED
15	STS runs	0.92456822	PASSED
16	RGB permutations	0.52880552	PASSED
17	Byte distribution	0.18849324	PASSED

Where 2.576 corresponds to the $Z_{(1-0.005)}$ value. Finally, the estimated minimum entropy can be obtained from $-log2(p_u)$.

Using this MCV, our bit sequence passed the test and achieved entropy of 7.974339 per byte or 0.999678 per bit, which is a sufficient amount of randomness to provide security. Therefore, the proposed TRNG successfully fulfills the criteria for NIST Random Bit Generators (RBG) and can be used for applications that require high security. Moreover, our proposed TRNG achieves slightly higher entropy per bit when compared to other designs implementation [14] (0.9993 per bit) and [16] (0.999 per bit) (Table 4).

4   Conclusion

In this work, we presented a novel entropy extraction based on synchronous edge sampling for the building block of a generic, high-throughput, low-area True Random Number Generator (TRNG) called AnyTRNG. Its implementation on Artix-7 FPGA utilized only 4 LUTs and 7 FFs, thus fitted in two slices, making the design compact. Furthermore, AnyTRNG offers better throughput compared to previous work, with up to 100 Mbps or higher depending on the system's clock frequency. We have evaluated the entropy quality of AnyTRNG using the NIST 800-90B, yielding an approximate min-entropy of 0.9996 per bit. In addition, AnyTRNG has passed statistical tests with all 15 tests from NIST 800-22 and Dieharder.

References

1. An, H.S., Shin, K.W.: Correlation power analysis attack on lightweight block cipher lea and countermeasures by masking. J. Korea Inst. Inf. Commun. Eng. **21**(7), 1276–1284 (2017)
2. Awaludin, A.M., Larasati, H.T., Kim, H.: High-speed and unified ECC processor for generic Weierstrass curves over GF(p) on FPGA. Sensors (2021). https://doi.org/10.3390/s21041451
3. Bassham, L.E., et al.: A statistical test suite for random and pseudorandom number generators for cryptographic applications. Technical report, NIST Special Publication 800-22 revision 1a (2010). https://doi.org/10.6028/nist.sp.800-22r1a
4. Boakye-Boateng, K., Kuada, E., Antwi-Boasiako, E., Djaba, E.: Encryption protocol for resource-constrained devices in fog-based IoT Using one-time pads. IEEE Internet Things J. (2019). https://doi.org/10.1109/JIOT.2019.2893172
5. Brederlow, R., Prakash, R., Paulus, C., Thewes, R.: A low-power true random number generator using random telegraph noise of single oxide-traps. In: Digest of Technical Papers - IEEE International Solid-State Circuits Conference (2006). https://doi.org/10.1109/isscc.2006.1696222
6. Brown, R.G., Eddelbuettel, D., Bauer, D.: Dieharder: a random number test suite. Open Source Software Library (2013, under development)
7. Choe, J.Y., Shin, K.W.: A self-timed ring based TRNG with feedback structure for FPGA implementation. In: 2020 International Conference on Electronics, Information, and Communication (ICEIC), pp. 1–4 (2020). https://doi.org/10.1109/ICEIC49074.2020.9051375
8. Ginosar, R.: Metastability and synchronizers: a tutorial. IEEE Des. Test Comput. (2011). https://doi.org/10.1109/MDT.2011.113
9. Govindan, V., Chakraborty, R.S., Santikellur, P., Chaudhary, A.K.: A hardware trojan attack on FPGA-based cryptographic key generation: impact and detection. J. Hardw. Syst. Secur. **2**(3), 225–239 (2018). https://doi.org/10.1007/s41635-018-0042-5
10. Heydari, P.: Analysis of the PLL jitter due to power/ground and substrate noise. IEEE Trans. Circuits Syst. I Regul. Pap. **51**(12), 2404–2416 (2004). https://doi.org/10.1109/TCSI.2004.838240
11. Kalanadhabhatta, S., Kumar, D., Anumandla, K.K., Reddy, S.A., Acharyya, A.: PUF-based secure chaotic random number generator design methodology. IEEE Trans. Very Large Scale Integr. (VLSI) Syst. **28**(7), 1740–1744 (2020). https://doi.org/10.1109/TVLSI.2020.2979269
12. Li, X., Stanwicks, P., Provelengios, G., Tessier, R., Holcomb, D.: Jitter-based adaptive true random number generation for FPGAs in the cloud. In: 2020 International Conference on Field-Programmable Technology (ICFPT), pp. 112–119 (2020). https://doi.org/10.1109/ICFPT51103.2020.00024
13. Marsaglia, G: Diehard: a battery of tests of randomness (1996). http://stat.fsu.edu/geo/diehard.html. Accessed 11 June 2021
14. Nalla Anandakumar, N., Sanadhya, S.K., Hashmi, M.S.: FPGA-based true random number generation using programmable delays in oscillator-rings. IEEE Trans. Circuits Syst. II Express Briefs **67**(3), 570–574 (2020). https://doi.org/10.1109/TCSII.2019.2919891
15. Nannipieri, P., et al.: True random number generator based on Fibonacci-Galois ring oscillators for FPGA. Appl. Sci. **11**(8), (2021). https://doi.org/10.3390/app11083330

16. Petura, O., Mureddu, U., Bochard, N., Fischer, V., Bossuet, L.: A survey of AIS-20/31 compliant TRNG cores suitable for FPGA devices. In: 2016 26th International Conference on Field Programmable Logic and Applications (FPL), pp. 1–10 (2016). https://doi.org/10.1109/FPL.2016.7577379

17. Rozic, V., Yang, B., Dehaene, W., Verbauwhede, I.: Highly efficient entropy extraction for true random number generators on FPGAs. In: 2015 52nd ACM/EDAC/IEEE Design Automation Conference (DAC), pp. 1–6 (2015). https://doi.org/10.1145/2744769.2744852

18. Sivaraman, R., Rajagopalan, S., Sridevi, A., Rayappan, J.B.B., Annamalai, M.P.V., Rengarajan, A.: Metastability-induced TRNG architecture on FPGA. Iran. J. Sci. Technol. Trans. Electr. Eng. **44**(1), 47–57 (2019). https://doi.org/10.1007/s40998-019-00234-2

19. Tehranipoor, F., Wortman, P., Karimian, N., Yan, W., Chandy, J.A.: DVFT: a lightweight solution for power-supply noise-based TRNG using dynamic voltage feedback tuning system. IEEE Trans. Very Large Scale Integr. (VLSI) Syst. **26**(6), 1084–1097 (2018). https://doi.org/10.1109/TVLSI.2018.2804258

20. Tokunaga, C., Blaauw, D., Mudge, T.: True random number generator with a metastability-based quality control. IEEE J. Solid-State Circuits **43**(1), 78–85 (2008). https://doi.org/10.1109/JSSC.2007.910965

21. Turan, M.S., Barker, E., Kelsey, J., McKay, K.A., Baish, M.L., Boyle, M.: Recommendation for the entropy sources used for random bit generation. Technical report, NIST Special Publication 800-90B, January 2018. https://doi.org/10.6028/nist.sp.800-90b

22. Vega, A., Bose, P., Buyuktosunoglu, A.: Rugged Embedded Systems: Computing in Harsh Environments. Morgan Kaufmann, Burlington (2016)

23. Wieczorek, P.Z., Gołofit, K.: Dual-metastability time-competitive true random number generator. IEEE Trans. Circuits Syst. I Regul. Pap. **61**(1), 134–145 (2014). https://doi.org/10.1109/TCSI.2013.2265952

24. Xilinx: 7 Series FPGAs Clocking Resources User Guide (2018). https://www.xilinx.com/support/documentation/user_guides/ug472_7Series_Clocking.pdf. Accessed 10 June 2021

25. Yang, B., Rožic, V., Grujic, M., Mentens, N., Verbauwhede, I.: ES-TRNG: a high-throughput, low-area true random number generator based on edge sampling. IACR Transactions on Cryptographic Hardware and Embedded Systems (2018). https://doi.org/10.46586/tches.v2018.i3.267-292

26. Zheng, X., Xu, C., Hu, X., Zhang, Y., Xiong, X.: The software/hardware co-design and implementation of SM2/3/4 encryption/decryption and digital signature system. IEEE Trans. Comput. Aided Des. Integr. Circuits Syst. **39**(10), 2055–2066 (2020). https://doi.org/10.1109/TCAD.2019.2939330

Hardware Security

Masked Implementation of PIPO Block Cipher on 8-bit AVR Microcontrollers

Hyunjun Kim[1], Minjoo Sim[1], Siwoo Eum[1], Kyungbae Jang[1], Gyeongju Song[1],
Hyunji Kim[1], Hyeokdong Kwon[1], Wai-Kong Lee[2], and Hwajeong Seo[1(✉)]

[1] IT Department, Hansung University, Seoul 02876, South Korea
[2] Department of Computer Engineering, Gachon University,
Seongnam, Incheon 13120, Korea
waikonglee@gachon.ac.kr

Abstract. PIPO is a lightweight block cipher and shows better performance than other block cipher algorithms on low-end microcontrollers (e.g. 8-bit AVR). In addition, PIPO block cipher can utilize the efficient masking method by minimizing the number of non-linear operations. Therefore, PIPO block cipher can prevent side-channel attacks, efficiently. In this paper, we propose an efficient first-order masking technique using a 2-byte random mask by taking an advantage of PIPO block cipher. We present a new OR operation masking technique. Among functions of PIPO, the masked S-layer with 23 AND operations, 5 OR operations, and 46 XOR operations is used. Operations of PIPO block cipher are implemented in AVR assembly languages. The proposed implementation showed 1.5× faster performance enhancements compared to the unprotected C implementation in the encryption process and 2.2× faster performance enhancements compared to the unprotected optimized assembly implementation.

Keywords: PIPO block cipher · Masked implementation · 8-bit AVR microcontrollers · Side channel attack

This work was partly supported by Institute for Information & communications Technology Promotion (IITP) grant funded by the Korea government (MSIT) (No. 2018-0-00264, Research on Blockchain Security Technology for IoT Services, 25%) and this work was partly supported by the National Research Foundation of Korea (NRF) grant funded by the Korea government (MSIT) (No. NRF-2020R1F1A1048478, 25%) and this work was partly supported by Institute of Information & communications Technology Planning & Evaluation (IITP) grant funded by the Korea government (MSIT) (No. 2021-0-00540, Development of Fast Design and Implementation of Cryptographic Algorithms based on GPU/ASIC, 25%) and this work was partly supported by Institute for Information & communications Technology Planning & Evaluation (IITP) grant funded by the Korea government (MSIT) (<Q|Crypton>, No. 2019-0-00033, Study on Quantum Security Evaluation of Cryptography based on Computational Quantum Complexity, 25%).

H. Kim (Ed.): WISA 2021, LNCS 13009, pp. 171–182, 2021.
https://doi.org/10.1007/978-3-030-89432-0_14

1   Introduction

Side-channel analysis is an attack technique that obtains a secret key through the unintended information, such as power consumption and electromagnetic waves, while cryptographic modules are working. For this reason, the cryptographic engineer should pay attention on countermeasures against side channel attack for secure implementations. A masking technique, known as an effective countermeasure against side-channel attacks, computes a random value on the sensitive information to hide the information. Secure and scalable masking techniques have been proven through several studies. However, there is room to improve the performance in the implementation.

PIPO block cipher is a lightweight cipher developed for efficient masking implementation and it is designed for limited resources in the IoT environment by minimizing the number of non-linear operations [1]. With this nice feature, the PIPO block cipher can efficiently utilize the masking method, which is a side-channel analysis response technique. The PIPO block cipher outperforms other lightweight 64-bit block ciphers using 128-bit keys in terms of 8-bit AVR implementations. Since the cost of masking is lower than that of other 64-bit lightweight ciphers, the increase in execution time is small when the masking technique is utilized. Therefore, PIPO block cipher can apply side-channel response techniques efficiently to the IoT environment with limited resources. It is very costly to generate a random value of high entropy used for masking. Low non-linearity of PIPO block cipher helps to minimize the masking cost. The masking application should optimize the randomness for a specific masking device, such as an AND gate, or make it work efficiently while reducing the amount of new randomness.

1.1   Our Contributions

We aimed to maximize the advantage of PIPO block cipher to utilize the masking. As a first step, we performed a power analysis attack on the PIPO block cipher [1]. The original paper discusses masking techniques, but it does not attack the PIPO before the masking protection. Through this process, the necessity of countermeasures against PIPO side channels is confirmed. To reduce the cost of generating random values, we propose an efficient first-order masking technique using two 8-bit masks. The mask value is generated in the first time. PIPO uses non-linear operations (i.e. AND and OR operations). For the safe and efficient masking of AND and OR operations, ISW masking technique is used for AND operation, and a new technique for the masking OR operation is proposed. The proposed new OR operation masking is based on the technique of Gross et al. and uses fewer instructions than the existing ones. The masked S-layer with 23 AND operations, 5 OR operations, and 46 XOR operations is designed for the PIPO's masking. There is no additional operations in the rest of the functions except for the initial mask value generation, the process of masking the input plaintext and round key, and the S-layer. When the proposed method is implemented in an assembly code, compared to the existing assembly code implementation reference code, the overhead of proposed method is 120%.

2   PIPO Algorithm

PIPO is a lightweight block cipher algorithm announced at ICISC'20 [1]. It consists of S-Layer using a new S-box and bit permutation using bit rotation in units of bytes. PIPO's new S-Box is cryptographically superior and is designed to be efficient. The differential and linear branching numbers of nonlinear functions is designed to be high, allowing safe use of efficient and low-spreading bit permutations in lightweight environments. A bit slicing implementation using only 11 non-linear bitwise operations and 23 linear bitwise operations is also presented. It outperforms existing lightweight block ciphers in side-channel protection and unprotected environments in 8-bit AVR microcontrollers due to byte-unit bit slicing operations and a small number of non-linear bit operations. In the side-channel analysis, the non-linearity of cryptographic algorithms and their actual implementation affect the attack success [2]. In this paper, we utilized masking considering PIPO's new S-box implementation of bit slicing.

3   Masked PIPO

We applied Boolean masking with the goal of defending against the primary side-channel attack. In Boolean masking, non-linear functions require additional techniques to manage mask values. In PIPO, the AND operation and the OR operation correspond to this. We considered safe and efficient AND and OR masking without using a new random mask. $\oplus$ is an XOR operation, $\wedge$ is an AND operation, $\vee$ is an OR operation, $m0$ and $m1$ are random mask values, and $a_1 = m_0$, $b_1 = m_1$, $q = q_0 \oplus q_1$, $m_2 = m_0 \oplus m_1$.

3.1   Masked XOR Operation

In Boolean masking, the XOR operation can maintain the masking state without performing additional operations. In the case of XORing two masked values, it can be protected with a mask value $m2$ as shown in the following equation.

$$q_0 = a \oplus m_0, q_1 = b \oplus m_1, q = q_0 \oplus q_1 = (a \oplus m_0) \oplus (b \oplus m_1) = (a \oplus b) \oplus m_2$$

When two mask values are the same, the state of the mask is removed. And different mask values must be used. In this paper, the same mask state is implemented by using masks of mask states m_0, m_1, and m_2. The mask value is not removed when the same two values are calculated. Since the remaining mask values are obtained by XORing two mask values, the mask can be easily managed even with three mask values.

3.2 Masking of and Operation

The masking of AND operation uses the same technique as the existing PIPO. The formula below is the AND operation masking of the existing PIPO using two masks [3].

$$q = a \wedge b = (a_0 \oplus a1)(b_0 \oplus b_1) \quad = a_0 \wedge b_0 \oplus a_0 \wedge b_1 \oplus a_1 \wedge b_0 \oplus a_1 \wedge b_1$$
$$= q_0 \oplus q_1 = (a \oplus m_0) \oplus (b \oplus m_1) = (a \oplus b) \oplus m_2$$
$$q_0 = a_0 \wedge b_0 \oplus m_2 \oplus a_0 \wedge b_1 \oplus a_1 \wedge b_0 \oplus a_1 \wedge b_1, q1 = m2$$

The mask value after the operation is changed to a new mask value. Considering the case where mask values are the same, two input values have different masking states, and the mask value after the operation is an XOR value of the input mask values. There are no additional mask values.

Biryukov et al. realized a masked AND gate that does not require new randomness. Based on this, Gross et al. created a new AND mask structure as follows [4].

$$q_0 = (a_0 \wedge b_0 \oplus (a_0 \wedge b_1 \oplus b_1)) \oplus (a_1 \wedge b_0 \oplus [m_0 \vee m_1]), q_1 = a_1$$

$[m0 \vee m1]$ is a fixed value and can be used equally in one operation. After the operation, it is masked with a single mask $(m0)$. It is easy to manage the mask state. The operation process is also more efficient than [4]. However, we applied the technique to PIPO, but our experimental CPA attack revealed the real key. Therefore, in the proposed technique, the existing PIPO AND masking technique was used instead of the corresponding masking technique.

3.3 Masking of or Operation

The OR operation masking is based on the AND masking technique of Gross et al. [4], and a new OR masking technique is used as shown in the following equation.

$$q_0 = (a_0 \wedge b_0) \oplus (a_0 \vee b_1) \oplus ((a_1 \vee b_0) \oplus ((a_1 \wedge b_1) \oplus a_1 \oplus b_1)) = (a_0 \wedge b_0) \oplus (a_0 \vee b_1) \oplus ((a_1 \vee b_0) \oplus$$
$$([m_0 \vee m_1] \oplus b_1)) q_1 = a_1 = m_1$$

The AND masking technique of Gross et al. does not use a new random mask and operates using 1 AND, 2 ORs, and 4 XORs. It uses fewer operations than PIPO's existing technique using 4 ANDs and 6 XORs. $[m0 \vee m1]$ is a fixed value and can be used equally in one operation. For the masking technique to be safe, values of the intermediate operations must be statistically identical regardless of the values of the intermediate operations. As shown in Table 1, in the proposed method, the Hamming weight of the intermediate operation is the same regardless of the secret value to be hidden. Therefore, the proposed OR operation masking is statistically identical, and actual operation values are not revealed.

Table 1. Security of the proposed masked OR; $t1 = (a_0 \wedge b_0), t2 = (a_0 \vee b_1), t3 = (a_1 \vee b_0), t4 = [m_0 \vee m_1] \oplus b_1, t5 = t3 \oplus t4, t6 = t1 \oplus t2$.

a_0'	b_0	a_1	b_1	a	b	ab	$t1$	$t2$	$t3$	$t4$	$t5$	$t6$	$q0$
				Secrets			TT(Truth table)						
0	0	0	0				0	0	0	0	0	0	0
0	0	1	1	0	0	0	0	1	1	0	1	1	0
1	1	0	0				0	1	1	0	1	1	1
1	1	1	1				1	1	1	0	1	0	1
TT Hamming Weight							1	3	3	1	2	2	2
0	0	0	1				0	1	0	0	0	1	1
0	0	1	0	0	1	1	0	0	1	0	1	0	1
1	1	0	1				0	1	1	0	1	1	0
1	1	1	0				1	1	1	1	0	0	0
TT Hamming Weight							1	3	3	1	2	2	2

a_0	b_0	a_1	b_1	a	b	ab	$t1$	$t2$	$t3$	$t4$	$t5$	$t6$	$q0$
				Secrets			TT(Truth table)						
0	1	0	0				0	1	1	0	1	1	0
0	1	1	1	1	0	1	0	0	1	1	0	0	0
1	0	0	0				0	1	0	0	0	1	1
1	0	1	1				1	1	1	0	1	0	1
TT Hamming Weight							1	3	3	1	2	2	2
0	1	0	1				0	1	1	0	1	1	0
0	1	1	0	1	1	1	0	0	1	1	0	0	0
1	0	0	1				0	1	0	0	0	1	1
1	0	1	0				1	1	1	0	1	0	1
TT Hamming Weight							1	3	3	1	2	2	2

3.4 Masking Scheme

Fig. 1. Proposed masked encryption process.

In order to minimize the cost for generating a random mask value used in the masking technique, the proposed technique proposes PIPO masking using only a 2-byte random mask. For the efficient operation, the masking state of the input and output of the function operating in the round is kept constant. The state of the mask used in the implementation of this paper is shown in Table 2.

The proposed method can be divided into a mask initialization step and an encryption step. In the initialization step, as in Algorithm 1, 8-bit random mask values, $m0$ and $m1$ are generated, and 8 mask values are generated by combining them. The generated mask $m2 = m0 \oplus m1$, and the remaining mask values are generated as in line 4–10 of Algorithm 1. This mask is a pre-work to keep the mask state of the value input to the round function the same as the previous round and the next round, and these values are masked by the round key. The first 64 bits of the round key are masked with $m2, m2, m2, m1, m2, m2, m2$, and $m2$, respectively. For remaining round keys, $m1, m3, m4, m5, m6, m7, m8$, and $m9$ are masked in order (Table 3).

In the encryption process, the input plaintext is first masked with the value of the Masking row of the table. Next, the same process as in the existing PIPO is performed except that a masked S-Layer is used. In the final step, the encryption is completed by removing the masking state.

Table 2. Masking state proposed PIPO masking.

	X[0]	X[1]	X[2]	X[3]	X[4]	X[5]	X[6]	X[7]
AddMask	m_1	m_0	m_0	m_0	m_1	m_0	m_0	m_1
AddRK out	m_0	m_1	m_1	m_2	m_0	m_1	m_1	m_0
S-Layer out	m_2	m_1	m_2	m_0	m_1	m_1	m_2	m_1
R-Layer out	m_2	$m_1 \ggg 7$	$m_2 \ggg 4$	$m_0 \ggg 3$	$m_1 \ggg 6$	$m_1 \ggg 5$	$m_2 \ggg 1$	$m_1 \ggg 2$
Remove mask	m_0	m_1	m_1	m_2	m_0	m_1	m_1	m_0

Table 3. Performance comparison.

Method	C (cycles)	ASM (cycles)
[3]	2,321	1,576
Proposed method	6,169	3,460
Overhead factor	2.7	2.2

4   Implementation

In this Section, we describes the implementation of the proposed technique. The application of the masking technique causes a lot of overhead in the speed of the existing algorithm. We implemented the proposed technique in C language and optimized it to minimize overhead and implemented it in AVR assembly. In Atmel Studio 7.0 version, the clock cycle of the encryption process was calculated by operating it in the simulation environment of the ATmega128 board. In the C language implementation 6,169 cycles and 3,460 cycles were shown in the assembly implementation. At this time, the random value generation used in the mask value was not considered because there are various methods.

4.1   8-bit AVR Microcontrollers

With the growth of the Internet of Things (IoT), many low-cost platforms are being used for sensors, actuators and smart devices. In the IoT environment, it is necessary to have a certain level of security for a safe communication environment. A commonly used 8-bit microcontroller AVR has a RISC architecture with 32 general-purpose registers. Typically, one arithmetic instruction requires one clock cycle, while memory access and 8-bit multiply instructions require two clock cycles. Instructions used to implement the optimized PIPO block cipher are summarized in Table 4.

4.2   Mask Initialization

As seen in Algorithm 1, 8 new mask values are generated with 2 random values. It is added to the rounded key to make the rotated mask state to the same state as

Table 4. Summarized instruction set of AVR microcontrollers for optimized PIPO block cipher; Rd: Destination register, Rr: Source register.

Instruction	Operands	Description	Operation	#Clock
AND	Rd, Rr	Logical AND	Rd ← Rd & Rr	1
OR	Rd, Rr	Logical OR	Rd ← Rd | Rr	1
EOR	Rd, Rr	Exclusive OR	Rd ← Rd ⊕ Rr	1
MOV	Rd, Rr	Copy Register	Rd ← Rr	1

Algorithm 1. Initmask.

Input: 8-bit random values (r1, r2)
Output: m1, m2, m3, m4, m5, m6, m7, m8, m9
1: m0 = r1
2: m1 = r2
3: m2 = m0 ⊕ m1
4: m3 = (m1 >>> 1) ⊕ m1
5: m4 = (m2 >>> 4) in ⊕ m1
6: m5 = (m0 >>> 5) ⊕ m2
7: m6 = (m1 >>> 2) ⊕ m0
8: m7 = (m1 >>> 3) ⊕ m1
9: m8 = (m2 >>> 7) ⊕ m1
10: m9 = (m1 >>> 6) ⊕ m0

---

the AddRK out row in Table 2. With one operation of this pre-step, add-key and L-layer in the proposed method work the same as the existing operation without overhead. The clock cycles generated here are 1,074 cycles in the C language implementation and 604 cycles in the assembly implementation, accounting for 17% of the total.

4.3   Encryption Round

In the encryption process of the proposed method, Add key and L-layer operate without additional operation as a pre-operation of Mask initialization described above. The Add Mask step to mask the plaintext input to the existing algorithm and Remove Mask to remove the mask value after encryption operation are added. And Masked S-Layer with a masking technique applied to the S-layer is used. In the Add Mask step, the received plaintext is masked by XORing the values. In the Remove Mask step, the value is masked by XORing it. 8 XOR operations are added in the Add Mask stage and 8 operations are added in the Remove Mask stage. C implementation of S-layer works like Algorithm 4. S-layer's nonlinear operation and operation and or operation are changed to secand and secor, and additional xor operation is performed. The mask state is not removed in line 33 and line 34. As shown in Algorithm 2, SecAND operates in 12 clock cycles using 12 instructions. As shown in Algorithm 3, SecOR operates in 11 clock cycles using 11 instructions. As a result, the Masked S-layer assembly takes 208 cycles.

Algorithm 2. SecAND in AVR assembly.

Input: temp regis-ters: r4, r5, data registers: a_0, b_0, mask registers: a_1, b_1, m($a_1 \oplus b_1$)	Output: r4 1: MOV r4, b_0 2: AND r4, a_0 3: EOR r4, m 4: MOV r5, a_0	5: AND r5, b_1 6: EOR r4, r5 7: MOV r5, a_1 8: AND r5, b_0 9: EOR r4, r5	10: MOV r5, a_1 11: AND r5, b_1 12: EOR r4, r5

Algorithm 3. SecOR in AVR assembly.

Input: temp regis-ters: r4, r5, r6, data registers: a_0, b_0, mask registers: a_1, b_1, m($a_1 \vee b_1$)	Output: r4 1: MOV r4, m 2: EOR r4, b_1 3: MOV r5, b_0 4: OR r5, a_1	5: EOR r5, r4 6: MOV r4, b_0 7: AND r4, a_0 8: MOV r6, a_0 9: OR r6, b_1	10: EOR r4, r6 11: EOR r4, r5

5   Experiment

5.1   Experiment Environment

10,000 waveforms from round 1 to round 3 were collected using ChipWhisperer-Lite in ATxmega128 MCU, which is an 8-bit processor, for PIPO-64/128 implemented by bit slicing.

5.2   Power Analysis of Unprotected PIPO

In PIPO, the S-box is implemented and operated by the block-unit bit slicing technique. Considering this, after the S-Box operation, the CPA attack was performed by targeting the upper first bit of the median value [5]. Figure 1 shows the result of acquiring the first 8 bits of the key of the first 64-bit transposed round. It can be seen that the attack was successful by showing the highest correlation coefficient at 0x05, which is the actual key value among the guessed key values. By repeating the same process eight times, the key of the first 64-bit transposed round can be found. If you attack the middle value of the S-Box operation of the second round based on the information found, you can find out the key value of the second transposed round. The original key value can be found by transposing the obtained two round kit values to their original state and performing XOR with the round constant.

8-bit Intermediate Value Attack After S-Box Operation. We first performed a CPA attack using the first 8-bit value after the S-box operation as an intermediate value. Figure 2 is the result of attacking the 1-byte partial key. If the attack is performed properly, the correct value of the guess key (85), should come out as the highest correlation coefficient value. However, as a result of the attack, the guess key with the highest correlation coefficient was 77. In addition, high correlation coefficients were shown at 72, 80, and 85. Unlike the original prediction, 85 did not have the highest correlation coefficient, so an accurate

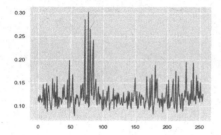 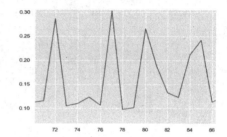

Fig. 2. Attack result (left) and attack analysis result (right) using 8-bit value after S-Box operation as an intermediate value.

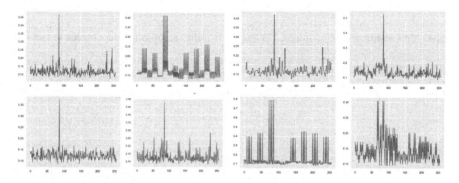

Fig. 3. Result of performing 1 bit CPA attack after S-Layer operation.

attack could not be performed with the attack method using the 8-bit value after the S-Layer operation as the median value.

1-Bit Attack of 8-Bit Median Value After S-Box Operation. We judged that the cause of the inaccurate attack result in 8-bit S-box attack is that the S-box of PIPO is implemented by bit slicing in block units, and taking this into account, we performed the attack on each bit of the value after the S-box operation. As a result, it was confirmed as shown in Fig. 3 that characteristic attack results were obtained for each bit. As can be seen in Fig. 3, in the most significant bit, the fourth, fifth, and sixth bits, the highest correlation coefficient value is one, and the round key value to be obtained can be obtained at the point where the high correlation coefficient value is obtained. On the other hand, it was confirmed that the second upper bit, the third, the seventh, and the least significant bit had two or more identical correlation coefficient values. The attack on the 4-th bit showing the highest correlation coefficient was possible with at least 70 waveforms.

Leak Point Analysis. A CPA attack was performed to determine where the power waveform leak occurred. Figure 4 is the result of performing CPA for

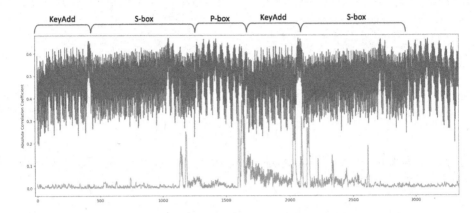

Fig. 4. The result of performing CPA for each point using an 8-bit correct guess key.

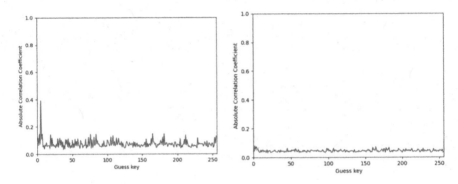

Fig. 5. CPA attack results on PIPO before protection (left) and CPA attack results on PIPO with masking (right).

each point using an 8-bit correct guess key and outputting it. Blue is the power consumption waveform of the 1st and second rounds of PIPO, and orange is the result of displaying the high correlation coefficient by performing CPA for each point. A leak occurred in S-box operation and P-box operation in round 1, keyAdd operation in round 2, and S-box operation (Fig. 5).

5.3   Power Analysis of the Proposed Masked PIPO

In order to check whether the proposed masking technique is safe against the primary side-channel analysis attack, the attack was performed in the same way as the power analysis for the existing PIPO. Figure 2 shows the results of the CPA attack against the masked PIPO. The correlation coefficients of all guess keys were low, and the value showing the highest correlation coefficient is irrelevant to the actual value. Therefore, the proposed method is safe for primary side-channel analysis.

Algorithm 4. S-layer in C code.

Input: $u8\ X[8]$, $m0$, $m1$, $m2$.
Output: $u8\ X[8]$.
1: $u8\ T[3] = \{0, \};$
2: $u8\ temp = 0;$
3: $u8\ c = m0|m1;$

4: $secand(temp, X[7], X[6], m0, m1, m2);$
5: $X[5] = X[5] \oplus temp;\ //(m1 \oplus m2) = m0$

6: $secand(temp, X[3], X[5], m2, m0, m1);$
7: $X[4] = X[4] \oplus temp;\ //m0 \oplus m1 = m2$
8: $X[7] = X[7] \oplus X[4];\ //m0 \oplus m2 = m1$
9: $X[6] = X[6] \oplus X[3];\ //m1 \oplus m2 = m0$

10: $secor(temp, X[5], X[4], m0, m2, c);$
11: $X[3] = X[3] \oplus temp;\ //m2 \oplus m0 = m1$
12: $X[5] = X[5] \oplus X[7];\ //m0 \oplus m1 = m2$

13: $secand(temp, X[5], X[6], m2, m0, m1);$
14: $X[4] = X[4] \oplus temp;\ //m2 \oplus m1 = m0$

15: $secand(temp, X[1], X[0], m1, m0, m2);$
16: $X[2] = X[2] \oplus temp;\ //m1 \oplus m2 = m0$

17: $secor(temp, X[1], X[2], m1, m0, c);$
18: $X[0] = X[0] \oplus temp;\ //m0 \oplus m1 = m2$

19: $secor(temp, X[2], X[0], m0, m2, c);$
20: $X[1] = X[1] \oplus temp;\ //m1 \oplus m0 = m2$
21: $X[2] = X[2];\ //m0$

22: $X[7] = X[7] \oplus X[1];\ //(m1 \oplus m2) = m0$
23: $X[3] = X[3] \oplus X[2];\ //m1 \oplus m0 = m2$

24: $X[4] = X[4] \oplus X[0];\ //m0 \oplus m2 = m1$
25: $T[0] = X[7];\ //m0$
26: $T[1] = X[3];\ //m2$
27: $T[2] = X[4];\ //m1$

28: $secand(temp, X[5]; T[0], m2, m0, m1);$
29: $X[6] = X[6] \oplus temp;\ //m0 \oplus m1 = m2$

30: $T[0] = T[0] \oplus X[6];\ //m0 \oplus m2 = m1$

31: $secor(temp, T[2], T[1], m1, m2, c);$
32: $X[6] = X[6] \oplus temp;\ //m2 \oplus m1 = m0$

33: $T[1] = X[5] \oplus m0;\ //m2 \oplus m1 = m0$

34: $secor(temp, X[6], T[2], m0, m1, c);$
35: $X[5] = X[5] \oplus temp;\ //m2^m0 = m1$

36: $secand(temp, T[1], T[0], m0, m1, m2);$
37: $T[2] = T[2] \oplus temp;\ //m1 \oplus m2 = m0$

38: $X[2] = X[2] \oplus T[0];\ //m0 \oplus m1 = m2$
39: $T[0] = X[1] \oplus T[2];\ //m2 \oplus m0 = m1$
40: $X[1] = X[0] \oplus T[1];\ //m2 \oplus m0 = m1$
41: $X[0] = X[7] \oplus m1;\ //m2$
42: $X[7] = T[0];\ //m1$
43: $T[1] = X[3];\ //m2$
44: $X[3] = X[6];\ //m0$
45: $X[6] = T[1];\ //m2$
46: $T[2] = X[4];\ //m1$
47: $X[4] = X[5];\ //m1$
48: $X[5] = T[2];\ //m1$

6   Conclusions and Future Work

We proposed a side-channel analysis of the lightweight block cipher algorithm PIPO and an efficient first-order masking technique. As a result of the CPA attack targeting the provided and collected waveforms, a successful CPA attack was performed with a bit-by-bit attack on the 8-bit median value of the S-box operation. And we propose an efficient first-order masking technique for PIPO. For masking, a 2-byte random mask is used to minimize the cost of generating a mask, and for this, a new OR operation masking is proposed. Among the functions of PIPO, Masked S-layer with 23 AND operations, 5 OR operations, and 46 XOR operations added is used, and the rest performs the same operation and operates efficiently. The safety of the proposed side-channel countermeasures against CPA attacks was confirmed through experiments. And as a result of implementing the assembly code in the AVR environment, the new masking technique showed 50% and 120% overhead respectively compared to the reference c code and the optimized assembly code provided by [1]. The proposed method aimed at efficient primary masking for PIPO for IoT environment with few resources. PIPO is also efficient for high-order masking with few non-linear operations. In the future, we plan to apply efficient high-order masking for PIPO to protect side-channel attacks in various environments.

References

1. Kim, H., et al.: PIPO: a lightweight block cipher with efficient higher-order masking software implementations. In: Hong, D. (ed.) ICISC 2020. LNCS, vol. 12593, pp. 99–122. Springer, Cham (2021). https://doi.org/10.1007/978-3-030-68890-5_6
2. Tian, Q., O'neill, M., Hanley, N.: Can leakage models be more efficient? Non-linear models in side channel attacks. In: 2014 IEEE International Workshop on Information Forensics and Security, WIFS 2014, pp. 215–220, April 2015
3. Ishai, Y., Sahai, A., Wagner, D.: Private circuits: securing hardware against probing attacks. In: Boneh, D. (ed.) CRYPTO 2003. LNCS, vol. 2729, pp. 463–481. Springer, Heidelberg (2003). https://doi.org/10.1007/978-3-540-45146-4_27
4. Gross, H., Stoffelen, K., Meyer, L., Krenn, M., Mangard, S.: First-order masking with only two random bits, pp. 10–23, November 2019
5. Prouff, E.: DPA attacks and S-Boxes. In: Gilbert, H., Handschuh, H. (eds.) FSE 2005. LNCS, vol. 3557, pp. 424–441. Springer, Heidelberg (2005). https://doi.org/10.1007/11502760_29

Parallel Implementation of PIPO Block Cipher on 32-bit RISC-V Processor

YuJin Kwak[1], YoungBeom Kim[2], and Seog Chung Seo[2]([✉])

[1] Department of Information Security, Cryptology, and Mathematics,
Kookmin University, Seoul, South Korea
`youjk@kookmin.ac.kr`
[2] Department of Financial Information Security, Kookmin University,
Seoul, South Korea
`{darania,scseo}@kookmin.ac.kr`

Abstract. In ICISC 2020, 64-bit PIPO lightweight block cipher was presented. The main design goals of PIPO are the implementation-friendly and the ease of designing side-channel protection techniques. Until now, the performance of PIPO has been investigated only on 8-bit AVR environment. Thus, optimization strategies on various embedded devices need to be investigated for PIPO's wide usage in various IoT applications. For filling this gap, in this paper, we present an optimized software implementation of PIPO cipher on 32-bit RISC-V processor being widely considered as an alternative embedded processor for ARM processors. For optimal performance, we propose several novel techniques: optimal register scheduling for minimizing the number of memory accesses, data parallel processing approach by using 32-bit register set, and combined internal process. In result, our software shows 128.5% improved performance on PIPO-64/128 basis than the simple ported version of RISC-V. In addition, our implementation showed 393.52% improvement over the encryption performance of the PIPO reference code, despite including the key scheduling process. As far as we know, this is the first optimal implementation of PIPO block cipher on RISC-V environment.

Keywords: PIPO · Optimization · 32-bit RISC-V · Embedded · Efficient implementation · Parallel implementation

1 Introduction

In ICISC 2020, a 64-bit lightweight PIPO block cipher was proposed for secure communication in IoT environment [1]. PIPO block cipher consists of an S-Layer designed with bit slicing and an R-Layer which is a permutation process.

This work was partly supported by Institute of Information & communications Technology Planning & Evaluation (IITP) grant funded by the Korea government (MSIT) (No. A2021-0270, 6G autonomous security internalization-based technology research to ensure security quality at all times, 50%) and the National Research Foundation of Korea (NRF) grant funded by the Korea government (MSIT) (No. 2019R1F1A1058494, 50%).

© Springer Nature Switzerland AG 2021
H. Kim (Ed.): WISA 2021, LNCS 13009, pp. 183–193, 2021.
https://doi.org/10.1007/978-3-030-89432-0_15

It has the advantage of providing security with fewer rounds compared to other lightweight ciphers [2–6]. In addition, PIPO block cipher can be implemented for countermeasures against side-channel attacks with relatively low computational cost. Low-end devices are particularly vulnerable to side-channel implementation [7–10]. Therefore, PIPO block cipher has great advantages from an optimization point of view. In particular, PIPO block cipher is designed specifically for the 8-bit AVR environment so that it achieves a small code size and high performance compared to the existing lightweight ciphers [1,2].

RISC-V is a open source architecture developed at UC Berkeley. RISC-V have advantages that users can freely design and apply it through the open modular instruction set and hardware structure. Due to these characteristics, many companies are currently developing RISC-V architecture. In addition, as interest in RISC-V architecture as a sensor node increases, research on the application of various cryptographic systems and protocol demonstration in RISC-V architecture is being actively conducted [3,11–14].

In this paper, we present the first optimized implementation of PIPO block cipher in RISC-V architecture. The various optimization methods are introduced by analyzing RISC-V architecture and overall structure of PIPO block cipher.

Organization. Section 2 describes PIPO block cipher and RISC-V Architecture; also, we describe some related block cipher implementations on RISC-V environment. In Sect. 3, we present a new optimization methods for PIPO block cipher on RISC-V. Section 4 evaluates our software with respect to speed and memory consumption. Finally, Sect. 5 concludes this paper with future works.

2 Preliminaries

2.1 Overview of 64-bit PIPO Block Cipher

PIPO (Plug-In and Plug-Out) is Korea block cipher presented at ICISC 2020, an international major security conference [1]. PIPO provides reference codes implemented as a Bit-slicing method and Table Look Up method to be applicable to various platforms or programming languages. In particular, it boasts excellent performance in the implementation of 8-bit AVR platform. In addition, it is expected to be highly portable to multiple platforms such as big data, cloud, database, and blockchain by proving the security of side-channel analysis.

PIPO performs encryption and decryption in units of 64-bit blocks, and the number of rounds varies according to the size of the key. One round of PIPO's encryption process consists of S-Layer, R-Layer, and AddRoundKey. Figure 1 schematically illustrates the overall structure of PIPO encryption algorithm. S-Layer is a non-linear layer that transforms using an 8-bit S-box. PIPO's Sbox is designed using an unbalanced bridge structure and provides an efficient bit-slicing implementation method in 8-bit Sbox. R-Layer is a linear layer process that rotates left by n-bit for each byte sequentially from the least significant byte. Rotate left by 0, 7, 4, 3, 6, 5, 1, 2-bit in order from the least significant byte.

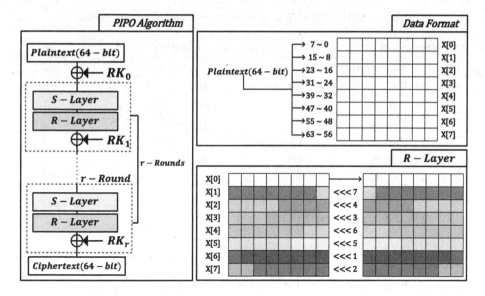

Fig. 1. PIPO algorithm [1]

$$K^{128} = K_1||K_0, RK_i = K_{i \bmod 2}(K_i = 64 \; bits, i = 0 \sim 13) \tag{1}$$

$$K^{256} = K_3||K_2||K_1||K_0, RK_i = K_{i \bmod 4}(K_i = 64 \; bits, i = 0 \sim 15) \tag{2}$$

Key schedule process performed before encryption process uses 2 or 4 master keys, respectively, depending on the key size according to the even and odd rounds. To generate a round key, XOR (eXclusive OR) master key and Rcon. Equation 1 is PIPO-64/128 key schedule process, and Eq. 2 is PIPO-64/256 key schedule process.

2.2 RISC-V Architecture

RISC-V is a new computer architecture based on RISC(Reduced Instruction Set Computer) that has been under development at UC Berkeley since 2010 [15]. RISC-V supports a free, open instruction set architecture based on open standards collaboration. In addition, since the hardware structure and ISA(Instruction Set Architecture) of RISC-V are freely available, it is possible to extend without restriction through the ISA configured in a modular way, and the freedom of hardware and software development is guaranteed [16]. Because of these advantages, many companies are actively investing in RISC-V development. Interest in RISC-V in the IoT environment has also been increasing by these aspects.

RISC-V consists of 32 registers. Register size is supported in 32-bit and 64-bit with the same instruction set according to the RV32I and RV64I models. In this paper, the RV32I model that supports 32-bit registers is used. A characteristic of RISC-V is that the integer ISA is like other RISC processors, but there is

Table 1. 32-bit RISC-V assembly instructions (*cc*: clock cycle)

Asm	Operands	Description	Operation	cc
LB	Rd, Ra(+Imm12)	Load bytes	Rd ← Ra(+Imm12)	2
SB	Rd, Ra(+Imm12)	Store bytes	Ra(+Imm12) ← Rd	2
ADD	Rd, Rs1, Rs2	Add	Rd ← Rs1 + Rs2	1
AND	Rd, Rs1, Rs2	And	Rd ← Rs1 & Rs2	1
XOR	Rd, Rs1, Rs2	eXclusive OR	Rd ← Rs1 ^Rs2	1
OR	Rd, Rs1, Rs2	OR	Rd ← Rs1 | Rs2	1
SLL	Rd, Rs1, Rs2	Shift left logical	Rd ← Rs1 « Rs2	1
SRL	Rd, Rs1, Rs2	Shift right logical	Rd ← Rs1 » Rs2	1
BNE	Rs1, Rs2, Ra(+Imm12)	Branch not equal	if(Rs1 != Rs2) PC ← PC + Ra(+Imm12 « 1)	1/2

no delay slot for branches, and it supports instructions of variable length. Also, unlike other embedded devices, RISC-V does not have a status code for the operation result [17]. Therefore, there is a characteristic that a conditional jump instruction exists for this purpose. Table 1 specifies the clock cycle and execution method for RISC-V instructions.

RISC-V uses FreedomStudio, an optimized development environment [18]. FreedomStudio is an integrated development environment that targets SiFive-based processors and can be used to write and debug software. FreedomStudio is based on Eclipse and is bundled with a pre-built RISC-V GCC Toolchain, OpenOCD, and freedom e-sdk.

2.3 Block Cipher Implementations on RISC-V

There are several implementations of crypto systems on RISC-V environment. [3] proposed an optimization method on RISC-V using AES-based Table and Bit-slicing. By using T-table, AES was efficiently implemented. However, since T-table-based AES implementation is not secure against side-channel attacks such as timing attack, an optimization method using the Bit-slicing technique was also proposed in [3] AES-128 based on T-table achieves 57 CPB.

In addition, [3] presented some optimal techniques of ChaCha20 and Keccak-f[1600] on RISC-V. Every round in ChaCha20 includes 4 quarter rounds and every quarter round consists of 4 extras, 4 XORs, and 4 turns. Since RISC-V's basic ISA does not have a rotation instruction, every rotation instruction must be replaced with two shift instructions and an OR instruction; therefore ChaCha uses 20 single cycle commands to comprise the quarter round. By the optimal method, the Implementation of ChaCha20 achieves 27.9 CPB on RISC-V platforms. Keccak-f[1600] is implemented using efficient register scheduling and bit interleaving. [3] also uses Lane Complementing's method. Through this technique, Keccak-f achieves 68.9 CPB.

[14] presented the benchmark results of the Korea block cipher algorithm on RISC-V. [14] provided the performance of ARIA, LEA, and PIPO encryption results for one block. As a benchmarking technique of RISC-V, [14] are benchmarking using efficient register scheduling and minimize memory access to plain text. By using this, in RISC-V, ARIA achieved a performance of 295.0 CPB, LEA achieved a performance of 48.4 CPB, and PIPO achieved a performance of 259.8 CPB.

3   Proposed PIPO Implementation on RISC-V Platform

In this section, we present a parallel optimal implementation of the first PIPO in a RISC-V processor. Section 3.1 overall introduces our parallel strategy, and the remaining subsections introduce detailed implementation details.

3.1   Overview of Optimization Strategy

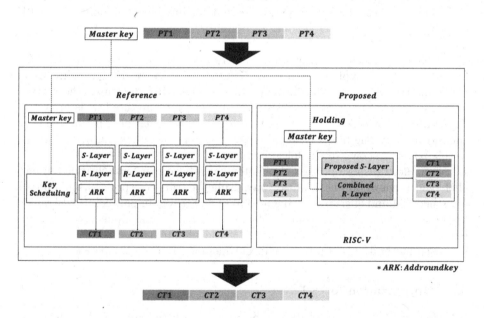

Fig. 2. Overview of optimization strategy

Figure 2 shows the overview of our optimization strategy. We propose three optimization strategies for efficient PIPO execution on 32-bit RISC-V processor. Followings are our strategies for optimizing the performance of PIPO.

- *Processing multiple data blocks in parallel*
  Since the size of each register in our target RISC-V processor is 32-bit, it is efficient to encrypt·decrypt 4 plaintexts, simultaneously. By using this, we design register scheduling and parallel logic.

- *Minimizing the number of memory access*
  By holding the master key on a register, memory access to the round key is minimized; also we efficiently load 4 plaintexts with minimal instructions. It requires only two memory accesses to load one plaintext and loads 32-bit data at a time. Therefore our implementation can load all 4 plaintexts in just 8 instructions.
- *Combining internal computation processes*
  we integrate the AddRoundKey process with the existing R-Layer, using a property that the simplicity of PIPO's AddRoundKey operation and the master key held in the register. Therefore, only very simple XOR operations are added to the R-Layer.

3.2   Proposed Parallel Logic

Our main idea is the minimization of memory access in encryption process. Compared to the register-only operation on the ALU, the memory access requires more clock cycles. Thus, encryption should be implemented only with ALU operation through register holding of plaintexts used for encryption to reduce memory access.

PIPO is designed for implementation in 8-bit AVRs. So it would be inefficient to only encrypt one block of PIPO in RISC-V, which provides 32-bit registers. Therefore, we will ultimately implement PIPO to match the register features provided by RISC-V. Because 32-bit registers are used, it is more efficient in terms of memory access if multiple blocks are encrypted in parallel than encrypting only one block. Therefore, the register scheduling method proposed in this paper is shown in the following Fig. 3.

After the transpose process, 4 plaintexts can have registers scheduled in parallel logic as shown in Fig. 3. In this way, using the transpose process, 4 plaintexts are scheduled and encrypted using a total of 8 registers in parallel. It rearranges the ciphertext scheduled in parallel logic so that a normal ciphertext can come out after all operations are completed. If the plaintext is scheduled using the proposed method, it will provide efficient memory access and operation.

3.3   Optimization for S-Layer

In Reference, the implementation of S-Layer is a single byte as a starting point. However, our implementation follows parallel logic, so there are considerations. The first is an independent computation of 4 plaintexts in one register. Since the S-Layer process is based on bit operation, each plaintext is independently calculated in our proposed parallel logic. That is, each plaintext has no effect. The second is the use of temporary registers considering operands. In our implementation, the 3 temporary variables in the reference code are replaced with 4 registers. Temporarily 1 register each in S_5^1, S_5^2, S_3 constituting S-Layer, and one additional register is used to store the intermediate value. Through this, the S-Layer for 4 plaintexts is calculated at the same time.

	Plaintext1		Plaintext2		Plaintext3		Plaintext4	
R_0	pt_1^0	...	pt_1^7	pt_2^0	...	pt_2^7	pt_3^0	...	pt_3^7	pt_4^0	...	pt_4^7
R_1	pt_1^8	...	pt_1^{15}	pt_2^8	...	pt_2^{15}	pt_3^8	...	pt_3^{15}	pt_4^8	...	pt_4^{15}
R_2	pt_1^{16}	...	pt_1^{23}	pt_2^{16}	...	pt_2^{23}	pt_3^{16}	...	pt_3^{23}	pt_4^{16}	...	pt_4^{23}
R_3	pt_1^{24}	...	pt_1^{31}	pt_2^{24}	...	pt_2^{31}	pt_3^{24}	...	pt_3^{31}	pt_4^{24}	...	pt_4^{31}
R_4	pt_1^{32}	...	pt_1^{39}	pt_2^{32}	...	pt_2^{39}	pt_3^{32}	...	pt_3^{39}	pt_4^{32}	...	pt_4^{39}
R_5	pt_1^{40}	...	pt_1^{47}	pt_2^{40}	...	pt_2^{47}	pt_3^{40}	...	pt_3^{47}	pt_4^{40}	...	pt_4^{47}
R_6	pt_1^{48}	...	pt_1^{55}	pt_2^{48}	...	pt_2^{55}	pt_3^{48}	...	pt_3^{55}	pt_4^{48}	...	pt_4^{55}
R_7	pt_1^{56}	...	pt_1^{63}	pt_2^{56}	...	pt_2^{63}	pt_3^{56}	...	pt_3^{63}	pt_4^{56}	...	pt_4^{63}

Fig. 3. Four plaintext scheduling using parallel logic in RISC-V

3.4   Optimization for R-Layer

R-Layer uses the rotation operator to shuffle the bits of each byte. We have to think about two parts of the R-Layer process. First, there is no rotation operator that handles carry in RISC-V. Therefore, we have to think about the handling of carry when performing the rotation operation. Second, we use parallel logic. Since we are encrypting 4 plaintexts using parallel logic, we need to perform rotation operation in one register in units of bytes. Therefore, in our implementation, we propose a method of constructing the R-Layer by processing the rotation operation using 4 plaintexts scheduled in parallel logic in RISC-V.

When performing the rotation operation, the carry part should be considered. We use a method of masking the data loaded onto each register to handle carry. This method can be useful in register with parallel logic from the 32-bit. Figure 4 are illustrates how to configure a rotation using a bit-masking in RISC-V that we offer.

The main idea is that when right rotation 3-bits in one byte, the actual process that takes place within a byte is that the left 3-bit and right 5-bit are swapped into one chunk. Figure 4 is an example using one register among 8 registers. It has one register which first bytes of the plaintext output after performing the S-Layer process are collected. We first proceed with the masking process, which divides chunks by considering carry.

The example shows the process of rotating 3-bits to the right of each of the 4-byte; therefore, we will perform an operation that swaps the right 3-bit chunk and the left 5-bit chunk for each byte. First, in order to divide chunks while considering carry, in the masking process, 0xE0 and 0x1F are operated by AND operator for each byte. Then, for 4 bytes, a 3-bit chunk on the left and 5-bit chunk on the right are generated respectively. A shift operation is performed to exchange the chunks of the left 3-bit and the right 5-bit. If the OR operation is performed on the two chunks that have performed the shift operation, the register that has performed the rotation operation for each byte is calculated. In

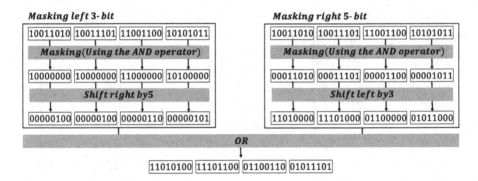

Fig. 4. Rotation operation using masking in RISC-V

this way, our proposed method has the advantage that it can be extended and applied to 16-bit and 64-bit processors, including 32-bit processors.

3.5   Combinded AddRoundKey

To proceed with the encryption process in PIPO, a round key is required for every round. A round key is generated from one master key through a key schedule process in advance. Since this function generates additional computational load independent of the encryption process, we propose a method to optimize the computational amount of key schedule process.

PIPO's key schedule process generates a round key through XOR operation of the master key and Rcon. In RISC-V, PIPO's key schedule function consumes 1146 clock cycles. To reduce the additional load caused by key schedule, the AddRoundKey function and the key schedule process are combined within the encryption process. We have implemented AddRoundKey to proceed with a simple XOR operation by storing the round key in the register. In this case, there is no process of loading the round key, which reduces the number of memory accesses. This operation is integrated into R-Layer. At this time, it should be noted that the master key used for even rounds and odd rounds is different.

4   Performance Analysis

Table 2 compares the performance of the proposed PIPO implementation with the reference PIPO implementation and other block cipher implementations on 32-bit RISC-V processor. To measure the correct performance, we used SiFive's HiFiveRevB board equipped with 32-bit RISC-V processor. HiFiveRevB board has a 320 MHz frequency, 16 KB RAM, and 32 MB flash memory. As a development tool, we used SiFive's FreedomStudio (ver. 2020) using GCC Toolchain: gcc version 10.1.0 and gcc version 8.3.0. For fair comparison, we build our software and the reference PIPO implementation with −O3 compile option.

Table 2. Comparison of other block cipher implementations on RISC-V (*CPB*: Cycles Per Byte, code size measured by byte).

Reference	Algorithm	Plaintext	Security	*CPB*	Code size
This work	PIPO	64-bit	128-bit	**113.7***	10816
			256-bit	**136.7***	12352
Kim et al. (Ref) [1]			128-bit	561.13	896
			256-bit	600.38	896
Ko Stoffelen [3]	Table-AES	128-bit	128-bit	57.0	4352
	ChaCha20 enc	512-bit		27.9	12960
	Keccak-f[1600]	-		68.9	7936
Kwak et al. [14]	PIPO	64-bit	128-bit	249.1	6124
	ARIA	128-bit		291.0	8192
	LEA			46.4	2432

*Includes key schedule process

For the comparison to the reference PIPO implementation [1] which was originally developed on 8-bit AVR MCU, we build it to a 32-bit RISC-V processor. Regarding the reference code, when performance was measured only for the encryption process, 561.13 CPB for PIPO-64/128 and 600.38 CPB for PIPO-64/256 were measured. Our work proposes a merged key scheduling process. Despite the inclusion of the key scheduling process, our implementation has a performance improvement of 393.52% and 339.19% for PIPO-64/128 and PIPO-64/256, respectively, compared to the implementation built with the reference code.

In Table 2, we also compare our implementation with other ciphers implementations on the same target devices. In case of Korean block ciphers PIPO, ARIA, and LEA, Kwak et al. implemented them on 32-bit RISC-V with some optimization techniques and benchmarked their performance (The core parts were written in assembly codes) [14]. The PIPO Reference implementation is assembled and ported to RISC-V. The implementation proposed in [14] had a performance improvement over the default implementation, the reference implementation built simply on RISC-V, as the ported implementation. The proposed PIPO implementation outperforms Kwak et al.'s ARIA and PIPO implementations by 159.45% and 128.5%, respectively.

However, it still shows lower performance than LEA, which is an ARX structure composed of only simple bit operations. 32-bit addition operation of LEA shows high efficiency in embedded devices with 32-bit registers, including the RISC-V environment. Implementation of the partitioning of LEA in 32-bit units removes the load on carry operations that have to be considered in other devices; therefore, the actual process is only simple XOR and rotate operation. We further investigated the implementation of LEA in the AVR environment. The encryption performance of LEA in the AVR platforms achieved 190 CPB in the initially proposed code [4], and 167 CPB in the additionally optimized paper [19].

PIPO's performance in PIPO's proposal paper is 197 CPB, which is basically lower than LEA [1]. On the other hand, in the AVR processor, which is one of the most constrained environments in terms of code size, PIPO shows the best performance. Algorithmic performance differences are maintained even in the RISC-V environment. However, our implementation achieves lower performance than benchmarked LEA in a RISC-V environment, but is competitive compared to ARIA and benchmarked PIPO. The code size for parallelization uses only 0.03% in the RISC-V environment with the most commonly used 32 MB of flash memory. Therefore, from a practical applicability standpoint, the memory cost is negligible. For a higher performance improvement over the proposed implementation, ISA of RISC-V needs to be further designed. Currently, parallel instruction development for RISC-V is in progress. If development is completed in the future and commercialization takes place in earnest, there is a possibility that the proposed PIPO software will be further optimized.

5   Conclusion

With the development of 5G technology, the importance of high-speed of data communication and security in embedded devices is being stressed. However, the embedded environment has limited resources unlike the high-end computer, so it is challenging to apply the reference implementation of the computation-intensive cryptography. Thus, it is necessary to optimize the crypto implementation considering the characteristics of each embedded environment. In this paper, we propose an optimization method for the PIPO block cipher algorithm in the 32-bit processor RISC-V architecture. Our optimization methods include parallel logic implementation, S-Layer optimization method, rotation instruction implementation method considering the characteristics of RISC-V architecture, and R-Layer configuration that merges the key schedule process and AddRoundKey process. Efficient PIPO in RISC-V architecture suggest implementation plan. Our PIPO-64/128 and PIPO-64/256 optimization implementations provide performance improvements of 393.52% and 339.19% over the existing reference code, respectively. In the future, we plan to conduct the optimized implementation of lightweight block ciphers such as SPECK, SIMON, and SKINNY for secure communication in an IoT environment.

References

1. Kim, H., et al.: PIPO: a lightweight block cipher with efficient higher-order masking software implementations. In: Hong, D. (ed.) ICISC 2020. LNCS, vol. 12593, pp. 99–122. Springer, Cham (2021). https://doi.org/10.1007/978-3-030-68890-5_6
2. Kim, H.: A new method for designing lightweight S-boxes with high differential and linear branch numbers, and its application. Cryptology ePrint Archive, Report 2020/1582 (2020). https://eprint.iacr.org/2020/1582
3. Stoffelen, K.: Efficient cryptography on the RISC-V architecture. IACR Cryptol. ePrint Arch. **2019**, 794 (2019)

4. Hong, D., Lee, J.-K., Kim, D.-C., Kwon, D., Ryu, K.H., Lee, D.-G.: LEA: a 128-bit block cipher for fast encryption on common processors. In: Kim, Y., Lee, H., Perrig, A. (eds.) WISA 2013. LNCS, vol. 8267, pp. 3–27. Springer, Cham (2014). https://doi.org/10.1007/978-3-319-05149-9_1

5. Hong, D., et al.: HIGHT: a new block cipher suitable for low-resource device. In: Goubin, L., Matsui, M. (eds.) CHES 2006. LNCS, vol. 4249, pp. 46–59. Springer, Heidelberg (2006). https://doi.org/10.1007/11894063_4

6. Roh, D., et al.: Revised version of block cipher CHAM. In: Seo, J.H. (ed.) ICISC 2019. LNCS, vol. 11975, pp. 1–19. Springer, Cham (2020). https://doi.org/10.1007/978-3-030-40921-0_1

7. Kizhvatov, I.: Side channel analysis of AVR XMEGA crypto engine. In: Serpanos, D.N., Wolf, W.H. (eds.) Proceedings of the 4th Workshop on Embedded Systems Security, WESS 2009, Grenoble, France, 15 October 2009. ACM (2009)

8. Golder, A., Das, D., Danial, J., Ghosh, S., Sen, S., Raychowdhury, A.: Practical approaches toward deep-learning-based cross-device power side-channel attack. IEEE Trans. Very Large Scale Integr. (VLSI) Syst. 27(12), 2720–2733 (2019)

9. Reinbrecht, C., Susin, A., Bossuet, L., Sigl, G., Sepúlveda, J.: Side channel attack on NoC-based MPSoCs are practical: NoC Prime+ Probe attack. In: 2016 29th Symposium on Integrated Circuits and Systems Design (SBCCI), pp. 1–6 (2016)

10. Schwarz, M.: Keydrown: eliminating keystroke timing side-channel attacks. CoRR, abs/1706.06381 (2017)

11. Campos, F., Jellema, L., Lemmen, M., Müller, L., Sprenkels, D., Viguier, B.: Assembly or optimized C for lightweight cryptography on RISC-V? In: Krenn, S., Shulman, H., Vaudenay, S. (eds.) CANS 2020. LNCS, vol. 12579, pp. 526–545. Springer, Cham (2020). https://doi.org/10.1007/978-3-030-65411-5_26

12. Marshall, B., Newell, G.R., Page, D., Saarinen, M.J.O., Wolf, C.: The design of scalar AES instruction set extensions for RISC-V. IACR Trans. Cryptogr. Hardw. Embed. Syst. 2021(1), 109–136 (2021)

13. Tehrani, E., Graba, T., Si-Merabet, A., Danger, J.-L.: RISC-V extension for lightweight cryptography. In: 23rd Euromicro Conference on Digital System Design, DSD 2020, Kranj, Slovenia, 26–28 August 2020, pp. 222–228. IEEE (2020)

14. Kwak, Y., Kim, Y., Seo, S.C.: Benchmarking Korean block ciphers on 32-bit RISC-V processor. J. Korea Inst. Inf. Secur. Cryptol. (JKIISC) 31(3), 331–340 (2021)

15. Waterman, A., Lee, Y., Patterson, D.A., Asanovic, K.: The RISC-V instruction set manual. Volume I: Base user-level ISA. EECS Department, UC Berkeley, Technical report, UCB/EECS-2011-62, 116 (2011)

16. Waterman, A.S.: Design of the RISC-V instruction set architecture. Ph.D. thesis, UC Berkeley (2016)

17. Lee, J.: Simulation and synthesis of RISC-V processor. J. Inst. Internet Broadcast. Commun. 19(1), 239–245 (2019)

18. Chat Room. RISC-V architecture. Image (2017)

19. Seo, H., An, K., Kwon, H.: Compact LEA and HIGHT implementations on 8-Bit AVR and 16-Bit MSP processors. In: Kang, B.B.H., Jang, J.S. (eds.) WISA 2018. LNCS, vol. 11402, pp. 253–265. Springer, Cham (2019). https://doi.org/10.1007/978-3-030-17982-3_20

No Silver Bullet: Optimized Montgomery Multiplication on Various 64-Bit ARM Platforms

Hwajeong Seo[1]([⊠])(iD), Pakize Sanal[2], Wai-Kong Lee[3], and Reza Azarderakhsh[2,4]

[1] IT Department, Hansung University, Seoul, South Korea
[2] Department of Computer and Electrical Engineering and Computer Science,
Florida Atlantic University, Boca Raton, FL, USA
{psanal2018,razarderakhsh}@fau.edu
[3] Department of Computer Engineering, Gachon University,
Seongnam, Incheon 13120, Korea
waikonglee@gachon.ac.kr
[4] PQSecure Technologies, LLC, Boca Raton, USA

Abstract. In this paper, we firstly presented optimized implementations of Montgomery multiplication on 64-bit ARM processors by taking advantages of Karatsuba algorithm and efficient multiplication instruction sets for ARM64 architectures. The implementation of Montgomery multiplication can improve the performance of (pre-quantum and post-quantum) public key cryptography (e.g. CSIDH, ECC, and RSA) implementations on ARM64 architectures, directly. Last but not least, the performance of Karatsuba algorithm does not ensure the fastest speed record on various ARM architectures, while it is determined by the clock cycles per multiplication instruction of target ARM architectures. In particular, recent Apple processors based on ARM64 architecture show lower cycles per instruction of multiplication than that of ARM Cortex-A series. For this reason, the schoolbook method shows much better performance than the sophisticated Karatsuba algorithm on Apple processors. With this observation, we can determine the proper approach for multiplication of cryptography library (e.g. Microsoft-SIDH) on Apple processors and ARM Cortex-A processors.

This work was partly supported by Institute for Information & communications Technology Promotion(IITP) grant funded by the Korea government (MSIT) (No. 2018-0-00264, Research on Blockchain Security Technology for IoT Services, 25%) and this work was partly supported by the National Research Foundation of Korea(NRF) grant funded by the Korea government(MSIT) (No. NRF-2020R1F1A1048478, 25%) and this work was partly supported by Institute of Information & communications Technology Planning & Evaluation (IITP) grant funded by the Korea government(MSIT) (No. 2021-0-00540, Development of Fast Design and Implementation of Cryptographic Algorithms based on GPU/ASIC, 25%) and this work was partly supported by Institute for Information & communications Technology Planning & Evaluation (IITP) grant funded by the Korea government(MSIT) (<Q|Crypton>, No. 2019-0-00033, Study on Quantum Security Evaluation of Cryptography based on Computational Quantum Complexity, 25%).

© Springer Nature Switzerland AG 2021
H. Kim (Ed.): WISA 2021, LNCS 13009, pp. 194–205, 2021.
https://doi.org/10.1007/978-3-030-89432-0_16

Keywords: Montgomery multiplication · ARM64 processor · Public key cryptography · Software implementation

1   Introduction

The modular reduction is the fundamental building block of conventional public key cryptography (e.g. RSA [15], El-Gamal [5], and ECC [10,13]) to post-quantum cryptography (e.g. RLWE [12], SIDH [4], and CSIDH [2]). One of the most well-known modular reduction techniques is Montgomery algorithm [14]. This approach replaces the complicated division operation for the modular reduction in relatively simple multiplication operations. For this reason, efficient implementations of Montgomery multiplication on target processors have been actively studied. In this paper, we firstly introduce the optimized Montgomery multiplication on ARM64 processors and show the impact on public key cryptography protocols (i.e. CSIDH)[1]. Furthermore, we found that recent Apple processors provide the multiplication instruction with very low latency. This nice feature leads to the new direction to implement the multiplication on Apple processors (i.e. simple schoolbook approach rather than sophisticated Karatsuba algorithm with additional routines). With this observation, we can improve the performance of cryptography libraries based on Karatsuba algorithm (e.g. Microsoft-SIDH) on recent Apple processors by replacing the multiplication to the schoolbook method[2].

1.1   Contribution

- **Optimized Montgomery multiplication on ARM64 architecture.** This paper presents the optimized implementation of Montgomery multiplication by taking advantages of Karatsuba algorithm and efficient multiplication instruction sets of ARM64 architectures. The proposed implementation is evaluated on both ARM Cortex-A and Apple A processors for benchmarking tests.
- **Efficient implementation of CSIDH on ARM64 architecture.** The implementation of CSIDH is accelerated through the proposed Montgomery multiplication. Full protocols of CSIDH-P511 are evaluated on 64-bit ARM Cortex-A and Apple A processors. In order to prevent the timing attack on the protocol, the implementation ensures the constant timing.
- **In-depth performance evaluation on ARM64 architecture.** Depending on ARM64 architectures (i.e. ARM Cortex-A and Apple A), same program code leads to different performance results. We analyze the performance of Montgomery multiplication and CSIDH on both architectures. Finally, we show that Karatsuba algorithm is not the best solution across all ARM64 architectures, since it introduces a number of addition operations than schoolbook methods.

---

[1] The proposed method is applicable to RSA, and ECC, as well.
[2] https://github.com/microsoft/PQCrypto-SIDH/tree/master/src.

Algorithm 1. Montgomery Reduction

Require: An m-bit modulus M, Montgomery radix $R = 2^m$, two m-bit operands A
    and B, and m-bit pre-computed constant $M' = -M^{-1} \bmod R$
Ensure: Montgomery product $(Z = (A \cdot B) \cdot R^{-1} \bmod M)$
  1: $T \leftarrow A \cdot B$
  2: $Q \leftarrow T \cdot M' \bmod R$
  3: $Z \leftarrow (T + Q \cdot M)/R$
  4: **if** $Z \geq M$ **then** $Z \leftarrow Z - M$ **end if**
  5: **return** Z

The remainder of the paper is structured as follows: We review the related
work on Montgomery multiplication, Karatsuba algorithm, and ARM64 processors in Sect. 2. We present the optimized implementation of Montgomery multiplication on ARM64 processors and its use cases (i.e. CSIDH) in Sect. 3. In
Sect. 4, we present results on various 64-bit ARM platforms (ARM Cortex-A
and Apple A processors). We end with conclusions in Sect. 5.

2 Related Works

2.1 Montgomery Multiplication

Montgomery multiplication consists of multiplication and reduction parts. The
multiplication can be implemented in different ways by altering the order of
operands and intermediate results. The operand-scanning method performs a
multiplication in a row-wise manner. This approach is suitable for processors
with many registers to retain long intermediate results as many as possible.
The alternative approach is the Comba (i.e. product-scanning) method [3]. Partial products are computed in a column-wise manner and only small number of
registers is required to maintain the intermediate result. Furthermore, since all
partial products of each word of the result are computed and added, consecu-
tively, the final result word is obtained directly and no intermediate results have
to be stored or loaded in the algorithm In [6], a hybrid-scanning method combining two aforementioned methods is presented. Afterward, several optimized
implementations for multiplication were suggested by caching operands [7,16].
However, the complexity of partial products for N-word multiplication is N^2.

Karatsuba algorithm computes a N-word multiplication with only three $N/2$-
word partial products compared to four $N/2$-word that are required by aforementioned multiplication methods [9]. The number of partial products is estimated
by $N^{log_2 3}$, which is a great improvement compared to N^2 of the standard multiplication. The previous multiplication on ARM64 processors mainly utilized
the Karatsuba algorithm for optimal performance since it reduces the number
of complicated multiplication.

Montgomery algorithm was firstly proposed in 1985 [14]. Montgomery algorithm avoids the division in modular multiplication by introducing simple shift
operations (i.e. division by 2). Given two integers A and B and the modulus M,

Table 1. Comparison of Montgomery multiplication on 64-bit ARMv8 Cortex-A processors.

Implementation	Multiplication	Montgomery Reduction	Application
Liu et al. [11]	Karatsuba	–	–
Seo et al. [17]	Karatsuba	Product Scanning	SIKE
Seo et al. [19]	Karatsuba	Product Scanning	SIKE
Jalali et al. [8]	Operand Scanning	Operand Scanning	CSIDH, RSA, ECC
This work	Karatsuba	Karatsuba	CSIDH, RSA, ECC

to compute the product $P = A \cdot B \bmod M$ in Montgomery method, operands A and B are firstly converted into Montgomery domain (i.e. $A' = A \cdot R \bmod M$ and $B' = B \cdot R \bmod M$). For efficient computations, Montgomery residue R is selected as a power of 2 and constant $M' = -M^{-1} \bmod 2^n$ is pre-computed. To compute the product, following three steps are conducted: (1) compute $T = A \cdot B$; (2) perform $Q = T \cdot M' \bmod 2^n$; (3) calculate $Z = \frac{(T+Q \cdot M)}{2^n}$ and (4) compute final reduction $Z \leftarrow Z - M$ if $Z \geq M$. Detailed descriptions of Montgomery reduction is available in Algorithm 1.

There are two approaches, including separated and interleaved ways, for Montgomery multiplication. The interleaved approach reduces the number of memory access for the intermediate result, but many implementations on ARM64 selected the separated approach. The separated implementation can employ the most optimal approach for multiplication and reduction operations each. In this paper, we also selected the separated approach. Both multiplication and Montgomery reduction parts are optimized with Karatsuba algorithm. In particular, we utilized the Karatsuba based Montgomery reduction by [18].

In Table 1, the comparison of Montgomery multiplication on 64-bit ARMv8 Cortex-A processors is given. Previous works [11,17,19] target for Montgomery friendly prime and it's application is limited to only SIKE due to the special prime form. On the other hand, the proposed Montgomery multiplication is targeting for random prime and it's applications are CSIDH, RSA, and ECC.

2.2   64-Bit ARMv8 Processors

ARMv8 is a 64-bit architecture for high-performance embedded applications. The 64-bit ARMv8 processors support both 32-bits (AArch32) and 64-bits (AArch64) architectures. It provides 31 general purpose registers which can hold 32-bit values in registers w0-w30 or 64-bit values in registers x0-x30. ARMv8 processors started to dominate the smartphone market soon after the release in 2011 and nowadays they are widely used in various smart phones (e.g. iPhone and Samsung Galaxy series) and laptop (e.g. MacBook Air and MacBook Pro). Since the processor is used primarily in embedded systems, smart phones and laptop computers, efficient and compact implementations are of special interest in real world applications. ARMv8 processors support powerful 64-bit wise unsigned integer multiplication instructions. Proposed implementation of modular multiplication uses the AArch64 architecture and makes extensive use of the following multiply instructions:

- MUL (unsigned multiplication, low part):
  MUL X0, X1, X2 computes X0 ← (X1 × X2) mod 2^{64}.
- UMULH (unsigned multiplication, high part):
  UMULH X0, X1, X2 computes X0 ← (X1 × X2)/2^{64}.

The two instructions above are required to compute a full 64-bit multiplication of the form 128-bit ← 64 × 64-bit, namely, the MUL instruction computes the lower 64-bit half of the product while UMULH computes the higher 64-bit half.

For the addition and subtraction operations, ADDS and SUBS instructions ensure 64-bit wise results, respectively. Detailed descriptions are as follows:

- ADDS (unsigned addition):
  ADDS X0, X1, X2 computes {CARRY,X0} ← (X1 + X2).
- SUB (unsigned subtraction):
  SUBS X0, X1, X2 computes {BORROW,X0} ← (X1 − X2).

Further details of ARMv8-A architecture can be found in official documents [1].

3 Proposed Implementations

3.1 Optimization of Montgomery Multiplication

One of the most expensive operation for public key cryptography is modular multiplication. In this paper, we present the optimal modular multiplication implementation in the separated way for 64-bit ARM architectures.

First, the multi-precision multiplication is performed by following the Karatsuba algorithm. 2-level Karatsuba computations are performed for 512-bit multiplication on 64-bit ARM architectures (i.e. $128 \rightarrow 256 \rightarrow 512$) [17]. Karatsuba's method reduces a multiplication of two N-limb operands to three multiplications, which have a length of $\frac{N}{2}$-limb. These three half-size multiplications can be performed with any multiplication techniques that we covered before (e.g., operand scanning method or product scanning method). Taking the multiplication of N-limb operand A and B as an example, we represent the operands as $A = A_H \cdot 2^{\frac{N}{2}} + A_L$ and $B = B_H \cdot 2^{\frac{N}{2}} + B_L$. The multiplication $P = A \cdot B$ can be computed according to the following equation by using additive Karatsuba's method:

$$A_H \cdot B_H \cdot 2^n + [(A_H + A_L)(B_H + B_L) - A_H \cdot B_H - A_L \cdot B_L] \cdot 2^{\frac{n}{2}} + A_L \cdot B_L \quad (1)$$

We further optimized the memory access by using general purpose registers to retain operands as many as possible since the access speed of register is much faster than that of memory. In particular, Karatsuba multiplication needs

Table 2. Register utilization for Montgomery reduction on ARM64.

Modulus M	Quotient Q	Temporal registers	Constant M'
8	4	15	1

to update operands but these operands are used in following computations. In this case, we keep operands in general purpose registers to avoid frequent memory loading operations where the memory access incurs read-write-dependency problems.

Multiplication and reduction operations are implemented in one function to avoid the function call and register push/pop instructions. Furthermore, the intermediate result of 512-bit multiplication is 1024-bit wise and this can be stored in 16 general purpose registers (i.e. $16 = 1024/64$) in the ideal case. By maintaining the whole intermediate result in general purpose registers, 16 memory load and 16 memory store operations are optimized away.

However, part of intermediate results are stored in STACK memory since Karatsuba approach requires a number of registers to retain operands and intermediate results. The stored result is directly used in the following modular reduction operation.

For the computation of Montgomery reduction, the product ($Q \leftarrow T \cdot M'$ mod R) is performed (Step 2 of Algorithm 1) in ordinary way. Afterward, the product $Q \cdot M$ is computed in a hybrid way (Step 3) [18]. The complexity of N-word original Montgomery reduction is $N^2 + N$ word-wise multiplications, while the hybrid Montgomery reduction is $\frac{7N^2}{8} + N$ word-wise multiplications. In particular, the hybrid Montgomery reduction consists of two 256-bit Montgomery reduction in product-scanning approach and two 256-bit (1-level) Karatsuba multiplication operations (i.e. $128 \rightarrow 256$).

28 out of 31 registers are utilized for 512-bit Montgomery reduction on the ARM64 architecture. The detailed register utilization is given in Table 2. When we perform the hybrid Montgomery reduction ($\frac{T+Q \cdot M}{2^n}$), computations ($Q_L \cdot M_L$ and $Q_H \cdot M_L$) are performed in sub-Montgomery reduction and others ($Q_L \cdot M_H$ and $Q_H \cdot M_H$) are performed in Karatsuba multiplication, where L and H represent lower and higher parts of operand.

In Algorithm 2, the optimized implementation of 256-bit sub-Montgomery reduction on ARM64 processors is given. Partial products of reduction are performed in the product-scanning way. Three ARM64 instructions (MUL, UMULH, and ADD) are mainly utilized for partial products. Since multiplication operations require 6 clock cycles in Cortex-A series, the utilization of result directly incurs pipeline stalls [17]. In Line 1 of Algorithm 2, the quotient (Q0) is generated with 64-bit wise. This is simply performed with single mul instruction. In Line 2~5, the quotient (Q0) is directly utilized, which incurs pipeline stalls. In Line 6~7, the result of multiplication (T0 and T1), which is computed in Line 2~3, is accumulated to the intermediate result. This approach avoids the read-write dependency. In Line 10, the register is initialized with xzr instruction and the carry is obtained in C0 register. In Line 11, the quotient (Q1) is generated but it is not utilized directly. In particular, the accumulation step (Line 12~15) is performed with partial products in previous steps. This does not incur the read-write dependency. Following computations (after Line 16 to end) are performed in the similar way (i.e. read-write dependency free).

Algorithm 2. Optimized implementation of 256-bit sub-Montgomery reduction on ARM64 processors.

Input: Modulus (M0-M3), intermediate results (C0-C3), constant (M_INV), temporal registers (T0-T3).
Output: Intermediate results (C0-C3), quotient (Q0-Q3).

```
 1: mul  Q0, C0, M_INV                              { Q0 ← C0 × M' }

 2: mul  T0, Q0, M0                                 { T ← Q × M }
 3: umulh T1, Q0, M0
 4: mul  T2, Q0, M1
 5: umulh T3, Q0, M1

 6: adds C0, C0, T0              { Accumulation of intermediate result }
 7: adcs C1, C1, T1
 8: adcs C2, C2, xzr
 9: adcs C3, C3, xzr
10: adc  C0, xzr, xzr

11: mul  Q1, C1, M_INV                              { Q1 ← C1 × M' }
12: adds C1, C1, T2
13: adcs C2, C2, T3
14: adcs C3, C3, xzr
15: adc  C0, C0, xzr

16: ...                                             { Omit }

17: mul  T2, Q3, M3
18: umulh T3, Q3, M3
19: adds C1, C1, T0             { Accumulation of intermediate result }
20: adcs C2, C2, T1
21: adc  C3, C3, xzr
22: adds C2, C2, T2
23: adcs C3, C3, T3
```

After the sub-Montgomery reduction, the remaining part is performed with the Karatsuba algorithm [17]. The additive Karatsuba algorithm performs the addition on the operand. This updates operands which cannot be used again. In the proposed implementation, we cached the operand in registers and this avoids the memory access for the operand re-loading. Afterward, one sub-Montgomery reduction and one Karatsuba multiplication are performed. Lastly, the final

Table 3. Comparison of ARMv8-A cores on ARM Cortex-A processors.

Company	ARM	
Platform	Odroid-C2	Raspberry-pi4
Core	Cortex-A53(@1.5 GHz)	Cortex-A72(@1.5 GHz)
OS	Ubuntu 16.04	Ubuntu 20.10
Released	2014	2015
Revision	ARMv8.0-A	ARMv8.0-A
Decode	2-wide	3-wide
Pipeline depth	8	15
Out-of-order	×	O
Branch prediction	Conditional	O
Execution ports	2	8

reduction is performed in the masked way in order to ensure the constant timing implementation. Firstly the intermediate result is subtracted by the modulus. When the borrow bit is captured, it sets the masked modulus. Otherwise, the modulus is set to zero. The result is subtracted by the masked modulus.

In conclusion, the proposed 512-bit Montgomery multiplication is performed in two steps as follows:

$$2 - level\ Karatsuba\ multiplication\ \rightarrow\ hybrid\ reduction\ (1 - level\ Karasuba)$$

3.2 Acceleration of Public Key Cryptography

The proposed implementation of Montgomery multiplication is efficiently optimized. We can directly apply the proposed Montgomery multiplication to the CSIDH library by [8]. CSIDH is a variant of isogeny-based cryptography that offers (conjecturally) post-quantum secure non-interactive key exchange with tiny public keys and practical performance.

We checked the improved CSIDH implementation based on the proposed Montgomery multiplication passed the CSIDH tests and public-key validations. Furthermore, the conventional public key cryptography based on random prime (RSA and ECC) can also take advantages of the proposed method.

4   Evaluation

The proposed implementation is evaluated on the various ARM64 architectures, which is largely divided into ARM Cortex-A and Apple A series. Detailed specifications for each processor are given in Table 3 and 4.

In Table 5 and 6, the comparison of clock cycles for 512-bit Montgomery multiplication and constant-time CSIDH-P511 on 64-bit ARM architectures is given. Proposed implementations of 512-bit modular multiplication achieved performance enhancements than the school-book method [8] by 1.25× and 1.23×

Table 4. Comparison of ARMv8-A cores on Apple A processors.

Company	Apple		
Platform	iPad mini5	iPhone SE2	iPhone12 mini
Core	A12(Vortex@2.49 GHz)	A13(Lightning@2.65 GHz)	A14(Firestorm@3.10 GHz)
OS	iPadOS 14.4	iOS 14.4	iOS 14.4
Released	2018	2019	2020
Revision	ARMv8.3-A	ARMv8.4-A	ARMv8.4-A
Decode	7-wide	8-wide	8-wide
Pipeline depth	16	16	–
Out-of-order	0	0	–
Branch prediction	–	–	–
Execution ports	13	13	–

on Odroid-C2 and Raspberry-pi4, respectively. Since the approach is a generic method, we can apply the proposed method to larger operand sizes without difficulties. Furthermore, Montgomery multiplication is the fundamental operation in PKC. For the case study, we ported the implementation of Montgomery multiplication to CSIDH implementation. The performance of key exchange is improved by $1.16\times$ and $1.23\times$ than previous works on Odroid-C2 and Raspberry-pi4, respectively.

On the other hand, proposed implementations on Apple platforms show the opposite performance result. The schoolbook method based 512-bit modular multiplication achieved performance enhancements than proposed method by $0.71\times$, $0.65\times$ and $0.69\times$ on iPad mini5, iPhone SE2, and iPhone12 mini, respectively. The performance of key exchange is degraded by $0.71\times$, $0.64\times$, and $0.72\times$ than previous works on Odroid-C2 and Raspberry-pi4, respectively.

Table 5. Comparison of clock cycles ($\times 10^6$) for Montgomery multiplication (for 512-bit) and (constant-time) CSIDH-P511 on 64-bit Odroid-C2 and Raspberry-pi4.

Implementation	Odroid-C2			Raspberry-pi4		
	Timing [cc$\times 10^6$]		[8]/Opt	Timing [cc$\times 10^6$]		[8]/Opt
	[8]	Opt		[8]	Opt	
Montgomery multiplication	1,309 cc	1,044 cc	1.25	973 cc	792 cc	1.23
Alice key generation	14,374	12,392	1.16	11,892	9,864	1.21
Bob key generation	14,386	12,392	1.16	12,098	9,916	1.22
Validation of Bob's key	58	50	1.16	43	35	1.21
Validation of Alice's key	58	50	1.16	43	35	1.21
Alice shared key generation	14,252	12,628	1.13	11,570	10,099	1.15
Bob shared key generation	14,544	12,555	1.16	12,453	10,114	1.23
Alice total computations	28,684	25,070	1.14	23,504	19,998	1.18
Bob total computations	28,988	24,998	1.16	24,594	20,065	1.23

Table 6. Comparison of clock cycles ($\times 10^6$) for Montgomery multiplication (for 512-bit) and (constant-time) CSIDH-P511 on 64-bit iPad mini5, iPhone SE2, and iPhone12 mini.

Implementation	iPad mini5			iPhone SE2			iPhone12 mini		
	Timing [cc×10^6]		[8]/Opt	Timing [cc×10^6]		[8]/Opt	Timing [cc×10^6]		[8]/Opt
	[8]	Opt		[8]	Opt		[8]	Opt	
Montgomery multiplication	167 cc	233 cc	0.71	154 cc	235 cc	0.65	150 cc	214 cc	0.69
Alice key generation	1,210	1,694	0.71	1,086	1,692	0.64	1,131	1,548	0.73
Bob key generation	1,212	1,681	0.72	1,086	1,693	0.64	1,132	1,557	0.73
Validation of Bob's key	8	11	0.71	7	11	0.65	7	10	0.72
Validation of Alice's key	8	11	0.71	7	11	0.66	7	10	0.72
Alice shared key generation	1,216	1,705	0.71	1,090	1,690	0.64	1,127	1,572	0.72
Bob shared key generation	1,214	1,681	0.72	1,084	1,706	0.64	1,135	1,546	0.73
Alice total computations	2,434	3,410	0.71	2,183	3,393	0.64	2,265	3,130	0.72
Bob total computations	2,433	3,373	0.72	2,177	3,409	0.64	2,274	3,113	0.73

Table 7. Comparison of cycles per instruction on ARM64.

Platform	MUL	UMULH	ADD	MUL/ADD	UMULH/ADD
Odroid-C2	2.37	3.93	0.90	2.62	4.34
Raspberry-pi4	3.02	4.03	0.64	4.65	6.20
iPad mini5	0.57	0.57	0.42	1.34	1.34
iPhone SE2	0.49	0.49	0.37	1.31	1.31
iPhone12 mini	0.55	0.51	0.37	1.47	1.38

In Table 7, the comparison of cycles per instruction on ARM64 is given. The timing is measured with the average cycles after performing 1,000 times of each iteration without read-write dependency. The timing also includes function call and push/pop instructions. In ARM Cortex-A series, ratios of $\frac{MUL}{ADD}$ and $\frac{UMULH}{ADD}$ are 2.62~4.34 and 4.65~6.20 for Odroid-C2 and Raspberry-pi4 boards, respectively. This shows that the multiplication operation is more expensive than the addition operation on the target ARM Cortex-A architecture. For this reason, Karatsuba algorithm, which replaces multiplication operations into addition operations is effective on ARM Cortex-A series. On the other hand, ratios of $\frac{MUL}{ADD}$ and $\frac{UMULH}{ADD}$ on Apple A series are 1.34, 1.31, and 1.47~1.38 for iPad mini5, iPhone SE2, iPhone12 mini, respectively. This is unique features of advanced ARM architectures. Unlike previous architectures, multiplication operations are efficiently performed and the complexity between addition and multiplication is narrow. This leads to different conclusion (i.e. best implementation technique) in Apple A series.

In Table 8, the number of instructions for Montgomery multiplication methods is given. The schoolbook method (i.e. operand-scanning) requires 297 addition, 265 multiplication, and 134 memory access instructions, respectively. Compared with the Karatsuba algorithm, 225 addition instructions are optimized away but it requires 51 multiplication and 64 memory access instructions, more

Table 8. Number of instructions for 512-bit Montgomery multiplication methods.

Implementation	ADD/SUB	MUL/UMULH	LDR/STR
Schoolbook Method [8]	297	265	134
Karatsuba Algorithm	522	214	70

than the Karatsuba approach. Due to the efficient multiplication instruction on Apple A processors, reducing the number of multiplication by sacrificing the addition operation is not effective. For this reason, even though processors based on ARM64 architecture, the implementation technique should be different depending on cycles per multiplication instruction. This observation is useful for optimization of public key cryptography on ARM64 architecture. For example, Montgomery multiplication of Microsoft-SIDH library is based on the Karatsuba algorithm. This library can be improved by using operand-scanning method on Apple A products.

5   Conclusion

In this paper, we presented optimized Montgomery multiplication implementations for the 64-bit ARM Cortex-A processors. Proposed implementations utilized the Karatsuba algorithm and ARMv8-A specific instruction sets. This work shows that proposed implementations on ARM Cortex-A platforms are more efficient than previous works.

However, the platform with low multiplication latency (e.g. Apple A processors) achieved the better performance with the schoolbook method. This is because the evaluation of previous works is usually conducted on ARM Cortex-A processors. With the observation on this paper, the implementation should be evaluated on various ARM platforms for fair comparison and practicality.

The obvious future work is improving the Microsoft-SIDH library on Apple A processors by utilizing the schoolbook method or other approaches (i.e. product-scanning and hybrid-scanning). Furthermore, we will investigate the multiplication method for various integer lengths. Lastly, the proposed implementation will be the public domain and other cryptography engineers can directly use them for their cryptography applications.

References

1. ARM: ARM architecture reference manual: ARMv8, for ARMv8-A architecture profile (2020)
2. Castryck, W., Lange, T., Martindale, C., Panny, L., Renes, J.: CSIDH: an efficient post-quantum commutative group action. In: Peyrin, T., Galbraith, S. (eds.) ASIACRYPT 2018. LNCS, vol. 11274, pp. 395–427. Springer, Cham (2018). https://doi.org/10.1007/978-3-030-03332-3_15

3. Comba, P.G.: Exponentiation cryptosystems on the IBM PC. IBM Syst. J. **29**(4), 526–538 (1990)
4. Costello, C., Longa, P., Naehrig, M.: Efficient algorithms for supersingular isogeny diffie-hellman. In: Robshaw, M., Katz, J. (eds.) CRYPTO 2016. LNCS, vol. 9814, pp. 572–601. Springer, Heidelberg (2016). https://doi.org/10.1007/978-3-662-53018-4_21
5. ElGamal, T.: A public key cryptosystem and a signature scheme based on discrete logarithms. IEEE Trans. Inf. Theory **31**(4), 469–472 (1985)
6. Gura, N., Patel, A., Wander, A., Eberle, H., Shantz, S.C.: Comparing elliptic curve cryptography and RSA on 8-bit CPUs. In: Joye, M., Quisquater, J.-J. (eds.) CHES 2004. LNCS, vol. 3156, pp. 119–132. Springer, Heidelberg (2004). https://doi.org/10.1007/978-3-540-28632-5_9
7. Hutter, M., Wenger, E.: Fast multi-precision multiplication for public-key cryptography on embedded microprocessors. In: Preneel, B., Takagi, T. (eds.) CHES 2011. LNCS, vol. 6917, pp. 459–474. Springer, Heidelberg (2011). https://doi.org/10.1007/978-3-642-23951-9_30
8. Jalali, A., Azarderakhsh, R., Kermani, M.M., Jao, D.: Towards optimized and constant-time CSIDH on embedded devices. In: Polian, I., Stöttinger, M. (eds.) COSADE 2019. LNCS, vol. 11421, pp. 215–231. Springer, Cham (2019). https://doi.org/10.1007/978-3-030-16350-1_12
9. Karatsuba, A.: Multiplication of multidigit numbers on automata. In: Soviet physics doklady, vol. 7, pp. 595–596 (1963)
10. Koblitz, N.: Elliptic curve cryptosystems. Math. Comput. **48**(177), 203–209 (1987)
11. Liu, Z., Järvinen, K., Liu, W., Seo, H.: Multiprecision multiplication on ARMv8. In: 2017 IEEE 24th Symposium on Computer Arithmetic (ARITH), pp. 10–17. IEEE (2017)
12. Lyubashevsky, V., Peikert, C., Regev, O.: On ideal lattices and learning with errors over rings. In: Gilbert, H. (ed.) EUROCRYPT 2010. LNCS, vol. 6110, pp. 1–23. Springer, Heidelberg (2010). https://doi.org/10.1007/978-3-642-13190-5_1
13. Miller, V.S.: Use of elliptic curves in cryptography. In: Williams, H.C. (ed.) CRYPTO 1985. LNCS, vol. 218, pp. 417–426. Springer, Heidelberg (1986). https://doi.org/10.1007/3-540-39799-X_31
14. Montgomery, P.L.: Modular multiplication without trial division. Math. Comput. **44**(170), 519–521 (1985)
15. Rivest, R.L., Shamir, A., Adleman, L.: A method for obtaining digital signatures and public-key cryptosystems. Commun. ACM **21**(2), 120–126 (1978)
16. Seo, H., Kim, H.: Multi-precision multiplication for public-key cryptography on embedded microprocessors. In: Lee, D.H., Yung, M. (eds.) WISA 2012. LNCS, vol. 7690, pp. 55–67. Springer, Heidelberg (2012). https://doi.org/10.1007/978-3-642-35416-8_5
17. Seo, H., Liu, Z., Longa, P., Hu, Z.: SIDH on ARM: faster modular multiplications for faster post-quantum supersingular isogeny key exchange. In: IACR Transactions on Cryptographic Hardware and Embedded Systems, pp. 1–20 (2018)
18. Seo, H., Liu, Z., Nogami, Y., Choi, J., Kim, H.: Hybrid Montgomery reduction. ACM Trans. Embed. Comput. Syst. (TECS) **15**(3), 1–13 (2016)
19. Seo, H., Sanal, P., Jalali, A., Azarderakhsh, R.: Optimized implementation of SIKE round 2 on 64-bit ARM Cortex-A processors. IEEE Trans. Circuits Syst. I Regul. Pap. **67**(8), 2659–2671 (2020)

ARMed Frodo

FrodoKEM on 64-Bit ARMv8 Processors

Hyeokdong Kwon[1], Kyungbae Jang[1], Hyunjun Kim[1], Hyunji Kim[1], Minjoo Sim[1], Siwoo Eum[1], Wai-Kong Lee[2], and Hwajeong Seo[1(✉)] [iD]

[1] IT Department, Hansung University, Seoul 02876, South Korea
[2] Department of Computer Engineering, Gachon University, Seongnam, Incheon 13120, Korea
waikonglee@gachon.ac.kr

Abstract. FrodoKEM is one of Post-quantum Cryptography, which is selected Round 3 alternate candidates of Public-key Encryption and Key-establishment Algorithms at NIST Post-quantum Cryptography Standardization. FrodoKEM uses AES algorithm for generate pseudo-random matrix, and also uses matrix-multiplication. At that time, a huge computational load occurred to the pseudo-random number generation and matrix-multiplication operation, reducing the overall performance of the FrodoKEM scheme. In this paper, we propose the parallel matrix-multiplication and built-in AES accelerator for AES encryption on ARMv8 processors, and applied these techniques to the FrodoKEM-640 scheme. To implement the parallel matrix-multiplication, vector registers (i.e. 128-bit wise) and vector instructions (i.e. NEON) are used. The proposed parallel matrix-multiplication can be generated 80 element of output matrix at once. As a result, the matrix-multiplication has $43.8\times$ faster than the normal matrix-multiplication in the best-case, the implementation FrodoKEM-640 with all of proposed techniques has $10.22\times$ better performance in maximum than previous C only implementation.

Keywords: Post-quantum cryptography · FrodoKEM · 64-bit ARMv8 processors · Software implementation

This work was partly supported by Institute for Information & communications Technology Promotion (IITP) grant funded by the Korea government (MSIT) (No.2018-0-00264, Research on Blockchain Security Technology for IoT Services, 25%) and this work was partly supported by the National Research Foundation of Korea(NRF) grant funded by the Korea government(MSIT) (No. NRF-2020R1F1A1048478, 25%) and this work was partly supported by Institute of Information & communications Technology Planning & Evaluation (IITP) grant funded by the Korea government(MSIT) (No.2021-0-00540, Development of Fast Design and Implementation of Cryptographic Algorithms based on GPU/ASIC, 25%) and this work was partly supported by Institute for Information & communications Technology Planning & Evaluation (IITP) grant funded by the Korea government(MSIT) (<Q|Crypton>, No.2019-0-00033, Study on Quantum Security Evaluation of Cryptography based on Computational Quantum Complexity, 25%).

ⓒ Springer Nature Switzerland AG 2021
H. Kim (Ed.): WISA 2021, LNCS 13009, pp. 206–217, 2021.
https://doi.org/10.1007/978-3-030-89432-0_17

1   Introduction

As the technology of quantum computers improved, classical cryptography algorithms are threatened. Cryptography algorithms based on mathematical hard problems can be easily broken by quantum algorithms. In order to resolve these issues, the National Institute of Standards and Technology (NIST) in the United States of America has held a contest to standardize post-quantum cryptography in preparation for the quantum computer era. Among them, FrodoKEM was selected as a Round 3 alternate candidate. FrodoKEM is a Public Key Encryption (PKE) algorithm based on Learning With Errors (LWE). Since the algorithm is based on very conservative mathematical problems, the execution timing is slower than other lattice based cryptography. In this paper, we challenge to the optimal implementation of FrodoKEM on 64-bit ARMv8 processors. The target processor is widely used in modern smartphone, tablet, and laptop computers. Detailed contributions are follow.

1.1   Contributions

- **Matrix-multiplication with parallel operations.** Matrix-multiplication is used in Key generation, Encapsulation, and Decapsulation of FrodoKEM-640 schemes. The size of matrix seed A is $640*640$, and error matrix s is $640*8$ or $8*640$. At this point, the matrix-multiplication occurs large computational loads, because the matrix size is huge. We propose the implementation by using vector registers (i.e. 128-bit wise) and vector instructions (i.e. NEON) of ARMv8 architectures, for the parallel matrix-multiplication. The proposed implementation does not transpose matrices, but it loads values used for each output generation in vector registers. The regularity of the value loaded for all rounds exists in the matrix multiplication and we made the value loading, accordingly. Therefore, the proposed parallel matrix-multiplication can calculate 80 number of output values at once. The existing matrix-multiplication $A * s$, and $s * A$ takes average 2,228.5 ms, and 2,557.7 ms for 50 repetitions (each repetition has 200 iterations), respectively on the Apple A10X Fusion processor (@2.38 GHz). However, the proposed parallel matrix-multiplication takes only 80.0 ms, and 58.4 ms, respectively. This is about a 27.9×, and 43.8× performance improvements for $A * s$ and $s * A$, respectively.
- **High-speed random number generation with AES accelerator based AES encryption.** To generate random numbers, FrodoKEM-640 scheme utilizes AES-128 encryption algorithm. We pursued higher efficiency by replacing software based AES implementation with the high-speed AES accelerator supported by ARMv8 processors. This approach improved the performance significantly. Finally we combined aforementioned methods to achieve the highest performance of FrodoKEM on ARMv8 processors.
- **First FrodoKEM implementation on 64-bit ARM processors** 64-bit ARM processors are widely used in smartphone, tablet, and laptop. For this reason, benchmarking on the target processor should be regarded. To the best of our knowledge, this is the first FrodoKEM implementation on 64-bit ARM

Table 1. Type of register packing of ARMv8 processors.

Type	Unit	Data Quantity	Specifier
Byte	8-bit	16 or 8	16B or 8B
Half-word	16-bit	8 or 4	8H or 4H
Single-word	32-bit	4 or 2	4S or 2S
Double-word	64-bit	2 or 1	2D or 1D

processors. We believe that this can be beneficial for following researchers to evaluate the performance of FrodoKEM.

2   Backgrounds

2.1   FrodoKEM

The FrodoKEM algorithm was firstly announced 2016 ACM SIGSAC conference [1]. This is one of lattice-based cryptography. It is mainly based on Learning With Errors (LWE) that can resist to quantum adversaries. In 2017, FrodoKEM was submitted to the NIST post quauntum cryptography standardization conference. In 2021, it is selected as alternate candidates in public-key encryption field in Round 3 of competition, with other 4 kinds of algorithms including BIKE [2], HQC [3], NTRU Prime [4], and SIKE [5].

FrodoKEM designed for IND-CCA security at 3-levels, FrodoKEM-640, FrodoKEM-976, and FrodoKEM-1344, where these algorithms target Level 1, 3, and 5 in the NIST call for proposals, respectively. FrodoKEM consists of 3-steps, including Key generation, Encapsulation, and Decapsulation.

FrodoKEM uses either AES or SHAKE algorithm to generate pseudo-random numbers, and generated pseudo-random numbers are used to the public matrix. Since FrodoKEM stores pseudo-random numbers as a matrix, the matrix-multiplication is used internally. At this time, since the size of the matrix is very large, $640 * 640$, $976 * 976$, and $1344 * 1344$, for level 1, 3, and 5, respectively. This shows that huge computational overheads occurs during the matrix-multiplication. In order to improve the performance of matrix-multiplication, we proposed parallel matrix-multiplication by using ARMv8 vector registers and instructions.

2.2   ARMv8 Processor

ARMv8 processor has 31 of 64-bit general purpose registers (i.e. scalar registers), and 32 of 128-bit vector registers [6]. Before using vector registers, the data packing process is required. At this point, the arrangement specifier is used for the packing unit. Table 1 shows supported data packing in the target architecture. The matrix-multiplication of FrodoKEM uses 2 byte-wise operation. The arrangement specifier (8H), which indicates 8 half words, is used.

2.3 Related Works

In this section, we introduce the optimized implementation of another Post Quantum Cryptography on ARMv8 processors, which is the target processor of this paper.

Sanal et al. [7] implemented the CRYSTALS-Kyber on the 64-bit ARM Cortex-A processor, which is one of ARMv8 family. They presented optimized Number Theoretic Transform (NTT), noise sampling implementation, and AES accelerator based implementation. Performance enhancements of proposed implementation are 1.72×, 1.88×, and 2.29× for key generation, encapsulation, and decapsulation than reference implementations, respectively.

Nguyen et al. [8] shows optimized implementations of CRYSTALS-Kyber, NTRU, and Saber on Apple M1 microcontroller and Cortex-A72 processor. The proposed implementation uses NEON instruction (vector instruction) to implement parallel polynomial-multiplication. Results show that on the Apple M1 environment, the encapsulation has 1.37–1.60×, 2.33–2.45×, 3.05–3.24×, 6.68× better performance than C language implementation for Saber, Kyber, NTRU-HPS, and NTRU-HRSS, respectively. The decapsulation shows faster than C implementation that 1.55–1.74×, 2.96–3.04×, 7.89–8.49×, and 7.24×, for Saber, Kyber, NTRU-HPS, and NTRU-HRSS, respectively.

Jalali et al. [9] proposes the SIKE algorithm on the ARMv8 processor. The main contribution is mixed implementation of field arithmetic design with the parallel implementation technique. Consequently, the proposed implementation achieved overall 10% higher performance than previous work.

3 Parallel Matrix-Multiplication

In this section, we show the parallel matrix-multiplication method on the 64-bit ARMv8 processor. For the optimal implementation, efficient register scheduling and instructions are utilized.

3.1 Instruction Set

64-bit ARMv8 processor has various instructions. These instructions can be classified into two types: scalar instructions and vector instructions. Vector instructions provide the parallel operation. Table 2 summarizes instructions which are used for the proposed implementation.

3.2 Register Scheduling

To efficiently utilize limited registers, optimal register scheduling is required. Table 3 shows the register scheduling according to the matrix-multiplication implementation. In the register notation, X is a scalar register, V is a vector register, and the number (n) is register number, respectively.

Table 2. List of instructions for parallel-implementation of Matrix-Multiplication; Xd, Vd: destination register (scalar, vector), Xn, Vn, Vm: source register (scalar, vector, vector), Vt: transferred vector register, T: Arrangement specifier, i: Index.

asm	Operands	Description	Operation
ADD	Vd.T, Vn.T, Vm.T	Add vector	Vd ← Vn + Vm
CBNZ	Xt, (Label)	Compare and Branch on Nonzero	Go to Label
LD1	Vt.T, [Xn]	Load multiple single-element structures	Vt ← [Xn]
LD1	Vt.T[i], [Xn]	Load one single-element structures	Vt[i] ← [Xn][i]
LD1R	Vt.T, [Xn]	Load one single-element structures and Replicate	Vt ← [Xn][i]
LDR	Xt, [Xn]	Load register immediate	Xt ← [Xn]
MOV	Xd, #imm	Move immediate (scalar)	Xd ← #imm
MOVI	Vt.T, #imm	Move immediate (vector)	Vt ← #imm
MUL	Vd.T, Vn.T, Vm.T	Multiply	Vd ← Vn * Vm
RET	{Xn}	Return from subroutine	Return
ST1	Vt.T, [Xn]	Store multiple single-element structures	[Xn] ← Vt
STR	Xt, [Xn]	Store register immediate	[Xn] ← Xt
SUB	Xd, Xn, #imm	Subtract immediate	Xd ← Xn - #imm

Table 3. Register scheduling for the matrix-multiplication. X: Scalar registers, V: Vector registers, n: Register number.

Type	Registers	Usage
A * s	V0–V9	8 of $A[i]$ values and intermediate results
	V10–V19	Output of matrix-multiplication
	V31	$s[i * 640 * k]$ values
	X0	Output address
	X1	Matrix A address
	X2	Matrix s address
	X4–5	Loop index
s * A	V0–V9	$A[i * 640 + 80 * k]$ values and intermediate results
	V10–V19	Output of matrix-multiplication
	V31	8 of $s[i]$ values
	X0	Output address
	X1	Matrix A address
	X2	Matrix s address
	X3–5	Loop index

3.3 Matrix Multiplication: $A * s$

Upper part of Fig. 1 shows the matrix-multiplication of A and s of FrodoKEM-640. A is a 640*640 matrix and s is a 640*8 matrix. For this reason, the *output* is a 640*8 matrix. To calculate the value of one *output*, 640 operations between matrix A and matrix s are required.

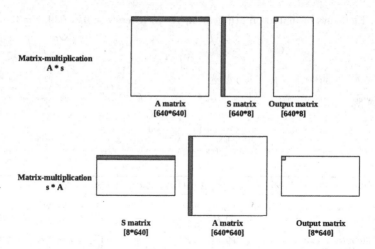

Fig. 1. (Upper) matrix-multiplication of $A * s$; (lower) matrix-multiplication of $s * A$.

In the $A * s$ matrix-multiplication operation, the value of the column component of the A matrix is used and the value of the row component of the s matrix is used. Each value is multiplied, and one output value is generated by adding them together.

For instance, each *output* value can be generated following equation.

$$\text{Output}[0] = \text{A}[0] * \text{s}[0] + \text{A}[1] * \text{s}[1] + \ldots + \text{A}[639] * \text{s}[639]$$
$$\text{Output}[1] = \text{A}[640] * \text{s}[640] + \text{A}[641] * \text{s}[641] + \ldots + \text{A}[1279] * \text{s}[1279]$$
$$\ldots$$
$$\text{Output}[i * 8 + k] = \text{A}[i * 640 + 0] * \text{s}[k * 640 + 0] + \text{A}[i * 640 + 1] *$$
$$\text{s}[k * 640 + 1] + \ldots + \text{A}[i * 640 + 639] * \text{s}[k * 640 + 639]$$

Since each value is 16-bit wise, 8 values can be stored in one vector register. Therefore, 80 vector registers are required to generate single *output* value in ideal cases. However, only 10 registers can be used at once due to limit of vector registers. Also, an operation causes inefficiency when adding each element. Some vector instructions provide a pair-wise operation that adds values inner values from single vector register. Since there are 8 values to be added, not only the number of additions increases, but also the register utilization decreases.

To solve this problem, we changed the operation order. Table 4 summarizes the value used for each index to calculate the matrix-multiplication $A * s$. Every $A[0]$ element is multiplied by $s[n * 640 + 0]$ (n is maximum value of k). All of $A[1]$ elements are operated with $s[n * 640 + 1]$. As a result, all $A[m]$ values are computed with $s[n * 640 + m]$. The *output* can be calculated by adding up all column elements of Table 4. Instead of assigning values to vector registers linearly, we assign values to follow this rule.

We used 10 vector registers to store A values (V0–V9) and 1 vector register (V31) to store s value. A registers are multiplied with the s register. These results are saved to A registers. Afterward, multiplied results are added to intermedi-

Table 4. Elements of matrix-multiplication $A*s$, where $i = 0 \sim 639, k = 0 \sim 7, j = 0 \sim 649$.

	i = 0			i = 1		
	k = 0	k = 1	k = n	k = 0	k = 1	k = n
j = 0	A[0]*s[0]	A[0]*s[640]	A[0]*s[n*640+0]	A[640]*s[0]	A[640]*s[640]	A[640]*s[n*640+0]
j = 1	A[1]*s[1]	A[1]*s[641]	A[1]*s[n*640+1]	A[641]*s[1]	A[641]*s[641]	A[641]*s[n*640+1]
j = m	A[m]*s[m]	A[m]*s[640+m]	A[m]*s[n*640+m]	A[640+m]*s[m]	A[640+m]*s[640+m]	A[640+m]*s[n*640+m]
	i = 2			i = o		
	k = 0	k = 1	k = n	k = 0	k = 1	k = n
j = 0	A[1280]*s[0]	A[1280]*s[640]	A[1280]*s[n*640+0]	A[o*640]*s[0]	A[o*640]*s[640]	A[o*640]*s[n*640+0]
j = 1	A[1281]*s[1]	A[1281]*s[641]	A[1281]*s[n*640+1]	A[o*640+1]*s[1]	A[o*640+1]*s[641]	A[o*640+1]*s[n*640+1]
j = m	A[1280+m]*s[m]	A[1280+m]*s[640+m]	A[1280+m]*s[n*640+m]	A[o*640+m]*s[m]	A[o*640+m]*s[640+m]	A[o*640+m]*s[n*640+m]

Algorithm 1. *Innerloop* of Matrix-multiplication $A*s$.

```
Input: A  address  =  [x1],        21: LD1R V2.8h, [x1]          45: MUL.8h V8, V31, V8
       s  address  =  [x2], Loop   22: ADD X1, X1, #1280         46: MUL.8h V9, V31, V9
       counter = [x5]              23: LD1R V3.8h, [x1]
Output: 80 output values           24: ADD X1, X1, #1280         47: ADD.8h V10, V10, V0
 1: LD1 V31.h[0], [x2]             25: LD1R V4.8h, [x1]          48: ADD.8h V11, V11, V1
 2: ADD X2, X2, #1280              26: ADD X1, X1, #1280         49: ADD.8h V12, V12, V2
 3: LD1 V31.h[1], [x2]             27: LD1R V5.8h, [x1]          50: ADD.8h V13, V13, V3
 4: ADD X2, X2, #1280              28: ADD X1, X1, #1280         51: ADD.8h V14, V14, V4
 5: LD1 V31.h[2], [x2]             29: LD1R V6.8h, [x1]          52: ADD.8h V15, V15, V5
 6: ADD X2, X2, #1280              30: ADD X1, X1, #1280         53: ADD.8h V16, V16, V6
 7: LD1 V31.h[3], [x2]             31: LD1R V7.8h, [x1]          54: ADD.8h V17, V17, V7
 8: ADD X2, X2, #1280              32: ADD X1, X1, #1280         55: ADD.8h V18, V18, V8
 9: LD1 V31.h[4], [x2]             33: LD1R V8.8h, [x1]          56: ADD.8h V19, V19, V9
10: ADD X2, X2, #1280              34: ADD X1, X1, #1280
11: LD1 V31.h[5], [x2]             35: LD1R V9.8h, [x1]          57: SUB X2, X2, #4095
12: ADD X2, X2, #1280              36: ADD X1, X1, #1280         58: SUB X2, X2, #4095
13: LD1 V31.h[6], [x2]                                           59: SUB X2, X2, #2048
14: ADD X2, X2, #1280              37: MUL.8h V0, V31, V0
15: LD1 V31.h[7], [x2]             38: MUL.8h V1, V31, V1        60: SUB X1, X1, #4095
16: ADD X2, X2, #1280              39: MUL.8h V2, V31, V2        61: SUB X1, X1, #4095
                                   40: MUL.8h V3, V31, V3        62: SUB X1, X1, #4095
17: LD1R V0.8h, [x1]               41: MUL.8h V4, V31, V4        63: SUB X1, X1, #513
18: ADD X1, X1, #1280              42: MUL.8h V5, V31, V5
19: LD1R V1.8h, [x1]               43: MUL.8h V6, V31, V6        64: SUB X5, X5, #1
20: ADD X1, X1, #1280              44: MUL.8h V7, V31, V7        65: CBNZ X5, innerloop
```

---

ate result registers (V10-V19). At the final round, the *output* is obtained from intermediate result registers. We call this step as *innerloop*. Algorithm 1 shows the implementation of matrix-multiplication $A*s$ *innerloop*. One *innerloop* can be calculated 80 *output* values. In Algorithm 1, line 1–16 loads s values to V31 vector register. *LD1* instruction can be loaded 1 value to specific place on the vector register. *ADD* instruction is using for moving pointer address. At this time, 1280 pointer is moved to load a value that is apart by 640 index, because the value of s is 16-bit. For this reason, V31 has $s[0]$, $s[640]$, $s[1280]$, $s[1920]$, $s[2560]$, $s[3200]$, $s[3840]$, and $s[4480]$ values at the first round. Line 17–36 loads A values to V0-V9 vector registers. *LD1R* instruction can be loaded single value and copies it through the register. For example, V0 has 8 of $A[0]$ values at the first round. *ADD* is used for same objective in line 1–17. Line 37–46 performs multiplication $A*s$, and stored results to V0-V9. Lastly, line 47–56 adds intermediate results to V10-19. In line 57–65, the address pointers are reordered and

Algorithm 2. *Outerloop* of Matrix-multiplication $A * s$.

Input: *Output* address = [x0]	8: MOVI V14.16b, #0	18: ADD X1, X1, #3330
A address = [x1], s address	9: MOVI V15.16b, #0	
= [x2], Loop counter = [x4]	10: MOVI V16.16b, #0	19: ST1.8h V10-V13, [x0],
Output: 5120 *output* values	11: MOVI V17.16b, #0	#64
1: STR, X2, [sp]	12: MOVI V18.16b, #0	20: ST1.8h V14-V17, [x0],
2: MOV X4, #64	13: MOVI V19.16b, #0	#64
		21: ST1.8h V18-V19, [x0],
3: MOV X5, #640	14: *innerloop* algorithm	#32
4: MOVI V10.16b, #0	15: LDR X2, [sp]	22: SUB X4, X4, #1
5: MOVI V11.16b, #0		23: CBNZ X4, *outerloop*
6: MOVI V12.16b, #0	16: ADD X1, X1, #4095	
7: MOVI V13.16b, #0	17: ADD X1, X1, #4095	

iterated by the *innerloop* through the condition. *Innerloop* iterate 640 times. afterward, it moves to *outerloop*.

The *Outerloop* returns *output* values and resets parameters for next 80 *output* values. Algorithm 2 shows the implementation of matrix-multiplication $A * s$ *outerloop*. In line 1–2, the first address pointer from X2 on the stack is stored. And then the *outerloop* counter is set to 64, because single *innerloop* can be generated by 80 *output* values. In order to get 5,120 *output* values, 64 *innerloop* iterations are needed. In line 1–2, *outerloop* is not included. In line 3 *innerloop* counter is set to 640. In line 4–13, intermediate result registers are initialized to 0. In line 14, *innerloop* Algorithm 1 is performed. In line 15, s value pointer is restored. In the end of round *innerloop*, next *innerloop* needs the $s[0]$ value at the first. The first s address is stored on the stack in line 1 of Algorithm 2. It is restored by calling it again from stack. In line 16–18, address pointers are reordered. In line 19–21, 80 *output* values are returned. In line 22–23, the loop counter is checked and the iteration is continued.

3.4   Matrix Multiplication: S * a

The matrix-multiplication of $s * A$ is similar to $A * s$, except the matrix form. The result of $s * A$ takes transpose of $A * s$ matrix form. It is shown in Fig. 1 Below. The overall operation structure is the same as $A * s$. Every s value is required for the calculation and the *output* is identical to s values used in $A * s$. Table 5 shows each round of element, the each *output* value can be calculated by adding up all the multiplied results of Table 5 column. We can find the rule that $A[0]$, $A[1]$, ... $A[639]$ is multiplied by $s[0]$. $A[640]$, $A[641]$, ... $A[1279]$ is multiplied by $s[1]$. Thus, $A[i]$, $A[i+1]$, ... $A[i+639]$ is multiplied by $s[i/640]$ (i is a multiple of 640 and the maximum value is 408,960). This is different from $A * s$ where variables are linear in memory. The register scheduling is equivalent to $A * s$, but can be implemented more simply to load values to be used in operations. Algorithm 3 shows the implementation of *innerloop* for the matrix-multiplication $s * A$.

Table 5. Elements of matrix-multiplication $s * A$, where $i = 0 \sim 639, k = 0 \sim 7, j = 0 \sim 649$.

	i = 0			i = 1		
	k = 0	k = 1	k = n	k = 0	k = 1	k = n
j = 0	A[0]*s[0]	A[0]*s[640]	A[0]*s[n*640+0]	A[1]*s[0]	A[1]*s[640]	A[1]*s[n*640+0]
j = 1	A[640]*s[1]	A[640]*s[641]	A[640]*s[n*640+1]	A[641]*s[1]	A[641]*s[641]	A[641]*s[n*640+1]
j = m	A[m*640]*s[m]	A[m*640]*s[640+m]	A[m*640]*s[n*640+m]	A[m*640+1]*s[m]	A[m*640+1]*s[640+m]	A[640+m]*s[n*640+m]

	i = 2			i = o		
	k = 0	k = 1	k = n	k = 0	k = 1	k = n
j = 0	A[2]*s[0]	A[2]*s[640]	A[2]*s[n*640+0]	A[o]*s[0]	A[o]*s[640]	A[o]*s[n*640]
j = 1	A[642]*s[1]	A[642]*s[641]	A[642]*s[n*640+1]	A[640+o]*s[1]	A[640+o]*s[641]	A[640+o]*s[n*640+1]
j = m	A[m*640+2]*s[m]	A[m*640+2]*s[640+m]	A[m*640+2]*s[n*640+m]	A[m*640+o]*s[m]	A[m*640+o]*s[640+m]	A[m*640+o]*s[n*640+m]

Algorithm 3. *Innerloop* of Matrix-multiplication $s * A$.

Input: A address = [x1],
s address = [x2], Loop
counter = [x5]
Output: 80 *output* values
1: LD1.8h V0-V3, [x1], #64
2: LD1.8h V4-V7, [x1], #64
3: LD1.8h V8-V9, [x1], #64

4: LD1R V31.8h, [x2], #2

5: MUL.8h V0, V31, V0
6: MUL.8h V1, V31, V1

7: MUL.8h V2, V31, V2
8: MUL.8h V3, V31, V3
9: MUL.8h V4, V31, V4
10: MUL.8h V5, V31, V5
11: MUL.8h V6, V31, V6
12: MUL.8h V7, V31, V7
13: MUL.8h V8, V31, V8
14: MUL.8h V9, V31, V9

15: ADD.8h V10, V10, V0
16: ADD.8h V11, V11, V1
17: ADD.8h V12, V12, V2

18: ADD.8h V13, V13, V3
19: ADD.8h V14, V14, V4
20: ADD.8h V15, V15, V5
21: ADD.8h V16, V16, V6
22: ADD.8h V17, V17, V7
23: ADD.8h V18, V18, V8
24: ADD.8h V19, V19, V9

25: ADD X1, X1, #1120

26: SUB X5, X5, #1
27: CBNZ X5, *innerloop*

$$\text{Output}[0] = A[0] * s[0] + A[640] * s[1] + \ldots + A[408960] * s[639]$$
$$\text{Output}[1] = A[1] * s[0] + A[641] * s[1] + \ldots + A[408961] * s[639]$$

$$\ldots$$

$$\text{Output}[k * 640 + i] = A[1 * 640 + i] * s[k * 640 + 0] + A[2 * 640 + i] *$$
$$s[k * 640 + 1] + \ldots + A[639 * 640 + 639] * s[k * 640 + 639]$$

The *innerloop* of matrix-multiplication $s * A$ can be generated 80 *output* values. In line 1–3, A values are loaded to V0–V9. In line 4, s values are loaded to V31. For example, $A[0]$, $A[1]$, $A[2]$, $A[3]$, $A[4]$, $A[5]$, $A[6]$, and $A[7]$ values are loaded to V0 vector register, and $s[0]$ value is stored to V31 vector register then copied by 8 times. In line 5–24, it performs the matrix-multiplication and intermediate results are stored to V10–V19. These steps are identical to the matrix-multiplication $A * s$. In line 25, the A address pointer is moved. In line 26–27, the condition is checked and the *innerloop* is iterated depending on the condition.

Algorithm 4 shows *outerloop* of the matrix-multiplication $s * A$, it has 2 kind of loop point (A and B). In line 1–2, *output* is stored and A address pointer is stored to stack. In line 3, the number of A loop is defined. In line 4–5, the loop label A is set and loop count B is initialized. The loop label setting does not take the operating time. In line 6–7, loop label B is set and the number of *innerloop* iteration is initialized. In line 8–17, intermediate result registers are initialized to 0 value. In line 18, *innerloop* of Algorithm 3 is performed. In line 19, A address

Algorithm 4. *Outerloop* of Matrix-multiplication $s * A$.

```
Input: Output address = [x0]    11: MOVI V13.16b, #0
       A address = [x1], s address  12: MOVI V14.16b, #0        23: ADD X0, X0, #1120
       = [x2], Loop counter A =  13: MOVI V15.16b, #0
       [x3], Loop counter B = [x4]  14: MOVI V16.16b, #0        24: SUB X4, X4, #1
Output: 5120 output values      15: MOVI V17.16b, #0        25: CBNZ X4, Move to LOOP
  1: STR, X1, [sp], #16         16: MOVI V18.16b, #0            POINT B
  2: STR, X0, [sp], #-16        17: MOVI V19.16b, #0
  3: MOV X3, #8                                             26: SUB X2, X2, #4095
                                18: innerloop algorithm     27: SUB X2, X2, #4095
  4: SET LOOP POINT: A                                      28: SUB X2, X2, #2050
  5: MOV X4, #8                 19: LDR X1, [sp]
                                                            29: LDR X0, [sp, #16]!
  6: SET LOOP POINT: B          20: ST1.8h V10-V13, [x0],   30: ADD X0, X0, #160
  7: MOV X5, #640                   #64                     31: STR X0, [sp], #-16]!
                                21: ST1.8h V14-V17, [x0],
  8: MOVI V10.16b, #0               #64                     32: SUB X3, X3, #1
  9: MOVI V11.16b, #0           22: ST1.8h V18-V19, [x0],   33: CBNZ X3, Move to LOOP
 10: MOVI V12.16b, #0               #32                         POINT A
```

pointer is restored. In line 20–22, *output* results are stored. In line 23, *output* address pointer is adjusted, because next loop generates $output[i + 640]$. The A pointer address is already increased by 80*2 in a post-increment mode at line 20–22. In line 23, the pointer increased to 620*2. In line 24–25, the loop-counter B is checked and it returned to the *LOOP POINT B*. In line 26–28, the s pointer is moved to $s[0]$. In line 29–31, the *output* address pointer is reordered and stored to the stack pointer. In line 32–33, the condition is checked and *LOOP POINT A* is iterated.

3.5 Using High-Speed AES Accelerator

To generate pseudo-random matrix, FrodoKEM-640 scheme utilized AES-128 or SHAKE-128 algorithm. In particular, 64-bit ARMv8 processors support the AES accelerator. We utilized the built-in AES accelerator for AES-128 encryption. This replaced inefficient software based implementation to hardware-aided implementation. Finally, we achieved high-speed implementation of pseudo-random number generation based on AES-128 algorithm.

4 Evaluation

In this section, we evaluate the proposed implementation and previous reference C implementation (PQClean; representative post-quantum cryptography library in C language)[1], because to the best of our knowledge this is the first implementation of FrodoKEM on 64-bit ARMv8 processors. The implementation was developed through the Xcode 12.5 framework. Performance measurements were performed on Apple A10X Fusion processor (@2.38 GHz) that is one of ARMv8 family. In addition, the performance measurement uses the time taken for 200 iterations of each algorithm with ms unit, and average of 50 iterations

[1] https://github.com/PQClean/PQClean.

Table 6. Comparison of matrix-multiplication in terms of execution timing (unit: ms).

Type	A * s	s * A
Reference C implementation [1]	2228.5	2557.7
This work	**80.0**	**58.4**

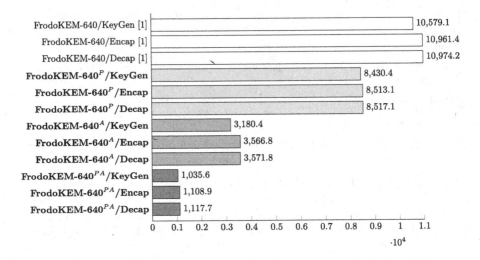

Fig. 2. Performance comparison on ARMv8 processors (unit: ms).

is used to reduce the deviation. Therefore, the total number of operation of the algorithm is 10,000 times.

The first performance comparison is the execution timing of matrix-multiplication. Performance results are shown in Table 6. Results show that matrix-multiplication operations ($A*s$ and $s*A$) in a parallel-way are 27.9× and 43.8× faster performance than previous implementation, respectively. The performance gap is the difference in number of outputs generated by 640 iterations. The previous implementation can be generated single output at once. On the other hand, the proposed parallel matrix-multiplication can be calculated with 80 outputs at once. Therefore, the parallel matrix-multiplication goes through fewer iterations compared to the previous implementation. In addition, vector instructions have a better operation performance than scalar instructions.

Second, after applying the proposed method parallel matrix-multiplication and AES accelerator to FrodoKEM, the performance comparison is performed with the C only implementation FrodoKEM. Figure 2 shows the performance measurement and comparison results between C only implementation, parallel matrix-multiplication based implementation, AES accelerator based implementation, and implementation with all proposed options. Basically, the performance difference between each step (Key generation, Encapsulation, and Decapsulation) is not very noticeable. Therefore, only the performance comparison between the applied techniques is checked. As a result of comparing C only implementation and matrix-multiplication in a parallel-way, a performance difference of 1.25× occurs for Key generation, and 1.29× both for Encapsulation and Decapsulation. The performance difference between C only implementation and implementation with AES accelerator is 3.33×, 3.07×, and 3.07× for Key generation, Encapsulation, and Decapsulation, respectively. This is because the computational load occupied by pseudo-random generation in lattice-based cryptography is enormous. Consequently, the implementation applying both techniques has 10.22×, 9.88×, and 9.82× faster performance for Key generation, Encapsulation, and Decapsulation compared to the C only implementation, respectively.

5 Conclusion

In this paper, we introduced implementation techniques of parallel matrix-multiplication for FrodoKEM-640. The proposed method uses vector registers and vector instructions of ARMv8 processors. This calculated the matrix-multiplication in a parallel-way. As a result, the proposed parallel matrix-multiplication operations ($A * s$ and $s * A$) are overall 27.9× and 43.8× faster than C only implementation on the A10x Fusion processor, respectively. When applied to FrodoKEM-640, the performance of FrodoKEM is improved by 1.25× for Key generation and 1.299× for Encapsulation and Decapsulation, than C only implementation on same processor, respectively. In addition, FrodoKEM with AES accelerator has 3.33× performance compared to C only implementation in best case. When both techniques were applied, the performance enhancement is up to 10.22× that of the C only implementation.

References

1. Bos, J., et al.: Frodo: take off the ring! practical, quantum-secure key exchange from LWE. In: Proceedings of the 2016 ACM SIGSAC Conference on Computer and Communications Security, pp. 1006–1018 (2016)
2. Aragon, N., et al.: BIKE: bit flipping key encapsulation (2017)
3. Melchor, C.A., et al.: Hamming quasi-cyclic (HQC). NIST PQC Round **2**, 4–13 (2018)
4. Bernstein, D.J., Chuengsatiansup, C., Lange, T., van Vredendaal, C.: NTRU Prime: reducing attack surface at low cost. In: Adams, C., Camenisch, J. (eds.) SAC 2017. LNCS, vol. 10719, pp. 235–260. Springer, Cham (2018). https://doi.org/10.1007/978-3-319-72565-9_12
5. Azarderakhsh, R., et al.: Supersingular isogeny key encapsulation, Submission to the NIST Post-Quantum Standardization project (2017)
6. Gouvêa, C.P.L., López, J.: Implementing GCM on ARMv8. In: Nyberg, K. (ed.) CT-RSA 2015. LNCS, vol. 9048, pp. 167–180. Springer, Cham (2015). https://doi.org/10.1007/978-3-319-16715-2_9
7. Sanal, P., Karagoz, E., Seo, H., Azarderakhsh, R., Mozaffari-Kermani, M.: Kyber on ARM64: Compact implementations of Kyber on 64-bit ARM Cortex-A processors. Cryptology ePrint Archive. https://eprint.iacr.org/2021/561
8. Nguyen, D.T., Gaj, K.: Optimized software implementations of crystals-kyber, ntru, and saber using neon-based special instructions of armv8 (2021)
9. Jalali, A., Azarderakhsh, R., Kermani, M.M., Campagna, M., Jao, D.: ARMv8 SIKE: optimized supersingular isogeny key encapsulation on armv8 processors. IEEE Trans. Circuits Syst. I Regul. Pap. **66**(11), 4209–4218 (2019)

Quantitative Analysis on Attack Capacity in Meltdown-Type Attacks

Seokmin Lee[1], Taehun Kim[2], and Youngjoo Shin[2(✉)]

[1] School of Computer and Information Engineering, Kwangwoon University, Seoul, South Korea
leesk212@kw.ac.kr
[2] School of Cybersecurity, Korea University, Seoul, South Korea
{taehunk,syoungjoo}@korea.ac.kr

Abstract. In recent years, modern CPUs have been suffering from Meltdown-type attacks. These attacks are delivered by exploiting transient execution created by a faulting load operation. A secret value is encoded into the cache by transient instructions, which in turn is deduced from a microarchitectural covert channel such as Flush+Reload. Recent studies on these attacks mainly focus on finding new vulnerable microarchitectural structures, while lacking interest in how many transient instructions can be executed in the transient execution. If attackers know the exact *attack capacity*, i.e., the maximum number of instructions available within a transient execution window, they will be able to maximize information leakage by executing additional transient instructions. In order to devise security solutions against Meltdown-type attacks, it is of crucial importance to measure and evaluate the attack capacity. In this paper, we quantitatively analyze the attack capacity in terms of the number of μops, the latency of transient instructions, and the size of the Reorder Buffer (ROB). Specifically, we present our method in detail that measures the capacity by reconstructing the original implementations of Meltdown-type attacks. We analyze the attack capacity by conducting experiments with various CPU models and identify several elements that affect the capacity. Based on our findings, we propose two methods that reinforce the Meltdown-type attacks.

Keywords: Meltdown-type attack · Transient attack capacity · Reinforcing microarchitectural covert channel

1 Introduction

CPU vendors pursue maximizing the performance of their processors by aggressively utilizing instruction-level parallelism. In most cases, the performance improvement caused an increase in the overall complexity, which consequently introduced a transient execution attack such as Meltdown [7] and Spectre [5]. It is a microarchitectural attack that exploits vulnerabilities in speculative and out-of-order executions of modern CPUs. When transient instructions are created by a faulting load, their execution affects the CPU in the microarchitectural

© Springer Nature Switzerland AG 2021
H. Kim (Ed.): WISA 2021, LNCS 13009, pp. 218–228, 2021.
https://doi.org/10.1007/978-3-030-89432-0_18

state. Although the transiently executed instructions will be rolled back later, the changed microarchitectural state still remains. According to Canella et al.'s taxonomy [2], transient execution attacks are generally classified into two classes: Meltdown-type [1,3,7,9–12] and Spectre-type [4–6,8].

Both types of attacks share a common structure in which transient instructions are executed by attackers. An attacker who makes use of more transient instructions in his/her attack might cause more harmful effects to a victim. Hence, it is necessary to figure out *the attack capacity*, i.e., the maximum number of available instructions within the transient execution window, for designing security solutions. In particular, we have the following questions:

Do current attack implementations fully utilize transient instructions? If not, what is the extent of the maximum number of transient instructions available to attackers?

In this paper, we answer the question by quantitatively analyzing the attack capacity of transient execution attacks, especially of Meltdown-type attacks, under various experimental settings. In order to conduct experiments, we reconstructed the original implementations of two Meltdown-type attacks; Meltdown [7] and ZombieLoad [10] attack, so that we can easily measure the capacity by varying the number of transient instructions. These two attacks deal with the exception by using a signal handler or an exception suppressing technique, i.e., Intel TSX. As the capacity of the transient execution attack is influenced by the characteristics of transient instructions, we also conducted the experiment under different kinds of arithmetic instructions, i.e., multiplication and addition. With the experimental result, we reveal the exact capacity of Meltdown-type attacks according to the number of μops, the latency of the instructions, the size of ROB, and exception handling methods. Based on the analysis, we propose several methods to reinforce Meltdown and ZombieLoad attacks. Specifically, the reinforced attacks can leak multiple bytes in continuous and discontinuous locations at a time.

Contributions. The main contributions of this paper are as follows:

1. We reveal that the attack capacity is correlated with the number of μops, the latency of transient instructions, and the size of ROB through our measurement method.
2. We quantitatively analyze the implementations of Meltdown with ZombieLoad in terms of their attack capacity.
3. We present two methods that reinforce Meltdown-type attacks by rebuilding the microarchitectural covert channel.

Outline. Section 2 provides some preliminaries about our analysis. Section 3 gives an overview of the experiment setting for measuring the attack capacity. Section 4 presents the result of experiments according to the attacks, microarchitectural elements, and transient instruction features. Section 5 describes how our analysis result can be used to reinforce the Meltdown-type attack. Finally, we conclude this paper in Sect. 6.

2 Background

In this section, we provide some background knowledge about data load, microarchitectural covert channel and Meltdown-type attacks.

2.1 Data Load

A load instruction is processed in a pipeline with three steps. First, the instruction is fetched into a front-end of the pipeline. Second, it is decoded into μops and dispatched to a load buffer and ROB. Third, a virtual address is translated to the physical address in an execution engine, i.e., a back-end of the pipeline. The virtual address is divided into two parts; the top 36 bits of the address are translated to the Virtual Page Number (VPN), and the bottom 12 bits are used as the virtual page offset. While the bottom 12 bits are not changed, a Translation Lookaside Buffer (TLB) is retrieved to translate a VPN into a Physical Page Number (PPN). If a page table entry exists in the TLB, the physical address is available to be used immediately. Otherwise, the page table entry has to be retrieved by a page miss handler through a page table walk over 4 level-page tables. Once the physical address has been prepared, the requested data is retrieved in the L1D cache. If the data is found, it is served immediately. Otherwise, the data is retrieved from lower levels of cache and memory.

2.2 Microarchitectural Covert Channel

A covert channel is an unauthorized communication channel that bypasses system security policies. That is, a sender transmits confidential information to a receiver through the covert channel across the security boundaries. The microarchitectural covert channel makes use of microarchitectural components such as a cache. As the recently accessed data has been already loaded on the cache, subsequent accesses to the data will take shorter than access to data not in the cache. The microarchitectural covert channel exploits such timing difference by using probe_array, a buffer in a sender's memory. probe_array consists of 256 elements, where the size of each element is 4 KB. The sender encodes the secret value into the specific cache line of probe_array within a transient execution window, i.e., microarchitectural level, and the receiver recovers the secret value by finding out which cache line has been changed with regard to its state. In this technique, the receiver usually makes use of *Flush+Reload* [13], one of cache side-channel techniques. The receiver first flushes a specific address from the cache, waits for a certain amount of time, and reloads to determine whether the load is from the cache or not by measuring the access latency. This way, the receiver can obtain the secret without any restrictions from hardware-enforced security boundaries.

2.3 Meltdown-Type Attack

Meltdown[7] and ZombieLoad [10] attack can be classified as Meltdown-type attack according to the Canella et al.'s taxonomy [2]. These attacks, unlike

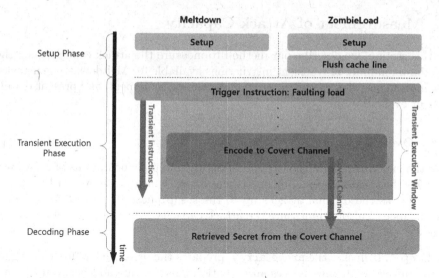

Fig. 1. Three phases in Meltdown and ZombieLoad attacks

Spectre-type attacks, rely on transient instructions introduced by out-of-order execution while handling the CPU's exception. The flow of the Meltdown-type attack is illustrated in Fig. 1. Once a faulting load instruction has been executed, transient instructions are executed subsequently, i.e., *a transient execution window* is opened. Before the faulting instruction retires from the ROB, transient execution will affect both architectural and microarchitectural states. Although architectural changes in registers or memory will be rolled back immediately, the microarchitectural state leaves unchanged. Meltdown-type attacks exploit this phenomena. The remaining microarchitectural state is encoded into the `probe_array` and the corresponding secret is then deduced through the microarchitectural covert channel (cf. Sect. 2.2).

Figure 1 shows that those attacks proceed in the same phases except in the setup phase. The reason of the difference in the setup phase is that ZombieLoad targets the Line Fill Buffer (LFB) where arbitrary data in transit resides, while Meltdown targets the cache. In order to mount ZomebieLoad attack, an attacker needs to be co-located with a victim on the same physical core. When the victim performs a load operation, the data is moved to the L1D cache from memory through the LFB. The attacker flushes the cache line via an user-accessible virtual address, i.e., a non-privileged address. Then, the attacker makes an access to the same cache line via a kernel address, i.e., a privileged address, which in turn triggers a microcode assist. In vulnerable processors, the microcode assist may read the stale value from the LFB. Hence, the attacker can transiently find out the remaining victim's data.

3   Measurement of Attack Capacity

In this section, we describe our method to measure the attack capacity, i.e., the maximum number of transient instructions available for Meltdown-type attacks. We give an overview of our experiment for the measurement, and present details on our evaluation method.

3.1   Overview

For the experiment, we reconstructed the original implementations of Meltdown and ZombieLoad attacks. Our implementations, which are shown in Fig. 2, run the same as the original attacks up to the setup phase (cf. Sect. 2.3). Then, it begins its execution to measure the attack capacity, which consists of 5 steps as follows:

- **Step 1:** It flushes the `probe_array`, prepares the privileged address to trigger a faulting load, and chooses an exception handling method between a signal handler and exception suppression method.
- **Step 2:** It creates a transient execution window by executing the faulting load instruction, which attempts to access to non-authorized privileged address.
- **Step 3:** It repeatedly executes the transient number of repetition is defined in the argument of `.rept` assembly directive.
- **Step 4:** It encodes the data into the corresponding cache line in `probe_array`.
- **Step 5:** It checks whether the secret is successfully recovered.

The execution result is considered to be a success if the secret has been successfully recovered in Step 5. We iterate the execution by 10,000 times to obtain averaged success rates. For each iteration of the experiment, we increase the number of repetition (defined in `.rept` argument) by 1 and restart the execution until the success rate reaches 0%. The attack capacity is decided based on the number of repetition that yields 0% of the success rate.

Table 1. Testing environments. ● and ✗ indicate whether the feature is supported by the CPU model or not. ✓ and - indicate whether the corresponding attack is available or not for the CPU model.

CPU	Supported Tech.		Meltdown		ZombieLoad	
	Intel TSX	Hyper-Threading	M-SIG	M-TSX	Z-SIG	Z-TSX
Core i5-6200U	✗	●	✓	–	✓	–
Core i7-6700K	●	●	✓	✓	✓	✓
Core i5-7200U	✗	●	✓	–	✓	–
Core i5-7400	✗	✗	✓	–	–	–
Core i7-8700K	●	●	✓	✓	✓	✓
Xeon E3-1270 v6	●	●	✓	✓	✓	✓
Xeon E5-2620 v4	●	●	✓	✓	✓	✓

```
1  // Declare the secret value
2  *(char *)var = 'M';
3  // Calculate physical address for trigger instruction
4  size_t phys = virt_to_phys(var);
5  // Flush probe_array buffer entries
6  for (i = 0; i <256; i++) flush(probe_array + i * 4096);
7  //
8  //
9  // Open transient execution window
10 asm volatile(
11     movzx (rcx), rax
12     .rept Number_of_Repetitions
13     Transient_Instruction_for_Measurement
14     .endr
15     shl $12, rax // rax is multiplied with 4096
16     movq (rbx,rax,1), rbx
17     :"b"(probe_array), "c"(phys)
18     :"rax"
19 );
20 // Check whether the data is encoded
21 if ( Flush_Reload(probe_array+'M'*4096) ) print("success");
22 else print("fail");
```

```
1  // Declare normal array
2  char mapping[4096] = {0,};
3  // Calculate physical address for trigger instruction
4  size_t phys = virt_to_phys(mapping);
5  // Flush probe_array buffer entries
6  for (i = 0; i <256; i++) flush(probe_array + i * 4096);
7  // Flush mapping
8  flush(mapping);
9  // Open transient execution window
10 asm volatile(
11     movzx (rcx), rax
12     .rept Number_of_Repetitions
13     Transient_Instruction_for_Measurement
14     .endr
15     shl $12, rax // rax is multiplied with 4096
16     movq (rbx,rax,1), rbx
17     :"b"(probe_array), "c"(phys)
18     :"rax"
19 );
20 // Check whether the data is encoded
21 if ( Flush_Reload(probe_array+'Z'*4096) ) print("success");
22 else print("fail");
```

(a) Meltdown attack   (b) ZombieLoad attack

Fig. 2. Code snippets that measure the attack capacity in Meltdown-type attacks.

3.2   Measurement Details

We conducted experiments on 8 different CPUs running Ubuntu 20.04 LTS (Linux kernel v5.8.0) with Kernel Address Space Layout Randomization (KASLR) and Kernel Page Table Isolation (KPTI) disabled. As shown in Table 1, we configure our experiment with four different types of Meltdown and Zombie-Load attacks. For M-SIG, we measure the attack capacity using a signal handler, while we use Intel TSX as M-TSX. Similarly, we use the signal handler and Intel TSX for Z-SIG and Z-TSX, respectively, to measure the capacity of ZombieLoad attack. M-TSX and Z-TSX are only available on five CPUs that support Intel TSX. On the other hand, Z-SIG and Z-TSX are available only for the CPU that supports Hyper-Threading. ZombieLoad attempts to leak a secret data from the LFB shared among logical cores. Hence, for ZombieLoad attack, a victim process has to repeatedly perform loading a secret data from memory to fill the LFB with the data while a spy process is simultaneously executing the attack to leak the secret from the LFB.

Figure 2 shows code snippets of our implementations that measure the capacity of Meltdown (Fig. 2(a)) and ZombieLoad (Fig. 2(b)) attacks. Before creating a transient execution window, our implementation proceeds similarly in preparing a physical address (line 4) and flushing probe_array (line 6), except the difference that for Meltdown attack, a local variable is defined (line 2 of Fig. 2(a)) and for ZombieLoad attack, an user-accessible address is flushed (line 8 of Fig. 2(b)). After the transient execution window has been opened, these two attacks follow the same execution flow. The transient execution attempts to load data at the privileged-address and then store the data into a rax register (line 11). After repeating the instruction as many as the number of defined in .rept directive, the data in rax is multiplied by 4096 to determine the index of probe_array. Then the value is encoded by making a memory access to the array index (line

16). Finally, the attack capacity is measured by checking whether the loaded value is successfully decoded or not (line 21).

4   Experimental Results

In this section, we present experimental results and details on our analysis.

4.1   Under Different Transient Instructions

We conducted experiments using three kinds of transient instructions: one ADD instruction and two MUL instructions with different types. The ADD and the first type of MUL instructions (denoted by MUL1) take two 64-bit registers as operands. Both yield one μop in a decoding stage, while they differ in latency by 1 and 3 cycles, respectively. As a lower latency instruction takes less time to retire, we expect the ADD instruction in the transient execution can be executed more than MUL1 instruction. The second type of MUL instruction (denoted by MUL2) uses a 64-bit register as an operand and yields 2 μops with latency of 3 cycles. Table 2 shows the attack capacity for the ADD instruction and the MUL2 instruction under various configurations. Transient instructions for measurement are decoded to μops which are stored in the ROB as many as the maximum number of ROB entries. Hence, using a transient instruction that yields less μops with the CPU that has more ROB entries will accommodate larger number of transient instructions in the attack. Figure 3 shows the experimental results. Figure 3(a) and 3(b) show that if the dependency among transient instructions is removed, more execution of transient instruction can be achieved. We attribute this observation to that the transient instructions without dependency can be executed in parallel through different execution ports.

Table 2. The sizes of transient attack capacity

CPU	ROB size	Type of T.I.	M-SIG	M-TSX	Z-SIG	Z-TSX
Core i5-6200U (Skylake)	224ops	ADD	152	–	94	–
		MUL	75	–	46	–
Core i7-6700K (Skylake)	224ops	ADD	143	139	95	85
		MUL	73	69	46	42
Core i5-7200U (Kaby Lake)	224ops	ADD	151	–	92	–
		MUL	73	–	46	–
Core i5-7400 (Kaby Lake)	224ops	ADD	144	–	–	–
		MUL	57	–	–	–
Core i7-8700K (Coffee Lake)	224ops	ADD	151	137	92	81
		MUL	74	68	46	42
Xeon E3-1270 v6 (Kaby Lake)	224ops	ADD	142	140	93	82
		MUL	65	68	46	38
Xeon E5-2620 v4 (Broadwell)	192ops	ADD	138	135	78	71
		MUL	67	65	37	36

T.I. - Transient Instruction

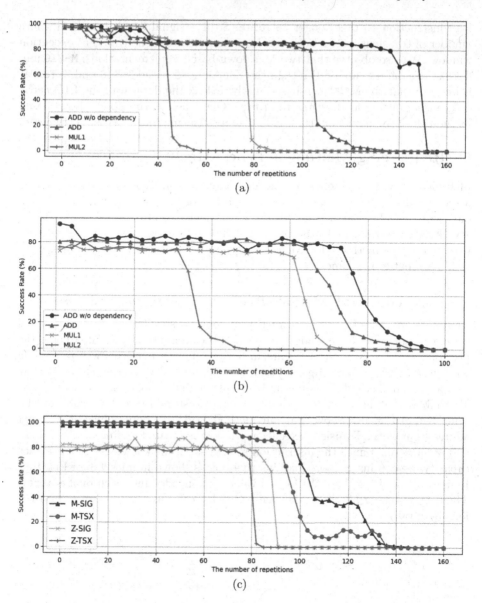

Fig. 3. The attack capacity: (a) The attack capacity of M-SIG on an Intel i5-7400. (b) The attack capacity of Z-SIG on an Intel Xeon E5-2620 v4. (c) The capacity with regard to an ADD instruction on an Intel i5-6700K.

4.2 Under Different Attacks and Exception Handling

As shown in Table 2 and Fig. 3(c), M-SIG and Z-SIG have larger attack capacity than M-TSX and Z-TSX. Because coping exception with signal handler incurs more intervention from an operation system than using Intel-TSX, it makes a faulting load instruction to take longer to retire. So if a signal handler is used, more number of transient instructions can be executed within the transient execution window. We also observe that two Meltdown-based implementations, M-SIG and M-TSX, have larger capabilities than the ZombieLoad based Z-SIG and Z-TSX. It is because that the Meltdown-based methods leak the data from the L1D cache before the faulting load retires from the ROB, whereas the ZombieLoad-based methods leak the data from the LFB as soon as the microcode assist is triggered.

5   Reinforcing Meltdown-Type Attack

Meltdown-type attack relies on the microarchitectural covert channel to leak a secret value. The covert channel used in the original attack implementation only leaks one byte at a time within a transient execution window. With the attack capacity that we learned through the analysis (cf. Sect. 4.1), we present two reinforcing methods for Meltdown-type attacks, which allow attackers to leak more bytes at a time.

5.1   Method 1: Leak Multiple Bytes at Discontiguous Addresses

This method is useful for an attack that looks a specific value in a physical memory, which can be extended to KASLR breaking attacks. Compared to the previous work, this method results in 4 times better performance by reading one-byte values at discontiguous addresses at once. Figure 4(a) shows a code snippet of our method. This method is implemented as follows. First, we define 4 variables that have different addresses and flush addresses of probe_array. Lines 3–6 of Fig. 4(a) show that our method loads one-byte values at different addresses at once, Transient execution window is created at line 3 in Fig. 4(a), and remains open until the instruction retires. With the knowledge of the attack capacity, we can insert more load instructions as shown in lines 4–6 of Fig. 4(a). In lines 11–14 of Fig. 4(a), the loaded values are encoded into each probe_array. Then, by checking all the cache lines of each probe_array, we can obtain the four-byte value.

```
 1 // %0,%1,%2,%3 = 4 physical address of char
 2 // %4,%5,%6,%7 = 4 probe array
 3 movzx  (%0), r10
 4 movzx  (%1), r11
 5 movzx  (%2), r12
 6 movzx  (%3), r13
 7 shl    $12, r10
 8 shl    $12, r11
 9 shl    $12, r12
10 shl    $12, r13
11 movq   (%4,r10,1), %4
12 movq   (%5,r11,1), %5
13 movq   (%6,r12,1), %6
14 movq   (%7,r13,1), %7
```
(a)

```
 1 // %0 = physical address of string
 2 // %1,%2,%3,%4 = 4 probe array
 3 movzx  (%0), r10
 4 movzx  1(%0), r11
 5 movzx  2(%0), r12
 6 movzx  3(%0), r13
 7 shl    $12, r10
 8 shl    $12, r11
 9 shl    $12, r12
10 shl    $12, r13
11 movq   (%1,r10,1), %1
12 movq   (%2,r11,1), %2
13 movq   (%3,r12,1), %3
14 movq   (%4,r13,1), %4
```
(b)

Fig. 4. The two methods of reinforcing Meltdown-type attack

5.2   Method 2: Leak Multiple Bytes at Contiguous Addresses

Unlike Method 1, this method leaks multiple bytes located at contiguous addresses such as strings in the memory at once. In the setup phase, the transient execution window is opened by making an access to the address where a string is stored (line 3 of Fig. 4(b)). Since MOVZX moves only one byte to word with zero-extension, the first MOVZX instruction (line 3 of Fig. 4(b)) can only load the first byte of the string. In order to leak the second byte in the transient execution window, a subsequent instruction performs loading with the address advanced by one byte from the base address (line 4 of Fig. 4(b)). The third and fourth byte of the string can be leaked in the same way (lines 5–6 of Fig. 4(b)). The loaded values are stored to registers, which in turn are recovered like Method 1.

6   Conclusion

In this paper, we quantitatively analyzed the attack capacity of transient execution attacks, especially of Meltdown-type attacks. Using the proposed measurement method, we revealed that the attack capacity is correlated to the size of ROB and the characteristics of an instruction executed within the transient execution window. Furthermore, we also analyzed the attack capacity according to two exception handling methods, i.e., signal handler and Intel TSX, in Meltdown and ZombieLoad attacks. Based on our analysis results, we present two methods that reinforce the Meltdown-type attacks by inserting more transient instructions that maximizes the attack capacity.

Acknowledgments. This work was supported by an Institute of Information & communications Technology Planning & Evaluation (IITP) grant funded by the Korean government (MSIT) (No. 2019-0-00533, Research on CPU vulnerability detection and validation).

References

1. Bulck, J.V., et al.: Foreshadow: extracting the keys to the intel SGX kingdom with transient out-of-order execution. In: 27th USENIX Security Symposium (USENIX Security 18), pp. 991–1008. USENIX Association, Baltimore, MD (2018)
2. Canella, C., et al.: A systematic evaluation of transient execution attacks and defenses. In: 28th USENIX Security Symposium (USENIX Security 19), pp. 249–266. USENIX Association, Santa Clara, CA (2019)
3. Canella, C., et al.: Fallout: leaking data on meltdown-resistant cpus, pp. 769–784. In: CCS 2019, Association for Computing Machinery, New York, NY, USA (2019)
4. Kiriansky, V., Waldspurger, C.A.: Speculative buffer overflows: Attacks and defenses. CoRR abs/1807.03757 (2018). http://arxiv.org/abs/1807.03757
5. Kocher, P., et al.: Spectre attacks: exploiting speculative execution. In: 2019 IEEE Symposium on Security and Privacy (SP), pp. 1–19 (2019)
6. Koruyeh, E.M., Khasawneh, K.N., Song, C., Abu-Ghazaleh, N.: Spectre returns! speculation attacks using the return stack buffer. In: 12th USENIX Workshop on Offensive Technologies (WOOT 18). USENIX Association, Baltimore, MD (2018)

7. Lipp, M., et al.: Meltdown: reading kernel memory from user space. In: 27th USENIX Security Symposium (USENIX Security 18), pp. 973–990. USENIX Association, Baltimore, MD (2018)

8. Maisuradze, G., Rossow, C.: Ret2spec: speculative execution using return stack buffers. In: Proceedings of the 2018 ACM SIGSAC Conference on Computer and Communications Security, pp. 2109–2122. CCS 2018, Association for Computing Machinery, New York, NY, USA (2018)

9. van Schaik, S., et al.: Ridl: rogue in-flight data load. In: 2019 IEEE Symposium on Security and Privacy (SP), pp. 88–105 (2019)

10. Schwarz, M., et al.: Zombieload: cross-privilege-boundary data sampling. In: Proceedings of the 2019 ACM SIGSAC Conference on Computer and Communications Security, pp. 753–768. CCS 2019, Association for Computing Machinery, New York, NY, USA (2019)

11. Stecklina, J., Prescher, T.: Lazyfp: Leaking FPU register state using microarchitectural side-channels. CoRR abs/1806.07480 (2018). http://arxiv.org/abs/1806.07480

12. Weisse, O., et al.: Foreshadow-NG: Breaking the Virtual Memory Abstraction with Transient Out-of-Order Execution. Technical report (2018)

13. Yarom, Y., Falkner, K.: Flush+reload: a high resolution, low noise, l3 cache side-channel attack. In: 23rd USENIX Security Symposium (USENIX Security 14), pp. 719–732. USENIX Association, San Diego, CA (2014)

Application Security

Adaptive Network Security Service Orchestration Based on SDN/NFV

Priyatham Ganta[1], Kicho Yu[2,3], Dharma Dheeraj Chintala[1],
and Younghee Park[1,3(✉)]

[1] Computer Engineering Department, San Jose State University, San Jose, USA
younghee.park@sjsu.edu
[2] Computer Science Department, Northeastern University, Shenyang, China
[3] Silicon Valley Cybersecurity Institute (SVCSI), San Jose, USA

Abstract. The integration of Software-Defined Network (SDN) and
Network Function Virtualization (NFV) is an innovative network architecture that abstracts lower-level functionalities through the separation
of the control plane from the data plane and enhances the management of
network behavior and network services in real time. It provides unprece-
dented programmability, automation, and control for network dynamics.
In this paper, we propose a flexible and elastic network security service
management system for timely reacting to abnormal network behavior
by orchestrating network security functions based on the technology of
SDN/NFV. In designing the system, we address key challenges associated
with scalability, responsiveness, and adversary resilience. The proposed
system provides a real time and lightweight monitoring and response
function by integrating security functions in the SDN/NFV domain. The
SDN automatically learns the network conditions to orchestrate security functions for effective monitoring against attacks. The system is
implemented based on an open-source SDN controller, RYU, and consists of three main agents; network monitoring, orchestration agents, and
response agents. Experimental results have shown that our approach
achieved low network latency with small memory usages for virtual intrusion detection systems.

1 Introduction

Software-defined networking (SDN) and Network Function Virtualization (NFV)
provide new ways to enable the introduction of sophisticated network control
for security and dependability. The advent of SDN/NFV has shifted the traditional perspective of the network from ossified hardware-based networks to
programmable software-based networks [10]. It introduces significant granularity, visibility, flexibility, and elasticity to networking by decoupling the control
plane in network devices from the data plane and through virtualization. A control program can automatically react to dynamic changes of the network state
and thus maintain the high-level policies in place. The centralization of the control logic in a controller with global knowledge of the network state simplifies the

© Springer Nature Switzerland AG 2021
H. Kim (Ed.): WISA 2021, LNCS 13009, pp. 231–242, 2021.
https://doi.org/10.1007/978-3-030-89432-0_19

development of more sophisticated network functions. This ability to program the network and to control the underlying data plane is therefore the crucial value proposition of SDN/NFV and opens new opportunities to implement responsive actions to networks under attack in a timely manner.

SDN/NFV shift traditional perspectives on defense methods in a new direction against attacks in real time. It provides programmability, flexibility, and scalability not possible in traditional computer networks, which facilitates logically centralized control and automation [10]. These capabilities provide insight into network behavior that can be used to automatically detect malicious network attacks. However, previous work has addressed specific attacks in the different layers of SDN instead of using both SDN and NFV to develop defense methods [11,17,19]. A few of the previous works have focused on the integrated security services between SDN and NFV. Furthermore, most previous works have studied the internal security problems of SDN or NFV in terms of software vulnerabilities. Now, it is important to develop a general centralized security service system that automatically reacts to unpredictable changes in the network states and initiates actions to deploy countermeasures against any attack in the intrusion detection and response systems. However, it has been passive to deploy hardware or software IDS in fixed locations that cause many disadvantages, such as low attack detection rates, low resource utilization, and little flexibility against zero-day attacks. For an effective defense system, a timely response action should be implemented and function properly in countering various attacks, especially on a real-time basis.

This paper proposes an adaptive network security orchestration system to dynamically and effectively deploy security functions and detect various attacks in real time. It is an intelligent and automatic framework integrated with SDN/NFV to be reactive to real time network behavior. This framework orchestrates virtual security functions into the network while monitoring real-time traffic to detect network attacks. The southbound interfaces that communicate with the switches deploy these security functions with the help of SDN. The proposed framework consists of three agents: a network monitoring agent, an orchestration agent, and a response agent. The network monitoring agent collects network statistical data to continuously monitor network states and evaluates the best routing path to monitor and detect network abnormalities in real time. The orchestration agent retrieves state information to dynamically deploy security functions for intrusion detection. The response agent dynamically changes network states to make the network safe while initiating an appropriate action into the network based on the reactive routing in SDN. The three agents keep interacting with the SDN controller for centralized monitoring and controlling of the entire network space. Our experimental results demonstrate the effectiveness of this framework to distribute virtual security functions with a reasonable network and system overhead. The results give us the insight to help the SDN controller with NFV properly react to known or unknown attacks by orchestrating a set of light security functions in real time.

Our first contribution is to propose an intelligent and autonomous orchestration system that can effectively react to network threats by utilizing SDN/NFV. In addition, we develop a lightweight orchestration agent by using containerization technology in order to deploy various security functions while monitoring network states. Finally, based on the programmability of SDN/NFV, we develop a resource-efficient security service system for real-time network intrusion detection and response system. Lastly, this paper implements the proposed system with open sources and evaluates the proposed framework in a real cloud environment.

The rest of the paper is organized as follows. Section 2 presents our new proposed framework. In Sect. 3, we evaluate our framework and show experimental results with the implementation details. In the rest of the sections, we discuss related work and state our conclusions.

2 System Architecture

This section presents our proposed framework to respond to network threats by using the orchestration service while leveraging the programmability and automation offered in SDN/NFV. The system consists of three main agents: a network monitoring agent, an orchestration agent, and a response agent, as shown in Fig. 1. First, the network monitoring agent has a traffic analyzer and a network measurement feature to keep track of real-time network status and conditions. Second, the orchestration agent determines the most appropriate reaction from real-time network states to monitor network behavior for intrusion detection. Lastly, the response agent takes reactive action to defend against network abnormalities for intrusion detection. A detailed explanation follows.

2.1 A Network Monitoring Agent

The network monitoring agent records statistical information and measures network usage in order to identify the current network state through the SDN controller. It analyzes traffic by byte rates and the number of packets according to each port and each protocol. It determines the network effective bandwidth to decide the number of security service functions per node while avoiding network congestion points. Network monitoring is an essential building block to initially understand the network situation and deploy a set of security functions to detect network abnormalities.

The SDN controller periodically polls statistical information from switches. The data includes topology information, switch information, and statistics about flow rules and packets. We compute the overall usage of the links in a network by using the number of bytes and the number of packets both for each port and each protocol to determine the routing path for incoming traffic. Also, the traffic classification module captures protocols that contribute the most traffic to the currently utilized bandwidth. Having identified these protocols, the corresponding flow rules are selected and pushed to the switch under consideration. As

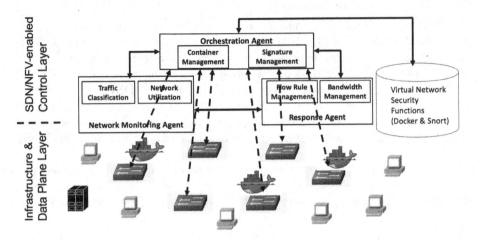

Fig. 1. System architecture

mentioned earlier, traffic classification is carried out in a fine-grained manner, that is, in a per-switch per-port manner, and this granularity makes it possible to deploy flow rules only on the switches that require them. Matching flow rule actions drop the selected packets and allow the same when the traffic rate for the particular protocol reduces. If the protocol-specific usage is relatively high, and the control is passed over to the flow-rule manager for threat responses, the drop action would be selected for the protocol with the highest protocol-specific usage. The system then observes the protocol-specific usage for subsequent iterations and then issues an allow flow rule on the switch to return it to normal behavior. It is important to understand that the flow rules are pushed on individual switches and not all of them, and hence even when a drop action is selected for a particular protocol on some switch, the rest of the network functions unchanged. Also, there are multiple routes present in the network for all the hosts, so the packets can still be routed using alternative paths. Protocol-specific network utilization is defined as how much bandwidth is occupied by a certain protocol (e.g. TCP, UDP, ICMP, HTTP, and DNS) out of the total current used bandwidth. This provides a method to identify specific network congestion locations for efficient orchestration services.

2.2   An Orchestration Agent

The orchestration agent aims to orchestrate virtual network security functions to edge devices dynamically based on the network traffic to that device. As shown in Fig. 1, the orchestration agent has two main components: container management and signature management. The container management monitors system resources and network utilization to determine the number of containers for orchestration services. The signature management decides a set of the Snort rules based on the input from the network monitoring agent. Finally, the agent can orchestrate a set of virtual security functions in SDN to monitoring real-time traffic and detect network attacks. The SDN controller keeps monitoring the network flow to orchestrate the virtual security functions on remote devices for intrusion detection. As multiple functions need to be executed on the same edge devices, it is important to design a lightweight orchestration service like container orchestration. The controller receives the network status information from the network monitoring agent and the orchestration agent deploys a container with a software-based IDS. To achieve this goal, it is significant to develop a lightweight orchestration service since the existing orchestration services require a lot of system resources. For example, Kubernetes and OpenShift have a minimum resource requirement of 8 Gigabytes of physical memory on the master and slave nodes. It is impossible to multiple security services on the same edge devices. To overcome resource limitations, we develop a new orchestration security service system by using Docker with Snort since the Docker needs only minimal physical memory as 256 megabytes. The Docker can be used to integrate and communicate with docker daemons running in remote hosts. To implement virtual security functions, this system utilizes Snort on the Docker. However, instead of including all the signature files in Snort, each signature file is dynamically loading into Snort according to protocol types. For example, under HTTP traffic, the security function includes only signature files related to TCP and HTTP by excluding other protocol-related signatures, such as DNS, UDP, or ICMPE. By dynamically controlling each security function, we can optimize the signature matching process in parallel by orchestrating these security services on the designated path in the network.

2.3   A Response Agent

The response agent is a reactive action to control network behavior when each security functions report alerts by using the reactive routing function of SDN. It has two reaction actions: bandwidth management and flow rule management. First, the Bandwidth Manager can be thought of as an interface for a southbound API to modify the bandwidth of the switch. The value of the bandwidth is determined by the orchestration agent, making it possible for the system to scale up and scale down the bandwidth as needed. The agent can select the best bandwidth based on the input of the network monitoring agent. There are many network attacks that can be countered by just modifying the network bandwidth to some extent. According to attack detection and congestion points, the SDN controller can control bandwidth according to the results of each security function. Second, the flow rule manager is another interface for a southbound API to update flow rules on the switch. This API sends an OpenFlow message to the particular switch to indicate the update in the flow table. With the help of this API, the framework can add, modify, and remove rules corresponding to various packets. When each security function detects attacks, the SDN controller can update flow rules in real time. For example, under the HTTP flooding attacks, the reactive action could be to limit or stop the incoming HTTP traffic to a particular switch or host in the network according to the report of the security functions.

3   Evaluation

This section evaluates our proposed orchestration system in terms of network efficiency and overhead in CloudLab, an open cloud infrastructure supported by NSF (National Science Foundation). We will discuss our implementation, experimental setup, and experimental results in the following sections.

3.1   Implementation

We implement the proposed system (i.e. application) based on RYU [1], an open-source SDN controller with Docker and Snort. RYU is an event-driven SDN controller developed in the Python programming language. It is modular and relatively simple to understand. The event-driven nature of the controller essentially boils down to the concept of event handlers and event listeners. The implementation of the framework spans across a library and an internal component integrated with the existing RYU code with Open vSwitch (OVS) and OVSDB. Docker is an application containerization technology that isolates the operating system from the application. This isolation helps us to run multiple applications of Snort, in parallel and each having its own secure environment called a container. There are three main components of the Docker Engine: Docker daemon, REST API, and client. In the current architecture, the proposed system is a client application running alongside the controller which is connected to docker daemons on all switches in the topology. To ensure a secure connection, a TLS handshake is enabled between the daemon and the client. Snort architecture consists of multiple modules. For Snort to read a packet on an interface to flag an alert or to allow the packet, all these modules should perform their operations consistently. For experimentation purposes, Snort will be packaged into a docker image with necessary configurations. It includes all the snort rules, community, and registered, categorized into 34 different sets based on their application layer protocol. A configuration file is also included for each set to specify rules. The container orchestration service is a python flask web service listening locally for any incoming requests from the controller process. It provides two services to set up the container and the bridge and then to start Snort. The docker API client will be used to trigger any deployment instructions to the docker daemon. Whenever a new packet arrives at the switch, an *ofp_event.EventOFPPacketIn* event is generated and a packet in handler will be triggered on this event. Details of the packet information like a switch IP address, port numbers, source, and destination addresses are extracted in the network monitoring agent. This extracted information is used to request the orchestration service to start Snort on the specified switch. Based on the information received, a specific Snort configuration file will be chosen according to protocol types. The docker API client will be used to get a container from the available list and execute necessary commands to run Snort with a selected configuration file in Inline mode. Snort is configured to report the alerts to a Unix socket. Simultaneously, a script is started to relay these alerts to the remote Ryu controller. As the existing container is used, a new thread is started to set up the container and bridge to allocate future requests.

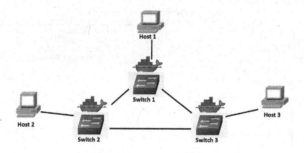

Fig. 2. Experimental setup in CloudLab

In the flow rule management, any packet entering the switch without corresponding flow rules in the switch will trigger the *packet_in_handler* code part in
RYU. Before starting the container, default flow rules should be added in order
to take care of switches where snort inside the container will not be started.
This situation might arise if there is already a container deployed in one of the
switches for this kind of flow. Once the generic flow rules are added, the request
to start snort inside a container is sent to the orchestration service along with
the flow parameters. If the service returns a positive response, the generic flow
rules will be deleted and the flow rules to forward every packet to the container
will be added onto the switch. If the response from the container is negative, no
operation will be done on the generic flow rules.

3.2   Environmental Setup

The proposed system is evaluated with a generic network topology with three
hosts and three switches on a cloud platform (called CloudLab) as shown in
Fig. 2. Cloudlabs is a cloud testbed built for experimenting with real-time cloud,
network, and orchestration scenarios and provides necessary transparency and
control over the nodes deployed in the environment. The switches used are virtual
machines with UBUNTU-18 installed and run OVS-Switch as a daemon. The
Ryu controller, with version 4.34, is run remotely from the topology. The docker
orchestration service, with docker server version 18.09.7 and API version 1.39,
is run alongside the Ryu controller in the same node. The system has a Ubuntu
machine running Ubuntu 16.04.1 LTS version, Intel(R) Xeon(R) CPU E5 with
2.4 GHz. Each switch has 16 GB of RAM with a quad-core processor and we
used Snort 2.9.7.o GRE with Ubuntu 18.04.3 LTS on Docker.

3.3   Experimental Results

We present the experimental results obtained from the evaluation of the proposed
system based on the following metrics: network latency and memory usage. Network latency is an important factor in evaluating the effectiveness of the proposed
framework and memory usage gives us an idea of the system resource requirement. The experimental results were obtained in the network topology shown

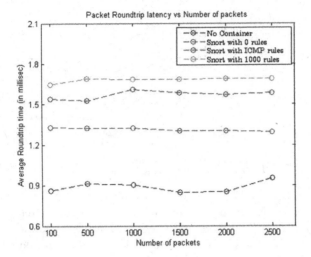

Fig. 3. Network latency in CloudLab

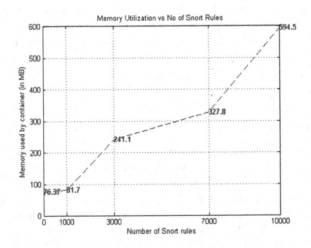

Fig. 4. Memory usage in CloudLab

in Fig. 2. Note that attack detection rates are mostly impacted by the Snort performance with the signature files, which is out of our research scope.

First, the network latency is calculated as the round-trip time (RTT) between two hosts in the network. The round-trip time accumulates the delay for each link in the path between two hosts. Network latency captures the delay in switch processing time, which includes flow rule and bandwidth update processing times. In Fig. 3, we measure network latency without containers or with containers depending on the number of Snort rules (i.e. attack signatures) to be matched with each packet. As shown in Fig. 3, the network latency increases with the orchestration service since it requires matching incoming packets with the attack signature for intrusion detection. When we deployed only the container with Snort without any rules, it shows an average of 1.4 ms round-trip time. With the Snort rules, the network latency was slightly increased and the increase was impacted by the number and the type of the Snort rules. It includes various factors: the switch capacity, the packet header processing time, the packet payload processing time, and so on. In particular, when every packet needs to compare bytes for malware with every rule configured in Snort, the network latency significantly increases according to the number of rules. However, the orchestration services can bring more benefits over such network overhead as we discussed in the previous sections.

Second, we evaluate the CPU and memory usage. The memory usage was obtained using the *top* terminal utility command. Figure 4 shows the physical memory used by the controller during the security orchestration service with different numbers of the Snort rules. CPU and memory utilization are noted while varying the number of rules. The memory utilization gradually increased depending on the number of the Snort rules. However, the CPU usage remained the same from 0.3% to 0.5% increases depending on the packet rates and the number of the Snort rules. Therefore, the memory utilization is gradually increased by increasing the number of the rules whereas the CPU utilization of the container remained similar in all cases.

4   Related Work

A number of approaches to security in SDN address controller specific attacks [11,17,19] by deploying additional defense modules within the SDN controller to keep track of various API calls or network traffic. The AEGIS [11] framework addresses security vulnerabilities that arise from SDN applications. It monitors API calls and usage of core controller modules to avoid any misuse. AVANT-GUARD [17] and FLOODGUARD [19] focus on delivering data plane solutions to SDN security.

Many previous approaches have utilized SDN features to detect network intrusions in SDN. Wang, et al. [18] were the first ones to propose a network security framework that relied solely on the features of SDN. They proposed DaMask a framework that uses deep learning to determine if the network is under attack and deploys network administrator input as the reactive measure against it. Lim et al. [9] discuss an SDN-based defense against DoS and DDoS attacks by botnets. The authors send a redirection message to thwart the botnet, which is powered by OpenFlow protocol to manage DDoS attacks. Braga, Mota and Passito [2] propose a lightweight DoS detection framework using NOX [8] controller. They use the concept of IP Flows [5] to detect network attacks.

Enterprise networks are populated with a large number of proprietary and expensive hardware-based network functions (NFs), or middleboxes [16], which provide key network functionalities, such as firewall, IDS/IPS, and load balancing. Hardware-based NFs present significant drawbacks including high costs, management complexity, slow time to market, and unscalability, to name a few [14,15]. Network Function Virtualization (NFV) was proposed as another new network paradigm to address those drawbacks by replacing hardware-based network appliances with virtualized (software) systems running on generic and inexpensive commodity hardware, and delivering NFs as network processing services. Different control frameworks for virtualized NFs have recently been proposed to address the *safe* scaling of virtual network functions [6,7,12,13]. In particular, Pico Replication [12], Split/Merg [13] and OpenNF [7] are all control frameworks over the internal state of NFs. Pico Replication provides APIs that NFs can use to create, access, and modify internal states. Split/Merg achieves load-balanced elasticity of virtual middleboxes, via splitting internal states of NFs among virtual middlebox replicas and re-route flows. However, neither Pico Replication nor Split/Merg are loss-free during NF state migration. OpenNF provides fine-grained control over movement within internal NF states and enables loss-free and order-preserving movement from one NF state to another. One significant drawback of OpenNF lies in the fact that it relies on the central controller to do heavy traffic buffering during state moves. This results in scalability and safety issues. A second drawback is the triangular routing of packets, which introduces large traffic overhead and latency. Jacobson et al. [6] proposed two enhancements to OpenNF: packet-reprocessing and peer-to-peer transfers. Although packet-reprocessing reduces the amount of traffic that needs to be buffered, it still relies on the controller to buffer in-flight traffic. Peer-to-peer transfer eliminates dependence on the controller to buffer, but still suffers from triangular routing issues. Our migration scheme neither depends on the controller to buffer, nor performs triangular routing. In addition, VNGuard [3] was recently introduced for effective provision and management of virtual firewalls based on NFV to safeguard virtualized environments. Also, NFV and SDN techniques have recently been used to overcome the inflexibility and inelasticity limitations of hardware-based DDoS defense appliances. In particular, Fayaz et al. [4] proposed Bohatei, a flexible and elastic virtual DDoS defense system, for effectively defending DDoS attacks.

5   Conclusion

The combination of SDN and NFV has changed our paradigm in networked systems with flexibility, scalability, and programmability. SDN enables us to control network behavior in real time and NFV allows us to utilize a virtual middleware for all services including security. This paper proposes an adaptive orchestration system to distribute virtual security functions in SDN for intrusion detection. The system consists of three components to manage a set of virtual security functions for intrusion detection and response. The virtual security functions are implemented with Docker and Snort. The proposed system defends network attacks autonomously and intelligently through real-time orchestration services. The goal of this framework is to protect the network from various network attacks through adaptive security orchestration services by using SDN/NFV. The SDN controller handles topology management by collecting switch statistics and by updating appropriate flow rules on the switches for intrusion response when the security functions raise alarms. Our experimental results increase network latency and memory usage depending on the number of the Snort rules inside each security function. To be efficiently and effectively matched with the signatures, the proposed system dynamically loads a set of the relevant rules depending on each traffic type. Our proposed framework makes a significant contribution in the direction of such intelligent and autonomous defense systems by using SDN and NFV.

References

1. Ryu SDN framework [software] (2014). https://osrg.github.io/ryu/
2. Braga, R., Mota, E., Passito, A.: Lightweight DDoS flooding attack detection using NOX/OpenFlow. In: IEEE Local Computer Network Conference, Denver, CO, pp. 408–415, October 2010. https://doi.org/10.1109/LCN.2010.5735752. https://dx.doi.org/10.1109/LCN.2010.5735752
3. Deng, J., et al.: VNGuard: an NFV/SDN combination framework for provisioning and managing virtual firewalls. In: IEEE Conference on Network Function Virtualization and Software Defined Networks (NFV-SDN 2015). IEEE (2015)
4. Fayaz, S.K., Tobioka, Y., Sekar, V., Bailey, M.: Bohatei: flexible and elastic DDoS defense. In: 24th USENIX Security Symposium (USENIX Security 15), pp. 817–832 (2015)
5. Feng, Y., Guo, R., Wang, D., Zhang, B.: Research on the active DDoS filtering algorithm based on IP flow. In: Fifth International Conference on Natural Computation, Tianjin, China, vol. 4, pp. 628–632, August 2009. https://doi.org/10.1109/ICNC.2009.550
6. Gember-Jacobson, A., Akella, A.: Improving the safety, scalability, and efficiency of network function state transfers. In: Proceedings of the 2015 ACM SIGCOMM Workshop on Hot Topics in Middleboxes and Network Function Virtualization, pp. 43–48. ACM (2015)
7. Gember-Jacobson, A., et al.: OpenNF: enabling innovation in network function control. In: Proceedings of the 2014 ACM Conference on SIGCOMM, pp. 163–174. ACM (2014)
8. Gude, N., et al.: NOX: towards an operating system for networks. SIGCOMM Comput. Commun. Rev. **38**(3), 105–110 (2008). https://doi.org/10.1145/1384609.1384625. https://doi.acm.org/10.1145/1384609.1384625
9. Lim, S., Ha, J., Kim, H., Kim, Y., Yang, S.: A SDN-oriented DDoS blocking scheme for botnet-based attacks. In: Sixth International Conference on Ubiquitous and Future Networks (ICUFN), pp. 63–68, July 2014. https://doi.org/10.1109/ICUFN.2014.6876752
10. McKeown, N., et al.: OpenFlow: enabling innovation in campus networks. SIGCOMM Comput. Commun. Rev. **38**(2), 69–74 (2008). https://doi.org/10.1145/1355734.1355746. https://doi.acm.org/10.1145/1355734.1355746
11. Padekar, H., Park, Y., Hu, H., Chang, S.Y.: Enabling dynamic access control for controller applications in software-defined networks. In: Proceedings of the 21st ACM on Symposium on Access Control Models and Technologies, SACMAT 2016, pp. 51–61. ACM, New York (2016). https://doi.org/10.1145/2914642.2914647. https://doi.acm.org/10.1145/2914642.2914647

12. Rajagopalan, S., Williams, D., Jamjoom, H.: Pico replication: a high availability framework for middleboxes. In: Proceedings of the 4th Annual Symposium on Cloud Computing, p. 1. ACM (2013)

13. Rajagopalan, S., Williams, D., Jamjoom, H., Warfield, A.: Split/merge: system support for elastic execution in virtual middleboxes. In: NSDI, pp. 227–240 (2013)

14. Sekar, V., Egi, N., Ratnasamy, S., Reiter, M.K., Shi, G.: Design and implementation of a consolidated middlebox architecture. In: Proceedings of the 9th USENIX Conference on Networked Systems Design and Implementation, p. 24. USENIX Association (2012)

15. Sherry, J., Hasan, S., Scott, C., Krishnamurthy, A., Ratnasamy, S., Sekar, V.: Making middleboxes someone else's problem: network processing as a cloud service. ACM SIGCOMM Comput. Commun. Rev. 42(4), 13–24 (2012)

16. Sherry, J., Ratnasamy, S., At, J.S.: A survey of enterprise middlebox deployments (2012)

17. Shin, S., Yegneswaran, V., Porras, P., Gu, G.: Avant-guard: scalable and vigilant switch flow management in software-defined networks. In: Proceedings of the 2013 ACM SIGSAC Conference on Computer & #38; Communications Security, CCS 2013, pp. 413–424. ACM, New York (2013). https://doi.org/10.1145/2508859.2516684. https://doi.acm.org/10.1145/2508859.2516684

18. Wang, B., Zheng, Y., Lou, W., Hou, Y.T.: DDoS attack protection in the era of cloud computing and software-defined networking. Comput. Netw. 81, 308–319 (2015). http://dx.doi.org/10.1016/j.comnet.2015.02.026. http://www.sciencedirect.com/science/article/pii/S1389128615000742

19. Wang, H., Xu, L., Gu, G.: FloodGuard: a DoS attack prevention extension in software-defined networks. In: 45th Annual IEEE/IFIP International Conference on Dependable Systems and Networks, pp. 239–250, June 2015. https://doi.org/10.1109/DSN.2015.27

A General Framework for Matching Pattern Hiding in Deep Packet Inspection

Jinghang Wen, Jia-Nan Liu$^{(\boxtimes)}$, Axin Wu, and Jiasi Weng

College of Cyber Security, Jinan University, Guangzhou, China

Abstract. Recently proposed proposals, such as BlindBox (SIGCOMM 2015), PrivDPI (CCS 2019) and Pine (ESORICS 2020), enable privacy-preserving deep packet inspection (DPI) on the encrypted traffic. Despite that they protect traffic privacy and/or rule privacy against enterprises and the third-party middleboxes, they might not be really satisfactory, due to the leakage of the *matching pattern*. The matching pattern refers to the matched token-rule pairs during the process of inspection, which can be learnt by the middleboxes, leading to the privacy leakage concerns. Our work aims to hide the matching pattern, thereby enhancing the privacy on top of the mentioned proposals. Specifically, we propose a general framework for matching pattern hiding in DPI and construct a concrete scheme by resorting to the DDH-based private set intersection cardinality technique under the proposed framework. Besides, we implement the constructed scheme, and conduct extensive evaluations which demonstrate the practical performance of the scheme.

Keywords: Traffic inspection · Middlebox privacy · Network privacy

1 Introduction

Deep packet inspection (DPI) is a technique that can perform detection on both the headers and the payloads of network traffic in real time. Enterprises usually utilize DPI for intrusion detection [28] and data exfiltration prevention [27] in their networks, and families also need DPI for parental filtering. Specifically, middlebox (MB) is a widely adopted network device for conducting DPI on the traffic transferred between a client and a server [15, 26]. But the rapid increasing of TLS traffic [10] naturally makes such network device hard to perform DPI on the encrypted traffic, which has been figured out by Naylor *et al.* [18,19]. As a result, TLS inspection enables deploying MB in a Man-in-the-Middle (MitM) way to decrypt, detect and re-encrypt the traffic before forwarding it to the destination [12]. Such a MitM method is practical without the need of modifying the existing TLS protocol, but it causes security and privacy concerns. In particular, it violates the end-to-end encryption security guarantee of the TLS protocol, compromising the traffic privacy between the two endpoints [4,8].

To address the above concerns, Sherry *et al.* [25] proposed BlindBox to perform DPI directly on the encrypted traffic, making MB able to detect while maintaining the privacy of the traffic, but leading to expensive computational costs.

© Springer Nature Switzerland AG 2021
H. Kim (Ed.): WISA 2021, LNCS 13009, pp. 243–254, 2021.
https://doi.org/10.1007/978-3-030-89432-0_20

To improve the efficiency of BlindBox, Ning *et al.* [22] introduced PrivDPI with reusable obfuscated rules that significantly cut down the computational overhead. After that, Ning *et al.* [21] further improved the performance of PrivDPI in Pine. In addition, Pine protects the privacy of rules against MB, by utilizing a pseudorandom function, which can resist brute force guessing on encrypted rules. This matters as security vendors like McAfee rely on the privacy of their rules to make them more competitive in the market as stated in [25].

Limitation of Previous Work. Although Pine can enhance the security and privacy of BlindBox and PrivDPI, it is still not really satisfactory as it might neglect the privacy leakage due to the exposed *matching pattern* which is denoted as the matched token-rule pairs and the total matched times of each rule. For example, given tokens ("2", "2", "3") and rules ("1", "2", "3"), the matching pattern refers to the matched pairs ("2"-"2", "3"-"3") and the matched times of each rule (0, 2, 1). Such pattern can be correlated to the access pattern in the area of searchable encryption [29]. Evidences can be found in [14], and attackers can exploit access pattern leakage to disclose significant amount of sensitive information with a very high accuracy. Similar to the access pattern leakage, the matching pattern leakage in DPI can also be utilized by attackers to disclose sensitive information, since the domain of rules is relatively small, and therefore it is easy to learn the most frequently matched rules. To hide the access pattern, proposals like [3,9,14] have been proposed, but might not be suitable to the setting of DPI. To our knowledge, there is no existing DPI scheme that can fully prevent the matching pattern leakage in the setting of DPI.

Our Contribution. We propose a privacy-preserving framework for hiding the matching patterns, by leveraging a cryptographic tool, named private set intersection cardinality (PSI-CA). We achieve our privacy goal that matching patterns are not revealed to MB, thereby fully protecting the privacy of traffic and rules. The main contributions of our work are summarized as follows.

- We introduce the notion of matching pattern in DPI and indicate that the matching pattern may lead to privacy leakage of rules and traffic.
- We present a general framework for matching pattern hiding in DPI with the help of PSI-CA.
- We construct a concrete matching pattern hiding DPI scheme under our proposed framework by utilizing a DPI scheme and a PSI-CA scheme.
- We evaluate the performance of our proposed scheme and the evaluation results show that our scheme is practical.

In the rest of our paper, we give the overview in Sect. 2 and our framework in Sect. 3. Then, the design details, the security analysis and evaluation results are presented in Sect. 4, Sect. 5 and Sect. 6, respectively. At last, we present the related work in Sect. 7 and conclude our work in Sect. 8.

2   Overview

This section starts with a general system architecture and the workflow of DPI, then presents the threat model we are concerned about, and lastly introduces the preliminaries we use in our design.

2.1   System Architecture and Workflow

The system architecture of a general DPI is consists of the following five entities: Rule Generator (RG), Middlebox (MB), Gateway (GW), client and server. We describe the system workflow, which is similar to Pine, at a high level as follows and provide Fig. 1 for illustration.

Initialization. Public parameters in the system are generated.

Setup. RG issues rule tuples for MB to perform detection. Meanwhile, the client and the server derive secret keys from the TLS session key for encrypting traffic tokens and masking common parameters.

Preprocessing. MB sends the masked rule tuples masked by its key to GW. Then, GW generates the masked reusable rules with the common parameters derived for the client and itself and sends the masked reusable rules back to MB. Finally, MB can recover the reusable rules.

Session Rule Preparation. MB generates the session rules for a specific session from the reusable rules with a secret key sent by the client.

Token Encryption. The client generates the undecryptable encrypted tokens from the payloads and sends them together with the regular TLS traffic, which is for the server to decrypt as the encrypted tokens could not be decrypted. Besides, the masked common parameters are sent to GW in the first round.

Gateway Checking. GW is required to check the validation of the masked common parameters in the first round before forwarding them to MB.

Traffic Detection. MB detects the traffic by trying to match its session rules and encrypted tokens one by one and records the malicious tokens. If no malicious token is detected, it forwards the TLS traffic and encrypted tokens to the server. The masked common parameters are sent together in the first round.

Traffic Validation. The server decrypts the traffic and verifies the validation of the connection with the common parameters to prevent malicious client.

2.2   Threat Model

As stated in [21], we describe three types of attackers as below according to the above system architecture.

Malicious Endpoint. We assume that at least one of the two endpoints must be semi-honest and will perform the protocol honestly. It is worth noting that if both the endpoints are malicious, they can encrypt the traffic with an agreed secret key, making MB unable to perform the traffic detection.

Attackers at the Gateway. Since GW is a network device located in the internal network, we assume it to be a semi-honest party, which exactly follows the protocol but may be curious about the traffic and rules.

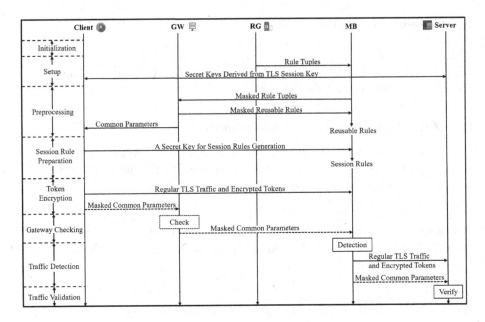

Fig. 1. System workflow.

Attackers at the Middlebox. MB is assumed to be semi-honest that may try to obtain the content of the encrypted traffic or the rules issued by RG but will perform the traffic detection exactly. Moreover, MB may attempt to infer information about the rules or traffic from the matching pattern.

2.3 Preliminaries

In this subsection, we give the preliminaries used in our paper as follows.

Private Set Intersection Cardinality (PSI-CA). Private set intersection (PSI) allows one of the two parties, each holding a set of items, to compute the intersection of the two sets without revealing any other information about their sets. PSI-CA is a variant of PSI, in which one of the parties learns only the intersection size while the other party learns nothing. It is worth mentioning that there is no duplicate in a set, otherwise it will lead to identical masked items and the adversary can learn more than what he is allowed to learn.

Decision Diffie-Hellman (DDH) Assumption. For a cyclic group G of order q with generator g, randomly and independently choose a, b and c from $\mathbb{Z}_p^*$, it is hard for an adversary to tell whether g^{ab} or g^c is an independently random value when given g, g^a and g^b.

Pseudorandom Function (PRF). A pseudorandom function is a one-way function $F : X \times K \to Y$. For each element x in the set X, with a secret key $k \in K$, it can generate an output $y \in Y$, where y is computationally indistinguishable from a truly random function.

Payload Tokenization. Payload tokenization is performed by deploying the window-based tokenization which follows the sliding window algorithm. Specifically, each token is 8 bytes in length and is derived from the payloads. For example, a payload "plain text" will be divided into three tokens "plain te", "lain tex" and "ain text".

3 Framework

In this section, we introduce our framework for matching pattern hiding in DPI. To avoid matching pattern leakage, we introduce the DDH-based PSI-CA to ensure MB learns only the intersection cardinality after detection. We select the DDH-based PSI-CA as it remains the best option when taking the simplicity, computation cost and communication cost into consideration as stated in [13].

The DDH-based PSI-CA is consists of three rounds as follows. In round 1, participant A exponentiates all the elements in its set using its key and sends them to participant B in shuffled order. In round 2, B exponentiates all the elements in the set received from A with its key and shuffles them. Then, it exponentiates all the elements in its own set using its key, shuffles them and sends these two sets to A. In round 3, A exponentiates elements in the set of itself received from B with the reverse of its key and gets the intersection cardinality of the two sets.

In our framework, we embed the round 1 of the DDH-based PSI-CA into the session rule preparation of DPI, the round 2 into the token encryption and the round 3 into the traffic detection. We present our framework as below.

Initialization. Public parameters are generated as usual.

Setup. RG issues rule tuples for MB and endpoints derive secret keys.

Preprocessing. MB derives reusable rules with GW.

Session Rule Preparation. MB first derives the session rules as usual. Then, it exponentiates the session rules with its secret key, as in the round 1 of the DDH-based PSI-CA, for the secrecy of the rules before sending the masked session rules to both the client and the server.

Token Encryption. The client first encrypts the tokens as usual. After that, it executes the round 2 of the DDH-based PSI-CA. It shuffles the encrypted tokens and exponentiates them with its secret key for the secrecy of the tokens. Then, it exponentiates the masked session rules received from MB using its secret key and shuffles them for matching pattern hiding. At last, it sends the masked encrypted tokens, the further masked session rules and the TLS traffic to MB.

Gateway Checking. GW checks the masked common parameters as usual.

Traffic Detection. MB first recovers the masked session rules from the further masked session rules by exponentiating the rules with the reverse of its secret key as in the round 3 of the DDH-based PSI-CA. Then, it performs detection by getting the intersection cardinality.

Traffic Validation. The server verifies the validation of the tokens.

With our framework, MB only learns the intersection cardinality as the rules are shuffled by the client every time. In another word, MB is unable to learn the matched token-rule pairs exactly, and therefore we successfully hide the matching pattern from MB.

4 Instance Details

In this section, we give an instance of applying our framework on a DPI scheme Pine [21] and a DDH-based PSI-CA scheme [6]. The details of our scheme, which is consists of eight phases, are shown below.

Initialization. Let $\mathcal{R}$ be the domain of rules. G is a multiplicative cyclic group with prime order p, $\prod$ is a random permutation and PRF is a pseudorandom function where $PRF : \mathcal{R} \times G \to \mathbb{Z}_p^*$. H and H' are two hash functions, where $H : \mathbb{Z}_p^* \to \mathbb{Z}_p^*$ and $H' : \mathbb{Z}_p^* \to \{0,1\}^\lambda$, and λ is the security parameter. Besides, n, v and u are the number of rules, tokens and max round times, respectively. $[n]$, $[v]$ and $[u]$ represent the set $\{1, \ldots, n\}$, $\{1, \ldots, v\}$ and $\{1, \ldots, u\}$, respectively.

Setup. GW first subscribes the rule service from RG. At the same time, GW and RG agree on a shared key $w \in \mathbb{Z}_p^*$, and use g^w as the key for the pseudorandom function PRF. Then, for $i \in [n]$, RG generates $r_{w,i} = PRF_{g^w}(r_i)$ and $R_i = g^{r_{w,i}+k_i}$ from the rule set $\{r_i \in \mathcal{R}\}_{i \in [n]}$, where k_i is randomly picked from $\mathbb{Z}_p^*$ for each rule r_i. After that, RG selects a signature scheme (*e.g.* Schnorr signature [24]) with sk as its secret key and pk as its public key to sign $\{R_i\}_{i \in [n]}$ with sk and get the signature set $\{\sigma_i\}_{i \in [n]}$. Next, RG sends the rule tuples $\{(R_i, \sigma_i, k_i)\}_{i \in [n]}$ to MB.

Meanwhile, the client and the server establish a regular TLS connection and derive a key k_{TLS} for encrypting traffic with the TLS handshake protocol. Then, the client and server generate two keys c, k_s and a key tuple set $\{(R_{c,i}, R'_{c,i})\}_{i \in [u]}$ in the same order from k_{TLS}, where $c, k_s, R_{c,i}, R'_{c,i} \in \mathbb{Z}_p^*$. Specifically, c is used to derive session rules via randomizing the reusable rules, k_s is for masking the common parameters, and $\{(R_{c,i}, R'_{c,i})\}_{i \in [u]}$ is for token encryption.

Preprocessing. In this phase, MB first sends $\{(R_i, \sigma_i)\}_{i \in [n]}$ to GW. Then, GW verifies the signature σ_i for $i \in [n]$ with pk. If any of them is invalid, GW terminates immediately. Otherwise, GW calculates $X = g^x$ and $Y = g^y$, where $x, y \in \mathbb{Z}_p^*$. Next, GW generates $X_i = (R_i \cdot Y)^x = g^{xr_{w,i}+xk_i+xy}$ for $i \in [n]$ and sends $\{X_i\}_{i \in [n]}$ and X to MB. After that, MB generates $K_i = \frac{X_i}{(X)^{k_i}} = g^{xr_{w,i}+xy}$ for $i \in [n]$ as the reusable rules. In addition, GW sets $I_0 = xy$, $I_1 = x$, $I_2 = g^w$ as the common parameters for token encryption and sends the parameter tuple (I_0, I_1, I_2) to all the clients within its domain.

Session Rule Preparation. At the beginning, the client sends $C = g^c$ to MB while the sever sends $C_s = c$ to MB. Then, MB verifies if $C = g^{C_s}$. If yes, it generates $S_i = (K_i \cdot C)^{C_s} = g^{c(xr_{w,i}+xy+c)}$ for $i \in [n]$. After that, it randomly picks R_m and R'_m from $\mathbb{Z}_p^*$ and calculates $M = g^{R_m}$. Finally, MB generates $h_{r,i} = H(S_i)$ and $a_i = (h_{r,i})^{R'_m}$ for $i \in [n]$ and sends M and the session rule set $\{a_i\}_{i\in[n]}$ to the client and the server. These session rules can be reused in different rounds of the same session.

Token Encryption. For each round, the client generates the token set $\{t_i\}_{i\in[v]}$ from the payload with the window-based tokenization method. Next, it gets the derived key tuple $(R_{c,k}, R'_{c,k})$ corresponding to this round from $\{(R_{c,i}, R'_{c,i})\}_{i\in[u]}$, where k is the current round number. Then, for the k th round traffic, it first computes $a'_i = (a_i)^{R_{c,k}}$ for $i \in [n]$ and generates the permuted rule set $\{\hat{a}_i\}_{i\in[n]}$, where $\{\hat{a}_i\}_{i\in[n]} = \prod(\{a'_i\}_{i\in[n]})$. After that, it generates $t_{w,i} = \text{PRF}_{I_2}(t_i)$, $T_{t,i} = g^{c(I_1 t_{w,i} + I_0 + c)} = g^{c(x t_{w,i} + xy + c)}$ for $i \in [v]$ and derives the permuted encrypted token set $\{\widehat{T_{t,i}}\}_{i\in[v]}$, where $\{\widehat{T_{t,i}}\}_{i\in[v]} = \prod(\{T_{t,i}\}_{i\in[v]})$. Next, it calculates $h_{t,i} = H(\widehat{T_{t,i}})$, $b_{c,i} = M^{R_{c,k}} \cdot (h_{t,i})^{R'_{c,k}}$ and $t_{c,i} = H'(b_{c,i})$ for $i \in [v]$. Finally, it sends $N = g^{R_{c,k}}$, $\{t_{c,i}\}_{i\in[v]}$ and $\{\hat{a}_i\}_{i\in[n]}$ back to MB for traffic detection. Besides, if this is the first round, the client will generate a parameter tuple $(C_{ks} = g^{k_s}, C_w = (I_2)^{k_s} = g^{wk_s}, C_x = g^{I_1 k_s} = g^{xk_s}, C_y = g^{I_0 k_s} = g^{xyk_s})$ for sharing the common parameters with the server, which will then be sent along with N, $\{t_{c,i}\}_{i\in[v]}$ and $\{\hat{a}_i\}_{i\in[n]}$.

Gateway Checking. The gateway checking will be conducted in the first round of the session, where a parameter tuple (C_{ks}, C_w, C_x, C_y) will be attached to the traffic for the server to obtain g^w, g^x and g^{xy} for traffic validation. To check whether g^w, g^x and g^{xy} are masked correctly, the GW verifies whether the equations $C_w = (C_{ks})^w$, $C_x = (C_{ks})^x$ and $C_y = (C_{ks})^{xy}$ hold.

Traffic Detection. For $i \in [n]$, MB computes $b_{m,i} = (N^{R_m})(\hat{a}_i)^{(R'_m)^{-1}} \bmod q$ and $t_{m,i} = H'(b_{m,i})$. Then, it calculates $|\{t_{m,i}\}_{i\in[n]} \cap \{t_{c,j}\}_{j\in[v]}|$ to get the intersection cardinality of the two sets. Every time there is a match, the counts will increase by one and MB finally get the total number of matched tokens, which can be utilized for MB to take actions. If no token is matched, it indicates that the traffic is valid and MB forwards N, $\{t_{c,i}\}_{i\in[v]}$, $\{\hat{a}_j\}_{j\in[n]}$ and the TLS traffic to the server. Specially, if this is the first round of the session, a parameter tuple (C_{ks}, C_w, C_x, C_y) will be sent to the server together.

Traffic Validation. In the first round of the session, the server checks whether the equation $C_{ks} = g^{k_s}$ holds when receiving the parameter tuple (C_{ks}, C_w, C_x, C_y). If the equation holds, it generates $g^w = (C_w)^{(k_s)^{-1}}$, $g^x = (C_x)^{(k_s)^{-1}}$ and $g^{xy} = (C_y)^{(k_s)^{-1}}$. Then, it decrypts the TLS traffic to generate the masked encrypted tokens as the client does and gets the same N, $\{t_{c,i}\}_{i\in[v]}$ and $\{\hat{a}_j\}_{j\in[n]}$. If all the results are the same as those received from MB, it indicates that the client is honest and the session can move on to the next round, otherwise the client is malicious and the connection should be terminated. It is worth mentioning that the server computes $((g^x)^{t_{w,i}} \cdot g^{xy} \cdot g^c)^c$ to get $T_{t,i} = g^{c(x t_{w,i} + xy + c)}$ as it learns g^x and g^{xy} instead of x and y.

5   Security Analysis

In this section, we present the security analysis of our scheme.

One Endpoint is Malicious. When the client is malicious, it generates the tokens from valid keywords, which are not relative to the actual traffic, to evade the detection from MB as these valid tokens will not match any rule. However, when the sever decrypts the traffic received from MB, it generates the tokens from the traffic and easily finds that the two token sets are different, which indicates that the client does not follow the protocol honestly. If the server is malicious and the client is semi-honest, the client generates the tokens from the traffic honestly and MB can discover the invalid tokens.

Attackers at the Gateway. GW in our scheme can neither decrypt the encrypted traffic and tokens nor perform the detection without the session rules. Therefore, it learns nothing about the traffic and rules.

Attackers at the Middlebox and Matching Pattern Hiding. MB is semi-honest, which is unable to decrypt the encrypted traffic, tokens and rules, but may be curious about the rules and traffic and try to collect the matching pattern during the detection. However, MB in our scheme needs a different masked session rule set, which is sent in shuffle order from the client, to perform detection in every round. Therefore, MB is unable to learn the matching pattern as it can no longer count the total matched times of each rule.

6   Implementation

In this section, we evaluate the efficiency of our scheme on a desktop (AMD Ryzen 5 5600X CPU 3.70 GHz 6 cores, 16 GB RAM and 512 GB SSD) under Windows 10 Pro 21H1. We build our experiments on the Java pairing-based cryptography library 2.0.0 [5] and select Type A pairings, which are constructed on the curve $y^2 = x^3 + x$, for implementation. Specifically, the initial parameters rBits and qBits are set to 160 and 512, respectively.

In our experiments, all the evaluations are conducted on the first-round connection as it is the most time-consuming. In addition, since the two schemes only differ in the session rules preparation phase, the token encryption phase and the traffic detection phase, we present the evaluation of these three phases under cases of different numbers of rules and tokens. For each case, we repeat the evaluation for 20 times and take the average as the final result of this case. Both the schemes are provided with the same rule set and token set, where there is no duplicate token in the token set as stated in the previous section.

Session Rules Preparation. As we can see, Fig. 2(a) shows the computational overhead of Pine and our scheme in session rules preparation, which is linear with the number of rules in the system, ranging from 500 to 1,500. It is truth that our scheme needs more time as our scheme needs to take one more exponentiation for every rule. These rules will be sent to the client and need to be masked for the secrecy of the rules, otherwise the client will learn the rules and can perform detection by itself.

Token Encryption. Since the number of rules will affect the computational overhead in token encryption phase in our scheme, we generate 1,000 rules in our system. As we can see from Fig. 2(b), the time of both the two schemes is

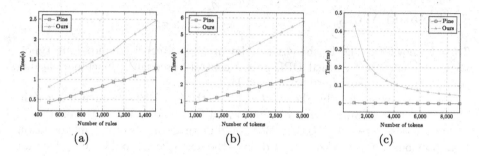

Fig. 2. Experiments results.

Table 1. Comparison with related schemes

Schemes	Traffic inspection	Rule privacy	Traffic privacy	Rule hiding	Brute force guessing	Matching pattern hiding
BlindBox [25]	✓	✓	✓	✗	✗	✗
PrivDPI [22]	✓	✓	✓	✓	✗	✗
Pine [21]	✓	✓	✓	✓	✓	✗
Ours	✓	✓	✓	✓	✓	✓

Traffic inspection: Inspection on encrypted traffic is enabled. Rule privacy: The privacy of rules is preserved from the endpoints and GW. Traffic privacy: The privacy of traffic is preserved from MB and GW. Rule hiding: Rules are not revealed to MB. Brute force guessing: The scheme can resist the brute force guessing on encrypted rules. Matching pattern hiding: Matching pattern is not revealed to MB.

linear with the number of tokens when the number of tokens ranges from 1,000 to 3,000. Obviously, our scheme requires more time for token encryption when given the same number of tokens. That is because the client in our scheme needs to conduct an additional exponentiation on each rule to bind its secret key to all the rules in the system and shuffle them for matching pattern hiding. In addition, each encrypted token still needs to be further processed by taking a multiplication and an exponentiation for MB to performance the detection.

Traffic Detection. We set the number of rules to 500 when evaluating the performance of traffic detection. Fig. 2(c) shows the traffic detection time per token when the number of tokens ranges from 1,000 to 9,000 while the number of rules is constant. It is not surprising that our scheme takes more time as MB in our scheme needs to perform a multiplication and an exponentiation on the encrypted rules before detection while MB in Pine can perform detection directly. It is worth noting that the computational overhead per token of our scheme drops quickly as the number of tokens increases.

In conclusion, our scheme is still practical though we introduce additional multiplications and exponentiations for matching pattern hiding. We consider such additional overhead is acceptable in real-world scenarios as we can provide stronger privacy guarantees than other schemes as shown in Table 1.

7 Related Work

To our knowledge, DPI schemes can be mainly categorized into four types: searchable encryption based DPI, access control based DPI, machine learning based DPI and trusted hardware based DPI.

BlindBox introduced by Sherry et al. [25] is the first DPI scheme using searchable encryption technique that can perform detection directly on the encrypted traffic. As was stated in [25], BlindBox could be three orders of magnitude faster than previous schemes. However, it derives the secret key through garbled circuit and oblivious transfer, which are prohibitively expensive. What is more, BlindBox only preserves the privacy of rules from the endpoints while leaving the rules all known to MB, which does not meet the requirement of security vendors. Therefore, Ning et al. [22] proposed PrivDPI that utilizes reusable obfuscated rules and optimizes the initial handshake to improve the performance of Blind-Box. Besides, PrivDPI preserves the privacy of rules from MB by masking the rules with randomnesses, though brute force attack can be launched when the domain of rules is relatively small. To address that, Ning et al. [21] introduced a pseudorandom function in their new scheme which is termed as Pine and further improved the efficiency.

Another searchable encryption based DPI scheme named Embark [17], proposed by Lan et al., further extends BlindBox to an outsourced MB setting. However, it introduces a gateway that learns all the traffic and rules. In addition, Ren et al. [23] proposed EV-DPI with two layers, where the first layer is for quick matching and the second layer supports exact matching. Lai et al. [16] also introduced a bandwidth-efficient protocol, allowing MB to perform detection with constant bandwidth overhead.

In addition to the above searchable encryption based schemes, there are still many other schemes based on other techniques. For example, Naylor et al. [20] proposed a scheme termed mcTLS, where MB is given the access rights to a portion of the encrypted traffic. Therefore, termed the access control. However, Bhargavan et al. [2] stated that mcTLS was insecure and proposed a formal model on analyzing the protocol. Besides, machine learning also seems appealing as it does not modify any existing protocol on the endpoints. Anderson et al. [1] found that malware's usage of TLS was distinct and could be effectively used in rules and machine learning classifiers. In addition, trusted hardware like Intel SGX has also been utilized in privacy-preserving DPI such as SGX-Box proposed by Han et al. [11] and LightBox proposed by Duan et al. [7].

8 Conclusion

In this paper, we introduced the notion of matching pattern and presented a general framework for matching pattern hiding in DPI by utilizing PSI-CA. To the best of our knowledge, we are the first to take the matching pattern in DPI into consideration. Moreover, we constructed a concrete matching pattern hiding scheme with our proposed framework and evaluated the efficiency of our scheme with different cases. The experiment results showed that our scheme is still practical while providing stronger privacy guarantees. Compared with the previous schemes, our scheme can prevent the matching pattern leakage while keeping the efficiency and functionality at the same time.

Acknowledgement. We are grateful to Prof. Jian Weng for the guidance and advice, and the anonymous reviewers for their insightful comments. This research was supported in part by the Key-Area Research and Development Program of Guangdong Province (Grant Nos. 2020B0101360001, 2020B0101090004), the National Natural Science Foundation of China (Grant Nos. 61902067, 62072215), the GuangDong Basic and Applied Basic Research Foundation (2020A1515111175), and the Foundation for Young Innovative Talents in Ordinary Universities of Guangdong (2018KQNCX255).

References

1. Anderson, B., Paul, S., McGrew, D.: Deciphering malware's use of TLS (without decryption). J. Comput. Virol. Hack. Tech. **14**(3), 195–211 (2018)
2. Bhargavan, K., Boureanu, I., Delignat-Lavaud, A., Fouque, P.A., Onete, C.: A formal treatment of accountable proxying over TLS. In: 2018 IEEE Symposium on Security and Privacy (SP), pp. 799–816. IEEE (2018)
3. Boneh, D., Kushilevitz, E., Ostrovsky, R., Skeith, W.E.: Public key encryption that allows PIR queries. In: Menezes, A. (ed.) CRYPTO 2007. LNCS, vol. 4622, pp. 50–67. Springer, Heidelberg (2007). https://doi.org/10.1007/978-3-540-74143-5_4
4. de Carnavalet, X.d.C., Mannan, M.: Killed by proxy: analyzing client-end TLS interception software. In: Network and Distributed System Security Symposium (2016)
5. De Caro, A., Iovino, V.: jPBC: Java pairing based cryptography. In: 2011 IEEE symposium on computers and communications (ISCC), pp. 850–855. IEEE (2011)
6. De Cristofaro, E., Gasti, P., Tsudik, G.: Fast and private computation of cardinality of set intersection and union. In: Pieprzyk, J., Sadeghi, A.-R., Manulis, M. (eds.) CANS 2012. LNCS, vol. 7712, pp. 218–231. Springer, Heidelberg (2012). https://doi.org/10.1007/978-3-642-35404-5_17
7. Duan, H., Wang, C., Yuan, X., Zhou, Y., Wang, Q., Ren, K.: LightBox: full-stack protected stateful middlebox at lightning speed. In: Proceedings of the 2019 ACM SIGSAC Conference on Computer and Communications Security, pp. 2351–2367 (2019)
8. Durumeric, Z., et al.: The security impact of https interception. In: NDSS (2017)
9. Goldreich, O., Ostrovsky, R.: Software protection and simulation on oblivious rams. J. ACM (JACM) **43**(3), 431–473 (1996)
10. Google: Https encryption on the web (2021). https://transparencyreport.google.com/https/overview?hl=en. Accessed 13 June 2021
11. Han, J., Kim, S., Ha, J., Han, D.: SGX-box: enabling visibility on encrypted traffic using a secure middlebox module. In: Proceedings of the First Asia-Pacific Workshop on Networking, pp. 99–105 (2017)
12. Huang, L.S., Rice, A., Ellingsen, E., Jackson, C.: Analyzing forged SSL certificates in the wild. In: 2014 IEEE Symposium on Security and Privacy, pp. 83–97. IEEE (2014)

13. Ion, M., et al.: On deploying secure computing: private intersection-sum-with-cardinality. In: 2020 IEEE European Symposium on Security and Privacy (EuroS&P), pp. 370–389. IEEE (2020)

14. Islam, M.S., Kuzu, M., Kantarcioglu, M.: Access pattern disclosure on searchable encryption: ramification, attack and mitigation. In: Ndss, vol. 20, p. 12. Citeseer (2012)

15. Kanizo, Y., Rottenstreich, O., Segall, I., Yallouz, J.: Designing optimal middle-box recovery schemes with performance guarantees. IEEE J. Sel. Areas Commun. 36(10), 2373–2383 (2018)

16. Lai, S., et al.: Practical encrypted network traffic pattern matching for secure middleboxes. IEEE Trans. Dependable Secure Comput. (2021)

17. Lan, C., Sherry, J., Popa, R.A., Ratnasamy, S., Liu, Z.: Embark: securely out-sourcing middleboxes to the cloud. In: 13th {USENIX} Symposium on Networked Systems Design and Implementation ({NSDI} 16), pp. 255–273 (2016)

18. Naylor, D., et al.: The cost of the "s" in https. In: Proceedings of the 10th ACM International on Conference on emerging Networking Experiments and Technologies, pp. 133–140 (2014)

19. Naylor, D., Li, R., Gkantsidis, C., Karagiannis, T., Steenkiste, P.: And then there were more: secure communication for more than two parties. In: Proceedings of the 13th International Conference on emerging Networking EXperiments and Technologies, pp. 88–100 (2017)

20. Naylor, D., et al.: Multi-context TLS (mcTLS) enabling secure in-network functionality in TLS. ACM SIGCOMM Comput. Commun. Rev. 45(4), 199–212 (2015)

21. Ning, J., et al.: Pine: enabling privacy-preserving deep packet inspection on TLS with rule-hiding and fast connection establishment. In: Chen, L., Li, N., Liang, K., Schneider, S. (eds.) ESORICS 2020. LNCS, vol. 12308, pp. 3–22. Springer, Cham (2020). https://doi.org/10.1007/978-3-030-58951-6_1

22. Ning, J., Poh, G.S., Loh, J.C., Chia, J., Chang, E.C.: PrivDPI: privacy-preserving encrypted traffic inspection with reusable obfuscated rules. In: Proceedings of the 2019 ACM SIGSAC Conference on Computer and Communications Security, pp. 1657–1670 (2019)

23. Ren, H., Li, H., Liu, D., Xu, G., Cheng, N., Shen, X.S.: Privacy-preserving efficient verifiable deep packet inspection for cloud-assisted middlebox. IEEE Trans. Cloud Comput. (2020)

24. Schnorr, C.P.: Efficient identification and signatures for smart cards. In: Brassard, G. (ed.) CRYPTO 1989. LNCS, vol. 435, pp. 239–252. Springer, New York (1990). https://doi.org/10.1007/0-387-34805-0_22

25. Sherry, J., Lan, C., Popa, R.A., Ratnasamy, S.: BlindBox: deep packet inspection over encrypted traffic. In: Proceedings of the 2015 ACM Conference on Special Interest Group on Data Communication, pp. 213–226 (2015)

26. Sherry, J., Ratnasamy, S., At, J.S.: A survey of enterprise middlebox deployments (2012)

27. Silowash, G.J., Lewellen, T., L Costa, D., Lewellen, T.B.: Detecting and preventing data exfiltration through encrypted web sessions via traffic inspection (2013)

28. Snort. https://www.snort.org/. Accessed 13 June 2021

29. Song, D.X., Wagner, D., Perrig, A.: Practical techniques for searches on encrypted data. In: Proceeding 2000 IEEE Symposium on Security and Privacy, S&P 2000, pp. 44–55. IEEE (2000)

A Privacy-Preserving Payment Model for EV Charging

Jane Kim[1], Soojin Lee[1], and Seung-Hyun Seo[2]([✉])

[1] The Department of Electronic and Electrical Engineering, Graduate School, Hanyang University, Seoul 04763, Korea
{rean5123,tssn195}@hanyang.ac.kr
[2] The Division of Electrical Engineering, Hanyang University (ERICA), Ansan 15588, Korea
seosh77@hanyang.ac.kr

Abstract. Due to the rapid spread of electric vehicles worldwide, the importance of building an efficient and safe electric vehicle charging system is increasing. In order to implement the decentralized vehicle network, blockchain technology is being leveraged in the electric charging system. However, since the blockchain ledger is public, the charging payment and authentication information is visible. While there have been attempts by blockchain-based charging systems to safeguard an electric vehicle's privacy and anonymity, the electric vehicle's identity can still be revealed by the electric vehicle service provider. Thus, we proposed a privacy-preserving payment model for electronic charging. We applied a traceable ring signature so that the electric charging station and the electric vehicle service provider cannot specify the electric vehicle within the ring group. When the EV reuses the token, it will be discovered during the tracing process. In addition, by using a blockchain-based smart contract, malicious user information can be stored and shared in a blockchain. As a result, secure token authentication and energy trading are possible.

Keywords: Blockchain · Charging system · Privacy · Traceable ring signature

1 Introduction

Recently, as interest in eco-friendliness has increased worldwide, demand for electric vehicles that emit less greenhouse gas than conventional vehicles is growing.

This research was supported by the MSIT (Ministry of Science and ICT), Korea, under the ITRC (Information Technology Research Center) support program (IITP-2021-2018-0-01417) supervised by the IITP (Institute for Information & Communications Technology Planning & Evaluation).
This research was funded and conducted under [the Competency Development Program for Industry Specialists] of the Korean Ministry of Trade, Industry and Energy (MOTIE), operated by Korea Institute for Advancement of Technology (KIAT). (No. P0002397, HRD program for Industrial Convergence of Wearable Smart Devices).

H. Kim (Ed.): WISA 2021, LNCS 13009, pp. 255–264, 2021.
https://doi.org/10.1007/978-3-030-89432-0_21

Automobile companies are jumping into the electric vehicle market, and electric vehicles are being spotlighted as a significant means of transportation for the next generation. According to the International Energy Agency (IEA), the share of electric vehicles (EVs) in the global automobile market, which currently stands at only 3%, will surge to 12% by 2030 [1].

As the number of electric vehicles rapidly increases, it is necessary to establish an efficient and safe electric charging infrastructure and energy trading system. A trusted third party can audit and verify transactions between EVs and electricity providers in a centralized system, but this system can be threatened with a single point of failure. Moreover, since many EVs move freely across the country in the vehicular network, charging stations and service providers must be distributed throughout the vehicular network to supply electricity electively. However, assuming there are malicious EVs or charging stations in the decentralized vehicular network, in this case, the contractual relationship between EVs and charging stations can be forged by manipulating charging or billing information. Therefore, the EV charging system must provide the integrity of the payment and charging information in the distributed vehicular network. Blockchain technology, which has the characteristics of ledger decentralization, data integrity, and secure P2P (Peer-to-Peer) transactions, is suitable for such distributed vehicle networks and smart grid environments. Therefore, studies applying blockchain to EV charging systems are being conducted [2,4–8,10]. However, since the blockchain ledger is transparently disclosed to all participants, personal information such as EV charging history, location, and charging amount is exposed. The exposed personal information will be possible to infer the EV driver's daily movement pattern and residence location. For example, if charging stations are installed in hospitals or workplaces, sensitive information such as the workplace and health status of the EV's driver may be revealed. Therefore, there is a need for an authentication and payment system that can protect users' personal information and location information when charging EVs. Several previous studies have tried to solve the privacy issue in blockchain-based EV charging models. Wang et al. [8] proposed a blockchain-based anonymous authentication and key agreement protocol using conditional identity anony-mity for smart grid systems. The anonymity of EVs is provided through pseudonyms, but electricity service providers can match the actual identity of the EVs with the pseudonyms. Xu et al. [10] presented an anonymous system using smart contract, zero-knowledge proof and ring signatures. Nevertheless, the EV's identity can be exposed while buying and using charging tokens. Gabay et al. [4] designed a privacy-preserving smart contract-based authentication scheme using pseudonym ID and zk-SNARKs. However, Gabay et al. [4]'s scheme is inefficient because the setting for verification must be updated every time a system participant leaves. Also, it has the problem of not changing the reservation when the EV is unable to charge at the scheduled time. In order to solve these limitations of previous works and protect vehicle privacy, it is necessary to study how to hide the identity of EVs from both EVSPs (Electric vehicle charging service providers) and CSs (Charging stations) in both the token buying stage and the token using stage. However, it is still necessary to identify a user when a token is used in a malicious manner. Otherwise, the anonymity of the system could be used for malicious purposes.

In this paper, we propose the payment model for electric charging systems based on blockchain. The EV purchases a charging token through a smart contract and presents the token to the CS when charging, and its validity is verified. Smart contracts provide efficient and transparent transactions by ensuring that the transaction code is executed only when the input parameters satisfy the given conditions. We also applied a traceable ring signature [3], which can detect if two signatures were produced by the same user, to ensure the anonymity of the EV's ID and to be traceable when malicious behavior is revealed in our model. If an EV uses the same token multiple times, the CS can learn the ID of the EV and know it is a duplicate use during the verification process. That is how the traceable ring signature scheme works. Therefore, it is impossible for a malicious EV to use a token that has already been used or secretly use another member's token.

The remaining content of this paper is organized as follows: In Sect. 2, we introduce the related work of EV authentication and a payment system for EV charging. Section 3 presents the overview of the proposed model and protocol. In Sect. 4, we describe the security and privacy analysis of the proposed model. Section 5 concludes this paper.

2   Related Work

Blockchain technology has been actively applied to EV authentication and payment systems for EV charging [2,4–8,10]. Lasla et al. [6] proposed a smart contract-based energy trading platform. Using a smart contract that includes an auction mechanism, secure trading between local renewable providers and EVs is possible without intermediaries. Huang et al. [5] proposed a blockchain-based decentralized, secure model by utilizing a lightning network for secure transactions between the EV and charging pile. However, in [6] and [5], there is the problem that the personal information of EVs, such as energy transaction details, is exposed to others.

In order to preserve the EV's privacy, there are several studies on blockchain-based EV authentication and payment models to provide vehicle anonymity [2,4,7,8,10]. Su et al. [7] proposed an EV charging system based on energy blockchain. The reputation-based Byzantine fault tolerance consensus algorithm was introduced and the decision process for energy trading between the EV and the aggregator was designed using contract theory. The author tried to protect the privacy of the vehicle through the blockchain and smart contracts, but the EV's energy transaction history is revealed on the blockchain and the charging pattern of the EV can be inferred. Wang et al. [8] proposed a blockchain-based anonymous mutual authentication for smart grid edge computing. The authors provided anonymity of EVs using a blinded public key in a blockchain network. However, an RA (Registration authority), acting as an electricity service provider, can link the actual identity of the public key.

Mohamed et al. [2] developed a blockchain-based anonymous payment system using zero-knowledge proof and a blind signature. Each charging coin is identified by a unique public key so the entire coin usage of the EV is not revealed. However, there is a possibility that F1 matches the coin owner and the EV by analyzing the EV's coin purchase patterns.

Xu et al. [10] proposed an anonymous blockchain-based system for the charging system. The EV pays the charging fee to the CS and schedules charging through a smart contract using zero-knowledge proof and a ring signature to provide anonymity. However, when the EV buys a token for charging and schedules the charging, the EV's certificate information is revealed in the blockchain, and it can expose the EV's identity. Gabay et al. [4] proposed a privacy-preserving authentication model that applied zero-knowledge proofs and a blockchain. In their scheme, when an EV makes a charging reservation, it creates a pseudonym and proves that it is a legitimate user using zero-knowledge proof. However, whenever an EV no longer participates in the service model, EVSPs and EVs must share a new function for zero-knowledge proof, which is an inefficient method.

To tackle the issues of the above studies, our proposed model aims to design a blockchain-based EV authentication and charging payment system in which the actual identity of the EV is not revealed to the EVSP as well as the CS during the charging and payment processes.

3   Smart Contract Based Privacy-Preserving Payment Model for EV Charging

In this section, we propose our payment model that consists of electric vehicle charging service providers (EVSP), charging stations (CS), and electric vehicle (EV), as shown in Fig. 1. The EVSP is a service provider that sells charging tokens to EVs. It creates smart contract code contracts with a CS. A CS is a charging station that verifies and authenticates the EV's token and executes the contract.

Our proposed model consists of four steps: (i) registration; (ii) Token Purchase for EV Charging; (iii) Token Use for EV Charging; and (iv) Refund for Unused Tokens for EV Charging. In the registration step, EVs and CS are registered with EVSP to use the EVSP's charging service. In the token purchase for the EV charging step, the EV selects a token and purchases it from the EVSP. The EVSP creates a smart contract with CS that exchanges the token and payment. The EV generates a token using information received from the EVSP. The EV can charge using the token at a registered CS. In the token use for the EV charging step, the EV verifies and authenticates the token. The CS can execute the contract, and payments are received from the EVSP. In the final refund for unused tokens for the EV charging step, the EV gets a refund from the EVSP for unused tokens. Figure 1 shows the overall model.

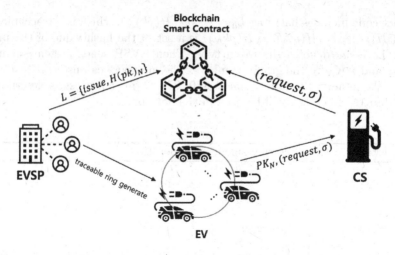

Fig. 1. Overall model

3.1 Registration

A user registers his EV with the EVSP to use the EV charging system. The user registration is performed in a similar way to general website membership registration by using the user's information such as name, EV model, and phone number. EVs that have registered can purchase the charging tokens, which are used to pay for electricity charging. CSs that want to sell electricity should also be registered with the EVSP, and only registered CSs can receive charging tokens from EVs. CS registration is carried out by registering business information and blockchain address. After registration, the EVSP shares the CS's ID and blockchain address with system participants.

3.2 Token Purchase for EV Charging

Once the users are registered, users pay the amount of the charge and a service fee for the token to the EVSP. It is assumed that the types of charging tokens provided by the EVSP are 20 kWh, 40 kWh, and 60 kWh. Users select the token type they want and make an online payment. Also, the EV users need to make a payment via a certain method such as a credit card, PayPal, Kakao Pay, etc. The EVSP can be seen as a registered user by the user's payment information. After the payment, the users generate (pk, sk) pair needed to generate the ring signature, and send the pk to the EVSP. Users request the token corresponding to the payment amount. The pk is public key and the sk is secret key. The EVSP makes a group in which N EVs participate as members and receives pk from the group members. At this time, all EVs in the same group purchase the same type of token. A $PK_N = (pk_1, ..., pk_N)$ is an ordered public key list for set N. The EVSP writes and deploys smart contract codes to public ethereum networks [9] that work tokens are to be exchanged for ether (ETH). Smart contract code includes hash tag $L_h = (issue, H(pk)_N)$, which is a traceable ring tag. A $H(pk)_N = (H(pk_1), ..., H(pk_N))$ is a set of the hash value of the public keys. The $issue$ denotes the token type. Then EVSP sends a smart contract address and PK_N to the group members. The members can use $(request, \sigma)$ as tokens. We assume that the $request$ is 0. The signing process is described in Algorithm 1. This token will be used in the next phases.

Algorithm 1: traceable ring signature generation

Input : $request = 0$, $L = (issue, PK_N)$, SK_N // $issue \in \{0,1\}^*$
Output: $\sigma(A_1, c_N, z_N)$
1: $h = H(L)$, $\sigma_i = h^{x_i}(x_i \in \mathbb{Z}_q)$
2: $A_0 = H'(L, request)$, $A_1 = (\frac{\sigma_i}{A_0})^{1/i}$ for all $j \neq i$, $\sigma_j = A_0 A_1^j \in G$
3: generate c_N, z_N on $(L, request)$
4: random $\omega_i \leftarrow \mathbb{Z}_q$, $a_i = g_i^\omega$, $b_i = h_i^\omega \in G$
5: for every $j \neq i$ random $z_j, c_j \leftarrow \mathbb{Z}_q$, $a_j = g^{z_j} y_i^{c_j}$, $b_j = h^{z_j} \sigma_j^{c_j} \in G$
6: $c = H''(L, A_0, A_1, a_N, b_N)$, $a_N = (a_1, \cdots, a_N)$, $b_N = (b_1, \cdots, b_N)$
7: $c_i = c - \sum_{j \neq i} c_j \pmod{q}$ and $z_i = \omega_i - c_i x_i \pmod{q}$
8: where $c_N = (c_1, \cdots, c_N)$, $z_N = (z_1, \cdots, z_N)$

3.3 Token Use for EV Charging

When the EV goes to the CS for charging, the CS creates a transaction to execute smart contract code, as shown in a Fig. 2. A Fig. 3 shows an example of token usage history in a smart contract. First, the EV sends the token $(request, \sigma)$, a public key set PK_N and the smart contract address to the CS for authentication. The PK_N is a public key set of the ring group, in which the EV is included. The CS checks whether the token is already submitted the blockchain or not. The CS refuses the charging if the token has already been submitted. If not, the CS verifies that the token contains a signature generated by one of the ring group members through Algorithm 2. Then, the CS validates the redundancy between each already used token and the token submitted by the EV through Algorithm 3. The output of Algorithm 3 is either pk or $indep$. When a different member generates the token, it outputs $indep$. Otherwise, it outputs pk of the EV, which means that there is the used token generated by the same EV. If all the results are $indep$, the verification is succeeded. Then the CS starts charging to the EV and executes a contract. If the token submitted by the same EV exists, Algorithm 3 reveals the pk of that EV. As a result, the CS could trace the identity of the malicious EV. The malicious EV cannot be charged and, the CS deploys the public key of the EV to the blockchain network.

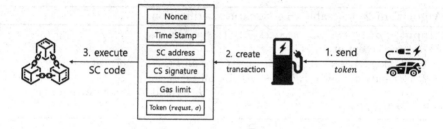

Fig. 2. Transaction for storing token

3.4   Refund for Unused Tokens for EV Charging

The EV that wants to get a refund for the token, sends the unused token and the smart contract address to the EVSP. The EVSP verifies and authenticates the token. If the token is valid, the EVSP self-executes the contract. The EV's payment will be canceled except service fee.

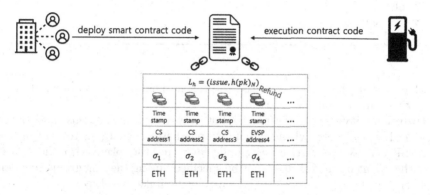

Fig. 3. Token usage history in a smart contract

4   Security and Privacy Analysis

In this section, we provide a security analysis of our proposed model.

1. **Anonymous authentication:** A curious EVSP or CS may want to find out the address of the EV that has used the token. The EVSP knows the identity of EVs when selling tokens, but when EVs use tokens for charging, the real identity is hidden within the ring group, so the EVSP cannot know which EVs used a specific token. Also, since the CS verifies the token using the public keys of the ring group, the exact identity of the EV cannot be specified. In addition, a curious EV may try to identify other EVs in the same ring group from the used token record, but the information indicating the EV who used the token is not used in the authentication process, so it is impossible to know

---

Algorithm 2: traceable ring signature verification

Input : $\sigma(A_1, c_N, z_N)$, request, $L = (issue, PK_N)$
Output: accept or reject
1: Check g, $A_1 \in G$, c_i, $z_i \in \mathbb{Z}_q$, $y_i \in G$ for all $i \in N$, if not, **return** *reject*
2: Compute $a_i = g^{z_i} y_i^{c_i}$, $b_i = h^{z_i} \sigma_i^{c_i}$ for all $i \in N$
3: Check $c = H''(L, A_0, A_1, a_N, b_N) \equiv \sum_{i \in N} c_i (\text{mod } q)$, if not **return** *reject*
4: **return** *accept*

Algorithm 3: traceable ring signature tracing

Input : $(request, \sigma)$, $(request', \sigma')$, tag L, $\sigma(A_1, c_N, z_N)$, $\sigma'(A_1', c_N', z_N')$
Output: *indep* or pk_i
1: Compute $\sigma = A_0 A_1^i \in G$ for all $i \in N$
2: **if** $\sigma' = \sigma_i'$ for all $i \in N$ **then**
3:     store pk_i in **TList**
4: **end if**
5: **if** #**TList** $= 1$ **then**
6:     pk_i
7: **else**
8:     *indep*
9: **end if**

---

which EV in the ring group used the token. Therefore, the proposed model provides anonymous authentication.

2. **Unlinkability:** A curious participant may try to link tokens used by the same EV. However, whenever an EV purchases a charging token from the EVSP, the EV generates a new public key to use the token. Also, the identity of the EV using the token cannot be specified among the ring group members. Therefore, the tokens used by EVs cannot be linked to each other.

3. **Resistance against stolen token attacks:** A malicious EV may try to use tokens issued to a ring group that it is not included in. However, in order to successfully authenticate the token, the EV must know the public key of all the ring group members and create a valid signature for the token. In the smart contract, only the hash value of the public key set of the ring group members are disclosed, so EVs that do not belong to the ring group cannot know the public key set. Even if the EV knows the public key set by chance, it cannot create a valid signature because it does not know the private key of the ring group members. In addition, a malicious EV may want to use the token of the EV participating in the same ring group. However, the EV does not know the private key of other ring group members, so it cannot use other people's tokens. Even if it is an EV of the same ring group as the EV using the token, the information indicating the EV using the token is not used in the authentication process, so it is impossible to know which EV in the ring group used the token.

4. **Resistance against double-spending attacks:** A malicious EV may try to spend the already used tokens with the CS. However, since all tokens used by the EV are recorded in the smart contract, the CS can detect that the tokens have been used. Therefore, duplicate use of tokens is not allowed. When signing with a different random number, the token value is changed. Nevertheless, the same signer is revealed in the verification process according to the traceable ring signature scheme's property. As a result, the proposed model prevents double-spending of charging tokens.

5. **Resistance against forging tokens:** A malicious EV can try to forge a token by generating a public key set of a virtual ring group without buying a token from the EVSP. However, the CS calculates hash values for the public key set of the ring group and compares them with the public key hash values stored in the smart contract distributed by the EVSP. If they are not identical, the transaction will be rejected. Because a malicious EV cannot infer the public key from the hash value of the public key, the EV cannot create a valid token by using an arbitrary public key set.

6. **Conditional traceability:** If the malicious EV uses the same token several times, the CS can calculate the public key of the EV that performed the malicious action through the tracing process of the traceable ring signature. Therefore, the CS can know the real identity of the EV and can restrict the EV's activities in the model.

5   Conclusion

In this paper, we proposed a privacy-preserving payment model for electric charging. Our model provides the EV's anonymity and the EV's authentication for the charging system. It allows the EV's secure verification for charging and needs no payment between the EV and the charging station because of the smart contract. Also, our model obscures token usage information from the EVSP; however, it can identify malicious users using used token traceability. Our model is effective against forged token attacks, double-spending attacks, and stolen token attacks to enable anonymous charging.

References

1. IEA: Global EV outlook 2021 (2021). https://www.iea.org/reports/global-ev-outlook-2021. Accessed 27 June 2021
2. Baza, M., Amer, R., Rasheed, A., Srivastava, G., Mahmoud, M., Alasmary, W.: A blockchain-based energy trading scheme for electric vehicles. In: 2021 IEEE 18th Annual Consumer Communications & Networking Conference (CCNC), pp. 1–7. IEEE (2021)
3. Fujisaki, E., Suzuki, K.: Traceable ring signature. In: Okamoto, T., Wang, X. (eds.) PKC 2007. LNCS, vol. 4450, pp. 181–200. Springer, Heidelberg (2007). https://doi.org/10.1007/978-3-540-71677-8_13

4. Gabay, D., Akkaya, K., Cebe, M.: Privacy-preserving authentication scheme for connected electric vehicles using blockchain and zero knowledge proofs. IEEE Trans. Veh. Technol. **69**(6), 5760–5772 (2020)
5. Huang, X., Xu, C., Wang, P., Liu, H.: LNSC: a security model for electric vehicle and charging pile management based on blockchain ecosystem. IEEE Access **6**, 13565–13574 (2018)
6. Lasla, N., Al-Ammari, M., Abdallah, M., Younis, M.: Blockchain based trading platform for electric vehicle charging in smart cities. IEEE Open J. Intell. Transp. Syst. **1**, 80–92 (2020)
7. Su, Z., Wang, Y., Xu, Q., Fei, M., Tian, Y.C., Zhang, N.: A secure charging scheme for electric vehicles with smart communities in energy blockchain. IEEE Internet Things J. **6**(3), 4601–4613 (2018)
8. Wang, J., Wu, L., Choo, K.K.R., He, D.: Blockchain-based anonymous authentication with key management for smart grid edge computing infrastructure. IEEE Trans. Ind. Inf. **16**(3), 1984–1992 (2019)
9. Wood, G., et al.: Ethereum: a secure decentralised generalised transaction ledger. Ethereum Proj. Yellow Pap. **151**(2014), 1–32 (2014)
10. Xu, S., Chen, X., He, Y.: EVchain: an anonymous blockchain-based system for charging-connected electric vehicles. Tsinghua Sci. Technol. **26**(6), 845–856 (2021)

Measuring Healthcare Data Breaches

Mohammed Alkinoon, Sung J. Choi, and David Mohaisen(✉)

University of Central Florida, Orlando, USA
mohaisen@ucf.edu

Abstract. Over the past few years, healthcare data breaches have grown rapidly. Moreover, throughout the COVID-19 pandemic, the level of exposure to security threats increased as the frequency of patient visits to hospitals has also increased. During the COVID-19 crisis, circumstances and constraints such as curfew imposed on the public have resulted in a noticeable increase in Internet usage for healthcare services, employing intelligent devices such as smartphones. The Healthcare sector is being targeted by criminals internally and externally; healthcare data breaches impact hospitals and patients alike. To examine issues and discover insights, a comprehensive study of health data breaches is necessary. To this end, this paper investigates healthcare data breach incidents by conducting measurements and analysis recognizing different viewpoints, including temporal analysis, attack discovery, security attributes of the breached data, attack actors, and threat actions. Based on the analysis, we found the number of attacks is decreasing, although not precluding an increasing severity, the time of attack discovery is long across all targets, breached data does not employ basic security functions, threat actions are attributed to various vectors, e.g., malware, hacking, and misuse, and could be caused by internal actors. Our study provides a cautionary tale of medical security in light of confirmed incidents through measurements.

Keywords: Healthcare data breaches · Data confidentiality · Data security · Data analysis

1 Introduction

The United States Department of Health and Human Services defines a data breach as an intentional or non-intentional use or disclosure of confidential health information. A data breach compromises privacy and security, resulting in a sufficient risk of reputation, financial, and other harm to the affected individuals [16]. Over the past few years, concerns related to healthcare data privacy have been mounting, since healthcare information has become more digitized, distributed, and mobile [7]. The medical records have transformed from paper-based into Electronic Health Records (EHR) to facilitate various digital system possesses. Medical EHR can be described as "a longitudinal electronic record of patient health information generated by one or more encounters in any care

© Springer Nature Switzerland AG 2021
H. Kim (Ed.): WISA 2021, LNCS 13009, pp. 265–277, 2021.
https://doi.org/10.1007/978-3-030-89432-0_22

delivery setting. Included in this information are patient demographics, progress notes, problems, medications, vital signs, past medical history, immunizations, laboratory data, and radiology reports" [10]. EHR enhances patient care by enhancing diagnostics and patient outcomes, improving patient participation, enhancing care coordination, practicing efficiencies, and cost savings [5]. Despite the numerous benefits of EHR, the transformation has inflated the security and privacy concerns regarding patients' information. The growing usage of Internet of Things (IoT) and intelligent devices affects the methods of communication in hospitals and helps patients quickly access their medical treatment whenever necessitated.

Nevertheless, the usage of such technologies is a fundamental factor that can cause security risks and lead to data breaches [13]. Broadly, healthcare data breaches are external and internal. External breaches are malicious, including at least one or more threat actions from cyber criminals such as hacking, malware, and social attacks. On the other hand, internal data breaches typically occur due to malfeasance by insiders, human errors, and negligence from employees. Data breaches have increased in the past decade. In comparison with other industries, healthcare is the worst affected [8]. Cybercriminals are targeting healthcare for two fundamental reasons: it is a rich source of valuable data, and its defenses are weak [3]. Medical records contain valuable information such as victims' home addresses and Social Security Numbers (SSNs). Adversaries utilize such information for malicious activities and identity theft, or exchange those medical records for financial profit on the dark web.

Contributions. For a better understanding of the landscape of healthcare data breaches against various attributing characteristics, we provide a detailed measurement-based study of the VERIS (Vocabulary for Event Recording and Incident Sharing) dataset. Among other characteristics, we temporally analyze data breaches and their growth over time. To understand attacks' intent, we analyze the type of breaches over various security attributes and characterize the threat actions, highlighting the attack vector employed for the breach. We hope that those characterizations will shed light on the trend and the attack vectors, thus providing directions for mitigating those breaches.

2   Data Source and Temporal Analysis

The object of this paper is to conduct a measurement of healthcare data breaches to understand trends and motives. To accomplish that, we used a trusted and reliable data called VERIS. In the past, there were numerous initiatives to accumulate and share security incidents. Nonetheless, commitment and participation have been minimal. Reasons behind that are many, including (i) the difficulty of categorization, (ii) the uncertainty of what to measure [15]. To facilitate data collection and sharing, VERIS is established as a nonprofit community designed to accommodate a free source of a common language for describing security incidents in a structured and repeatable way [15]. Due to the prevailing lack of helpful information, the VERIS dataset is an effective solution to the most critical and persistent challenges in the security industry. VERIS tackles this problem by offering organizations the ability to collect relevant information and share them responsibly and anonymously.

VERIS and Incident Attributes. VERIS's primary purpose is to create an open-source database to design a foundation that constructively and cooperatively learns from their experience to assure a more reliable measurement and managing risk system. VERIS is a central hub whereby information and resources are shared to maximize the benefits of contributing organizations. During the incident collection process, the VERIS community focuses on successfully implementing an intersection, namely the 4A's, which indicate the following: who is behind the incidents (actors), the action used by the adversary (actions), devices affected (assets), and how are they effected (attributes). An example of the 4A's for an incident can be as follows: internal (actor), hacking (action), network (asset), and confidentiality (attribute). VERIS designers estimate the needed information to be collected about an incident based on the level of threat, asset, impact, and control. If organizations understand the complete image of those risk aspects, they can learn to improve their management system to make the correct decisions. The power of VERIS is the collection of evidence during and after the incidents, besides providing helpful metrics to maximize risk management.

2.1   Distribution of the Incident's Timeline

We analyzed the timeline mapping of the incidents across the years. The VERIS dataset contains incidents that took place between the year 1971 until 2020. While a long period of time is considered, the time frame from 1971 until 2010 seemed to contain a low number of incidents, with only 272 (total) of them, per the VERIS dataset. Thus, to understand the actual trend in the active region,

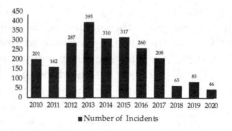

Fig. 1. The distribution of incidents

we limit ourselves to the year 2010 onward. This analysis is essential because it provides us with insights into the active period of breaches and attacks, and could hint on the underlying ecosystem. To this end, and upon this analysis, we found out the following (1) the per year number of incidents follows a normal distribution, with the peak at 2013. (2) 2013 was the highest year in the number of incidents, with 395 (16%), followed by 2015 with 317 (13%), and 2014 with 310 ($\approx$13%). (3) Contrary to the common belief that the number of attacks is increasing, we found that the number of breaches has been decreasing since 2013, per VERIS reporting, as shown in Fig. 1.

> **Takeaway.** *There is a decrease in the number of incidents per year, possibly due to the lax reporting. This decrease, however, does not preclude the possibility that each of those breaches is getting more severe than past breaches.*

2.2 Timeline Discovery for Data Breaches

Health organizations encounter various difficulties in attempting to keep patients' medical records safe. The *timeline discovery* affects both the patient and the hospital. The longer it takes for an organization to discover a data breach, the more significant harm it can cause. The damage cannot only result in data loss or the disclosure of information but also includes businesses. In the literature, it was shown that organizations take 197 days to identify a data breach and 69 days to contain it, on average [6]. That amount of time to detect a data breach is considered long and costs organizations millions of dollars. An organization containing the data breach incident in less than 30 days from the date it happened can save up to $1 million compared to others who fail to do so, per the same study. In healthcare, hospitals and organizations can suffer many consequences due to a data breach, including lawsuits from the affected individuals, as well as reputation and trust loss. In addition, healthcare organizations incur significant costs fixing the problem and protecting patients from additional harm.

We examined the response time for incidents affecting victims; the patients, customers, and employees. In the following, we present the results and contrast.

Results. We began by converting the timeline discovery into one unit (hours). Then, we calculate the cumulative distribution function (CDF) of incidents. Due to the extensive range of timelines, we used the logarithmic function to the discovery time range for simplicity and visibility, as shown in Fig. 2. Based on this analysis, we noticed that the discovery time of incidents for employees is significantly faster than for customers and patients. As we can see in Fig. 2, we discovered that 20% of the incidents for employees were discovered within four days or less. It took five days or less to discover the same percentage for customers, and up to six days to discover that for patients. Such results indicate the difference between the different categories breach discovery time, and perhaps the priorities associated with their discovery and protection, although all are relatively high. To further establish that, for 50% of the incidents, the discovery time was 2, 2.5, and 3 months for customers, employees, and patients, respectively. The patients represent most victims with 41%, and the discovery time for their data breaches extends to years (14 years to discover 100% of all incidents). While discovering 100% of incidents for customers require a longer time: up to 21 years. On the contrary, the discovery time of incidents for employees is much less because discovering 100% of the incidents for this category is about ten years.

> **Takeaway.** *Incidents discovery, even for most protected victims, can take many years, highlighting the lax security posture of healthcare organizations.*

| (a) Patients | (b) Employees | (c) Customers |

Fig. 2. CDF for the timeline discovery of different types of victims.

3   Security Attributes

The VERIS dataset uses pairs of the six primary security: confidentiality/possession, integrity/authenticity, and availability/utility as an extension of the CIA triad.

In this section, we attempt to investigate the compromised security attributes during the incidents by conducting the following: (i) analyzing the confidentiality leakage that occurred during data breaches, (ii) present the different data types, and note which is the most targeted by adversaries, (iii) determine the state of the compromised data at the time of the incidents.

Data Confidentiality. Confidentiality refers to the limit of observations and disclosure of data [15]. We start by examining the data confidentiality leakage that occurred during data breaches. This analysis is necessary because it examines the amount of compromised data and their varieties throughout the incidents. Using the VERIS dataset, we found that 1,045 out of total data 1,937 incidents had *information disclosure*, representing 54% of the total incidents, 882 had a *potential information disclosure*, representing 46%, while only two incidents that had *no information disclosure* at all and eight incidents are *unknown*.

We analyzed data that attackers often target. Based upon this analysis, we discovered the following: medical information exposed to higher disclosure compared to the other types of information, encompassing 1,413 incidents, representing 73%, while personal information appeared in second place, with 345 incidents, representing 18%. Lastly, payment information appeared in third place, having 61 incidents, representing 3%. Other targeted information include *unknown* (44; 2%), *banking* (33; 2%), *credentials* (23; 1%), and *others* (18; 1%).

> **Takeaway.** *Despite their variety in breaches, medical and personal information are the most targeted, with 91% of the incidents combined.*

Status of Breached Data. During the exposure or compromise process, we investigated the state of the data and whether it was encrypted, transmitted, or stored unencrypted during the attack. This categorization aims to understand the security controls while the data is at rest or in motion due to transformation. As a result of this investigation, we noticed 36% of the data was *stored unencrypted*, 30% *stored*, 25% *unknown*, 3% *printed*, 2% *transmitted unencrypted*, and 4% with other attributes.

> **Takeaway.** *The majority of breached data does not employ basic security functions, making it an easy target to adversaries for exploitation at rest or in transit.*

Data Integrity and Authenticity. Integrity refers to an asset or data to be complete and unchanged from the original state, content, and function [15]. Example of loss to integrity includes but is not limited to unauthorized insertion, modification, and manipulation. We wanted to discover the varied nature of integrity loss. Each time incidents occur, there can be at least one integrity attack. However, many losses can be associated with a single incident. Following the analysis, we noticed that most data integrity losses are due to altering behaviors containing 93 incidents, representing 31% of the overall. Software installation comes in second with 91 incidents, representing 30% of the known reasons. Other integrity related attacks include *fraudulent transmission* (18%), *data modification* (11%), *re-purposing* (3%), and *others* (6%).

Authenticity refers to the validity, conformance, correspondence to intent, and genuineness of the asset (or data). Losses of authenticity include misrepresentation, repudiation, misappropriation, and others. Short definition: Valid, genuine, and conforms to intent [15]. Based upon this analysis, we observed that the authenticity state was poorly reported at the time of the incidents.

Data Availability. Availability refers to an asset or data being present, accessible, and ready for use when needed [15]. A loss to availability includes deletion, destruction, and performance impacts such as delay or acceleration. We will show the varieties of the data available that might happen during the incidents. This analysis is necessary to understand the nature or type of availability or utility loss. Based on this analysis, we found that 769 incidents contained a loss of data regarding their effect on availability, representing 90% of the total incidents with the reported attribute. *Obfuscation*, and *interruption* are reported as remaining causes affecting availability, with 9% and 1% of all incidents, respectively.

> **Takeaway.** *Despite limited reporting, more than 20% of all the studied incidents suffer from integrity and authenticity attacks, due to a range of factors, magnifying the potential of attacks without data leaving the organization.*

4   Analyzing the Threat Actors

Threat actors are entities that can cause or contribute to an incident [15]. Each time an incident happens, there can be at least one of the three threat actors involved, but on some occasions, there can be more than one actor involved in a particular incident. Threat actor's actions can be malicious, or non-malicious, intentional or unintentional, causal or contributory [15]. VERIS classifies threat actors into three main categories, namely: external, internal, and partner. This

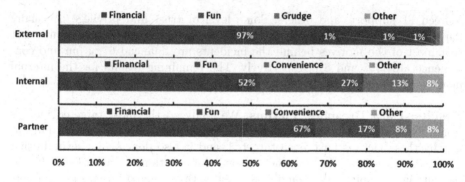

Fig. 3. Threat actors motives for external, internal, and partner actors.

classification excludes the contributory error that unintentionally occurs. For instance, if an insider unintentionally misconfigures an application and left it vulnerable to an attack. The insider would be not be considered as a threat actor if the applications were successfully breached by another actor [15].

On the other hand, an insider who deliberately steals data or whose inappropriate behavior (e.g., policy violations) facilitated the breach would be considered a threat actor in the breach [15]. This section will explain and analyze each category of the threat actors with their presence in incidents from our dataset. This analysis is essential because of the following reasons: (i) it provides us with an understanding of the reasons or motives that can leads actors to act, (ii) the analysis can provide knowledge for organizations to consider proper precautions to defend against how threat actors operate. Several motives can be a reason for a data breach, such as fear, ideology, grudge, espionage, convenience, fun, and financial. Based upon this analysis, we noticed that the financial motive is the primary motive for adversaries, followed by looking for fun.

External Actors. External threats originate from outside of an organization and its third-party partners [15]. Examples include criminal groups, lone hackers, former employees, and government entities. It is also comprised of God (as in "acts of"), "Mother Nature," and random chance. Typically, no trust or privilege is implied for external entities. We found out that 97% of the external actor motives are financial, 1% are for fun. Figure 3 shows the different motives of the actor's external motives.

Internal Actors. Internal threats originate from within the organization, which encompasses full-time company employees, independent contractors, interns, and other staff. Insiders are trusted and privileged (some more than others). Upon further analysis, we found that 52% of the internal motives for adversaries are financial, while 27% are for fun. Figure 3 presents the distribution of motives for internal motives.

Partner Actors. Partners include any third party sharing a business relationship with the organization, including suppliers, vendors, hosting providers, outsourced IT support, and others. Some level of trust and privilege is usually implied between business partners [15]. Based on this analysis, we found out that most of the motives behind the incidents are financial 67%; fun and convenience are 17% and 8% respectively. The remaining results for the internal motives distribution are shown in Fig. 3.

Results: Data Breaches Victims. We analyzed the most targeted victims from adversaries according to the number of incidents. Reasons often differ as to why these victims have been targeted, and it also depends on several other aspects such as location, specific personal information, or a high number of patients in a hospital. We found that most of the targeted victims are patients (88%), the customer came in second (5%), and 5% for employees. Other types of victims include students (interns) working inside healthcare organizations or third-party companies that share data with a specific entity. Figure 4 shows the most targeted victims in the incidents.

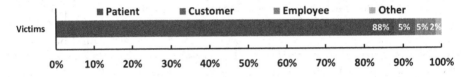

Fig. 4. Distribution of incidents by the different targeted victims from attackers.

Takeaway. *For the three threat actors combined, financial gain is the primary motive for adversaries to launch their attacks.*

5   Analyzing Threat Actions

In this section, we introduce our measurement and analysis of the threat actions used by adversaries during a data breach. This investigation intends to provide insight and the causes of threat actions and their occurrences in our dataset. The following section discusses the two types of threat actions: the different action varieties and the most used vectors by adversaries during an attack. The VERIS dataset classifies threat actions into seven primary categories: malware, social, hacking, misuse, physical, error, and environmental. Analyzing threat actions is essential due to the amount of risk associated with each of them every time an incident occurs. Generally, an incident usually contains a least one of the threat actions; however, most of the incidents will comprise multiple actions that often come with numerous categories.

Terminology Definitions. Below, we define several types of threat actions.

Malware Malicious software or malware is a computer code designed to disable, disrupt, or take control of the computer system by altering its state or function without the owner's informed consent [15]. Malware exploits technical flaws or vulnerabilities in hardware or software.

Hacking Refers to all attempts to intentionally access or harm information assets without (or exceeding) authorization by circumventing or thwarting logical security mechanisms. It includes brute force, SQL injection, crypt-analysis, denial of service attacks, etc. [15].

Social Social engineering criminals strive to exploit the users of these technologies by pretending to be something they are not to persuade others. Attackers utilize the trust to their advantage by misleading users into disclosing information that compromises data security. Social engineering tactics employ deception, manipulation, intimidation, and other techniques to exploit the human element, or users, of information assets, includes pretexting, phishing, blackmail, threats, scams, etc. [15].

Misuse The use of entrusted organizational resources or privileges for any purpose or manner contrary to intended is considered misuse. It includes administrative abuse, use policy violations, use of non-approved assets, etc. [15]. These actions can be malicious or non-malicious.

Physical Encompass deliberate threats that involve proximity, possession, or force. These include theft, tampering, snooping, sabotage, local device access, assault, etc. [15]. Natural hazards and power failures are classified into physical actions. However, VERIS restricts these events to intentional incidents only caused by human actors.

Error Error broadly encompasses anything done (or left undone) incorrectly or inadvertently. It includes omissions, misconfigurations, programming errors, malfunctions, etc. [15]. It does not include any intentional incidents.

Environmental The environmental category includes natural events such as earthquakes and floods and hazards associated with the immediate environment or infrastructure in which assets are located. The latter encompasses power failures, electrical interference, pipe leaks, and atmospheric conditions.

Results: Threat Actions Analysis. We measured the existence of each threat action category by calculating their varieties and vectors used in the incidents. We observed that ransomware represents 82% of the malware threat followed by others 8%. VERIS "other" to define any enumeration not represented by one of the categories in the data set. For the social threat actions category, with a percentage of 69%, phishing plays a large part in threat actions. The use of stolen credentials represents 80% of the hacking threat actions. With an increase in the number of employees, errors increased. Loss errors represent the main factor in this threat actions category representing 28%, followed by a disposal error of 27%. It is worth noticing that theft in the physical threat actions category with a percentage of 96%. Finally, privilege abuse in the misuse category with a rate of 59% is behind most of the threat actions in these two categories.

On the other hand, when we analyze the threat action vectors as shown in Fig. 6, we found out that the direct install represents 45% of the malware threat

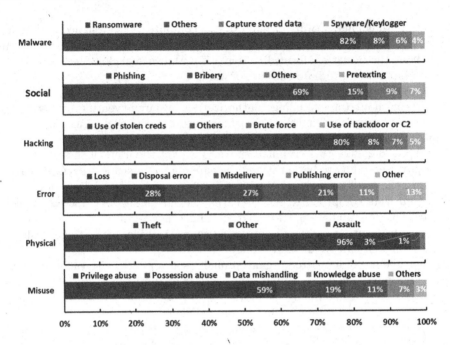

Fig. 5. Threat actions varieties.

actions. Email attachment is the second most common malware breach vector with 32%. The email vector represents 81% in the social category for other categories of threat actions, and web applications represent the primary vector with 81% of all hacking threat actions.

Carelessness is the primary vector with 92% of the error category. Although most data breaches using hacking by threat actors involve brute force, or the use of lost or stolen credentials [1], At the same time, LAN access is the most effective vector in the misuse category with 65%. It is clear that email and web application vectors represent the highest percentages among other vectors, and this is associated with the shift of valuable data to the cloud, including email accounts and business-related processes [1].

> **Takeaway.** *Despite the variety of vectors, ransomware is still the leading malware method involving 82% of the incidents.*

6   Related Work

Recently, several studies have been conducted aimed at analyzing data breaches in the healthcare sector. Choi *et al.* [2] estimate the relationship between data breaches and hospital advertising expenditures. They concluded that teaching hospitals were associated with significantly higher advertising expenditures in

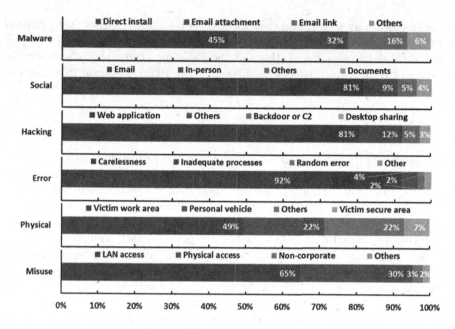

Fig. 6. Threat actions vectors.

the two years after the breach. Another study [9] investigated the privacy-protected data collection and access in IoT-based healthcare applications and proposed a new framework called PrivacyProtector to preserve the privacy of patients' data. Siddartha *et al.* [12] found that the healthcare industry is being targeted for two main reasons: being a rich source of valuable data, and its weak defenses. Another study [17] suggested a framework to examine the accuracy of automatic privacy auditing tools. Another study [12] suggested that current healthcare security techniques miss data analysis improvements, e.g., data format-preserving, data size preserving, and other factors.

Using a collection of two years of data, [14] characterized DNS requests and TLS/SSL communications to understand the threats faced within the hospital environment without disturbing the operational network. Another analysis in [11] shows that attackers mostly use hacking/IT incidents, and the email and network servers are the primary locations for confidential health data breach.

Most relevant to our work, the 2020 Data Breach Investigations Report [4] summarized the findings and determined that external actors are behind 80% of data breaches while 20% of data breaches involved internal actors. According to the same report, hacking is the action that was used in 45% of data breaches, followed by errors that were causal events in 22% of breaches. The rest of the actions used in data breaches are social attacks, malware, misuse by authorized users, and physical actions presented in data breaches. The report also shows that financially motivated breaches are more common than espionage by a wide margin. In contrast to our work, a study by [11] presents information on data breach incidents by sector, and they focused on the data breaches that occurred in the healthcare industry in the last five years because they account for 61.55% of the total data breaches. Authors of the following study have also compiled the data of healthcare breaches published by the HIPAA journal from 2010 to 2019 to authenticate their data.

7   Conclusion

While analyzing the timeline of the data set that comprised all the data breaches, the results showed that the highest number of incidents occurred from 2010–2020. Moreover, this long-term study revealed that health organizations are exposed to internal, external, and partner attacks. The financial is the primary motivation for the external, internal, and partner attackers. Without a doubt, there is a high cost associated with data breaches, the price for each stolen health record increases with time. Moreover, the victims include different types, but the primary victims are the patients, followed by the customers and the employees. Based on a long-term analysis of the data set, the actions used by the threat actors are classified into seven categories: malware, hacking, social, misuse, physical, error, and environmental. Ransomware motivated 82% of malware threat actors, and 45% of malware threat actions are directly installed. In the future, it would be worthwhile examining the correlation between security breaches and other indicators, including GDP, hospital size, etc.

Acknowledgement. This work was supported by NRF-2016K1A1A2912757, the UCF ORC Graduate Fellowship Program and Faculty Mentorship Program.

References

1. Introduction to the 2020 DBIR: Verizon Enterprise Solutions. Verizon Enterprise (2020). https://vz.to/3h5rva1
2. Choi, S.J., Johnson, M.E.: Understanding the relationship between data breaches and hospital advertising expenditures. Am. J. Managed Care **25**(5), 14–20 (2019)
3. Coventry, L., Branley, D.: Cybersecurity in healthcare: a narrative review of trends, threats and ways forward. PubMed (April 2018). https://doi.org/10.1016/j.maturitas.2018.04.008
4. Enterprise, V.: Verizon data breach investigations report (2020). https://vz.to/3w66fpa
5. HealthIT.gov: Benefits of ehrs (2017). https://bit.ly/3qA5X8S
6. IBM: Cost of a data breach report 2020 (2020). https://ibm.co/2TlDKX7
7. Kamoun, F., Nicho, M.: Human and organizational factors of healthcare data breaches: the swiss cheese model of data breach causation and prevention. Int. J. Heal. Inf. Syst. Inform. **9**(1), 42–60 (2014)
8. Liu, V., Musen, M.A., Chou, T.: Data breaches of protected health information in the United States. JAMA **313**(14), 1471–1473 (2015)
9. Luo, E., Bhuiyan, M.Z.A., Wang, G., Rahman, M.A., Wu, J., Atiquzzaman, M.: Privacyprotector: privacy-protected patient data collection in iot-based healthcare systems. IEEE Commun. Mag. **56**(2), 163–168 (2018)

10. Menachemil, N., Collum, T.H.: Benefits and drawbacks of electronic health record systems (2011). https://bit.ly/3x7XNXJ
11. Seh, A.H., et al.: Healthcare data breaches: insights and implications. Healthcare **8**, 133 (2020). https://doi.org/10.3390/healthcare8020133
12. Siddartha, B.K., Ravikumar, G.K.: Analysis of masking techniques to find out security and other efficiency issues in healthcare domain. In: Third International Conference on I-SMAC, pp. 660–666 (2019). https://doi.org/10.1109/I-SMAC47947.2019.9032431
13. Smith, T.T.: Examining data privacy breaches in healthcare. Walden University, Technical report (2016)
14. Vargas, L., et al.: Digital healthcare-associated infection: a case study on the security of a major multi-campus hospital system (2019). https://doi.org/10.14722/ndss.2019.23444
15. Veris community: Veris (2021). https://bit.ly/3jrTUbZ
16. Wikina, S.: What caused the breach? An examination of use of information technology and health data breaches. Perspect. Health Inf. Manag. **11**, 1h (2014)
17. Yesmin, T., Carter, M.W.: Evaluation framework for automatic privacy auditing tools for hospital data breach detections: a case study. Int. J. Med. Inform. **138**, 104123 (2020)

BadASLR: Exceptional Cases of ASLR Aiding Exploitation

Daehee Jang[(✉)]

Sungshin W. University, Seoul, South Korea
djang@sungshin.ac.kr

Abstract. Address Space Layout Randomization (ASLR) is de-facto standard exploit mitigation in our daily life software. The simplest idea of unpredictably randomizing memory layout significantly raises the bar for memory exploitation due to the additionally required attack primitives such as information leakage. Ironically, although exceptional, there are rare edge cases where ASLR becomes handy for memory exploitation. In this paper, we dig into such theoretical set of cases and name it as BadASLR. To evaluate if BadASLR can be an actual plausible scenario, we look into real-world bug bounty cases, CTF/wargame challenges. Surprisingly, we found multiple vulnerabilities in commercial software where ASLR becomes handy for attacker. With BadASLR cases, we succeeded in exploiting peculiar vulnerabilities, and received total 10,000 USD as bug bounty reward including one CVE assignment.

Keywords: Address space layout randomization · Memory exploit · Memory safety

1 Introduction

Modern software essentially adopts Address Space Layout Randomization (ASLR) to harden the memory from exploitation attempt. Especially when applied to 64bit system, ASLR makes infeasible to predict any virtual memory address from attacker's exploitation code. This forces attackers to additionally equip themselves with a stronger exploitation capability – information leakage. Thanks to ASLR, the difficulty of modern exploitation in large-scale software such as browsers and kernel has substantially increased. To exploit memory corruption bugs in such software, abusing strong information leakage bug is a must nowadays.

We emphasize that ASLR is a standard exploit mitigation technique protecting us for decades and this paper does intend to accuse its effectiveness. However, we summarize and analyze the rare and bizarre cases which, ironically, ASLR acts as a useful tool for successful exploitation and we refer such edge cases as BadASLR[1]. Understanding such BadASLR cases will advance the completeness of knowledge and provide thought provoking insights in future research.

---

[1] In this paper, for simplicity, we mention heap memory layout randomization techniques as part of ASLR. In general, ASLR is more specific term for randomizing the location of memory segments such as .text or library mapping.

© Springer Nature Switzerland AG 2021
H. Kim (Ed.): WISA 2021, LNCS 13009, pp. 278–289, 2021.
https://doi.org/10.1007/978-3-030-89432-0_23

There are four types of BadASLR:

- Type-I: Supporting heap layout manipulation for use-after-free and heap over-flow (technically, heap memory randomization is not exactly ASLR).
- Type-II: Stack-pivoting support in frame pointer null-poisoning.
- Type-III: Reviving exploitability of invalid pointer.
- Type-IV: Introducing wild-card ROP gadgets with diversified branch offset encoding.

BadASLR Type-I is regarding randomization in heap chunk allocation timing and their layout adjustment in attacker's advantage. Technically, the term ASLR indicates randomizing the address/order of memory segments at page granularity, but in this paper we include ASLR for all types of memory layout randomization including heap chunk positioning. BadASLR Type-II is about special type of stack-based buffer overflow that allows null-poisoning against saved stack frame pointers (e.g., RBP register value in x64). This type of special buffer overflow attack is plausible if the buffer is based on printable string. BadASLR Type-III is about randomization in mmap (page allocation) or dynamic library loading. This type of scenario is extremely unlikely in 64-bit address space environment but quite plausible in 32-bit virtual address space application. Finally, BadASLR Type-IV is conceptually far from other BadASLR cases. The scenario is regarding ASLR introducing more diverse ROP gadgets due to the randomly changing inter-segment distance. Depending on compiler/linker options, branch target addressing in position independent code might change its instruction encoding due to ASLR; which gives diversity in encoded branch target offsets. This issue only affects Intel CISC instruction set architecture where the instructions can split with byte granularity; thus any byte sequence inside instruction can be an ROP gadget.

Each BadASLR cases are first, theoretically discussed based on assumptions; and demonstrated with Proof-of-Concept codes/examples. Afterward, based on our theoretical analysis of BadASLR, we study real-world memory corruption exploits and CTF/wargame challenges to see if such ironical cases can actually happen in practice. Surprisingly, we found multiple real-world cases for BadASLR Type-I and Type-III. Four bugs we discovered was only possible to exploit it with the help of ASLR. In particular, we found a peculiar heap over-flow vulnerability in KMPlayer video parser and successfully exploited with CVE assignment (CVE-2018-5200) and 4,500 USD bug bounty reward.

2   BadASLR Explained

In this section, we categorize BadASLR into four types and explain their details in theory (we note, technically, the term ASLR is not accurate for type-1 case).

2.1   BadASLR Type-I: Aiding Free Chunk Reclamation

Heap spray is frequently utilized to enhance the reliability of memory corruption based exploit. There are multiple data types to spray inside heap depending

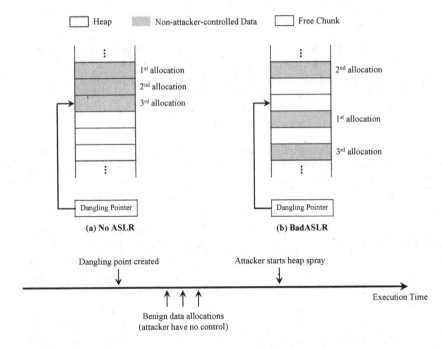

Fig. 1. BadASLR-(i) turning unexploitable use-after-free situation into highly exploitable situation.

on the exploitation environment. Although it is outdated, the basic data type for heap spray is the *NOP-sled* (and shellcode). Spraying the NOP-sled is only meaningful when the target application lacks Data Execution Prevention (DEP). Another type of data attackers typically spray inside heap is *objects* embedding pointers. These objects are sprayed in order to place at least one of them at proper memory position (e.g., free chunk reclamation). In theory, it is possible that ASLR (technically, it is called heap randomization but we refer it as ASLR to simplify terms) helping attacker to this end. We refer such counter-intuitive situation as BadASLR Type-I.

For example, in use-after-free, consider a hypothetical scenario where an application happens to allocate a chunk of pure data (e.g., image) immediately after a dangling pointer is created as illustrated in Fig. 1. In such case, use-after-free vulnerability becomes unexploitable as the inevitable execution flow immediately consumes the inadvertently freed (dangling-pointed) chunk. Same principle can be also applied to heap overflow vulnerability case.

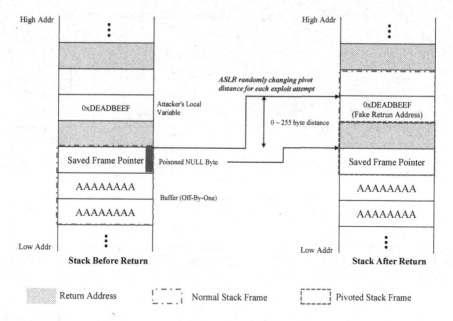

Fig. 2. BadASLR-(ii) turning off-by-one NULL byte poisoning against stack frame pointer into random byte (from 0 to 255 range) poisoning.

2.2 BadASLR Type-II: Aiding Stack Pivot in Frame Pointer NULL-Poisoning

As a specific case of off-by-one bug, null-poisoning is common in heap exploitation. For example, a single byte of metadata (e.g., size) corruption can lead things into chaos [15]. This technique can be equally applied to stack data structures. In fact, if stack canary is bypass-able or absent, off-by-one null-poisoning is a promising/reliable exploitation primitive to pivot the stack frame to initiate ROP attack.

One might ask why we need to pivot the stack before ROP. Consider if the stack buffer overflow is based on null-terminated ascii string. Building ROP chain with such restriction is often impossible because pointers usually require non-ascii bytes. In this situation, an alternative exploitation strategy is pivoting the stack where attacker already prepared the ROP chain.

Because most of the compilers insert stack frame's base address (e.g., the value of RBP register in x64) on the stack and chain them up for each function calls, even partially corrupting such saved frame pointer can pivot the stack and overlap the return address with attacker's local variable in other function frames (let us assume these local variables can be a working ROP chain). By null-poisoning the stack frame pointer, the parent function stack frame will pivot towards lower memory address up to 255 (or 65535 for lower two bytes poisoning) bytes thus can overlap with attacker's local variable in other stack frame. Figure 2 illustrates this scenario in detail.

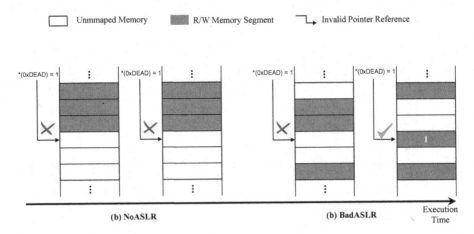

Fig. 3. BadASLR-(iii) giving a survival chance to invalid pointer reference. Totally unexploitable invalid pointer reference might become useful (with small chance) under ASLR.

The essence of BadASLR Type-II is that because modern ASLR changes stack base address and offset every time, the offset between pivoted stack frame and attacker's local variable (which aims to overwrite parent function's return address) can randomly change across executions within a predictable range of 255 or 65535 bytes. Therefore, with average 255 (or 65535) trials of exploitation attempt, attacker can eventually overlap his/her local variable at a proper ROP chain position regardless of the local variable's relative positioning inside the stack frame. Basically, in this hypothetical scenario, ASLR is converting the *NULL byte poisoning* primitive into more useful *random byte poisoning*. Without ASLR, NULL byte poisoning in this theoretical setup would be always exploitable with single exploitation attempt, or never exploitable if stack layout turns out unlucky. With ASLR, for every attack trial, attacker has small chance to succeed exploitation regardless of how the stack layout is positioned (as ASLR provide diversity in stack frame layout).

2.3   BadASLR-(iii): Reviving Invalid Pointer Reference

Invalid pointer refers to a virtual memory address with no accessible corresponding memory segment. Let us consider a hypothetical bug which allows an attacker to reference a fixed constant (say, `0x12345678`) as a pointer of an object (confusing constant and pointer). If the virtual address `0x12345678` has no valid segment mapping, without ASLR, this bug is never exploitable. However, ASLR opens a possibility for turning this bug into something exploitable with small chance. Because of ASLR, the address `0x12345678` is no longer guaranteed to be inaccessible considering ASLR moving memory segments including library mapping and other dynamically mapped segments (e.g., `MapViewOfFile` in Windows). This is unrealistic in 64bit address space, however, in 32bit address space the entropy of segment base address is quite small. Surprisingly, we found an actual real-world case of this unlikely exploitation scenario. We visualize this exceptional hypothetical scenario in Fig. 3 and discuss real-world case in Sect. 3.

2.4   BadASLR-(iv): Introducing Wild Card ROP Gadget

In theory, ASLR might contribute to increase the diversity of ROP gadgets in x86/64 position independent binaries such as shared objects. Position independent codes must handle out-of-segment branches such as imported library calls. Because the relative distance between position independent code and library call target is unknown at compile time and decided at runtime, branch offset for such call instructions must be updated at runtime as well. Usually, such calls utilize additional data structures known as procedure linkage table (PLT) and global offset table (GOT) to calculate the target address using a dynamically updated function pointer. However, depending on the compiler options, dynamic linker can also resolve such offset by updating the instruction code at runtime. In the latter case, ASLR introduces wild card ROP gadgets as a part of branch target offset encoding.

Depending on how compiler emits machine code, the branch target offset can change across execution to support ASLR. Because Intel is CISC machine, the changing bytes can act as a *wild card ROP gadgets* which can become any instruction attacker expects with some attack iteration. In fact, there are some crucial ROP gadgets composed only with 2 bytes such as stack pivot (e.g., xchg eax, esp; ret as **94 c3**). Admittedly, exploitation only viable with BadASLR-IV is unrealistic for some reasons: (i) it is likely that such small gadgets would be already available somewhere else in the code base (e.g., encoded constants or fixed relative offset) even without BadASLR primitive, (ii) in reality, there are multiple ways to construct ROP chains; thus an exploitation scenario only possible via BadASLR-IV is unrealistic. However, we find it is educative and interesting to explore such theoretical scenarios.

3   Evaluation

Based on our study, we report that BadASLR is extremely unlikely to be an exploitation primitive in large-scale, user interactive application such as browsers and kernel. However, we found that it can be a working exploitation primitive in small/non-user-interactive application such as multimedia/document parser.

3.1   Case Study: Heap Overflow in WPS Writer

WPS is an office suite software developed by Kingsoft [16]. We have discovered a heap overflow bug from WPS Writer exploitable with BadASLR Type-I. While initializing data for a special object (let us denote as **SOBJ**) in specific condition, the program accidentally calculates the size of the object twice bigger than it should be. As a result, the program initializes memory contents of **SOBJ** with a

```
typedef struct _tagSOBJ{
    unsigned int color;
    unsigned int font;
}SOBJ, *PSOBJ;
void Parse_Document(){
    ...
    PSOBJ p = (PSOBJ)malloc(sizeof(SOBJ));
    p->color = get_color();
    p->font = get_font();
    ...
    // blocks exploitation under no-ASLR
    alloc_useless_data();
    ...
    if( special_condition() ){
        // bug (heap overflow)
        p++;
    }
    ...
    p->color = get_color();
    p->font = get_font();
}
...
```

Fig. 4. Example C code to explain WPS bug.

miscalculated size and corrupts adjacent heap region. As a result, attacker can overwrite adjacent heap region with limited (fixed) length with data such as color code, font size such that attacker can specify in the input file. Figure 4 is the example C code for explaining this bug.

In file parser exploitation, there is no leeway over the heap allocation timing and overall heap memory management (de-allocation, re-allocation, etc.) because there is no continuous interaction between attacker's data and program.

In fact, in Windows 7 environment where LFH heap lacked ASLR primitive (e.g., allocation sequence is deterministic), the bug we discovered was never exploitable because the parser immediately allocates a useless data chunk at the precise position where attacker can overwrite (adjacent to SOBJ). Therefore, even attacker triggers buffer overflow, there is no meaningful target to overwrite. However, ironically, this bug became exploitable in Windows 8 environment where LFH adopted ASLR primitive in their chunk allocation policy. As free chunk for allocation is randomly chosen, it is unlikely that the useless data (immediately allocated after SOBJ allocation) will consume the *overwrite-able memory* before the execution flow reaches attacker's heap control.

Due to the BadASLR Type-I, it is highly likely that the overwrite-able heap region remains as a free space until attacker takes over control for heap allocation. Although we cannot control *when* to allocate our data, we had control over *how many*; which allow as to spray the heap to some extent. By adjusting proper heap-spray amount, with high probability, we were able to overwrite useful (in

Table 1. Average heap spray amount to reclaim a specific free chunk in randomized LFH heap bucket. N is the number of initial allocation, K is the percentage of randomly de-allocated chunks, SD stands for standard deviation. The average value is calculated based on 10 iteration.

Chunk size	N	K	Average spray amount	SD
50	1,000	20	216.8	61.3
		50	251.1	131.5
		80	270.0	231.9
	10,000	20	1559.8	705.0
		50	2611.0	1206.1
		80	3967.0	1879.1
	100,000	20	11423.0	3464.0
		50	14831.1	6021.3
		80	13533.4	9790.0
500	1,000	20	201.8	26.8
		50	158.6	104.0
		80	219.6	127.8
	10,000	20	1196.3	617.2
		50	3037.6	1044.4
		80	3360.8	1896.5
	100,000	20	8350.2	4125.8
		50	12695.1	5971.3
		80	15300.9	6719.8

terms of exploitation) objects embedding function pointers. Table 1 is an experiment result for finding minimal heap spray amount in randomization-enabled Windows 8.1 LFH heap. We allocate N chunks continuously, then randomly de-allocate K percent of them. Afterward, we randomly select a target free chunk (assuming as if dangling pointed, or overwrite-able) and spray the heap until our target gets reclaimed. The result suggests that we can practically reclaim the target free chunk despite of the randomized allocation sequence as heap defragments.

3.2 Case Study: Heap Overflow in KMPlayer

Similarly to WPS Writer exploitation, we discovered BadASLR Type-I case in KMPlayer as well. We reported this bug to vendor and got 4,500 USD as reward and also got CVE assignment (CVE-2018-5200 [1]). In this vulnerability, KMPlayer do not consider the edge case of H.263 video packet decoding (H.263 Sorenson Type). As a result, attacker can trigger heap overflow with crafted H.263 Sorenson encoded video. Attacker had full control over the length of attack payload, however, because the overflowing data is decompressed video stream, we had to overwrite the memory only with decompressed pixel values which gave us significant restriction in memory corruption.

Fortunately, we found out that we could spray the *overwrite-able* heap region with a specific object of size `0x24` and corrupt it in a exploitable way with our decompressed byte stream. Unfortunately, because the decompression starts *after* we spray the corruption target object (which has size 0x24), it was not possible to overwrite the target object without ASLR environment where heap chunks are sequentially allocated towards higher address in deterministic order. However, when ASLR is applied to heap chunk allocation, we could reliably overwrite our target object by precisely controlling the amount of heap spray and create an hole.

3.3   Case Study: Use-After-Free in HWP Parser

One of a use-after-free bug we have discovered from a document parser had BadASLR Type-I case. In our bug, when the parser encounters an invalid object, it frees the object and escapes the parsing loop. However, afterward, the program overlooks the prior exceptional de-allocation and reference VPTR (virtual pointer for C++ virtual table) pointer as if the object was never freed.

We can also see that immediately after terminating the main parsing loop, the program starts processing GUI elements. After the GUI processing, the logic continues and finally references the prior dangling pointer. We note that the execution flow of this logic is deterministic thus attacker has no control over it. Unfortunately for the attacker, GUI image data allocation step involves allocating heap chunk that has exactly same size as the dangling pointed object. Therefore, without ASLR in heap chunk allocation, the use-after-free in this example becomes impossible to exploit. However with BadASLR Type-I, with high chance, memory allocation in GUI processing will not immediately reuse the dangling pointed free chunk. Indeed, we were able to reliably exploit this bug and hijack the control flow in Windows 8 LFH environment (randomized allocation), but could not exploit the bug under Windows 7 or XP (deterministic sequential allocation). We reported this bug to vendor to fix it and got compensated with approximately 2,500 USD.

3.4   Case Study: Invalid Pointer Reference in HWP Parser

We found a use-after-free in HWP document parser while parsing V3 file format. Because V3 file format do not support various document components, allocating/controlling heap data is very limited. Therefore, although we found use-after-free, it was impossible to reclaim the dangling pointer with malicious data that we can control. As a result, the only choice for abusing this use-after-free bug is making the heap allocator to overwrite the dangling pointed region and corrupt data.

Fortunately, the dangling pointed object had virtual table pointer (VPTR) as first member variable thus we could corrupt the lower 2 bytes of VPTR pointer with *next offset* metadata which the LFH allocator manages. In this case, the

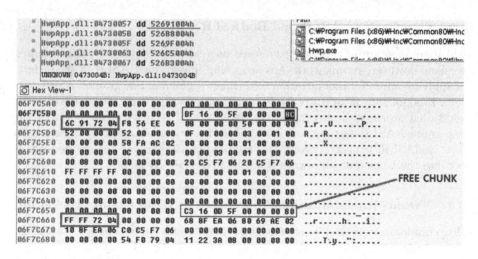

Fig. 5. Lower 16 bit of VPTR pointer (originally 0x472916c) is overwritten by 0xffff (0x472ffff at 0x6f7c660). Corrupted VPTR pointer deterministically points an invalid pointer 0x52691004 which is a fragment of pure data.

next offset was changed into **65535** which indicates the next chunk is out of range boundary. As a result, we could reference VPTR pointer who's lower 16bit is always corrupted with 0xFFFF. Figure 5 is the heap memory dump of this situation. Because VPTR is included as part of *text* section, the 0xFFFF overwrite shifted the pointer to point read-only literal constant **0x52691004** included in the same segment. Therefore, the initial use-after-free turned into *invalid pointer reference* bug. Without ASLR, there was no valid segment mapping at this address. However, because of ASLR we had a small chance (1 out of hundreds) to occasionally reference this pointer to finally execute our controlled heap memory region as function; thus allowing shellcode execution in no-DEP environment. This is an example case of BadASLR Type-III.

4   Discussion and Related Work

4.1   Good System Introducing New Bugs

Wressnegger et al. demonstrated in their paper (Twice the Bits, Twice the Trouble: Vulnerabilities Induced by Migrating to 64-Bit Platforms) that migrating a 32-bit application into 64-bit environment could introduce new bugs [2]. Such bugs are mainly caused by the confusing interpretation of **LONG** type variable which is considered 32bit in Windows however treated as 64bit in Linux environment. The paper found various example cases of such errors and evaluated the prevalence. We also present the paper in a similar sense but with different topic: edge cases of ASLR supporting exploitation.

4.2   Fine-Grained ASLR and BadASLR

ASLR we mention in this paper is based on real-world deployed coarse-grained version. However, recent works are proposing fine-grained ASLR [3–9]. Instead of applying address randomization to memory segments, fine grained ASLR pursuits randomizing location of basic blocks. Obviously, such attempt will incur additional overhead and complication in return of security efficacy. Under the fine-grained ASLR assumption, BadASLR theory remains equally effective. In fact, BadASLR Type-IV becomes even more plausible under fine-grained ASLR because the branch offset always change across the execution.

4.3   Various Randomization Approaches in Heap Chunk Allocation

Heap randomization and its exploit is the main issues covered in our evaluation. We only focused on heap randomization which shuffles the allocation order in free chunk selection which was deployed in real-world as part of Windows 8 non-deterministic LFH heap [10]. However, randomization in heap has been discussed in a number of prior studies, and their randomization method differs from one to another. For example, Bhatkar et al. and Qin et al., respectively randomize the base address of the heap, as shown in Refs. [11,13]. Additionally, there are others approaches that randomize heap chunk size during allocation phase [12,14].

5   Conclusion

In this paper, we presented BadASLR: a set of peculiar cases where ASLR counter-intuitively aiding memory exploitation. According to our study, there are four types of BadASLR in theory, and some of the cases were actually found in real-world exploitation.

Acknowledgement. This work was supported by the Sungshin Women's University Research Grant of 2021.

References

1. CVE-2018-5200.   https://nvd.nist.gov/vuln/detail/CVE-2018-5200.   KMPlayer 4.2.2.15 and earlier have a Heap Based Buffer Overflow Vulnerability
2. Wressnegger, C., Yamaguchi, F., Maier, A., Rieck, K.: Twice the bits, twice the trouble: vulnerabilities induced by migrating to 64-bit platforms. Proceedings of the 2016 ACM SIGSAC Conference on Computer and Communications Security, pp. 541–552 (2016)
3. Snow, K.Z., Monrose, F., Davi, L., Dmitrienko, A., Liebchen, C., Sadeghi, A.-R.: Just-in-time code reuse: On the effectiveness of fine-grained address space layout randomization. In: 2013 IEEE Symposium on Security and Privacy, pp. 574–588. IEEE (2013)

4. Davi, L.V., Dmitrienko, A., Nürnberger, S., Sadeghi, A.-R.: Gadge me if you can: secure and efficient ad-hoc instruction-level randomization for x86 and ARM. In: Proceedings of the 8th ACM SIGSAC symposium on Information, computer and communications security, pp. 299–310 (2013)
5. Hiser, J., Nguyen-Tuong, A., Co, M., Hall, M., Davidson, J.W.: ILR: where'd my gadgets go? In: 2012 IEEE Symposium on Security and Privacy, pp. 571–585. IEEE (2012)
6. Kil, C., Jun, J., Bookholt, C., Xu, J., Ning, P.: Address space layout permutation (ASLP): towards fine-grained randomization of commodity software. In: 2006 22nd Annual Computer Security Applications Conference (ACSAC 2006), pp. 339–348. IEEE (2006)
7. Li, J., Wang, Z., Jiang, X., Grace, M., Bahram, S.: Defeating return-oriented programming through gadget-less kernels. In: Proceedings of European Conference on Computer Systems, pp. 195–208 (2010)
8. Seo, J., et al.: SGX-shield: enabling address space layout randomization for SGX programs. In: NDSS (2017)
9. Wartell, R., Mohan, V., Hamlen, K.W., Lin, Z.: Binary stirring: self-randomizing instruction addresses of legacy x86 binary code. In: Proceedings of the 2012 ACM conference on Computer and communications security, pp. 157–168 (2012)
10. Valasek, C., Mandt, T.: Windows 8 heap internals. Black Hat USA (2012)
11. Qin, F., Tucek, J., Sundaresan, J., Zhou, Y.: Rx: treating bugs as allergies–a safe method to survive software failures. ACM SIGOPS Oper. Syst. Rev. **39**(5) (2005)
12. Kharbutli, M., Jiang, X., Solihin, Y., Venkataramani, Gu., Prvulovic, M.: Comprehensively and efficiently protecting the heap. ACM Sigplan Not. **41**(11), 207–218 (2006)
13. Bhatkar, S., DuVarney, D.C., Sekar, R.: Address obfuscation: an efficient approach to combat a broad range of memory error exploits. USENIX Security (2003)
14. Iyer, V., Kanitkar, A., Dasgupta, P., Srinivasan, R.: Preventing overflow attacks by memory randomization. In: 2010 IEEE 21st International Symposium on Software Reliability Engineering (ISSRE), pp. 339–347 (2010)
15. ShellPhish, How2Heap. https://github.com/shellphish/how2heap. Educational Heap Exploitation
16. KingSoft. https://www.wps.com/. WPS Complete office suite with PDF editor

Author Index

Printed in the United States
by Baker & Taylor Publisher Services